David Field Rennie

The British Arms in North China and Japan: Peking 1860; Kagosima 1862

David Field Rennie

The British Arms in North China and Japan: Peking 1860; Kagosima 1862

ISBN/EAN: 9783337166953

Printed in Europe, USA, Canada, Australia, Japan

Cover: Foto ©ninafisch / pixelio.de

More available books at **www.hansebooks.com**

THE BRITISH ARMS

IN

NORTH CHINA AND JAPAN:

PEKING 1860; KAGOSIMA 1862.

By D. F. RENNIE, M.D.,

SENIOR MEDICAL OFFICER OF THE FORCE IN THE NORTH OF CHINA; LATE SURGEON TO
HER MAJESTY'S LEGATION, AND TO THE LEGATION OF HIS MAJESTY
THE EMPEROR OF THE FRENCH AT PEKING.

LONDON:
JOHN MURRAY, ALBEMARLE STREET.
1864.

[*The Right of Translation is reserved.*]

LONDON:
BRADBURY AND EVANS, PRINTERS, WHITEFRIARS.

TO

LIEUT.-COL. EDWARD ST. JOHN NEALE, C.B.,

KNIGHT OF SAN FERNANDO;

FORMERLY SECRETARY OF LEGATION AT PEKING, AND LATTERLY
HER BRITANNIC MAJESTY'S CHARGÉ D'AFFAIRES IN JAPAN;

This Volume is Inscribed,

AS A TOKEN OF REGARD,

BY HIS SINCERE FRIEND,

THE AUTHOR.

PREFACE.

I have been induced to add the following Volume to the Works already published on the subject of China, by the consideration that our information regarding that vast Empire has been in a great degree confined to the Southern districts—in which, owing to the deterioration caused by intercourse with the Western nations, the character of the Chinese can be least favourably and least correctly estimated.

Being attached to the expeditionary force which marched to Peking, and being stationed in that city and at Tien-tsin for a considerable length of time, I had peculiar opportunities of observing the native character in a part of the country hitherto closed to European intercourse. Many of the events connected with the expedition to Peking I personally witnessed. When not myself present I had the advantage of receiving information on the spot from those immediately engaged, which I recorded in my daily journals written at the time. My connection with the British and French Legations placed me in the way of acquiring much interesting information, and has enabled me to record many facts about China, as well as traits of Chinese character, not generally known.

The delay which has occurred in the publication of these notes has arisen in the first place from my not having had any thought originally of giving them to the press, and secondly from my professional engagements with the army, which have greatly impeded the task of preparing my journal for publication.

An opportunity of visiting Japan about the time of the British expedition to Kagosima, has enabled me to add some account of that country, and of the state of feeling entertained towards the English and other Europeans by the Daimios and the Japanese generally. The present critical state of affairs renders valuable any addition to our scanty information regarding that remarkable country and people.

Having given special attention to the hygiene of the army, I am not inclined to endorse the generally received opinion that the expedition to North China was a remarkable sanitary success. The expedition was formed under peculiarly favourable sanitary conditions. The troops were selected out of men already seasoned in India. The force was afterwards weeded of its sick and weakly on three occasions before landing. The operations in the field were performed in the healthy season. Yet, with all these advantages, the amount of sickness and invaliding was very considerable. The direct application of sanitary science by the appointment of a medical officer, whose sole duty it was to contend with nuisances and to carry into effect sanitary reform, was not in my opinion attended with any great results. The sickness of the army while living in a pure, and, to all appearance, salubrious atmosphere, and its immunity from disease among the foulest odours of animal and vegetable decomposition, presented some astonishing paradoxes, which seem to shake the primary and simplest conclusions of sanitary science.

I shall be glad if the records of my experience in this respect can throw any light upon this difficult but important subject, which is but little understood, and from which, in my opinion, too much immediate result has been expected.

SHANGHAI,
    22nd August, 1863.

CONTENTS.

INTRODUCTION.
ORIGIN OF THE THIRD CHINESE WAR.

PAGE

The disaster at Taku—Its cause—Proposed ratification at Peking of the treaties of Tien-tsin—Arrival of the Plenipotentiaries at the Peiho—The Chinese refuse to open the river—Failure of the attempt to clear the passage—Assistance from the American Commodore—Gallantry of Admiral Hope—Moderate demands of the Government—Re-appointment of Lord Elgin and Baron Gros —The Author volunteers for service in China 1

CHAPTER I.

Arrive at Hong Kong—Aspect of affairs—Rejection of the ultimatum—Preparations for war—Occupation of Chusan—Friendly disposition of the natives—Hong Kong—Kowloon hired from the Chinese Government—Formation of a Chinese Coolie Corps— Arrangements for garrisoning Hong Kong and Canton . . . 8

CHAPTER II.

Kowloon—The Chinese Coolie Corps—Wreck of the "Isère"— Parade of the Coolies—The Happy Valley—Record of mortality in the 59th Regiment—Barracks of the Coolie Corps— Sir Hope Grant—Seik soldier and vegetable vendor—The Seik Cavalry—The Loodiannah Regiment—Shanghai threatened by the Taeping rebels 14

CHAPTER III.

Loss of Her Majesty's Troop-ship "Assistance"—Return of Transports owing to foul weather—Allied attack on pirates at Chusan —Sanitary condition of the Troops in Hong Kong—The "Winifred" Coolie ship—Chinese doctor—Mo'es of deserting from the Coolie Corps—Boat population near the Happy Valley—Quarrying by Chinese—Missionary children—State of Shanghai—The Taeping rebellion—Ascent of Victoria Peak—Arrival of Lord Elgin and Baron Gros—Fall of Soochow—Chinese tailors . . . 21

CHAPTER IV.

Embark in the "Weser"—Muster of the Crew—Punishments—M. Tao—Off the Yang-tse-kiang—Sisters of Charity—Uncertainty of Monsoon—Council for promoting deserving sailors—The Shantung Promontory — Che-foo — The French camp—Questionable seizure of junks—Chinese Jew—A Jewish colony . 33

CHAPTER V.

Che-foo Harbour—Trade—Climate—Health of the Troops—Interview with General Montauban—The French force—Market supplies—Chinese money-changers—Judicious treatment of the natives—Buddhist temple—Progress of the shopkeepers in French—Construction of the houses—Arrival of the "Calvados"—The Coolie Corps 40

CHAPTER VI.

Agriculture—Appearance of the Peasantry—Gunboats—Kit inspection—French mode of carrying ammunition—Its advantages over the English method—Watch-tower—Military air of the Coolies—Leave Che-foo—Talien-whan Bay—Camp of the Second Brigade—The Bell Tent—Capture of Junks—Interview with Sir Hope Grant—Auriferous quartz — Arrival of Lord Elgin—Sir Robert Napier 47

CHAPTER VII.

Trial of a Marine—Boat accident, and death of Captain Gordon—Visit of the French Commanders-in-Chief—Native houses—Stove bed-places — Village temple — Cartoons — Proposed hospital—Head man of the village— Gambling in the Coolie Corps—Their cookery and quarters—Ship whitewashed—Baggage ponies—Tea unknown to the peasantry—Dr. Thomson—Episode of the Disaster at the Peiho—Low state of health of the troops—Bell Tent—Weight of ammunition 57

CHAPTER VIII.

The Expedition sails for the Peiho—The anchorage sighted—The French Fleet arrives—First view of the Taku forts—Preparations for landing at Peh-tang—Landing effected—March through the mud—The Forts deserted—First shot of the Campaign—Military occupation of the town—The "Zouave" cattle ship—Mortality on board—Commencement of hostilities—Reconnaissance in the direction of Taku 67

CHAPTER IX.

Confusion at the landing-place—Head-quarters of the First Division—Uninterred coffins—The Hospital of the 31st Regiment—

CONTENTS. xi

PAGE

Valuable clothing—Order against looting—A Chinese family residence—The South Peh-tang fort—Explosive machines—State of Horse Transport Service—Mortality among the horses on board ship—State of Peh-tang after rain—Reconnaissance—Attempt of the Chinese to open Negotiations—Order for the advance of the Army—Sanitary paradox—Exertions of the Officers and Crews of the Gunboats 77

CHAPTER X.

March on Sinho—Artillery Waggons abandoned in the mud—The first Armstrong Gun—The Action of Sinho—Capture of Entrenchments—Tartar Cavalry retreat towards Taku—Sinho occupied—Tartar Vedettes — Junction with Second Division—Appearance of the Troops—Details of Action on the Right—Bivouac—Sinho—Tartar Tents—Dexterity of Tartar Horsemen—The Gingal—Breakdown of the Horse Transport Corps—The *Times* Correspondent—Coolies' contempt for Cash—Prisoners captured by the Tartars—Horses galled by ill-made pack-saddles—Papers found in the house of the Tartar General 86

CHAPTER XI.

Advance of the army upon Tang-koo—The Artillery open fire—Capture of the fort—Apparent non-efficiency of our fire—Scenes inside Tang-koo—Cavalry enclosure—Captured guns—Prisoners—Camp flooded—Punishment parade—Samshu—Military bridge—Armstrong guns—Exaggerated statements respecting their success—Cholera—Return of the Sergeant and Coolies captured on the 12th—Flag of truce—Preparations for the attack on the Northern Forts 93

CHAPTER XII.

Advance upon the Taku forts—Explosion of magazines—Upper North Fort taken—Aspect of the fort after its capture—A photographic group—The cavalier—The other forts hoist white flags—An armistice granted—Details of the capture of the upper North Fort—A Coolie in search of Sycee silver—Flags of truce arrive—A letter from the Governor-General—Mandarin conveying it speaks English—Termination of the armistice—The lower North Fort surrenders—Terrific thunder-storm—Return of the army through the mud 108

CHAPTER XIII.

Surrender and occupation of the South Taku Forts—Gallantry of the Chinese defence—The Chinese Coolie Corps—Capacity of the Chinaman to make an efficient infantry soldier—Defects in the Armstrong gun—Revisit the North Taku Fort—Burial scene—Admiral Hope proceeds to Tien-tsin—Visit opposite bank of river—Embark for Tien-tsin—Accident to the gunboat . . 121

CHAPTER XIV.

Steam up the Peiho—Vessels get aground—Obliging disposition of the villagers—Arrival at the Forts of Tien-tsin. Their appearance and construction—Occupation of Tien-tsin by Admiral Hope—Visit to the walled city—Civility of the inhabitants—A village deputation—Assault on a villager by a sailor—Sang-ko-lin-sin's commissariat arrangements—Appointment of Imperial Commissioners—Lord Elgin's arrival at Tien-tsin—Reinforcements sent to defend Shanghai—Departure from Tien-tsin 129

CHAPTER XV.

Arrive at Shanghai—State of affairs—Visit the European settlement and the Chinese city—Brigadier Jephson's interview with the Tautai—Tea-gardens—Baby Tower—Sail for Hong Kong—Chinese festival—Return to Shanghai—Chinese soldier's devotions—Chinese petition to Mr. Bruce—English shooting party—Sickness on board ship—Malaria and ague—The English in Japan—Arrive at Tien-tsin—News from Peking 140

CHAPTER XVI.

Summary of Occurrences on the Peiho—Communications between the Commissioners and Lord Elgin—Negotiations broken off—Advance towards Tung-chow—The Prince of I—Mr. Parkes' interview—18th September—Endeavours to recover the prisoners—The Prince of Kung—Advance towards Peking—Imperial Palace plundered—Prisoners returned—Anting Gate surrendered—Funeral of the murdered English—Destruction of Yuen-ming-yuen—Entry into Peking—Treaty signed—Character of the Chinese negotiations—Conduct of the Chinese on the 18th September—Opinion of Lord Elgin 158

CHAPTER XVII.

Tien-tsin—Housing of the Troops—Chinese shot by sentries—The sponge-cake man—Temple of the Oceanic Influences—City wall—Heavy rain—Seizure of houses—The Caugue—Committee of British Supply—Imperial decree—Chinese entertainment—Wounded Chinese soldiers—Magistrate—Return of Lord Elgin—Occurrences at Peking—Return of Troops—Reappearance of Trade—Chinese dinner—Indian followers—Departure of Baron Gros—Comte de Bastard—Departure of Lord Elgin—The mess-room of the 31st—The Peiho frozen—Sir Hope Grant—Arrival of the Indemnity Money 171

CHAPTER XVIII.

A Chinese druggist's shop—The remains of the prisoners—Quarters of the garrison—Soldiers' barrack-rooms at night—Ozone and its influence on health—Population and revenue of China—The

CONTENTS.

Chinese candle—French soldiers' inscriptions—Parental grief—Opium smoking—Peking—Cruelty to dogs—Chivalrous sports of officers—Visits to Chinese officials—Acts of violence—Insecurity of property entrusted to military guards—Chinese hawking—State of affairs at Peking and Je-ho—The Tien-tsin Fire Brigade—Chinese funeral obsequies—Public baths—Marriage procession—Effects of the looting of Yuen-ming-yuen on the French army. 195

CHAPTER XIX.

Frozen porter—Statistical fallacies—Indifference of local officials in respect to hostilities against the Government—Dead beggar—New Year pictures—Chinese hawking party—Scarcity of copper—Occasional resistance of the Chinese to extortion—Self-sacrifice—Distribution of money to indigent Chinese—Its disastrous results—Extreme cold—Serious illness and death of General Collineau—Procession to propitiate a weather divinity—Funeral of General Collineau—Sketch of his career—Outrage by English soldiers at Taku—Private of 67th in trouble 217

CHAPTER XX.

An opium smoking-shop—The kow-tow—Small-pox and rude inoculation—The Foundling Hospital—Chinaman executed—Funeral procession—Demolition of a house for sam-shu dealing—Pawnbroker's establishment—News from Peking—Juvenile gambling—Garrison theatre opens—Approach of the Chinese New Year—Mortality amongst the troops—A Foreign Office to be established at Peking—Severe cold—Preserved fish—A Chinese joke—Old furniture shops—The silver pheasant—A dying Mandarin—The Audience question—Lord Macartney and the kow-tow—Ushering in of the New Year—Chinese compliments of the season—The ancestral tablet 231

CHAPTER XXI.

New Year's Visit from Chang—Injudicious snowballing—Ingenious toymaker—Robberies—Literary examinations—Peking Foreign Office—Seal of the late Emperor for sale—French loot—Rent dispute—Funeral obsequies—Visit to Chang—Chinese theatre—Restaurants—Feast of Lanterns—Presentation of the Victoria Cross—Brigade drill—Chinese opinions thereon—Ice commences to break up—News from Mr. Morrison—Chinese General reduced to the ranks—Sang-ko-lin-sin—Effect of electrical changes on the sick—Health of the Seiks compared with that of Europeans—Legation Guards detailed for Peking—Break-up of the ice—Prussian Diplomatic Mission—Commercial prospects of Tientsin—The Legations proceed to Peking—Evacuation of Tien-tsin . 246

JAPAN.

INTRODUCTION 269

CHAPTER I.

Embark at Shanghai for Japan—Cholera in the Yang-tse-kiang—Aspect of the coast—First impressions of the European settlement—The French and Dutch flags fired on—Aspect of affairs at Yokohama—Rural scenery—The peasantry and their habitations—Position of the foreign settlement—The British Legation—A Japanese garden and gardener—H.M.S. "Centaur" expected 282

CHAPTER II.

The steamers "Elgin" and "Rajah"—Fire at Yeddo—Visit to the native town—Curiosity shops—Reconnaissance along the Tokaido—Kanagawa—Scene of Mr. Richardson's murder—Japanese grooms—A tea-house beauty—Japanese disciplined troops—Arrival of H.M.S. "Centaur" from Nagasaki—Action of the "Wyoming" with the vessels and forts of the Prince of Negato—Extreme heat and its fatal effects—An earthquake . . 290

CHAPTER III.

The Japanese custom-house system—Objections to the exposing of the sword blade—The Gaukiro—A Japanese entertainment—A Japanese game—Public baths—Freak of two French soldiers—Visit to the "Medusa"—Japanese shot and shell, whence obtained—Visit to the "Wyoming"—Terms of construction of Legation residences—H.M.S. "Coquette" sent to communicate with the French Admiral in the Straits 304

CHAPTER IV.

Seamen and marines land for battalion drill—The armament of the "Euryalus"—Remarks on the Armstrong gun—Arrival of a member of the Gorogio from Yeddo—His interview with the Foreign Ministers—Sanitary paradox at Yokohama—Japanese washermen—The Chinese in Yokohama—Comparison between the Japanese and the Chinese—Question of the descent of the former from the latter 311

CHAPTER V.

Return of the French Admiral—His proceedings in the Straits of Semonosaki—Daimios' retainers—Military character of the Japanese—A Chinaman's views regarding the hostilities—

CONTENTS. xv

PAGE

Captain Macdougall—The Governor of Kanagawa—Conference of Foreign Ministers — Visit to the barracks of the disciplined Japanese — Barrack-room drill — Disregard of national prejudices 320

CHAPTER VI.

The Gorogio's reply to the French Minister—An American sailor wounded by a Yaconin—The Tycoon and the Daimios—Agriculture—Rapid acquisition of the language by a foreigner—The peasantry—Inconsiderate conduct of equestrians—Naval conference respecting the inland sea question—Japanese shampooing—Its application to the treatment of disease—The blind in Japan—Origin of the Tycoons. 329

CHAPTER VII.

Report respecting the return of the Tycoon—Mode of committing suicide a branch of Japanese education—Fight between the betos and the Gankiro people—Attempt on the part of Japanese traders to procure rifled cannon—Japanese doctor and medical science—Diet of the natives—A profitable land speculation—Errors respecting the disposition of the peasantry—A Japanese official wounded—Return of the Tycoon—Hostile feeling towards foreigners at Miako—Aptitude of the Japanese for mastering the details of machinery—Purchase of the "Lyemoon" steamer—Fire-proof stores—Primitive state of society—Preparations for leaving Yokohama for Nagasaki—Peaceful news—Modes of travelling in Japan—Tattooing—Violent death of the murderer of Mr. Euskin 339

CHAPTER VIII.

Departure for Nagasaki—Division of exchange profits amongst the crew—The currency question in Japan—Encounter a portion of a typhoon—Nagasaki harbour—Peaceful aspect of affairs—The old Dutch settlement of Desima—Singular reception of the Dutch superintendent of trade by the Tycoon at Yeddo—Analogous position of the agents of the late East India Company at Canton—The Japanese town of Nagasaki—Effects of solar influence—Heat apoplexy—Occurrence of cholera at Nagasaki co-existent with salubrity of climate—Observations on cholera 353

CHAPTER IX.

Visit to the Japanese steam factory at Nagasaki—English tea establishment—Commercial relations of the Prince of Satsuma with foreigners at Nagasaki—Interview with two of Satsuma's high officers—Anxiety expressed by them to avert the visit of the British squadron to Kagosima—Leave Nagasaki—Arrive at Shanghai 372

CHAPTER X.

Kagosima—Attempt of the Tycoon's Government to detain the squadron—The letter of demands sent in to Satsuma—His minister's reply—Admiral Kuper's despatch—Two of Satsuma's officers voluntary prisoners—The Armstrong gun in naval warfare—Admiral Kuper unjustly censured—A traveller's experience of the British abroad 381

SUPPLEMENTARY CHAPTER.

Consular trial at Yokohama—Affairs in Japan in September, 1863—The Prince of Negato—The Tycoon unfolds his foreign policy—Threatening notice from the Loonins—The Satsuma difficulty amicably settled—Congratulatory despatch from the Tycoon—Shimadzo Sabooro's explanations—Indemnity for the "Pembroke" being fired at—The Tycoon's palace destroyed—Charges brought against him by Daimios—A second embassy to Europe—The first ambassadors' opinions of Europe and the Europeans—Arrival of the Japanese embassy at Shanghai—Concluding observations 396

THE BRITISH ARMS

IN

NORTH CHINA AND JAPAN.

JUST READY,

By the same Author,

PEKIN AND THE PEKINESE:

JOURNAL OF A RESIDENCE IN THE CAPITAL OF CHINA.

George's Sound, with the homeward Australian mail, touched at the Mauritius to coal. I was a passenger on board, and the first news which reached us, on dropping anchor in the harbour of Port Louis, was, that a serious reverse had befallen our arms—in conjunction with those of France—in China; that four gun-boats had been sunk by the fire of Chinese batteries in an ineffectual attempt to force the passage of the Peiho—and that 500 men had been killed or wounded in the attack upon the Taku forts which defend the entrance to the river. This news seemed so improbable —so completely at variance with all past experience of Chinese warfare—that we hesitated to believe it. It proved, however, but too true; the story is soon told, and with it the circumstances which led to the Third Chinese War.

CHAPTER X.

Kagosima—Attempt of the Tycoon's Government to detain the squadron—The letter of demands sent in to Satsuma—His minister's reply—Admiral Kuper's despatch—Two of Satsuma's officers voluntary prisoners—The Armstrong gun in naval warfare—Admiral Kuper unjustly censured—A traveller's experience of the British abroad 381

SUPPLEMENTARY CHAPTER.

Consular trial at Yokohama—Affairs in Japan in September, 1863—The Prince of Negato—The Tycoon unfolds his foreign policy—Threatening notice from the Loonins—The Satsuma difficulty

THE BRITISH ARMS

IN

NORTH CHINA AND JAPAN.

INTRODUCTION.

ORIGIN OF THE THIRD CHINESE WAR.

The disaster at Taku—Its cause—Proposed ratification at Peking of the treaties of Tien-tsin—Arrival of the Plenipotentiaries at the Peiho—The Chinese refuse to open the river—Failure of the attempt to clear the passage—Assistance from the American Commodore—Gallantry of Admiral Hope—Moderate demands of the Government—Re-appointments of Lord Elgin and Baron Gros—The Author volunteers for service in China.

On the 14th of October, 1859, the steamer from King George's Sound, with the homeward Australian mail, touched at the Mauritius to coal. I was a passenger on board, and the first news which reached us, on dropping anchor in the harbour of Port Louis, was, that a serious reverse had befallen our arms—in conjunction with those of France—in China; that four gun-boats had been sunk by the fire of Chinese batteries in an ineffectual attempt to force the passage of the Peiho—and that 500 men had been killed or wounded in the attack upon the Taku forts which defend the entrance to the river. This news seemed so improbable —so completely at variance with all past experience of Chinese warfare—that we hesitated to believe it. It proved, however, but too true; the story is soon told, and with it the circumstances which led to the Third Chinese War.

On the 26th of June, 1858, the treaty with China, negotiated by the Earl of Elgin, was signed at Tien-tsin, and on the day following the treaty negotiated on the part of France by Baron Gros.

In each a clause was introduced providing for the exchange of the ratifications at Peking, within one year from the dates of signature. With the view of this clause being duly carried out, the Honourable Frederick Bruce, C.B., brother of the Earl of Elgin, was appointed Her Majesty's Envoy Extraordinary and Minister Plenipotentiary in China, and directed to proceed by the way of the Peiho to Tien-tsin, and thence to Peking. Instructions from home were at the same time sent to Admiral Hope, the naval commander-in-chief in China, to provide a sufficient force to accompany Mr. Bruce to the mouth of the Peiho.

Mr. Bruce, on arriving at Shanghai, found the Commissioners Kweiliang and Hwashana, awaiting his arrival there, in place of being at some point near the capital. A communication was received from them, begging Mr. Bruce to delay his departure for Peking, and to discuss with them at Shanghai certain details connected with the treaty. Mr. Bruce declined to do so, but offered them steam conveyance to the Peiho to enable them to reach Peking at the same time that he would. This they declined, alleging that they had no authority for returning by sea.

In the meantime Admiral Hope assembled his fleet, numbering in all some nineteen vessels, in the Gulf of Pechili, at the Sha-lu-tien Islands, about twenty miles from the Peiho. On the 17th of June, 1859, he proceeded to the anchorage off Taku, in H.M. ship "Fury," and sent her gig on shore, with an interpreter, to intimate that the Ministers of England and France would shortly be there on their way to Peking. The boat was met at the beach by an armed rabble, who stated that they were militiamen, acting on their own responsibility, and that the forts were defended and the river staked with the view of affording them protection against pirates. They denied the presence of constituted authority, and alleged that they had no instructions regarding the arrival of the foreign Ministers, but offered to transmit any communication to Tien-tsin, and to bring back a reply. Admiral Hope again sent on shore, and requested that within three days they would remove such of the obstructions from the mouth of the river as would clear a passage for the vessels accompanying the Ministers. To this request they made no apparent objection, and further stated that they had sent a messenger to Tien-tsin to acquaint the authorities with what had occurred. Admiral Hope then returned to Sha-lu-tien, and the following day brought his fleet to anchor off the Peiho.

On the 20th of June, Mr. Bruce and Monsieur de Bourboulon, the French Minister, reached the Peiho. The same day Admiral Hope sent a boat to see if the obstacles had been removed from the river, and to deliver a letter to the Intendant of Tien-tsin. The same armed rabble came down to the bank and refused to allow the party to land. In place of having removed any of the obstacles, they had increased the defences, and when taxed with a breach of faith in so doing, denied having promised to clear them away—adhering at the same time to their original statement that they were militiamen, acting on their own responsibility, in the absence of regular civil or military authority.

After a long and anxious deliberation, the ambassadors determined, in their joint names, to request Admiral Hope to adopt whatever measures he might deem expedient for the opening of the river, so as to admit of their continuing their journey to Tien-tsin. This occurred on] the 21st of June, and nothing was done until the 24th ;* the Admiral having been engaged in the interval notifying to the Chinese

---

* On this day, Mr. Ward, the American Minister, went into Taku in a small steamer, and requested to be allowed to proceed on the mission which he had to Peking, but he was refused, and had to return.

that as they would not remove the obstacles, he should proceed to do so himself. Accordingly, on the night of the 24th, a portion of the defences were blown up, preliminary to the operations intended to be carried out next day at as early an hour as the tide would permit.

After a good deal of delay, caused by difficulties connected with the tide, on the afternoon of the 25th of June, about two o'clock, Admiral Hope succeeded in getting his gunboats in position close to the barriers, and commenced attempting their removal. The Taku forts immediately opened a fire, which proved so heavy and destructive, as in a comparatively short time to completely disable four gunboats.

The Chinese artillerymen served their guns with a degree of skill and deadly precision that our navy had never witnessed in previous contests with them. As the remainder of the attacking vessels were now all aground, it was thought necessary for their safety that the forts should be captured by storm. This was the most disastrous part of the affair. A battalion of Marines had been kept in reserve as a storming-party, and disposed of in junks out of range. The determination to employ them was come to late in the afternoon, but no ready means were available for bringing them up; the only vessels capable of crossing the bar being either sunk or aground. It was at this critical moment that Commodore Tatnall,* of the American Navy, rendered the important service of towing the reserves into action. The attempt to storm the forts ended in a total defeat; out of 1,100 men that went into action, 434 were either killed or wounded.†

---

* This gallant officer, hearing that the British Admiral was lying badly wounded, jumped into his barge, and through the thickest of the fire pulled to the "Cormorant," where Admiral Hope was. On the way he had his cockswain killed by his side, who had been with him thirty years; and while he was with the Admiral, the crew of the barge, like true sailors, amused themselves by taking a turn at the guns, which were short-handed.

† The French force was represented by about 100 men, landed from the "Duchala," the commander of which vessel was wounded.

The conduct of Admiral Hope in this disastrous engagement was characterised by an amount of personal gallantry and total disregard of self second to none in the records of our navy. An eye-witness has thus described it: "The 'Plover' went into action at 2·30, the Admiral standing on the top of the cook-house, myself and the French captain on the harness cask in front of him. By three o'clock he was badly wounded by a round shot taking away the fleshy part of the thigh; the lieutenant commanding and eight men were killed, and twenty-two badly wounded. She then dropped down for more men, and the Admiral left her, to hoist his flag in the 'Opossum.' All this time his wound had been unattended to, except what my little surgical knowledge pointed out. When we left the 'Plover' there were only nine of us with a whole skin left out of her crew; she was literally like a butcher's slaughter-house. We had not been long in the 'Opossum' before the Admiral was again wounded. We had managed to get him on the top of the cook-house again, and being weak from his wound, he was supporting himself by the mainstay, when a round shot took that away, and threw him on the deck, injuring him on the head and fracturing his ribs. Still he would not give in, and was placed on the gunwale, till at last, being quite exhausted, he fainted. I then got him into a French boat, and was taking him away, but he came to and asked me which was the ship furthest in, I said 'Cormorant.' 'Then take me there.' So we went to the 'Cormorant,' where, finding him perfectly unable to stand, I had the signal made for Captain Shadwell, the senior captain, who came on board and took charge."

On the 26th of June, Admiral Hope having reported to Mr. Bruce his inability to clear the passage of the river with the force at his disposal, the Ministers decided to consider their mission to Peking at an end for the present, and Mr. Bruce directed the Admiral to dispose of the remainder of his fleet in such manner as he thought best calculated to secure tranquillity at the various ports on the coast where trade with Europeans was carried on; and thus ended the attempt made by the plenipotentiaries of England and France to ratify the treaties of Tien-tsin, the failure to effect which constitutes the prologue of the Third Chinese War.

On reaching England in November, 1859, I found that though an extensive allied expedition was in process of organisation, with the object of re-establishing our *prestige* in China, nevertheless a strong feeling existed against war —a humane sentiment, shared in to such an extent by her Majesty's Government that terms of the easiest nature were transmitted to Mr. Bruce, to be forwarded to the Chinese Government as those, the acceptance of which would avert further bloodshed. They were simply—that the treaty of Tien-tsin should be ratified, and an apology made by the Chinese Government for the occurrence at Taku; the very lenient view being adopted, that the hostile proceedings of the garrison there had originated in a local misunderstanding, and not from specific instructions on the part of the Chinese Government.

Shortly after this determination was come to, information reached England showing that the Chinese Government, far from disavowing the proceedings at Taku, fully approved of all that had been done, those who had conducted the defence being rewarded, while posthumous honours were conferred on the slain. With such feelings on the part of the Government of China, the settlement of the question naturally assumed a more difficult and complicated character, and it was considered expedient by the Governments of England and France, that Lord Elgin and Baron Gros should return to China, and themselves complete the ratifications of their treaties, which it was thought would be rendered the more easy, owing to the personal influence which previous relations with high Chinese officials had given them. Should the ultimatum which Mr. Bruce was directed to send, and their own efforts fail, the matter was then to be placed in the hands of the military and naval commanders of the allied forces.

Major-General Sir James Hope Grant, K.C.B., distinguished for his services in India, was appointed Commander-in-Chief of Her Majesty's land forces in China, with the local rank of Lieutenant-General. About 10,000 men were added to the troops already in China. The command of the navy remained in the hands of Rear-Admiral Hope, C.B., who was promoted to the rank of Vice-Admiral in China.

General Cousin de Montauban, a cavalry officer of distinguished service in Algeria, was appointed to the command of the French expeditionary corps, amounting to about 8000 men, and Vice-Admiral Charner was appointed to conduct the naval portion of the French expedition.

Having been for the previous six years and a-half stationed in that somewhat isolated portion of the Australian continent known as the Swan River Settlement, I had never seen any active service, and as this expedition appeared to offer an opportunity of doing so, I made up my mind to relinquish my place on the home roster and volunteer for China; which I did on the 1st of December, 1859. My application was complied with, and I was placed under orders for China.

CHAPTER I.

Arrive at Hong Kong—Aspect of affairs—Rejection of the ultimatum—Preparations for war—Occupation of Chusan—Friendly disposition of the natives—Hong Kong—Kowloon hired from the Chinese Government—Formation of a Chinese Coolie Corps—Arrangements for garrisoning Hong Kong and Canton.

On the 4th of April, 1860, I embarked at Southampton in the P. and O. mail steamer "Pera." At Marseilles we were to have taken on board Lord Elgin and Baron Gros. In consequence, however, of the death of the Dowager Lady Elgin, their departure was deferred until the next mail.

The well-known route to Alexandria and thence by Suez to Aden and the Point de Galle, needs no description. We reached Galle in the "Candia" on the 5th of May. At this place the passengers for China were transferred to the "Madras." Among the passengers who here came on board from Ceylon was a gentleman, whose general aspect conveyed the impression of one in very bad health, but patient and unexacting in suffering. He asked me several questions about the troops on board, and expressed a fear that without some additional awning they would be but indifferently protected from the sun. Conversation then turned upon the China expedition, with all the details of which he showed an intimate acquaintance, expressing at the same time his satisfaction that his health had borne up long enough to enable him to see the last portion of the expedition despatched from Calcutta, in the organisation of which he had had the chief direction. These and other remarks led me to ask him if I was not speaking to Sir James Outram. He answered yes, but that he was not travelling under his own name. He then went on to explain that in compliance with the urgent wishes of his medical attendants he was trying the effects of a sea voyage for an attack of chronic bronchitis from which he had been suffering for six months: but that his health was too indifferent to admit of receiving that hospitality which he knew would be pressed upon him at the various places at which he had to touch ; and he was therefore passing under the name of Major Osborne. He purposed going to Singapore and then on to Batavia, returning to Calcutta. His only attendant was a boy of some twelve years, whose parents had perished at Lucknow, at the relief of which Sir James had found him, and taken him into his service.

After touching at Penang and Singapore—where Sir James Outram left us—we arrived at Hong Kong on the 20th of May, and dropped anchor in front of the town of Victoria.

We now learnt that all hopes of an amicable adjustment of the difficulties arising out of the affair at the Peiho were at an end. The ultimatum of Her Majesty's Government had been forwarded by Mr. Bruce, and its rejection, in the form of an insolent reply, received. Preparations were forthwith commenced for moving the expedition northward, and as a preliminary measure a force, consisting of the Marines, 67th and 99th regiments, with a battery of artillery and company of engineers, was despatched to act in conjunction with the French, and take possession of Chusan, which was given up without resistance on the 24th of April. When the troops landed, numbers of the inhabitants came down and met them, offering themselves as servants and compradores,* in that peculiar Anglo-Chinese dialect known as Pigeon† English. To all appearance a lively and very

* A word of Portuguese origin, used in the south of China for housesteward.

† The nearest approximation which the Chinese can make to the pronunciation of the word "business."

favourable recollection still existed of our occupation of the island during the first war. The troops were hardly established on shore before sign-boards began to re-appear which had been in use during the previous occupation; the inscriptions thereon being such as—E. Moses & Son, outfitters, from Aldgate Pump; Jim Crow, fashionable tailor, from Buckmaster's, London; *sobriquets* which the Chinese had adopted on the advice of their army friends, as first-class English names likely to attract attention and secure them extensive patronage.

An allied commission was appointed for the purpose of exercising, under the military commanders, a general supervision over the government and administration of the island, the Chinese authorities at the same time being permitted to retain their local powers of jurisdiction, under the supervision of the Commissioners. Intimation was given to the natives that the commission had been established and was ready to hear and redress any complaints that might be brought before it.

In the meantime the main portion of the expedition was assembling at Hong Kong, and at the period of my arrival the remaining troop and store ships were daily expected.

Hong Kong is an island of small size and irregular shape, situated just within the tropics. Its greatest length is about nine miles, while its average breadth is about three. The island is extremely mountainous, a central ridge from east to west extends the whole length, throwing off a series of high lands on each side. Near the western end Victoria Peak rises to a height of 1,825 feet. On the northern slope of these mountains the town of Victoria creeps up from the beach, the principal portion of it being built on the ascent to Victoria Peak: houses now extend up it to nearly one-fourth of its height. The eastern end of the island is equally mountainous, the two highest points being Mounts Pottinger and Parkes.

The harbour of Victoria can be approached from either

the east or the west. Vessels coming from the north take the eastern entrance, or Lymoon Pass, a narrow strait between the island and mainland. The western entrance, called Sulphur Channel, is that usually taken by vessels from the south. This channel, which is about a quarter of a mile wide, lies between Hong Kong and a little islet known as Green Island. The harbour of Victoria assumes a completely land-locked appearance, being shut in at both ends by the opposite coast of China, a promontory of which, the Kowloon peninsula, is distant from the town of Victoria only one mile.

Besides the harbour of Victoria, there are several other bays where good shelter for shipping is afforded. On the southern side Lytam harbour is a fine deep bay, formed by two peninsulas—the westward one called Wong-ma-kok, where Captain Da Costa, of the Royal Engineers, was murdered in 1847. On the western side of the neck of this peninsula is the military station of Stanley, where barracks have been erected and a species of sanatorium established, under the supposition that from being exposed to the south-west monsoon it would prove a more healthy station than Victoria during the summer months. This hope, however, has not been realised; the men having suffered as much, and on several occasions more, than the troops in barracks at Victoria.

On the 20th of May a considerable portion of the expedition was on board transports in Lytam harbour, where they had been directed by Admiral Hope to rendezvous, and there wait until the monsoon changed, and then sail for Talien-whan Bay, a harbour on a promontory in the Gulf of Pechili, about 200 miles from the Taku forts, which had been selected as the northern rendezvous of the British expedition. Some of the troops were on board transports in Victoria harbour, while others remained in camp on the Kowloon peninsula, a portion of which had been actually hired from the Chinese authorities for the purposes of the expedition, and an annual rental of 500 taels paid for it in advance—the proceeding involving a singular anomaly in the history of war.

The French expedition was assembling at Shanghai previously to occupying Che-foo, where it was to rendezvous in the north. The vessels touched at Hong Kong, but no troops were landed there.

During the operations against Canton, the Military Train had been composed of Chinese coolies. This corps had not been disbanded, and an extension and re-organisation of it for the expedition was in course of progress, under the superintendence of Major Temple, of the 12th Madras Native Infantry, who had hitherto commanded it. Enlistment was going on briskly enough, but the difficulty was in retaining the recruits afterwards, as numbers bolted as soon as they had received the advance of two months' pay granted them on embarking for service in the north.

The intention was, provided a sufficient number of coolies could be procured, to attach 500 to each regiment, in addition to those to be employed in connection with the first battalion of the Military Train recently arrived from England, which was now broken up into three battalions, and constituted into a Horse Transport Service.

The pack-saddles for this corps were manufactured at Hong Kong by Chinese artizans, and the utmost activity prevailed amongst the native population in furthering the equipment of the expedition—the patriotism of John Chinaman assuming a very negative character when brought in contact with the opportunity of making money, or, as they themselves express it, "catching dollars." The tailors, blacksmiths, and tinmen were particularly busy in manufacturing field clothing, horse shoes, and camp cooking utensils.

Sir Hope Grant was residing in Victoria, at "Head-Quarter House"—the official residence of the Commander of the Forces in China—and the flag of Admiral Hope (blue at the fore) was flying on board the "Chesapeake" frigate of fifty guns. The camp at Kowloon had been commanded by Sir Robert Napier, who was now at Shanghai, in communication with the French Commander-in-Chief.

To complete the expedition several transports had yet to arrive. One battalion of the Horse Transport Corps, under the command of Captain Grey of the Military Train, had been sent to Japan, to aid in the purchase and care of horses and cattle.

On the sailing of the expedition, it was arranged that Hong Kong and Kowloon should be garrisoned by the 21st Madras Native Infantry, and a provisional battalion formed of depots from the various European infantry regiments proceeding to the north; the men selected for this depot were those who, from physical or moral causes, were unfit to embark with a corps intended for field service; an arrangement which appears to me open to criticism, because, however expedient it may be to avoid the embarkation of sick, weakly, and intemperate men on active service, the collecting of them for garrison duty in such a climate as a Hong Kong summer, is a measure not admitting of ready justification.

H. M. 87th regiment, the 3rd and 5th Bombay Native Infantry, with one battery of artillery, were detailed to garrison Canton, under Brigadier-General Crawford, who, on the departure of Sir Hope Grant, was to command the troops in the south of China.

Arrangements were made by the military authorities, that the expedition on sailing should be accompanied by artists, and berths were told off for Signor Beato, the well-known photographer, and Mr. Wirgman, the artist of the *Illustrated London News*, with whose talented and faithful sketches of Chinese scenery and character the readers of that journal have been for several years familiar.

Such was the state of affairs on the 20th of May, the date from which my personal narrative of the progress of the expedition commences.

CHAPTER II.

Kowloon—The Chinese Coolie Corps—Wreck of the "Isère"—Parade of the Coolies—The Happy Valley—Record of mortality in the 59th Regiment—Barracks of the Coolie Corps—Sir Hope Grant—Seik soldier and vegetable vendor—The Seik Cavalry—The Loodiannah Regiment—Shanghai threatened by the Taeping rebels.

May 21st.—Went over to the Kowloon peninsula, leased to the British by the Chinese Government. Three companies of the 44th regiment were being embarked on board of the transports that are to convey detachments of the coolie corps to the north, on which full European guards will be required.

The Chinese who have hitherto enlisted are for the most part Hakkas,* from the neighbouring districts of Lu-non and Kwei-shin. They are rather a marauding people, as compared with other classes of the Chinese, and consequently will require to be closely looked after when the expedition lands in the north; as the looting propensities which they are pretty certain to indulge in, should the opportunity offer, may disturb the friendly relations which the Commanders-in-chief will seek to establish with the natives amongst whom the troops may be stationed.

The 400 coolies that are to be attached to each regiment going north will be superintended by one officer, two sergeants, and thirty steady old soldiers, selected from the regiment. Twelve Chinese physicians have been engaged at thirty dollars per head per month, to form the medical

* The term applied by the aborigines, or Punti people, of the southern parts of the Kwang-tung province, to settlers who have moved down from the more northern districts.

staff of the corps, the general superintendence of which has been placed under Assistant-Surgeon Turner, who has been attached to the corps since its first formation at Canton some three years ago.

May 23rd.—News received of the loss of the French transport, "Isère," at Amoy, on the 15th instant. She struck on a rock going into the harbour, under charge of a Chinese pilot, and went down with a large quantity of gunpowder, two rifled cannon, and the harness for the field artillery. No lives were lost, and hopes are entertained of recovering the harness and cannon. The quantity of gunpowder lost is stated to be four hundred tons.

May 25th.—Went on board the "Forerunner" to see my brother, about to sail with a detachment of his regiment for Talien-whan Bay. Three hundred of the Chinese coolie corps are on board, with a guard of 120 men of the 44th, under Major Hackett. While I was there the coolies were paraded three deep on deck. Their uniform consists of an ordinary Chinese shirt, made of nankin, with the number and section to which they belong stamped on it front and back. Their head-dress is a conical shaped wicker-work hat, made after the fashion of those worn by the Chinese troops. They all appeared on parade with fans, which they used vigorously: some pulling up their shirts and fanning their chests and backs alternately, others pulling up the legs of their capacious under garments for the same purpose. The parade consisted of arranging them according to their numbers and then counting the total, to make sure that none had jumped overboard during the night to swim on shore, as they had all received their advance of pay. A few nights ago, of ten that were sent on board one of the transports to act as hospital orderlies, only four were forthcoming the following morning, six having swum on shore during the night and probably immediately re-enlisted.

I went below and looked at their quarters. They occupy the lower deck, and sleep on mats. One-third of the number will always be on deck, with a similar proportion of the 44th. They have all boxes with them, containing various little articles of food to be used as luxuries during the voyage. Their regular food will be supplied by the Government in the form of a daily ration of rice and pork. When relieved from parade they seemed very happy, and busied themselves making arrangements for the voyage, stowing their boxes away, and getting their berths in order.

May 26th.—The transports, forty in number, that have sailed from Hong Kong within the last fourteen days, have hitherto been at the rendezvous in Lytam harbour on the southern side of the island; to-day, however, we hear that they have fairly got under way for the north, convoyed by Her Majesty's steamers "Odin" and "Sampson."

This afternoon I walked through the grave-yards in the Wang-ne-chung,* or, as it is called by the English, the "Happy Valley." The last time I visited it was in June, 1852. At that period, the 59th regiment, the head-quarters of which had only been twenty months on the island, had buried there 182 men. A plain Doric column erected in the Protestant cemetery bears the following inscription:—

Sacred to the Memory of all those of the 59th Regiment, who died between the 11th June, 1849, and 18th November, 1858.

Brevet-Lieut.-Colonel G. F. Boughey.

Captain E. B. S. Stanhope. Surgeon A. Campbell.
Lieutenant Hacket. Assistant-Surgeon Orr.
Lieutenant J. B. Cockrel. Assistant-Surgeon Danvers.
Surgeon C. W. Powell. Quartermaster M'Donald.

Sergeants	21
Corporals	14
Privates	466
Women	36
Children	107
	644

* "Stream of Yellow Mud."

This conveys but an imperfect idea of the actual mortality which the regiment suffered during its service in China, as it does not include those who were invalided and died either on the voyage home or after reaching England, from diseases contracted in Hong Kong.

At the upper part of the Happy Valley, beyond the race-course, temporary barracks have been erected for the Coolie corps, composed of a framework of bamboo covered with matting. In each barrack-room are ranges of beds, formed of boards on bamboo supports, on which are spread the usual Chinese sleeping mats. In front of the sleeping places, on both sides of the rooms are ranged open fires, without chimneys or any protection against fire, or any means of exit for the smoke. On these were placed pots and other culinary utensils, in which cooking was actively going on from one end of the barracks to the other. The coolies seemed quite contented and free from care, further than what the preparation of their food required: the only marvel is, that the whole place has not been burned down long ago.

On my way back to the town I met a soldier of the Military Train, preceded by a Chinaman, whom he was holding firmly by the tail, twisted two or three times round his hand. I learned on inquiry, that this was a recruit for the coolie corps, who had just received an advance of twenty-seven dollars, and had been showing great anxiety to make his purchases for the voyage in shops up narrow lanes, which from experience was known to be symptomatic of an intention to bolt, so the soldier had adopted this method of securing him. Until lately these Chinese recruits have been receiving only two months' pay in advance, but they struck for an additional month's pay, and the point had to be conceded, the securing of their services being of so much importance.

The "Sir William Peel," steamer, lately arrived from England with military stores, was selected to-day by Dr. Muir, the principal medical officer, and placed in charge of my brother Staff-Surgeon D. R. Rennie, to be fitted up as the hospital-ship of the second, or Sir Robert Napier's, division. Three batteries of artillery have arrived in Deep-Water Bay from India, and orders have appeared this evening for the sailing of the expedition on the 27th, 28th, and 29th. The Staff to embark on the 30th.

27th May—Sunday.—At the conclusion of service, standing near the door of St. George's Cathedral, shading himself from the fierce sun, under an umbrella, might have been seen a spare, somewhat lathy, and weather-beaten looking officer, above the middle height, and about fifty years of age, whose sword indicated him to be of the rank of a general officer. His accent unmistakeably pointed to the north of the Tweed as the country of his birth, and his breast bearing the ribbons of the first Chinese war—the campaigns of the Sutlej—of the Punjaub and of Oude, bore testimony to a long and active career of Eastern warfare; his moustache, shorn off at the angle of the mouth, and a clear space of one inch intervening between it and the whisker, showed a strict adherence to regulation: this was Lieutenant-General Sir James Hope Grant, K.C.B.—as gallant a soldier, with as kind a heart as it ever fell to the lot of an army to be commanded by.

Passing down the Queen's Road this afternoon, I noticed one of the sowars* of Probyn's Horse, endeavouring to conclude a bargain for a cucumber, with the proprietor of a vegetable stall. There was some hitch about the price, and as the most simple way of concluding the business, he threw down a halfpenny and walked off with the cucumber. The Chinaman was not to be done, however. Unawed by the formidable tulwar† hanging from his side and pistol sticking out of the waist-belt, he strode after him, and with a sturdy determined air seized the cucumber, and wrenched it out of his hand. The Seik, finding himself worsted, came back, picked up his copper, and quietly walked away.

* Native troopers.   † Native sabre.

May 28*th.*—Walked over the camp at Kowloon this afternoon, and looked at the Seik cavalry. The horses are picketed in front of the troopers' tents—their movements restrained by ropes round their fetlocks, attached to pegs sunk in the ground. By this means they are effectually prevented kicking one another, as they otherwise would do; being for the most part high-spirited Arabs. The full uniform of the Seik cavalry is French grey, but the field-dress consists of blue serge tunics, made according to the custom of the East, with red cotton cummerbunds, or sashes, round their waists, white cotton trousers and jack-boots. Probyn's Horse wear a slate-coloured turban, and Fane's, a red one. Their arms consist of tulwars, light bamboo-shafted lances, carbines and pistols. Their lances, from which flutter blue and red pennants, are stuck in the ground in front of their tents, giving the encampment a very picturesque appearance.

The costume of the Regiment of Loodiannah consists of tunics and trousers of Kah Kee (mud-coloured drill) and turbans of dark brown calico. Their belts and ammunition-pouch are of rough brown leather; their arms are the old regulation musket and bayonet. This regiment was to have formed part of the first brigade of the field force; but it has now been decided that it will not form a portion of the expedition to the Peiho, owing to some difficulties having been raised during its voyage to China connected with the manner in which the water was served out; the men objecting, if I am rightly informed, to its passing through a leathern hose, as opposed to their faith.

May 29*th.*—Owing to the illness of Staff-Surgeon Pain, I to-day assumed temporary medical charge of the provisional battalion, now quartered in the Moray Barracks.

May 31*st.*—Several cavalry transports got under way yesterday afternoon, but they have been unable to get out of the harbour, owing to the strong north-east monsoon still blowing.

Last night a desperate affair took place in the Chinese

district, near West Point. A band of robbers broke into the house of a Chinese merchant with intent to plunder, but being beaten off by the inmates they hurriedly retired, and while retreating were stopped by two constables, who demanded their passes—one policeman was immediately stabbed and expired on the spot, the other was wounded so seriously that his recovery is considered hopeless. The gang got clear off, and no clue likely to lead to their apprehension is known. Hong Kong has long formed a sort of Alsatia for the worst classes of the neighbouring maritime provinces. Robberies, with or without violence, are of daily occurrence.

News has been received to-day of the approach of the Taeping rebels towards Shanghai. So much alarm exists amongst the general trading community there, native and foreign, that the British and French ministers have issued a proclamation, stating "that they will call upon the commanders of Her Majesty's naval and military forces to take proper measures to prevent the inhabitants of Shanghai from being exposed to massacre and pillage, and to lend their assistance to put down any insurrectionary movements amongst the ill-disposed, and to protect the city against any attack." This has been circulated in Chinese, and troops have been landed to protect the foreign settlement, and, if need be, the Chinese city.

CHAPTER III.

Loss of Her Majesty's Troop-ship "Assistance"—Return of Transports owing to foul weather—Allied attack on pirates at Chusan—Sanitary condition of the Troops in Hong Kong—The "Winifred" Coolie ship —Chinese doctor—Modes of deserting from the Coolie Corps—Boat population near the Happy Valley—Quarrying by Chinese—Missionary children — State of Shanghai — The Taeping rebellion — Ascent of Victoria Peak—Arrival of Lord Elgin and Baron Gros—Fall of Soochow—Chinese tailors.

June 1st.—This forenoon I was standing in the back verandah of the hospital, looking at the bustle going on in the harbour, where steamers in constant succession were getting under way. Just as a large black troop-ship was leaving her moorings, an officer passing by casually remarked, "There they go, sailing on a Friday." The vessel in question was Her Majesty's steamer "Assistance." A few hours afterwards news was received of her total loss on the opposite side of the island, having struck on a rock as she was going into Deep-Water Bay, to take horse transports in tow for the north. There were on board 850 of the coolie corps, and a large quantity of stores and provisions. Where the accident occurred was not more than fifty yards from the shore ; fortunately no lives were lost. Though the rock was not marked on the chart, it is difficult to understand why the vessel was taken so close in shore. On the vessel striking it was with considerable difficulty that the coolies were prevented jumping overboard and making for the shore. In a short time they became reassured and were gradually landed. Only seven of the 850 that were landed deserted. Fortunately about 100 of the number were veterans that had served during the operations against

Canton, and from being fully alive to the advantages of the service, were probably instrumental in preventing a general bolt, as they had all received three months' pay in advance.

June 2nd.—Examined the arrangements for the sick on board the "Mauritius" steamer, detailed as the hospital ship of the first division, and placed in charge of Staff-Surgeon Dr. Lewins. She is divided into three compartments, and has accommodation in bunks for 220 men. She was fitted up at Deptford under the immediate superintendence of Dr. Mapleton, Deputy-Inspector-General of Hospitals, and nothing was left unprovided that foresight and the closest personal supervision could supply for the comfort and medical care of the sick.* An apparatus also has been provided by the owners for distilling 1400 gallons of water daily. She sails this afternoon for Deep-Water Bay, to take transports in tow for Talien-whan.

June 3rd.—The weather has become unfavourable for the progress of the expedition. The monsoon would seem not yet fairly to have changed, as a strong north-east wind is now blowing. Towards evening between twenty and thirty of the transports that have sailed for the north within the last few days were reported as having returned, unable to make head against the adverse breeze. The present makes the fifth successive day of rain we have had, in consequence of which a considerable reduction of temperature has taken place.

* Notwithstanding the care which was taken in the fitting out of this vessel, and the beautiful order she was kept in by her commander, Captain Cruickshank, her success as an hospital ship is doubtful. From some cause or other, she was the only vessel of the fleet—numbering over two hundred vessels—anchored off the Peiho, on board of which anything resembling epidemic fever broke out. This unhealthiness I am inclined to attribute to the fact of her having been put to the purposes of a stationary hospital ship, while her construction was more that of a floating ambulance —in a word, she had not adequate accommodation for the number of sick that, as a stationary hospital ship, were kept on board for prolonged periods.

June 4th.—News received from Chusan of a combined English and French attack on a piratical station, situated between the islands of Latea and Chusan. The allied force consisted of Her Majesty's gunboats "Bustard" and "Woodcock," the marines and two cutters' crews of Her Majesty's ship "Imperieuse," and one company of the 99th regiment, with the French gunboat "Alarme," and some Infanterie de la marine. The pirates were concealed in a narrow channel formed by three small islands on the west coast of Chusan, into which there are four openings admitting of ingress and egress. The "Bustard" went in at the southern entrance, and as soon as she was seen, several junks' crews jumped on shore, while others got up sail and made their way towards some of the other openings, where they were met by the "Alarme" and the "Woodcock," and driven back under a heavy fire. The gunboats then closed in on the junks, but the greater portion of their crews got on to the mainland of Chusan and escaped. It had been arranged that the land force was to be on the spot to capture them, but it arrived two hours too late, much to its disappointment, the naval attack having been made before the appointed time. The leader of the pirates, however, an Englishman, known as Fokie Tom, was killed, and his wife, a rather good-looking Malay girl, was, with some thirty or forty others, made prisoner. Twenty-six junks were captured, and taken to Tinghae—six were burnt on the spot.

June 6th.—On taking medical charge of the provisional battalion, I was instructed by the principal medical officer to furnish weekly a sanitary report of its condition; the last few days have accordingly been devoted by me to this object, and the results are of a very unfavourable character. I find in the Moray and the adjoining range of barracks occupied by the battalion, in active operation every one of those sanitary defects (as well as others of a specially local character) which a few years ago were brought under public notice by the Army Sanitary Commission as having exercised so destructive an influence on the health and longevity of soldiers serving in England.

I had an interview on the subject this forenoon with Sir Hope Grant, who has perused my report bearing yesterday's date, forwarded to him with strong comments by Dr. Muir, on consultation with whom he has directed that 220 men should be removed immediately from the barracks and sent to Stanley as a preliminary measure. My report has also been placed in the hands of the officer commanding the battalion, with instructions to see the various defects therein pointed out forthwith remedied.

It is extraordinary that such a state of things as recent investigations have brought to light, should have been allowed to exist at a station so long notorious for its unhealthy climate ; and when one reflects on the probabilities that the defects in question are not of recent origin, the conclusion is unavoidable—that a vast amount of mortality, disease, and general physical deterioration, has been attributed to climate, which, in reality, has been rather the result of defective hygiene.

June 8th.—Medically inspected the "Trimountain" transport, arrived from Madras with a troop of the King's Dragoon Guards, numbering sixty-three men, 101 native followers, and seventy horses. The ventilation I found to be very defective, the men having been compelled, owing to the closeness of the atmosphere below, to sleep during nearly the whole voyage on deck. To-day the weather has improved so much as to admit of twenty-nine transports sailing.

June 9th.—Visited on duty the "Winifred" transport, an iron sailing vessel of 1300 tons, about to start for the north with 550 of the Chinese coolie corps, in charge of 110 men of the 2nd and 44th regiments. The coolies occupy the forepart of the vessel. The atmosphere I found to be exceedingly close and foul. Upwards of a dozen of the coolies were sitting on deck, on the sick list, suffering from fever. I sent for the Chinese doctor who was on board and inquired into the health of his charge, questioning him as to the causes to which he attributed the sickness. He was a tall solemn-looking old man, with an acute and very intelligent countenance, and his views relative to the causes of the sickness then prevailing, as conveyed to me by a "Pigeon English" interpreter, were strictly correct, being to the effect that it resulted from "too many piecee men, too muchee hot," —over-crowding, in fact, having been going on to an injurious extent, owing to about one-third more men having been crammed between decks at night during the ship's stay in harbour than there was adequate accommodation for; as it was stated to be impracticable to leave them on deck during the dark, owing to the probability of their jumping overboard and escaping, now that they had all received their advance pay.

Those I saw between decks were busily employed in one way or other—such as unpacking their boxes, writing letters to their friends, combing and plaiting their tails, &c. They appeared cleanly, and their superintendents state that they are fond of washing themselves. The troops are separated from the quarter of the vessel where the coolies sleep, by a latticed barricade.

One of the coolies made his escape a few days ago in a somewhat ingenious manner after he had received his advance of twenty-seven dollars, previous to embarkation. He was going about the town in charge of a soldier attached to the corps, making purchases for the voyage; amongst other things he bought some pepper and immediately threw it in the soldier's eyes and bolted, getting clear off. Another artifice they have practised successfully on several occasions, is working their way into a crowd of brother celestials surrounding vegetable or sweetmeat stalls, and watching their opportunity when the soldier is not looking, and then slipping off their regimental jackets and mixing with the crowd, who at this season of the year are usually similarly attired as the individual is who has thus denuded himself of Her

Majesty's livery—namely, with nothing on beyond a pair of blue cotton pantaloons. When the soldier looks about for his friend, he sees his jacket lying on the ground and a crowd of Chinamen about him, dressed in the same manner and looking so much alike that he is utterly at a loss which to fix on, and thus they have several times managed to escape; in fact, so hopeless are the chances of their recapture, that latterly the soldiers, after the coolies have fingered their dollars in advance, seldom let go of their tails until they have them fairly on board ship.

This afternoon Admiral Hope sailed for the rendezvous at Talien-whan Bay, in Her Majesty's steamer "Inflexible." His flag-ship, the "Chesapeake" screw frigate, will follow in the course of a day or two.

Walked in the afternoon to the east end of the harbour. Passing round towards an inlet that terminates in the Happy Valley, aground in the mud were several hundred sampans,* crowded with human beings of all ages and kinds, apparently healthy and happy. At this point there is a native rope work and several boat-building establishments.

In the neighbourhood, extensive stone-cutting and quarrying operations were going on. I passed several parties engaged in excavating, splitting, and hewing large blocks of fine granite. Splitting is effected by introducing a series of iron wedges into holes cut with sharp-pointed chisels. About four or five are generally placed in a line, and struck one after the other with a heavy sledge-hammer until cleavage is effected.

Huge blocks of granite were in course of excavation from hills composed chiefly of red sandstone, mixed up with detritus of granite. I observed hereabouts numerous masons' sheds, with native workmen engaged fabricating grave-stones and monumental sculpture out of the granite, which is of a light grey colour, of fine grain and very compact—a beau-

* Small flat-bottomed boats, covered in with matting, in which whole families reside—frequently two generations.

tiful stone for building purposes, but laborious, I should say, to work.

At the termination of the eastern extreme of the harbour, is situated the large establishment of Jardine & Company, in connection with which there appears to be a small dock at present in course of construction. Returning thence, I met walking in the cool of the evening, such as it is at this season of the year, a missionary and his wife, accompanied by two Chinese female servants (aiyahs, as they are called in the East), having in charge six or eight little Chinese children, all looking charmingly neat and clean. They are children attached to one of the missionary establishments in Victoria, where they are being brought up as Christians.

June 11*th*.—Sir Hope Grant and his personal staff, with the heads of the commissariat and medical departments, embarked at noon for Shanghai, *en route* to Talien-whan Bay. The temperature is gradually increasing, the thermometer now standing close on 90° in the shade.

June 12*th*.—Went off with the quarter master-general to report on the fitness of the sailing-ship "Oriental," to convey 160 invalids to England. We found her accommodation unequal to the number that it is proposed to send in her.

June 15*th*.—The regiment of Loodiannah has been ordered to Shanghai to reinforce the marines who have been landed under Lieutenant-Colonel March, for the defence of the Chinese city and foreign settlement—an attack by the rebels being daily expected. Trade is for the time suspended, and the greatest consternation prevails amongst the Chinese population.

Thus it would seem, that the first practical use of the expeditionary force, bids fair to be, to support the government that we are proceeding to chastise, and if coming events cast their shadows before, the probabilities are that the ultimate application of this great expedition will be to prop up the Manchu dynasty and save it, decayed as it is, from being irrevocably overthrown.

To no purpose more important to the interests of peaceful commerce—to no purpose more beneficial, I will go the length of saying essential, to the interests and progress of Christianity in China could our arms be applied, than to the suppression of the Taeping rebellion—the curse of the country,—and the most hopeless and impracticable movement, in a moral, social, and political point of view, that deluded individuals were ever betrayed into believing to possess Christian or other elements capable of being moulded into a stable form of government.

What progress can Christianity make—with what favour can it be expected to be received—amongst a people in whose ideas its principles are identified with those professed by the followers of the Taeping or Christian king, which, in their practice, embrace nearly every crime to be found in the Newgate Calendar?

The Taeping rebellion may be disposed of in a few words—a vast scheme of obscenity, rapine, and disorganisation, mixed up with a gibberish, blasphemous in character and worse than a travestie upon the Christian faith, and directed by a man, originally a peasant called Hung-seu-tseuen, and now known as the Tien Wang, or heavenly king, who, in any European country, would simply have been arrested in his early career and placed in a lunatic asylum; as his whole history, for several years prior to his assumption of spiritual and temporal powers, is that of one whose intellect had become seriously deranged.

That madmen, more especially those whose insanity takes a religious form, will readily procure adherents prepared to commit any extent of folly or violence, we know from the history of our own country; and when such a movement is combined with every element of disorder that will render it attractive to the scum of a population numbering upwards of four hundred millions, its success need not be wondered at.

After all, it is only partial, and is formidable only from the imbecility and utter incapacity of the government. One fact connected with it speaks volumes—it is a movement viewed with aversion by the respectable classes in the empire, and it is doubtful whether there is a single Chinaman or other person of respectability associated with it, save the Reverend Issachar Roberts, the original spiritual instructor of the Tien Wang—an American missionary, whose claims to be continued amongst the class in question are becoming seriously endangered by his persisting in attaching himself to the Court of Nanking, preaching Christian doctrines and receiving pay from the Tien Wang, thereby continuing to give missionary countenance to the movement.*

June 16*th.*—This afternoon, about four o'clock, I started from the Moray Barracks to ascend to the top of Victoria Peak. I soon reached the range of buildings known as the Albany, now occupied as quarters by officers of the Colonial government. From this point the harbour looks a picturesque lake, dotted over with shipping of every variety. At five o'clock the summit of the hill leading to Victoria Peak was reached, and from it burst on the view the southern side of the island—the vast group of islands in its

* Two years after the above remarks were written, the Reverend Issachar Roberts nearly came to serious grief in Nanking; having had a misunderstanding with his Taeping proselytes, one consequence of which was, that an unfortunate Chinese servant he had with him was beheaded in his own room. The reverend gentleman himself, through the aid of some of his former friends, managed to effect his escape from Nanking without bodily injury, and is now (April, 1863) going about professing great animosity towards the Tien Wang and Taepingdom generally. He recently had an interview with Brigadier-General Staveley at Shanghai, from which it would seem, that, though at variance with the Court of Nanking, he still continues to hold friendly relations with the Boo Wang, the present Taeping ruler at Soochow; as he undertook to convey a letter to him from General Staveley, to procure the release of four Sepoys who were taken prisoners in May, 1862, and were then known to be still alive and in the hands of the Taepings. To this communication, I may add, the Boo Wang sent an evasive and somewhat impertinent reply.

vicinity, and the wide expanse of the China sea. Ascending the summit of the Peak, I reached the signal station, from which, in clear weather, vessels are seen fifty-five miles off. The Kowloon peninsula lies beneath, mapped out like a garden, now dotted over with military tents. The great extent of the town of Victoria is much better seen from here than from any other point of view; the roof of almost every separate house being distinctly visible. The town of Victoria straggles over an extent of nearly four miles water frontage.

June 21*st.*—This morning the English mail steamed into harbour decked in her gayest colours and flying the ensigns of England and France, thereby showing the presence on board of Lord Elgin and Baron Gros. The cause of their detention now became known, viz., the total loss in Galle harbour of the mail steamer "Malabar." At noon Lord Elgin and Baron Gros landed under a double salute from the Royal Artillery, and proceeded to Government House. Amongst the passengers who arrived with Lord Elgin was Mr. Bowlby, the talented and ill-fated special correspondent of the *Times*.

June 23*rd.*—Lord Elgin embarked for the north this afternoon in the "Feroze," a steamer of the Indian navy that has been waiting his arrival. He looked in robust health, his snow-white hair contrasting strongly with his sun-scorched face. The "Feroze" sailed this evening for Shanghai, whither Baron Gros follows to-morrow morning in a French steam-vessel.

News from Shanghai has been received, bringing accounts of the capture by the rebels of Soochow, one of the most flourishing cities in China, distant about ninety miles from Shanghai. Ho, the governor-general, has taken refuge there, and placed himself in communication with the allies, begging them to advance on Soochow and drive out the rebels, a proposition that could not be acceded to, although the Chinese city of Shanghai will be defended by the allies, should the rebels attack it, which is now almost certain, Soochow having fallen.

June 24*th.*—Having been relieved from the charge of the provisional battalion, I was preparing to start for Talien-whan in one of the horse transports recently arrived from India, when to-day I had the good fortune to meet Admiral Page, who hearing that I was going north, very kindly offered me a passage in the " Weser," that has just arrived from France with stores for the expedition. I gladly accepted the offer, being happy to escape the uncertainty always attending the progress of sailing vessels on the north-east coast of China. The "Weser" will go to Che-foo, where I shall have to wait until an opportunity occurs of getting across the Gulf of Pechili to Talien-whan.

June 25*th.*—The heat during the night was so great that sleep was impossible. This morning, between five and six, I strolled down with Dr. Gordon, C.B., who arrived two days ago to assume the duties of Deputy-Inspector-General of Hospitals at Hong Kong. Dr. Gordon was despatched at very short notice and had not time to procure certain requisites of his new rank. To ascertain whether such could be supplied in China, I went with him to Tung-cheong, a Chinese tailor, who undertook, without a moment's hesitation, to furnish what he wanted, and amongst other things to metamorphose a forage cap of the 10th Foot into a gold-laced Staff one, *à la* Buckmaster, for eight dollars. Martial clothing appeared to be Tung-cheong's special branch of trade, as he had a variety of military appointments on hand, including a stock of the various war medal ribbons, China not excepted—which, by the way, reminds me of " Cheap John," as he designates himself on his sign, a Chinaman opposite, who has exposed for sale in the window of his shop a complete supply of the hat ribbons used in the navy, with the names thereon, in gilt letters, of the various war vessels in China, at present numbering about seventy pennants—there not being a single commodity at all likely to be in demand, that the ever ready and watchful celestial does not endeavour to be in a position to supply. The gold lace, ribbons, and other military decorations which are supplied by the Chinese tailors in Hong Kong, are manufactured in Canton after English patterns, and really little or no difference is perceptible in the quality or appearance of the article.

The following anecdote I afterwards heard of Pun-lun, "dealer in silks, ivory, matting, fire-crackers, &c.," as his signboard declares:—When the troops touched at Hong Kong, on their way home from Peking, a quantity of the Summer Palace loot was hawked about by soldiers, and extensively purchased by all classes in Hong Kong. Pun-lun, with a quick eye for business, observing the great run there was on garments represented to be Imperial, sent to Canton and privately bought up all the Chinese *theatrical dresses* that could be procured, which he disposed of at Hong Kong at very high prices, as vestments warranted Imperial—clearing in the course of a few days upwards of three thousand dollars by the speculation.

While we were out heavy rains fell, after which the atmosphere seemed surcharged with moisture; the heat assuming a more than usually oppressive character and producing a sensation of debility, much greater than ever results from the direct rays of the sun. This peculiar heat I have always observed is accompanied by an increased amount of sickness.

CHAPTER IV.

Embark in the "Weser"—Muster of the Crew—Punishments—M. Tao—
Off the Yang-tse-Kiang—Sisters of Charity—Uncertainty of Monsoon
—Council for promoting deserving sailors—The Shantung Promontory
—Che-foo—The French camp—Questionable seizure of Junks—Chinese
Jew—A Jewish colony.

June 27th.—After a detention at Hong Kong of nearly six weeks, I embarked for the north this day at noon in the "Weser" transport, and on presenting the order for the passage, so kindly furnished me by Admiral Page, was received with the same kindness and courtesy that I have invariably experienced when thrown in contact with French officers, whether abroad or in their own country.

The "Weser" has on board the compartments and armaments of three gun-boats, with their respective complements of officers and men. The gun-boats will be landed at Che-foo, where they will be put together. The "Weser" will then be fitted up as an hospital ship, and employed in conveying invalids from China to Suez *en route* to France, an arrangement that in the end will probably be cheaper and more salutary than the adoption of an intermediate sanatorium at the Cape of Good Hope.

At six in the evening the crews of the "Weser" and the gun-boats were mustered on deck, and a short prayer said by one of the men. The punishments for the day were then read out and carried into effect,—the orders for the night were also given. The punishments differ somewhat from those adopted in our navy. The mildest one is placing men in a row, making them look at the sea in the same direction for a certain time; another is a sort of modification of mast-heading, namely, placing men in the shrouds with their faces to the sea for a couple of hours; a third is a stoppage of wine, which is considered a severe punishment.

June 28th.—Amongst the passengers there are six sisters of charity and a priest, going to join the Roman Catholic Mission at Ningpo. They mess with the commander of the "Weser," and on her arrival in the Yang-tse-Kiang, will be landed at Shanghai.

One of the passengers, Monsieur Tao, is a native of Shanghai, and having been educated there at the Catholic Mission, he was afterwards taken to Paris, and while there became known to General Montauban, who arranged that he should be sent out and attached to his staff as interpreter. He speaks French fluently, is quiet and prepossessing in his manners, conducting himself at table with as strict attention to its conventionalities as if his education had been altogether French. Though born and brought up at Shanghai, he could not make himself intelligible to the Chinese at Hong Kong, so great is the difference between the northern and southern dialects, though the written character is the same.

July 1st.—At sunset we anchored about fifteen miles from the light-ship in the mouth of the Yang-tse-Kiang, and twenty miles from the shore.

July 2nd.—This morning a Chinese pilot boarded us. He spoke pigeon English very fairly, and was a sturdy favourable specimen of a northern Chinaman. He had with him an ordinary pilot boat, and a crew of six. On being questioned about the probabilities of being able to land the sisters of charity at Shanghai, without taking the "Weser" farther up the river, he undertook to do so himself for sixty dollars, and his terms were accepted. The morning was dull and damp, a drizzly rain falling. Not a murmur was raised by these devoted females to entrusting themselves, accompanied only by one seaman and the priest, in a

Chinese boat twenty miles from land, amongst a rude crew belonging to a race that their nation was at war with.

There was a considerable swell on, and after some difficulty all were got into the boat, setting sail at ten in the morning with a fair wind up the wide waters of the Yang-tse-Kiang. When fairly away from the ship, one could not but be struck with their helpless position, should ideas of plunder or violence cross the minds of the boatmen in whose hands they completely were.

July 4*th.*—The wind continues dead ahead, and is of considerable strength—a warning to sailing vessels beguiled into trying the passage north under the belief that they must of necessity have a fair wind because it is the season of the south-west monsoon, supposed to have been blowing since June. The weather is fine, however, and the thermometer about seventy; the bracing air and clear atmosphere being a pleasant change from the muggy, suffocating heat of Hong Kong.

A council was held this forenoon by the captain and officers, for the purpose of determining the merits and claims to advancement of the petty officers and crew. This council is held twice a year, and the officers are at liberty to bring forward any suggestions they may have to make regarding the promotion of any of the men they may feel interested in.

July 5*th.*—This morning land was sighted at six o'clock. In two hours we were abreast of the Shantung Promontory.* The outline of the coast is here very irregular; numbers of small conical peaks forming the prominent features as we passed along.

At one o'clock the Peak of Che-foo, an elevation of about a thousand feet, came in sight about twenty-four miles

---

* The province of Shantung is celebrated as being the birthplace of Confucius and his disciple Mencius; the tomb of Confucius, who died 479 years before Christ, is still shown at Kink-fan, no great distance from Che-foo.

ahead. Shortly afterwards we made out a confused collection of houses on a hilly slope, which we concluded was the town of Che-foo.

Che-foo Point, marking the entrance to the anchorage, is now reached. A rocky and picturesque headland, with a scanty covering of mouldy-looking vegetation, without any trace of tree or brushwood.

To the right, the harbour opens out into a fine bay with a beautiful sandy beach, villages, and cultivated fields. The land in the immediate vicinity of the anchorage appears to rise by a gentle slope for several miles, and then abruptly terminate in a somewhat lofty range of hills.

The naval arrangements at Che-foo, up to the present time, have been conducted by Rear-Admiral Protet, whose flag is seen flying from the "Dryade," a magnificent frigate, specially constructed so as to carry guns on one deck, and troops or horses on the other. She is of unusual length, and has the round stern, characteristic of French naval architecture, her double line of ports being continued right round.

As we get closer to the anchorage, what has seemed to us an island and town, our glasses now make out to be a hill covered with the huts and tents of the troops. From a small fort or watch-tower at its summit the *tricolor* is seen fluttering in the breeze. Groups of soldiers are collected on the hill-side watching the vessel coming to anchor.

About six in the evening I went on shore with some of the officers. We landed on the beach to the south of the hill where the troops are encamped, and ascended it by a rude pathway leading towards the encampment. Neither the camp nor the soldiers looked the picture of neatness; the tents, for the most part, present a poor appearance, consisting of two sheets of canvas joined together, and supported across a longitudinal wooden rod about four feet from the ground, forming a covering like an inverted letter V (the *tente d'abri*), allowing three men to sleep in a row.

Sometimes two of these tents are joined together end to end, and enable six men to sleep together. They appeared well secured from water, by deep drains dug round them. The great advantage of these tents is, that as they are carried by the soldiers themselves, shelter at night can always be secured, whereas, in the case of the bulky tents used in our service, the shelter depends on the means of transport. Every French soldier on service with the expedition will carry a portion of his tent, two men carrying the canvas sheets, and a third the wooden supports, which, from being jointed, go into small bulk.

On our way to the top of the hill, we came to a small Buddhist temple where General Jamin has established his head-quarters. General Montauban was then dining with him, having arrived this forenoon from Shanghai. Passing amongst the tents of the chasseurs à pied, I observed a little garden fancifully laid out, having neatly designed in shells the imperial crown in the centre, with *Vive la France* on one side, and a light infantry bugle and "2nd" on the other.

A steamer which we had seen in the distance as we were entering the harbour, arrived in the evening. She had twelve junks astern, which had been seized as store-ships. Though they are forcibly taken possession of, the owners are informed, through interpreters, that they are merely taken on loan, and will be returned at a future period with an indemnity; four of the crew are also taken at the same time, and retained in the junks, being fed and looked after in consideration of their services. The English, it is stated, are seizing junks in a similar manner at Talien-whan.

As no declaration of war has in reality taken place, and the junks in question are the property of private traders, it appears to me doubtful whether such a proceeding is either justifiable, or in accordance with the humane wishes of the home governments that hostilities should be confined as much as practicable to the scene of the outrage of June,

1859, and pressure brought to bear on the government of China rather than on its people. Forty junks have already been seized, and are anchored off the group of islands in the harbour, under the guns of the "Andromache," moored opposite them as a guard-ship. As soon as the steamer came in with her prizes this evening, another went out on the same errand.

Amongst the natives I met on shore was one of tall stature and stout frame, with a florid complexion, and as perfect a Jewish physiognomy as it is possible to conceive. A colony of Jews, I believe, was discovered in Honan, the province adjoining Shantung, by the Jesuits, about two hundred years ago.*

* I have since ascertained that it was at Kai-fung-fu, a town on the Yellow River, and the capital of Honan, that the Jesuits made this discovery; and, further, that a mission of inquiry, consisting of two Chinese Christians, was sent from Shanghai in 1851, to visit and report on the state of those that remained, for the information of the London Society for Promoting Christianity amongst the Jews. The results of the visit are thus summed up by the Bishop of Hong Kong, in an introductory chapter to the narrative written by the two Chinese; a detailed notice of which will be found in the "Chinese Repository" for July, 1851.

"After a tedious journey of twenty-five days, they arrived at the site of the Jewish synagogue, facing to the eastward. Here, in the midst of a surrounding population, two thirds of whom were professors of Mohammedanism, and close adjoining to a heathen temple dedicated to the 'God of Fire,' a few Jewish families, sunk in the lowest poverty and destitution, their religion scarcely more than a name, and yet sufficient to separate them from the multitude around, exposed to trial, reproach, and the pain of long-deferred hope, remained the unconscious depositaries of the oracles of God, and survived as the solitary witnesses of departed glory. Not a single individual could read the Hebrew books; they had been without a rabbi for fifty years. The expectation of a Messiah seems to have been entirely lost. The rite of circumcision, which appears to have been observed at the period of their discovery by the Jesuits two centuries ago, had been totally discontinued. The worshippers within the synagogue faced towards the west; but whether in the direction of Jerusalem, or towards the suspended tablets of the emperors, no clear information was obtained. The synagogue itself was tottering in ruins; some of the ground had been alienated to pagan rites, and a portion of the fallen materials sold to the neighbouring heathen. Some time previously, they had petitioned the Chinese emperor to have pity on their poverty, and to rebuild their temple. No reply had been received from Peking, but to this feeble hope they still clung. Out of seventy family names or clans, only seven now remained, numbering about 200 individuals in all, dispersed over the neighbourhood. A few of them were shopkeepers in the city; others were agriculturists at some little distance from the suburbs; while a few families also lived in the temple precincts, almost destitute of raiment and shelter. According to present appearances, in the judgment of our native messengers, after a few years all traces of Judaism would probably have disappeared, and this Jewish remnant have been amalgamated with and absorbed into surrounding Mohammedanism."

CHAPTER V.

Che-foo Harbour—Trade—Climate—Health of the Troops—Interview with General Montauban—The French force—Market supplies—Chinese money-changers—Judicious treatment of the natives—Buddhist temple—Progress of the shopkeepers in French—Construction of the houses—Arrival of the "Calvados"—The Coolie Corps.

CHE-FOO may be described in general terms as a bay with a number of villages skirting its shores, about sixty miles to the north of the Shantung Promontory. The harbour is formed by a long neck of land known on English charts as Che-foo Head, running parallel to the main, and united to it by a narrow sandy isthmus about three miles long. The average depth of water is six fathoms, with a bottom of mud and shingle, affording good holding-ground. The harbour runs in a south-easterly direction, being six miles long and three and a half wide. The entrance is a little over a mile in width, and lies between a group of islands and the southern extreme of Che-foo Head.

Che-foo Harbour is much superior to that of Tang-chan, thirty miles to the south of it, the port of the Shantung province opened to trade by the treaty of Tien-tsin in 1858. Tang-chan was selected owing to its having been visited by the embassy of Lord Macartney in 1793. It can only be entered at high water, whereas vessels can come into Che-foo at all times.

A considerable trade has hitherto been carried on in grain with other parts of the Shantung province,* and also it is

* The Shantung province contains 65,000 square miles, and 30,000,000 of inhabitants.

stated with Corea and Japan. Some of the villages that skirt the shores of the harbour are near the beach, others a short distance inland, prettily placed amongst groves of trees, the rich foliage of which partly conceals them from view. The general character of the mainland at Che-foo is that of a gentle slope, gradually rising until it terminates in a curve of lofty and picturesque hills of a sombre green colour, contrasting strongly with the bright green of the maize fields that creep for a considerable distance up their slopes.

The climate, judging from present appearances, would seem to be unusually healthy, there being an almost total absence of sickness amongst the troops, and their general health since landing being stated to be much superior to what is usually the case in France. This probably results from the extreme dryness and purity of the atmosphere, notwithstanding the direct force of the sun, which during the day is very considerable. The troops have gradually been assembling here since the first of June, and only four deaths have taken place out of some seven thousand men, and one of those was from a wound received in a duel.

This morning (July 6th) I came on shore with Captain Cléret. He was accompanied by his chief artificer for the purpose of selecting a suitable spot for the construction of the gun-boats. We landed at a jetty near a wooden shed, ticketed "Bureau de direction du Port."

General de Montauban has established his head-quarters in a good-sized house situated in the rear of the hill, on the outskirts of the village, and apparently recently constructed for some public purpose. It is built of brick, and consists of a hall with dwelling-rooms and offices built round two squares. Here I was introduced to the General, who told me that on his arrival yesterday morning, he found a letter waiting for him from Sir Hope Grant, informing him that the English army would have to remove from Talien-whan Bay to Pe-tung, twelve miles from the Peiho, owing to difficulty in procuring water. As the letter had no date, he could not form an opinion as to whether the army had started or not; but said that in the course of a day or two he would send a steamer over to Talien-whan with a despatch for General Grant, by which opportunity I could go across.

The French force now at Che-foo is divided into two brigades, commanded by Generals Jamin and Collineau. The infantry number about six thousand three hundred men. The artillery consists at present of three batteries of rifled cannon (twelve-pounders), and one of mountain guns (four-pounders), also rifled. The engineer force consists of two companies of the corps de génie; the soldiers of which present the best appearance of any in camp.

There is a corps also of pontoniers attached to the artillery, and they are at present employed constructing a military bridge for service on the Peiho.

The force is not yet ready to take the field, the delay resulting chiefly from the unbroken condition of the horses when purchased. They have been procured for the most part from Japan, at a first cost of twenty-five dollars (five pounds sterling) per head. A number of them are in very bad condition, but on the whole, the artillery horses, which are a selection of the best, are in good order. The mountain battery is horsed by mules imported from Japan, where their cost was fifty dollars each. The officers and soldiers of the artillery seem to be occupied from morning until sundown breaking the ponies in; which, however, does not appear to be conducted on Mr. Rarey's principle, as I occasionally noticed a good deal of violence used. This is a source of delay and annoyance that the English force is not exposed to, regularly broken artillery horses having been brought from India, many of them veterans that had served in previous campaigns. There is an excellent watering-place for the horses under the wall of a small town about a quarter of a mile in the rear of the camp.

With the exception of an escort of fifty men for General Montauban, consisting of Spahis (Algerine cavalry) and chasseurs d'Afrique, there are no cavalry attached to the force. The Spahis are natives of Africa, and wear the Arab costume. They are armed with long muskets, which they carry slung across their back. Their heels are armed with long sharp-pointed steel spikes, the most murderous-looking weapons to which the name of spurs was ever applied. As far as appearance goes, they do not contrast favourably with the dashing look and martial bearing of the Seik cavalry.*

Abundant supplies of fresh pork, poultry, eggs, vegetables, and fruit are brought in for sale by the neighbouring population. A regular market has been established in the centre of the camp, and every morning several hundred Chinamen may be seen disposing of their supplies. The eggs are of large size, and are sold at a rate equal to four for a penny. Fowls are eight for a dollar, or sixpence apiece. Vegetables and fruit are hawked about the camp the whole day, chiefly onions, lettuces, radishes, cucumbers, apricots, plums, and walnuts. In the market-place, from sunrise to sunset, a line of money-changers are established, with portable bureaus in front of them, on which are deposited piles of the current coin of the realm, in the shape of the copper *tchen*, or cash, as they are termed in pigeon English. As purchasers pass, the money-changers clink a dollar, and, pointing to their native coin, call out *huit cent cinquante* with a remarkably good accent, indicating their readiness to give 850 cash in exchange for a dollar;† in fact, the whole popu-

---

* I am in possession of information however from an eye-witness, that at the action of Pa-li-chao, on the 21st September, where there was a detachment of Seik cavalry attached to General Montauban, an opportunity was offered of testing their respective merits in action, and that the comparison unquestionably was in favour of the Spahis.

† The cash is the only coin the Chinese have, and is a good deal adulterated with base metal. In the south of China their value is about

lation have now accommodated themselves to circumstances, and in the prospect of making money out of him all fear of the barbarian has been dispelled. These results are due to the judicious and humane manner in which the primary occupation has been conducted by General Jamin.

On the arrival of the first portion of the expedition about a month ago, the inhabitants fled into the interior, but General Jamin immediately ordered a proclamation to be circulated that private property would be respected, and that the people had nothing to fear, as the soldiers would not be allowed to enter the town. This soon became known, and in the course of a few days the natives began to come back and business was gradually re-established, though several of the houses and stores are still closed. The respectable portion of the female community have not yet ventured back, and it is probably as well that they should remain absent.

An interpretorial court has been established, and almost every morning applications are made by traders for indemnification for losses sustained by robberies during the first few days of the panic; and as a general rule, I am informed, their claims are listened to with consideration.

The mandarin of the town has been re-established in his authority, and adjudicates in the case of little squabbles between the soldiers and the natives; in most instances deciding against the latter. When a complaint is made, he immediately furnishes the authorities with a police officer, who aids them in arresting the offending party. This afternoon I visited the town on the beach, near the camp, entering by a sort of gateway, where a strong guard was posted to prevent soldiers entering. The main street consists of a line of shops differing but little from those seen in the south of China. At the doors of the principal ones, sentries are placed to protect them against attempts at looting. In

twenty for a penny, or one thousand to a dollar. They are perforated by a square hole at the centre, and thus strung together.

the joss-house* or Buddhist temple the main guard is established. The temple consists of three separate chapels, in two of which there are three well-carved grotesque-looking figures, and in the central chapel a female image of some beauty placed behind the folds of a curtain, reminding one strongly of figures of the Virgin in Roman Catholic countries, more especially where devotees have deposited relics at her shrine, there being a number of small junks hung up in the vicinity of the figure, offerings to the deity in hopes of securing safe and prosperous voyages. In the porch of the temple also a number of miniature junks were suspended.

Several of the shops were visited, and the progress which the owners had made in "pigeon" French was considerable. One man had mastered nearly all the ordinary numerals, and could say *Comment vous portez-vous*, and *Bon jour*, with all the ease possible.

The houses and shops appear of more substantial construction than those in the south of China, the result probably of the difference of climate. They are built of either dark-coloured brick or stones, well cemented; the masonry altogether being exceedingly good. The roofs are angular, and formed of dark-coloured tiling neatly arranged. The ceilings in some of the shops are composed of matting spread over a light framework of bamboo, in place of plaster-work. Most of the shops have court-yards in their rear; in many of them flowers in green porcelain pots are ranged on terraced benches, as in hot-houses in Europe.

The "Calvados," steam-transport, came in this evening from Shanghai, with 250 horses and a battery of artillery, recovered from the wreck of the "Reine des Clippers," a French transport recently burned near Macao, in which the whole of the winter clothing for the army was destroyed.

* A corruption of *Deos*, the Portuguese for God; hence "joss pigeon" —the generic term in Canton English for all devotional exercises.

As I passed the lines of the Corps Chinois, on my way to the beach, the bugle sounded, and forthwith the members of this distinguished corps emerged from their tents, formed themselves into line, and had their names called over, during which smoking was not prohibited in the ranks. Their number at present is 600, and 400 more are expected from Shanghai. A General Order has this day been issued by General Montauban prohibiting gambling amongst them, owing to the numerous breaches of the peace to which the practice has given rise; sums as high as thirty and forty dollars having changed hands. The Canton men are said to squabble a good deal with those from Shanghai. Only ten have as yet deserted.

CHAPTER VI.

Agriculture—Appearance of the Peasantry—Gun-boats—Kit inspection—
French mode of carrying ammunition—Its advantages over the English
method—Watch-tower—Military air of the Coolies—Leave Che-foo—
Talien-whan Bay—Camp of the Second Brigade—The Bell Tent—
Capture of Junks—Interview with Sir Hope Grant—Auriferous quartz
—Arrival of Lord Elgin—Sir Robert Napier.

July 7th.—This morning early I walked a little way into the country. Peasants were coming into market, and a good many were at work in the fields. I passed some fine crops of Indian corn, cultivated with great care and regularity—about fourteen inches being allowed to intervene between each stalk. The soil is everywhere light clay, and there is not an available portion of it that I passed but is devoted to the growth of the maize; the fields extending by terraces a considerable way up the base of the hills. Donkeys, fitted with pack-saddles, are extensively used for transport, and are of a fine breed, some of them being so large as almost to be mistaken for mules. The peasantry struck me as a taller and finer race, though not more muscular than the lower orders of Chinese in the south. In their dress and general customs there is no perceptible difference, with the exception that the moustache, which in the south is not worn until the position of grandfather has been attained, here may be seen decorating the faces of the comparatively young.

Through Monsieur Tao, I ascertained that the town or village which bears the name of Che-foo is on Che-foo Head, near its northern end. The one near the hill where the camp is, is called Yentai, and is the chief place of commerce. Tao explains why there are so many villages within short distances of each other in place of one large town, by the fact that in China all collections of houses coming within the term town or city, by law must be invested by a wall, and therefore the inhabitants of districts sufficiently populous to form a town, prefer a series of detached villages to an intramural residence. Tao states that the inhabitants perfectly understand why the French have landed, and that they will not long remain; that their object is to make a new treaty, force the passage of the Peiho, and thus avenge their defeat of last year: this, they add, is no business of theirs, but of the government, and so long as the French are ready to trade on fair terms, so are they.

On this side of the hills that surround Che-foo the climate is too dry for the cultivation of rice, but on their inland aspect considerable quantities are grown.

In the course of my walk I had numerous opportunities of observing the respect that the Chinese entertain for all kinds of manure, and I feel assured that Mr. Alderman Mechi would see nothing to grieve him were he to visit Che-foo.

The landing of the gun-boats has already commenced, and large shears for putting them up are in course of construction. Each gun-boat is in fifteen pieces, including machinery, and when complete, armament included, will weigh seventy-five tons and draw five feet of water. The hull of the vessel is in three pieces. The gun is a sixty-pounder rifled, and worked from an unprotected front in the bow of the boat, and from their being constructed of iron, the inference is that they are intended to operate at a distance sufficiently great to be out of the reach of ordinary shot. The compartments are fastened by screws and nuts, and were put together at Toulon in thirty-six hours. They are seventy-eight feet long and eighteen broad. The weight of the boiler is six tons and a half, and they are provided with a rudder at stem and stern.

At a kit inspection of the 102nd Regiment this afternoon, I was struck with the less fatiguing and less hurtful mode in which the French soldier carries his sixty rounds of ball ammunition, as compared with the method in our service. A single belt, fastened round the waist, carries his bayonet and cartouch-box, of small size, containing only twenty rounds, the remaining forty being carried in the knapsack—an arrangement which appears to me much superior to ours, which compels the soldier to carry forty rounds in a small portmanteau suspended by a cumbrous shoulder-belt, and further to fit on to waist-belt supporting the bayonet another leathern box containing twenty rounds, which, from being placed on the right side in front, bumps over the liver every time his movements are accelerated. To modify the pain arising from this, he has to tighten the belt to the utmost, thereby necessarily diminishing the cavity of the chest and abdomen. Reducing the natural space of organs, such as the lungs, the liver, and spleen, interferes with the circulation, and predisposes the soldier to heat apoplexy,* and other congestive diseases of warm climates—in a word, subjects the soldier to evils much the same as those which arise from tight lacing in the other sex.

Though the French cartouch-box is suspended from the waist, yet, from its position and small size, it does not cause the men anything like the same amount of inconvenience that the English soldier suffers ; at the same time it would be more desirable if the waist were left altogether free, and a moderate amount of ammunition, and the bayonet, suspended by light shoulder-belts, and the remainder carried in the knapsack or in some other way, without compressing the waist.†

* The term *coup de soleil*, by which this disease is generally known, implying it to result from the direct influence of the sun's rays, is a misnomer; as it is well known to occur with greatest severity under circumstances where the sun's action is not direct, such as in the barrack rooms at night, and on the march in sultry, cloudy weather.

† My attention was first drawn to the injurious effects of compressing

I visited the fort-like building on the top of the hill. It is a tower of observation, surmounted by a stone sentry-box made in the shape of a pagoda. These towers are stated to be of considerable antiquity. It is about thirty feet high, and has no entrance whatever, the top being reached by a ladder placed outside. On ascending, I found the interior earthed up to the battlements. The look-out house faces the sea, and commands an extensive view.

While at the jetty waiting for a boat to return to the "Weser," some three hundred of the coolie corps marched down in military order, to carry up stores landed from the " Calvados." A good number of them seemed to have acquired a martial spirit, shouldering their bamboos like muskets, keeping step, and marching exceedingly well, appearing to afford material capable of being moulded into well-drilled soldiers.

On returning to the " Weser," about four in the afternoon, I found that the " Forbin," a steam corvette of 1000 tons, armed with four large guns, had been placed under orders to start immediately for Talien-whan Bay, with a despatch for Sir Hope Grant, from General de Montauban, and that Admiral Charner had directed a passage to be given me. As the " Forbin's " steam was up, and her anchor a-peak, I had not a moment to lose, and taking a hurried leave of my friends in the "Weser," * proceeded on board, where I

the waist in men from observations made by me when surgeon of the convict establishment in Western Australia. Dissection revealed, in the case of convicts from among the labouring class, the frequency of very remarkable adhesions between the organs situated in the region over which the waist-belt presses. I was disposed to attribute such adhesions to the practice of using narrow leathern belts, tightly applied, in lieu of braces. And this practice, by diminishing the space within the abdominal cavity, may have much to do with causing a very common surgical disease. This question, as having an important bearing upon the hygiene of all classes, and not least of the soldier in the East, deserves close attention. All tight girding, by "body belts," "cummerbunds" (the cholera belt of India), &c., appears to me open to grave objection.

* It was with feelings of no ordinary regret that a few months after-

again met with the greatest courtesy and kindness. The only other passenger was Colonel Foley, C.B., Her Majesty's Commissioner at French head-quarters, going over for a trip to Talien-whan, to see what was going on, and to return next day.

In the evening, I learnt from one of the officers that when the "Forbin" was in the Gulf of Pechili, about two months ago, taking soundings and making observations on the coast, some communication took place with a low-rank mandarin, who stated that it was quite impossible now to take the Taku forts, as they had recently been surrounded by ditches forty-five feet wide, and from fifteen to fifty feet deep; also, that the entrance to the river near the forts was obstructed by eleven rows of barriers, two being of iron stakes, three of stone, three of sunken junks, and the remainder of wood; further, that the river was kept open for junk navigation by a series of zig-zags, which, though available to themselves, would be altogether useless to us in the event of an attack by sea.*

At 7 P.M. the crew were mustered, and prayers read by one of the crew. At day-light to-morrow morning we expect to be off the entrance to Talien-whan Bay.

July 8th.—On going on deck, a little after day-break, we were just entering Talien-whan Bay; † the entrance is marked by two islands, the larger one known as the outer Shantai Island. Between it and the mainland on the left, there is a clear passage of five miles, on steaming through which a fine harbour and forests of masts opened to view.

Talien Bay is situated in the province of Lian-tung.

---

wards I heard of the total loss of the "Weser," from striking on a rock not previously known, at the entrance of the harbour of Saigon, in Cochin China. The officers and crew lost everything save their lives.

* Formidable as the defences at the Peiho were subsequently found to be, this was a very exaggerated account of them.

† Properly, Talien Bay; Whan meaning Bay in Chinese.

It was surveyed in February, 1860, by English officers. Within it are several small bays, the largest of which, on the south side, has been named Victoria Bay.

Here the "Forbin" anchored. I left her, and proceeded to the "Granada" steamer to report myself to the principal medical officer. I was directed to take up my abode on board the "Mauritius," hospital ship; and after depositing my baggage there, I went on shore with Dr. Cass, the surgeon of the "Forbin," who was anxious to see one of the English camps.

The first division of the expeditionary force is encamped on shore, in two brigades, about a mile distant from each other.

We landed close to the camp of the 60th Rifles, brigaded with the 2nd Queen's and the 15th Punjaubees. The Seiks, many of whom are remarkably fine men, were cooking their breakfasts, consisting chiefly of rice and curry stuff. Their dress is dark mud-coloured drill, with turbans of the same colour, and the bayonet and cartouch-box are suspended by belts of untanned leather, in colour suiting the clothing, which is made according to the pattern worn by the European infantry. I noticed that they have adopted a less fatiguing and hurtful mode of wearing their waist ammunition pouches than that which regulation compels the European to adopt. In place of having it in front on the right side, they slide it along the waist-belt until it reaches the hollow of the back, where it rests on the larger pouch suspended by the shoulder-belt, and thus relieve their waists of that constriction and inconvenience which I have already alluded to as so objectionable. On passing through the camps of the 2nd and 60th, I ascertained the number of men detailed for each tent to vary from fourteen to sixteen, an amount of overcrowding that cannot but prove injurious should the men be exposed to it for any length of time; more especially as the tents are the common bell * pattern,

---

* The "Bell tent" is the one in common use in the English army. It

which do not afford the same facilities for ventilation as the Indian tent.

Sir John Michel commands on this side of the bay, and has his head-quarters at a village a short distance from the camp of the Punjaubees. In this village (which has been abandoned by the inhabitants) five hundred of the coolie corps are at present quartered. The greater portion of the army is on the opposite side of the bay, the shipping of the respective corps being at anchor opposite the encampments.

A short distance from the shore a number of junks are lying, each bearing a number, and "Commissariat" marked in large black letters. These junks have been taken possession of from unsuspecting and unoffending traders, under circumstances similar to those described at Che-foo. The intention was to have given up the cargoes to the owners, and merely retain the vessels on compulsory hire; but unfortunately, owing to the somewhat too dashing manner in which the seizures were effected by the navy, the crews fled, leaving their junks and cargoes in the hands of the captors. Large quantities of valuable property, including grain, beans, oil, rice, &c., and, in some instances, Manchester goods, have thus become exposed to indiscriminate waste and plunder.

It is to be regretted that the services of these junks could not have been secured without entailing a loss so serious as that which has resulted to the unfortunate

is a cone, supported by a central pole, towards which the feet of the men converge at night. These tents have only one entrance, and their ventilation is chiefly derived from what is called the fall, a circular curtain, about ten inches deep, running round the bottom of the tent, which is generally lifted up during the day; at night, however, the men invariably sleep with it down, to keep their heads out of the night air, and generally close the front aperture also. The "Indian tent" is supported by two upright poles and one horizontal. The men sleep six on each side, and, from having an opening at each end, ventilation at night can be better secured.

owners, owing to the cargoes, in most instances, having been allowed to become the property of any who chose to help themselves. Some of the owners are now turning up and complaining bitterly of the way in which we have "pilonged" (stolen) their property.

I had a long conversation with Sir Hope Grant in reference to the progress the French were making at Che-foo, a point at present of considerable interest, as affecting the probable period for a movement towards the Peiho.

While I was on board the "Granada," Colonel Ross, the Assistant Quarter-Master-General, showed me a piece of quartz, supposed to be auriferous, that he had picked up on the top of the range of hills overlooking the camp of the first brigade. I examined it carefully, and saw distinctly a minute spec of metal presenting the external indications of gold, which there is every reason to suppose it to be, Dr. Home having subjected it to the nitric-acid test. A good deal of loose quartz exists on the summit of the hills, also in the water-courses leading from them, but as yet, this is the only auriferous specimen that has been picked up, though Colonel Ross has searched with some care for others.*

July 9th.—At nine this morning the "Feroze" was seen steaming into the anchorage, with the English ensign flying at the main — the sign that she was the bearer of Her Majesty's plenipotentiary. Immediately on her anchoring, boats were seen leaving the "Chesapeake" and the "Granada," conveying respectively Admiral Hope and General Grant to visit Lord Elgin.

A report is in circulation to-day that a number of coolies have deserted from the opposite side of the harbour, and that some of them have been murdered by the native population. The facts would seem to be these:—Some coolies

---

* A few days afterwards, I heard of another piece having been picked up amongst some ballast taken in at Odin Bay by one of the store transports.

were lent to the navy, and being ill treated by the sailors, they bolted into the country. A portion of them have returned, but a good many are still missing, and hence the conclusion that they have been made away with by the inhabitants.

July 10*th*.—Communication with the opposite side is carried on by means of small steamers that have been sent from India for service on the Peiho; they are essentially river boats, and are known in the fleet by the *sobriquet* of the "penny-boats." One starts every morning shortly after daybreak from alongside the flag-ship, and goes the round of the various bays where ships are at anchor. I crossed the bay in one of them called the "Tonze" this morning. I went to the "Sir William Peel" steamer, the hospital-ship of the second division, to see my brother, under whose charge she is. I found the arrangements for the sick very good; the vessel being fitted with iron bedsteads in place of wooden bunks. I landed with my brother, and passed through the camps of the Buffs and the 8th Punjaubees towards the crest of a hill, where I found my younger brother with a detachment of the 44th.

I availed myself of the present opportunity to send to Sir Robert Napier a letter of introduction which Sir James Outram had been kind enough to give me, and in the course of the day had a long and interesting conversation with him on matters relating to the Indian army, with the opinions of Sir James Outram respecting which circumstances had rendered me conversant.

While I was with him, Mr. Swinhoe, the interpreter attached to his division, came in with a proclamation he had translated into Chinese, cautioning the natives against selling spirits to the troops; to ensure due respect to which, it was necessary that the General should append his seal, the Chinese attaching more importance to that than to a signature.

Sir Robert Napier enjoys a high reputation as an able and scientific soldier. He was chief of the staff under Sir James

Outram during the series of operations which terminated in the relief of Lucknow; having previously served during the campaigns of the Sutlej and Punjaub. He is a Colonel of Bengal Engineers, and holds the local rank of major-general in China.

CHAPTER VII.

Trial of a Marine—Boat accident, and death of Captain Gordon—Visit of the French Commanders-in-Chief—Native houses—Stove bed-places—Village temple—Cartoons—Proposed hospital—Head man of the village—Gambling in the Coolie Corps—Their cookery and quarters—Ship whitewashed—Baggage ponies—Tea unknown to the peasantry—Dr. Thomson—Episode of the Disaster at the Peiho—Low state of health of the troops—Bell tent—Weight of ammunition.

July 12*th.*—This morning a gun was fired from the "Impérieuse," and at the same time the union jack was hoisted at the mizen, intimating that a court-martial had assembled on board. A Marine of the name of Dalliger had, on the 9th instant, attempted a double murder on board the gunboat "Leven" while at sea. He had come on board the "Leven" with a very bad character, and the corner of his certificate cut off. Lieutenant Hudson, the commander, thinking that possibly kindness might make something of the man, employed him as his cabin steward. Happening, however, to miss some liquor, and believing Dalliger to have taken it, he directed him to be punished. While Mr. Hudson was lying on his sofa after breakfast, Dalliger came into the cabin and endeavoured to get his punishment remitted, on the ground of his being wrongly accused. Mr. Hudson refused to alter his determination. Dalliger then, without making any further remark, walked into the sleeping berth and took down a loaded revolver, and coming behind Mr. Hudson shot him through the back of the neck. He then went on deck and called for Mr. Ashton, the second master, stating that the commander wished to see him. As Mr.

Ashton was coming up from below, Dalliger stood at the top of the ladder and took deliberate aim at him, the bullet passing through the right ear, lodging in the shoulder. He was found guilty on his trial, and sentence of death was passed upon him by the court-martial.

A sad accident occurred last evening to a boat from the "Impératrice" steamer on her way over from Victoria Bay, resulting in the death of Captain Gordon of the Madras Engineers. The day was wild, a sudden squall struck the boat when half-way across the harbour, or about five miles from the shore. She turned bottom upwards—the whole party, however, managed to cling to her—but before help came Captain Gordon had sunk from exhaustion.

July 13*th*.—This morning Admiral Charner and General Montauban arrived in the "Saigon" on a visit to the English camp. Lord Elgin and Sir Hope Grant accompanied them to Odin Bay, where arrangements had been made for an inspection of the artillery and cavalry at eleven o'clock. The King's Dragoon Guards, Probyn's Horse, Fane's Horse, and a demi-battery of Armstrong guns, were drawn up on the beach. Lord Elgin was received with a salute of nineteen guns and the French commanders-in-chief each thirteen guns. The Seik sports of tent-pegging and practice with the Armstrong guns were the novelties exhibited.

Landing on the beach near a small village about the centre of the bay, where it is proposed to establish an hospital, I accompanied Dr. Galbraith to examine some houses that have been selected with this intention; but they appeared to us both to be by no means adapted for the purpose—promising to be damp in wet weather, having earthen floors, while the odour with which they seemed at present impregnated, and which does not appear of a character admitting of very ready removal, cannot be viewed as propitious to either the comfort or recovery of the sick. The houses in the village are of stone construction, substantially built, and the roofs thatched with the stalk of the millet, with the exception of a few feet round the chimney, where, as a protection against fire, tiles are employed. The bed-places are fixtures, built of brick and extending from wall to wall. In breadth they average from four to six feet, and have a flue passing through them from the cooking stove, from which it may be inferred that during winter the natives are exposed to considerable extremes of cold.*

The village "Joss House" has been converted into the brigade office. On the walls I observed some rude cartoons, apparently illustrative of a naval engagement. These, I learned, are historical drawings commemorative of the defeat of the Western Barbarians at the Peiho in June, 1859; also, that a prominent figure on the deck of one of the gunboats, with the arms thrown up and the face painted black to indicate fear, is intended to represent Admiral Hope. In this temple there are several grotesque-looking deities, some-what battered about the faces, the result, probably, of playful familiarities on the part of military visitors.

In the evening I revisited the proposed hospital build-ings, and found that considerable progress had been made since the morning in clearing them out. Large quantities of lumber with which they were filled have been thrown into the court-yard, amongst which large jars, such as are represented in the tale of the Forty Thieves, were conspicu-ous. These jars, I believe, are usually employed for the transport of tea oil. Amongst the *débris* lying about I observed a quantity of books, the remains, evidently, of what once had been an extensive library. I took one of them and asked an interpreter (Mr. Adkins) what it related to. He told me it was an odd volume of a work on phi-losophy, and that the owner of the house had been to him complaining of the manner in which the complete set, worth a hundred taels (about £30) had been destroyed by soldiers coming in and taking odd volumes to light their pipes.

* This form of stove bedstead is called *a caugue*, and is in general use in the north of China, amongst the rich as well as the poor.

The houses in question have been hired from the owner at a price to be fixed by ourselves. I was present at a conversation on the subject between Mr. Adkins and the head man of the village, a tall, fine-looking man, with an expression of countenance altogether un-Chinese. He smoked his pipe with great *nonchalance* during the earlier part of the interview, then wiped the mouth-piece and presented it to Dr. Galbraith, who, out of compliment, took a few whiffs.

In the rear of the village, and close by where it is the intention to form a sick depôt on the departure of the expedition for the Peiho, we are now busy throwing up a line of entrenchments, terminating at each extreme in a redoubt mounting three traversing guns. The coolie corps are employed on this work as military labourers, and every day are proving themselves more and more useful.

July 16th.—Several hundred of the coolie corps are quartered in a neighbouring village, and in the yard fronting one of the houses occupied by them, I observed a circle of about fifty, some sitting, others standing, all either gambling or watching attentively the progress of the game. It was dark, and they were playing by a light formed by burning a quantity of wick in a metallic saucer full of oil, and shaped somewhat like a lamp. Some were staking dollars, and others only "cash." One coolie, while I was looking on, won ten dollars at a chance. From what I could make out of the game, it appeared to be a combination of dice and cards. A certain number of the latter were at the disposal of the players, on each card was a certain device, similar to a series of devices on a large square-shaped die, which was exposed at certain periods of the game. The players selected their cards, and placed the sums of money they intended staking upon them. The proprietor having previously adjusted the die (concealed under his clothes in a small square box made of brass), hands it to one of the players, who removes the cover from it, and those whose cards correspond with the exposed surface of the die are the winners. The coolies played in a quiet and systematic manner, talked but little, and were apparently quite free from excitement.

July 18*th*.—This evening I revisited the village occupied by the coolie corps, and found that, with few exceptions, the whole of the houses were in military occupation by the coolies. They looked happy and sleek, and were busy preparing their evening meal, the viands employed being of no mean description, embracing pork, sucking pigs, ducks, fowls, kid, rice, green vegetables, &c., the latter however in comparatively small quantity, boiled rice being the great substitute for the potato and other vegetables of the European. The culinary department appeared to be conducted in a careful and artistic manner, the meat being cut up with remarkable neatness and expedition.

I examined the houses in which they are lodged, and from the numbers of them that have been allowed to congregate in very limited spaces, it is not surprising that so much sickness prevails amongst them. It will be necessary to leave between 200 and 300 of them behind under medical treatment when the expedition sails.

July 19*th*.—This morning I found the "Sir William Peel" in course of being whitewashed externally; Sir Robert Napier having been informed by the commander of the "Impératrice" steamer that, while laying down the electric cable in the Red Sea, he succeeded in reducing the temperature of his ship fifteen degrees by whitewashing her, suggested that the experiment should be tried on the "Sir William Peel." I do not myself anticipate any very marked diminution of temperature, as the vessel is a wooden one, though the temperature of ships of iron construction, such as the "Impératrice," may be a good deal lessened by the process referred to.* Iron vessels however, I am of opinion,

---

* All the vessels of the Peninsular and Oriental Company are now painted black. The colour might with great advantage be changed to white.

ought never to be selected for hospital purposes in warm climates, owing to their higher temperature.

July 20th.—Breakfasted at the camp with Sir Robert Napier, who had been out on horseback from four A.M., endeavouring to purchase baggage ponies at the neighbouring villages without much success, having procured only two. He was dressed in the rough-and-ready style adopted on field service in the East—felt helmet and puggery, blue flannel patrol jacket, moleskin breeches, and jack-boots; his sword, an Indian tulwar remounted, and girded close up by a common brown leather belt with buckle, devoid of military ornament.

While we were at breakfast, the owners of the ponies accompanied by the head man of their village arrived, and sat down in front of the tent. Sir Robert sent out a cup of tea and some bread to the head man. He did not seem at first to understand what the tea was, but being persuaded to taste it, he approved of it so much that, after finishing it, he walked into the tent, and indicated by signs that some more of it, as well as some of the bread and meat on the table, would be acceptable to his retainers outside. He was allowed to take what he wanted, which he faithfully distributed amongst his followers. It is a curious fact that the natives of this portion of the Chinese empire neither grow, import, nor make use of tea in any form, otherwise than as oil, prepared from the seed of a species of tea-plant which they import from the south.

After breakfast, another native arrived with a pony, which he made signs that he wished to sell. On Sir Robert Napier asking him the price, he opened and shut both hands seven times, meaning seventy dollars. Sir Robert went through a similar performance, limited to four times, forty dollars being about the average given for ponies in this district. Up went his hands again six times. Sir Robert still adhered to four. He then tried five, and ultimately took his forty dollars, and walked off perfectly satisfied. While negotiations were going on, an Indian servant came forward with a light, which he was in the act of handing to the General; the peasant, however, intercepted it, and with the most perfect self-possession, lighted his pipe, and then passed it on to Sir Robert Napier.

Prior to leaving the camp, I sat for an hour in his tent, with Surgeon-Major Dr. Thomson, talking over the news brought by last mail of serious disturbances in New Zealand, respecting which, from his long residence in the colony, Dr. Thomson is naturally much interested, and seems to entertain a hope that, in the event of troops being ordered there from China on the conclusion of the campaign, he may be enabled to accompany them.*

I returned to the "Sir William Peel," and at dinner heard from an officer of the Marines, a story doing credit to the feelings of some of the Canton coolie corps that were with the force on board the gunboats at the Peiho disaster last year. So long as the firing was going on the coolies were in high spirits, clapping their hands and *hye-yahing* † with great glee as they watched the shot flying about; but as the firing slackened, and they saw gunboat after gunboat going down, they became much depressed. When the affair was over, several of them were observed to refuse their food; and when asked the reason, one came forward as spokesman and said, "How can catchee chow-chow, when five piecee gunboat makee die;" an amount of sensitiveness, if real, that could hardly have been expected from them; nevertheless, the kindness with which they have been for the most part treated, may in this instance have developed feelings of unfeigned regret at our misfortune, combined,

---

* This hope was not destined to be realised. He died while principal medical officer of the Second Division, with the army before Peking, and his remains now lie in the Russian cemetery, a little way to the north of the city. Dr. Thomson is well known as the author of the "Story of New Zealand," one of the best works that have yet appeared on that country.

† Hye-yah is the ordinary Chinese exclamation of surprise.

perhaps, with a certain degree of dread that the worst was not over, and that they might ultimately fall into the hands of the authorities at Taku.

In the evening I returned to Victoria Bay in the "Forester" gunboat, and heard that the 26th was the day fixed for the sailing of the expedition; the result of deliberations held yesterday by the allied commanders-in-chief at Che-foo. Further, that the plan of operations which had been originally determined on was abandoned, and that both armies are to land at the same time at Peh-tang: the original intention was, that the English only should land at Peh-tang, which is twelve miles to the north of the Peiho, while the French went to a landing-place called Chi-kan, some miles to the south of it; both armies were then to advance, and simultaneously take in reverse the forts on both sides of the river. This plan has been found impracticable; Colonel Schmitz, General Montauban's chief of the staff, having returned from a careful reconnaissance made on the 16th instant, and reported that, though men might be landed, it would be impossible to get horses or artillery on shore, owing to the amount of shallow water and mud.

July 25*th.*—Before leaving Talien-whan, I reported to the principal medical officer upon the health of the troops during their encampment on shore. A large amount of sickness prevailed, pointing to some untraced morbific influence. The symptoms closely resembled those which prevail at Hong Kong,—fevers, dysentery, &c. Yet the position was remarkably healthy; there was no intemperance, as intoxicating liquors could not be obtained beyond the rations. The army had been weeded of its weakly and sick at Hong Kong, the troops having at the first been selected in India as men of known robust health. The lowest amount of sickness occurred in the 99th Regiment; and I observed that that regiment alone is furnished with the Indian tent; the rest of the infantry use the bell tent.

To this fact I attribute the low state of health during encampment at this place. This is a subject worthy of close attention, as seriously affecting the hygiene of troops in the field. A bell tent, twelve feet in diameter and eleven in height, contains in the gross about 400 cubic feet. From this considerable deductions have to be made on account of the arms, accoutrements, &c., which are collected in the tents at night. As fourteen men are assigned to each tent, the amount of air per man is very small. Of course, a canvas tent can never be so closely shut as a barrack-room. In the latter, the above conditions would be intolerable; but even in a tent, when the entrance is closed, and the lower part is shut to the ground, the supply of air is far below the point desirable for health. I also observed two practices which I believe to be by no means unimportant collateral causes of atmospheric impurity. The men procure oil and wick, with which they extemporise large flaming lamps in tin cans, &c., overheating their tents, and consuming their fresh air just at the time when it is most desirable to keep the atmosphere as pure as possible, namely, the two hours preceding their turning in for the night; and, secondly, it is a common habit with the men to sit up in their beds smoking during the hours set apart for sleep.

It is but right to state that Dr. Muir gave me a verbal answer to my report, to the effect that at the commencement of the campaign he had recommended that the number in each tent should not exceed eight, but that the military authorities had decided that the exigencies of the service would not warrant any reduction being made in the numbers (from fourteen to sixteen) usually detailed for bell tents on field service.

The sick that are sent on board the hospital ship bring their arms and ammunition with them. To-day I had the belts and pouches weighed. The large cartouch-box and shoulder-belt weigh six pounds; the waist pouch with bayonet and belt weighs five pounds; in all eleven pounds that the soldier is burdened with about his shoulders and waist in carrying ammunition alone. The small waist pouch, with two packets of cartridges of $14\frac{1}{2}$ ounces each, itself weighs four pounds, and I have already noticed the serious objections to which it is open.

CHAPTER VIII.

The Expedition sails for the Peiho—The anchorage sighted—The French Fleet arrives—First view of the Taku forts—Preparations for landing at Peh-tang—Landing effected—March through the mud—The Forts deserted—First shot of the Campaign—Military occupation of the town—The "Zouave" cattle ship—Mortality on board—Commencement of hostilities—Reconnaissance in the direction of Taku.

July 26th.—At three this morning the "Mauritius" got her steam up, and at daylight crossed over to Hands Bay to tow the "City of Poonah" to sea, and give her an offing of five miles.

As we entered the harbour at Hands Bay we passed several ships waiting to be towed to sea. While we were endeavouring to find the "City of Poonah" amidst the crowd of vessels that filled the harbour, the scene began to change, and the "Carthage" steamer (known by the red ring round her funnel, which has served hitherto to indicate her as the head-quarter commissariat vessel, with the treasury chest on board), was seen making her way to sea with the "Dalhousie" and "Queen of the East" in tow. In the course of a few minutes the scene became one of a lively and exciting character. From the various anchorages in the bay, wherever the eye turned, columns of smoke were seen rising like miniature volcanoes. At this moment, coming into harbour with a fair wind under full sail was the "Anglo-Saxon," laden with cattle from Japan.

The "Mauritius," with the "City of Poonah" astern, has now reached the outside of Talien-whan, and anchored there is the "Impericuse," flying the Rear-Admiral's flag, watching the vessels making their exit. Outside the harbour the scene has assumed a character even more exciting than within, as here the steamers are casting off their vessels, and returning to tow others out.

Having given the "City of Poonah" a sufficient offing, the "Mauritius" returned to the harbour to tow the "Winifred" hospital store-ship to the new anchorage off the Peh-tang Ho.

Outside the harbour, a little way round its western point, in two little bays, I observed villages similar to those inside Talien-whan, cereal crops forming the characteristic vegetation in their immediate vicinity, while highlands with sheep pasturage abounded in the rear. Small groups of villagers were sitting in front of their houses watching the departure of the fleet, while a few fishermen in sampans were quietly pursuing their vocation, apparently regardless of the busy scene then in course of enactment in the waters near them.

July 27*th*.—About 3 P.M. we sighted the anchorage. About the same time a dense cloud of smoke in our rear indicated the approach of the French fleet. In the distance, in the direction of the Peiho, the masts of six vessels were visible, stated to be a Russian and American squadron of observation.

Since we left Talien-whan Bay the weather has been beautiful, but it has now become very warm, and we shall probably find the temperature increase as we approach the shore, from which we are distant at present about twenty miles.

July 28*th*.—At daybreak the French fleet was seen at anchor some little way off, having been unable to reach its proper position before dark. About 8 A.M. it got steam up and sailed in to its point of rendezvous. As it sailed past it presented a very imposing aspect, from the large size of the vessels and their being all steamers. I counted over thirty vessels flying the *tricolor*. They came in in three divisions, each division headed by the flag-ship of one of the Admirals.

At noon I counted ninety vessels under full canvas bearing down on the anchorage, a fine strong and fair wind having set in. The sight was a magnificent one, not likely soon to be witnessed again. About this time a number of junks that had been cruising in the neighbourhood, though at a very respectful distance, made sail in the direction of the Peiho, in all probability to report our approach.

No accident of any kind has occurred, and the strong southerly wind that is blowing has brought in nearly the whole of the sailing vessels. The gunboats and the junks, however, have not yet arrived.

July 29th.—This morning at nine o'clock, Her Majesty's surveying vessels "Actæon" and "Cruiser" sailed in the direction of the Peiho. In the course of the forenoon we heard that it had been ascertained that Peh-tang was altogether deserted, the troops having been withdrawn for the defence of Taku.

July 30th.—At 10 A.M., while on the bridge looking out for land, I saw in the distant haze three dark masses, apparently equidistant from each other and of symmetrical shape, looming obscurely above the horizon. I looked at them through my glass, and concluded they were the Taku forts. Soon all the glasses in the ship were directed towards them, and considerable difference of opinion prevailed as to what they were. In a short time, however, all doubts were removed, for as the haze somewhat cleared and we approached nearer, the outline of the forts, with their embrasures, was distinctly made out, looking in the distance as if their construction was of light-coloured stone, like the bastions of Malta, and presenting certainly an imposing aspect. As we got closer a long line of very low coast and four other bastions came in view.

Two American and four Russian men-of-war are now lying in the anchorage with us, and a great deal of saluting has been going on during the day, which no doubt our friends on shore have construed into one of those distant "awe-inspiring demonstrations" which they themselves are so fond of indulging in.

Late in the afternoon it became known that the Commanders-in-Chief had determined to land a portion of the troops to-morrow, and take possession of the town of Peh-tang, where not much, if any, resistance is anticipated. The troops detailed to land amount to about 1800 men. This force will be accompanied by an equal number of French troops, with four of their mountain guns.

July 31*st.*—Last night the weather became very unsettled, and about nine o'clock a circular storm, accompanied by clouds of sand, passed over the fleet, and struck some vessels, causing them to heel over considerably, while others were altogether untouched.

As the weather continues threatening, and Peh-tang is some ten miles off, all idea of landing the troops to day has been abandoned, owing to the risk that would be run in attempting to tow boats in the heavy sea that is at present on. The ships' launches, however, were all down at an early hour, and remained ready to start, until the Admiral sent a steamer round the fleet to give notice that they would not be required to day.

August 1*st.*—The day opened with heavy rain, and the general aspect of the weather continued unsettled. The sea, however, had considerably gone down, and the activity going on in the harbour from an early hour betokened the intention no longer to defer the landing. At 9 A.M. the signal was made from the flag-ship for the various launches to take up their positions alongside the transports that were to furnish the landing-party—similar preparations were observed in progress in the French fleet.

About noon, in the midst of a drizzly rain, Sir Hope Grant joined Admiral Hope on board the "Coromandel," while the officers of the staff embarked in the "Leven." In

LANDING EFFECTED.

a few minutes the "Coromandel" was under way, steaming for the shore, the gunboats, seventeen in number, following in regular line, each towing six launches filled with troops. The "Algerine" gunboat, with the flag of Admiral Jones, brought up the rear.

The French were in motion at the same time, on the starboard quarter—several steamers and despatch gunboats towing junks and launches filled with troops as close as they could be packed.

As the flotillas approached the shore they sank below the horizon, and to trace their further progress it was necessary to go aloft. From the mizen-top of the "Mauritius," with the aid of a good glass, I saw them cross the bar at the mouth of the river. In the distance, the low line of coast, and the forts defending the approach to the town of Peh-tang, were seen. The sea had now become calm and the weather fine, though the atmosphere was not very clear. About two o'clock the gunboats came to anchor some distance from the forts, and in an hour afterwards there were indications that the landing had commenced, apparently without opposition. As evening closed in, the gunboats were still lying where they originally anchored, and the landing seemed to have been effected without the expenditure of a single shot.

The second brigade forms the landing party, composed of the 2nd Queen's, the 2nd battalion of the 60th Rifles, the 15th Punjaub Infantry, a detachment of artillery, with rockets, and the 10th company of Royal Engineers.

August 2nd.—Towards the afternoon some of the gunboats engaged in the landing returned to the fleet to carry on the disembarkation, and from them we learn the following details of the landing:—

The Peh-tang forts are three miles from the mouth of the river, and the gunboats anchored about a mile and a quarter below them. The embrasures appeared masked, but no troops could be seen, with the exception of a detachment of

Tartar cavalry stationed on a causeway, that seemed to run from the town of Peh-tang in the direction of Taku. At three in the afternoon, Sir Hope Grant and General Montauban determined on landing a reconnoitring party of 400 men, half French, half English, with the view of examining the approaches to the causeway. The French were the first on shore; the boats conveying the English having grounded on nearing the river bank, compelling the men to disembark in the water and wade on shore—on reaching which, it was found to be a mud flat, extending on every side, into which the men sank over their ankles at each step.

Immediately on the troops landing the Tartar horsemen retired along the causeway towards Taku, and the disembarkation of the remainder of the force was proceeded with.

The allies now advanced towards the causeway, nearly an hour being spent in making their way through the mud, which continued without break the whole way. On the causeway being reached, according to previous arrangement, the English took their position on the side nearest the town while the French formed on the left.

The causeway enters the town by a gate in an embankment of mud which invests its rear. A few feet from the outside of the gate, the causeway has been cut across and bridged over, to enable the tide to flow from one side of it to the other, and thus prevent its being flooded. This gate was taken possession of without any resistance. By this time it was nearly dark, and further operations were deferred until morning. The troops then proceeded to bivouac on the muddy causeway, without tents or other covering than that afforded by the blanket which each man carries, and the water-proof sheet issued to every three soldiers.

In the meantime an advanced picket from the party at the gate approached the outskirts of the town, and found the inhabitants standing at the doors of their houses in great

THE FORTS DESERTED. 73

alarm. They supplied the soldiers with water, and seemed anxious to render them what assistance they could.

When this intelligence reached the outside of the gate, Mr. Parkes, who accompanies Sir Hope Grant as interpreter, went forward, and having ascertained from one of the townspeople that the forts were deserted, he undertook to visit them. The General having given his consent, Mr. Parkes, accompanied by a few men of the Rifles, and an officer of the quartermaster-general's department (Captain Williams, of the Royals), about 10 P.M. passed through the town of Peh-tang. The people were in a state of the greatest alarm, and there did not appear the most remote indication of an intention to resist.

The information about the forts being undefended was found to be correct, and the guide who accompanied Mr Parkes pointed out to him some spots which contained explosive machines. Having ascertained all that was necessary, he rejoined the force outside the town.

About two o'clock this morning the first shot of the campaign was fired. Some Tartar vedettes approached a picket of the Rifles, who immediately fired. When daylight came it was found that they had killed a horse.

At 4.30 A.M. Sir Hope Grant and General Montauban, accompanied by their staffs, rode through the town to the fort, and having ascended the bastion they were able to take a general survey of the country around, which presented nothing to the eye but one vast morass of mud— leaving them no resource but to take military possession of the town, and turn the unfortunate inhabitants out, without house or home, which dire necessity was in course of being carried out when the gunboats left.

The "Zouave," cattle-ship, arrived this afternoon from Chusan with eighty-five oxen on board, the remains of 250 that she had started with some ten days ago. A number of goats also were shipped, among which the mortality has been equally great. This result I have little doubt is to be traced to the ignorance of the requirements of animal life which has characterised their shipment;—the form of disease being of that pestilential type which dense over-crowding seldom fails to generate.

With regard to the survivors of this cargo, the question arises how far animal food, arriving under such circumstances, can be considered wholesome aliment, when there is every probability that the whole of it is more or less tainted with the atmospheric poison which has proved so fatal to the others, and that the death by disease of no small proportion of them will be anticipated by the commissariat butcher's knife.

That unwholesome animal food may have played an important part in the production of the febrile diarrhœa which was so prevalent at Talien-whan, I think very probable, more especially when taken in connection with the fact, that while as many as seventy-eight, and even over a hundred, men a day in a European regiment were frequently affected with it, the Seiks, who do not use beef at all, and mutton but once weekly, were entirely free from it.*

August 3rd.—Daylight this morning found us steaming up the Peh-tang Ho, a low mud flat, devoid of vegetation on each side; in front a slight narrowing of the river at one of its bends, defended on both banks by forts; immediately beyond which, on the south side, a crowded mass of low-roofed houses, built of mud, is seen—which is the town of Peh-tang.

We came to anchor a little way above the forts, alongside the town; the houses of which come down to within a short

---

* That the case of the "Zouave" was not an isolated one, and that a similar mortality was the rule, not the exception, may be inferred from the fact which I give on the authority of an officer of the commissariat, that from calculations based on the number of oxen purchased, and the number that actually arrived alive and in a state fit for the butcher, it had been ascertained that the fresh beef served out to the army in Talien-whan cost in all about twelve shillings per pound.

distance of the river side. On the opposite bank there is a suburb of considerable extent, which has also been taken possession of.

While the disembarkation of baggage and artillery was going on from the gunboats, between seven and eight in the morning, an unusual commotion was observed on board the "Coromandel" and the French vessels—officers and men were ascending the tops, and something was evidently going on in the direction of the causeway in the rear of the town. Shortly afterwards firing was heard in the distance.

I went on shore and heard that a reconnoitring party of 2000 English and French had gone out about four in the morning along the causeway towards Taku, and that when between three and four miles out they had got involved with the enemy, and had sent in for reinforcements.

I took a course up the main street in the direction of the firing with Captain Cruickshank, who landed with me. The street was ankle-deep, in some places nearly knee-deep, in mud.

Passing through the town we proceeded along the causeway for about four miles, when we met the force returning to camp, and learnt the following particulars :—The object of the reconnaissance was to discover how far the road was practicable for the advance of the army towards Taku, as the result of an inspection of the country made yesterday from the "Coromandel" for several miles up the river had been unsatisfactory, nothing but mud and swamps, with reeds growing in them, being visible for miles around.

The force left Peh-tang at four in the morning, the French being in advance, the English following in support. As the column approached a ruined temple a few Tartar vedettes were seen, who immediately retired. The force then pushed on. Presently a Tartar outpost, stationed near some deserted houses that were seen in front, opened fire. The French were ordered to deploy on each side of the causeway, and jumping into the mud, they immediately advanced in skirmishing order and drove the outposts in, who retired behind the houses. The mountain guns were now ordered to the front; on their firing shell into the houses, the Tartars speedily withdrew. The column advanced for about half a mile, when a large entrenched camp invested by a crenellated mud wall was seen, in front of which the cavalry, whose numbers were now considerably increased, advanced and manœuvred with some degree of skill, threatening the left flank of the English, who immediately changed front in that direction. Some skirmishing took place, and instructions were sent for to Peh-tang, as nothing beyond a reconnaissance had originally been intended.

On the Commanders-in-Chief and the reinforcements reaching the ground, it was determined not to push matters further at present, as we had no cavalry on shore.

The number of the enemy's cavalry in the field appears to be a matter of considerable uncertainty, some estimating it at 2000, others as high as 5000. Brigadier Sutton, however, on the way back to Peh-tang, told me that in his opinion it did not exceed 1500 at the outside, and that 1200 was probably nearer the mark. Estimating the strength of a body of horsemen in motion, especially at a distance, is stated to require considerable experience, which Brigadier Sutton, as an old cavalry officer, possesses.

The men as they marched back looked a good deal fatigued. They had their trousers rolled up as high as they could, and their mud-stained limbs showed the nature of the ground they had been in. The Tartar cavalry were seen manœuvring on the plain in the rear, but making no signs of approaching the causeway or otherwise interfering with the troops retiring.

Some appeared to be dissatisfied with the day's proceedings, on the ground that the French had been premature in involving themselves with the enemy, but that after the affair had proceeded the length which it did, it would have been better to have stormed the camp than retire the troops.

CHAPTER IX.

Confusion at the landing-place—Head-quarters of the First Division—Uninterred coffins—The Hospital of the 31st Regiment—Valuable clothing—Order against looting—A Chinese family residence—The South Peh-tang fort—Explosive machines—State of Horse Transport Service—Mortality among the horses on board ship—State of Peh-tang after rain—Reconnaissance—Attempt of the Chinese to open Negotiations—Order for the advance of the Army—Sanitary paradox—Exertions of the Officers and Crews of the Gunboats.

August 5th.—The landing-place presents a scene of no ordinary confusion; heaped in masses are lying all sorts of military stores and munitions of war, amongst which figure prominently guns and their carriages, pontoons, ammunition waggons, casks, kegs, scaling-ladders, wheel-barrows, pick-axes, shovels, &c.

During the night it has rained heavily at intervals, and the landing-place can be compared only to a swamp; to say that it is ankle-deep in mud does not express its state. Officers and men are going about without shoes, trousers rolled up to their knees. Detachments of the coolie corps are employed conveying bales of compressed hay and other stores into houses that have been told off for the purpose in the neighbourhood. The bank of the river hereabouts is strewed with matting, broken crockery, and other *débris* thrown out of the houses to make room for the stores.

The town bears unmistakeable evidence of the destructive character of a military occupation, especially in the French quarter, where attempts have been made to lessen the depth of mud by macadamising the streets with bricks procured by pulling down portions of the houses. Down one of these streets, strewed with the carcases of dogs wantonly butchered, broken porcelain and shattered furniture, I made my way to the Southern Fort, where Sir Hope Grant has established his head-quarters in a bell tent on the top of the cavalier.

I called on Dr. Muir, who, with Staff-Surgeon Dr. Home, is residing in one of the casemates in the curtain connecting the two cavaliers, and received instructions from him to be on shore on the 9th; the present intention being, that the army shall move forward on the 10th, and attack the Tartar entrenchments that obstruct the march on Taku.

Through the kindness of Surgeon-Major Dr. Telfer, I was offered a lodging for the night at the head-quarters of the first division, established in a temple at the end of the main street. It consists of a series of buildings, arranged in the form of three-sided courts, one behind the other. Sir John Michel occupies the chief hall of the temple, in which there are several gaudily painted figures that look like deified warriors, and a number of coffins arranged on the top of one another, containing bodies, the final interment of which has been delayed by the relatives, until what they consider a lucky period should arrive. Corpses are thus kept uninterred in temples, and store-houses set apart for the purpose, frequently for many years. From odours in their vicinity, the coffins in question do not appear to be altogether airtight. They are formed of massive slabs of wood, nearly half a foot thick, and some of them are lacquered on the outside.

In the construction of Peh-tang, its builders have been to a great extent obliged to accommodate themselves to the resources of the neighbouring country—the bulk of the town being constructed of mud, made more cohesive by having chopped straw mixed up with it. Though the town, when glanced at in a general way, has a very poor appearance, there are numbers of by no means contemptible houses, built of brick, and laid out according to the custom of the country in courts facing the south, in each of which there is generally a large water-jar.

In one of these buildings, near General Michel's head-quarters, the officers and sick of the 31st regiment are quartered. In the portion used as an hospital, there are massive presses of a dark wood, like mahogany, with brass hinges and clasps. They are at present filled with costly silks, satins, and furs, for the most part made up in the form of robes, the silk outside and the fur inside, being apparently the winter wardrobe of a person of wealth and position.

At present there is an order against looting, which, however, would seem to be more honoured in the breach than the observance, and the restriction might as well be withdrawn, as far as the interests of the unfortunate owners are concerned, any chance of property of the least value ever finding its way back to them being too remote to be entertained. The silks and furs in the hospital of the 31st are only safe for the time, as their removal would be too overt a violation of a general order, the breaking of which on the part of the soldier subjects him to flogging. From all accounts, notwithstanding the poor appearance of the place, a large amount of valuable property has fallen into the hands of the occupying force.

A little way below the hospital of the 31st, the officers of the 15th Punjaubees have quartered themselves in a pawnbroker's shop, in which room after room is filled to the ceiling with goods of more or less value, all neatly arranged and ticketed with great care and regularity.

Towards sundown, the first division staff dined in the court-yard fronting Sir John Michel's quarters. The mess arrangements were of the most simple character; no adjuncts being brought into use beyond the resources found at hand in the temple, yet luxurious, I have no doubt, compared with what the General and several of his staff have frequently had to put up with in the course of service at the Cape. Whatever the shortcomings may be in some respects, a water-tight roof, good seats and tables, and plenty of earthenware, would seem to be some of the advantages of campaigning in China.

August 6th.—Visited Brigadier Crofton, R. A., who occupies a house nearly opposite General Michel's head-quarters, apparently the residence of a person of the higher class. It consists of three court-yards, branching off from which there are numerous side buildings and offices. In one of the courts there is a small vineyard. The central court communicates with the female apartments, the bed-rooms on one side, and the nurseries on the other. The walls of the rooms are decorated with odd pictures, chiefly caricatures; one of the pictures is a representation of the signing of the treaty of Nanking, which, on the whole, is tolerably well executed, the uniforms of the English officers being pourtrayed with remarkable fidelity.

August 8th.—I revisited the fort where the English head-quarters are established, and made the following notes of its construction.

The fort may be described as an oblong enclosure, covering about ten acres, the front portion consisting of two casemated cavaliers, distant from each other about one hundred and fifty yards, and connected by a crenellated curtain, with loop-holes at short intervals for gingals or matchlocks. From the flanks of the cavaliers, a curved curtain extends for a short distance, and is continued in the form of a crenellated wall all round the rear of the fort, forming its enclosing wall. On the outside there is a moat of some width, filled with water, across which, by a draw-bridge, the fort is entered.

Each cavalier is ascended by an inclined plane, and the part where the embrasures are, though protected above, is quite open to the rear.

The connecting curtain has four large casemates, evidently

intended for guns of considerable size. Between each of these there is a smaller casemated embrasure, with a very small external opening, affording almost complete protection to men working the guns.

In the flanking curtain to the south, there are two large and five small casemates, their thickness averaging about twelve feet. The large ones are at present occupied by officers, and the smaller ones are used as servants' quarters and cook-houses.

The north bastion continues to be occupied by the Commander-in-Chief.

Within the inclosure of the fort, about a thousand horses, including Probyn's Seik cavalry, are at present picketed.

In the rear of the fort, just within the walls, there is a small temple, apparently for the use of the garrison; and in the northern angle there are a number of buildings that look like barracks.

With the exception of a few very primitive pieces of ordnance, formed of wood, bound by iron hoops, and covered with a strong coating of hide, all the guns have been removed for the defence of the approaches to Tien-tsin by the Peiho.

Several large shells and tin cases were lying about within the fort. These had been dug up by the Sappers on their position being pointed out by the native guide who warned Mr. Parkes respecting them. The shells were found filled with powder and placed in tin cases. These again were deposited in pits, covered over with matting and a thin coating of earth, to resemble the ground adjacent. A man's weight thrown upon one of these traps would have dropped him into the pit, whereupon, by an arrangement of a lanyard communicating with a flint lock attached to the shell it would have exploded, probably with considerable damage to those in its vicinity. Thanks to the Chinaman, no opportunity was offered for their destructive qualities being practically tested.

G

Yesterday a lighted slow match, communicating with a considerable quantity of gunpowder, was discovered in a house occupied by the Royal Artillery. A memorandum was immediately issued, ordering a careful search to be made throughout the quarters for the discovery of similar attempts.

The Military Train and the infantry of the Second Division are landing to day. Connected with the prospects of the efficiency of the former, strange scenes are stated to be witnessed at the landing place, such as horses intended for the transport service being so weak as to require the aid of the coolies to be carried on shore. Whether this is an exaggeration or not, it is certain that owing to the great mortality at sea, and the bad condition in which the surviving horses have arrived from Japan, the serious break down of the horse transport service is a contingency looked forward to almost as a matter of certainty.

One day when crossing Talien-whan Bay, an officer of the Military Train on board the gunboat mentioned to me that he had just returned from Japan in the "Kate Hooper" with the remnant of some 250 horses that had formed the freight of the vessel, the mortality amongst which had been so great that in one day he had thrown seventy overboard, a wholesale slaughter attributable to the same cause as that which has produced like results in the cattle ships, namely, an apparent unacquaintance with the fact that food and water alone are insufficient for the maintenance of animal life, and that similar pestilential diseases are generated by the overcrowding of animals as of men in limited spaces. The fittings of the vessels would appear also to have been in some instances defective, from the fact of horses that survived the voyage being received with their lower jaw-bones laid bare, caused by lurches of the vessel throwing them forward on iron bars that had been injudiciously fitted across the front of the stalls, apparently without reference to the height of the animal they were intended to contain.

August 9th.—This morning I left the anchorage in one of the boats of the "Mauritius," to remain permanently on shore. The weather was dull and threatening: rain was falling in torrents.

Having no definite place of shelter, beyond permission from the Quartermaster-General to pitch a tent within the enclosure of the fort, I went down there to see how far this might be practicable, and to report my arrival to the principal medical officer. With some difficulty I was able to reach the fort, the street leading to it being at the time a running stream, in many places more than knee deep in mud and water. The open space within the fort had become a lake, and everybody and everything looked as cheerless as they well could. No prospect existing of getting a quarter there, I retraced my steps to the town, where, learning that the 44th had landed, I waded through several rivulets in the form of narrow streets, until I found where the regiment was quartered, under the impression that my brother might be able to give me room. However, when I saw the very limited accommodation which he, along with some six or eight others had, in a small house divided into two narrow partitions, into which the rain was beating both by the windows and the doors, I concealed the object of my visit. On returning to the landing-place, I was relieved from my difficulties by Major Fisher, R.E., who kindly gave me a part of his quarter in the court of a house occupied by the Royal Engineers.

The state of the weather renders the proposed advance of the army to-morrow impossible, and it is therefore now quite uncertain what day the force will be able to move.

At daybreak this morning, prior to the weather changing, a reconnaissance was made along a road that crosses the mud to the right of the causeway a short distance from the town, and which is believed to lead to Tien-tsin. This road, though very indifferent, has been decided on as practicable for artillery in dry weather. It extends for about four miles from Peh-tang, passing over a good deal of broken marshy ground, and terminates on a good hard plain, where there is an abundance of excellent water.

A few days ago a gunboat was sent up the river about five miles for the protection of a spot where better water can be procured than in the town. Near the place some Tartar cavalry are posted on the left bank of the river, and Admiral Hope being anxious to avoid unnecessary collision and bloodshed, sent his interpreter, Mr. Morrison, on the 5th, with a flag of truce to the Tartar camp, to explain the object for which the gunboat is placed there, and to caution them not to approach too near, as they would be fired at, should they do so.

This occurrence it appears has been construed by the Governor-General of Chili, who is at present at Taku, into a friendly overture from the allied ambassadors, and he accordingly has addressed communications to them of a pacific character. These, it is stated, cannot be entertained after the unequivocal terms in which the ultimatum has been rejected; nor indeed is there any reason to suppose that the Governor-General has any authority to negotiate, otherwise he would not have delayed intimating that such were his powers until the accidental occurrence in question.

August 11*th*.—The weather is now showing signs of clearing, and orders have appeared for the advance of the army at daybreak to-morrow.

It would be difficult to indicate a more filthy and foul-smelling locality than Peh-tang has been found to be, and situated as it is, on the bank of a river, with nothing but vast mud flats for miles around, it was expected that the troops would suffer severely from malarious disease; such, however has not been the case, their health having been much superior to what it was in the beautiful climate and pure atmosphere of Talien-whan. All idea of bringing sanitary science into practical operation was from the first given up as hopeless, and nature allowed to take her course.

The result would seem to confirm the opinion I have already expressed, that in matters relating to military hygiene there is a tendency to over-estimate as causes of disease certain atmospheric impurities of local origin, as well as to attribute endemic disease to the external air that soldiers breathe, when it is rather due to the internal.

The prospect of moving to-morrow appears to be hailed with satisfaction by all, and by none more than by the officers and crews of the gunboats, whose exertions in the landing of the expedition have been of no ordinary nature, involving work almost incessant night and day, the intervals for rest falling a long way short of those usually deemed requisite for the support of nature. Nothing, I believe, but the feeling that every day's exertion has been expediting the approach of the day when they hope to have an opportunity of avenging their disaster of last year, has supported them during an amount of fatigue and loss of sleep which, without some strong mental impulse, they probably would have been unable to bear. The gunboats are now stripped of their spars and rigging, and are like gladiators ready for the fight.

CHAPTER X.

March on Sinho—Artillery Waggons abandoned in the mud—The first Armstrong Gun—The Action of Sinho—Capture of Entrenchments—Tartar Cavalry retreat towards Taku—Sinho occupied—Tartar Vedettes—Junction with Second Division—Appearance of the Troops—Details of Action on the Right—Bivouac—Sinho—Tartar Tents—Dexterity of Tartar Horsemen—The Gingal—Breakdown of the Horse Transport Corps—The *Times* Correspondent—Coolies' contempt for Cash—Prisoners captured by the Tartars—Horses galled by ill-made pack-saddles—Papers found in the house of the Tartar General.

August 12*th*.—I rose this morning about half-past two, and found the coolie corps, under Major Temple, mustering by the light of lanterns on the bank of the river near the landing place. Soon the bugle-calls of the various corps were heard in different directions, and with the earliest dawn of day the town was alive with armed men. Three days' cooked provisions had been served out to each man, and the whole force was preparing to move, with the exception of the 99th regiment, which remains to garrison Peh-tang.

At 4 o'clock A.M., the troops of the Second Division, under Major-General Sir Robert Napier, commenced defiling through the gate opening on the causeway, along which they proceeded for about a quarter of a mile, and then diverged to the right, taking the road already described.

Owing to the very heavy nature of the ground after leaving the causeway, three hours elapsed before the column was clear of the town and fairly on the line of march. The cavalry brigade being for the day attached to General Napier's division, commenced to move at seven o'clock, under Brigadier Pattle;—the King's Dragoon Guards leading, followed by Probyn's Horse, Stirling's Battery, and Fane's Horse.

As soon as the cavalry brigade had left the causeway clear, the first division under Sir Hope Grant and General Michel, and the French under General Montauban, commenced leaving the town.

Having been appointed to the medical charge of the artillery of the first division, I remained with the principal medical officer (Surgeon-Major Telfer), to accompany the field hospital equipage and dhoolies,* detailed in orders to follow in the rear of the French main column. The other medical officers were on the line of march with their respective regiments, each of them accompanied by a certain number of light canvas stretchers for removing the wounded to the rear. We were joined by Un-chung-fung, the senior Chinese physician of the coolie corps, who as head of his own particular department proceeded with us.

As we passed the road to the right of the causeway, along which the second division and the cavalry had gone, a number of artillery waggons were seen stuck fast in the mud. They belonged to Milward's battery, and had been left behind, being too heavy to be moved through ground into which even the infantry sank over their ankles.

To the right, a considerable way a-head, the rear of General Napier's division was just getting out of sight, while on the causeway in front, the infantry and artillery of the first division, with a French force, were slowly advancing towards the entrenched works in front of which the reconnaissance of the 3rd instant took place.

* The Dhoolies were made by Chinese artizans at Hong-Kong. They proved heavy and cumbrous, and by no means adapted for carrying sick or wounded on a campaign. They also soon got out of repair; owing to the snapping of the ironwork by which the bed-frames were swung from the bamboo bearing-poles. Fortunately they were hardly required on the line of march, otherwise their inutility would have been seriously apparent. The Indian Dhoolies are swung by woodwork, and are consequently not so liable to get out of repair from such accidents.

As we were proceeding along the causeway, about eleven o'clock the report of a gun was heard on the right. This inaugurated a new epoch in artillery—it was the first war-shot from an Armstrong gun : Milward's battery was then opening fire on a large force of cavalry that the second division had sighted on its left. Clouds of smoke were now seen rising to the right, gun after gun was heard, and in a short time a heavy fire of musketry from the infantry of the second division. About the same time the booming of guns in front indicated that the first division and the French were also engaged.

I now rode on to the front, and passed from the causeway on to good hard clay soil. The infantry brigades were advancing in close column on each side of the road, and a heavy fire of artillery and rockets was going on in front against an advanced work, fronting the principal entrenchment some distance in the rear.

Sir Hope Grant was in front, in person directing the operations. Desborough's and Barry's batteries were in line to the right. The French artillery was on the left, also a French and Madras rocket battery. In the rear of the guns the Royals and part of the 31st were extended in skirmishing order, under Brigadier Staveley. This advanced work seemed defended chiefly by cavalry, who opened out to the right and left, and made a demonstration as if they were going to attack. The fire from the artillery quickly dispersed them. The guns, which had opened at about half-a-mile from the position, were now advanced to within 500 yards, and silenced a very ineffective gingal fire which had up to this time been kept up. The advance was then sounded, and the work taken possession of, the Tartars having retired to their inner entrenchment.

Sir Hope Grant led the way through the work. Inside of it there was a number of white calico tents, a good deal riddled with shot, a few horses killed or wounded, and some dismounted gingals. The concentrated fire to which this entrenchment had been exposed did not seem to have been attended with very serious results, unless, as is supposed, the Tartars removed their killed and wounded before retreating, which I do not think probable. Five casualties only were found inside the work; one body was fearfully mutilated. The man appeared to have been struck in the chest by a shell at the moment of explosion—one arm was blown completely off, and the hand tightly grasped a piece of fuse. Another man was found pinned to his horse by a rocket.

Passing this entrenchment without halting, the artillery again advanced in line, followed by the Royals in skirmishing order, towards the principal works fronting Sinho. As the line approached, a gingal fire was opened, and a few balls passed hissing over our heads. Brigadier Staveley ordered the Royals to lie down, and the guns were wheeled round. After a few shots, the cry of "There they go!" was heard, and looking to the left a line of cavalry was seen issuing from the rear of the entrenchment, proceeding at a gallop along a causeway leading in the direction of Taku. Colonel Barry was requested to try his Armstrongs on the retreating column. Two or three shots were sent after them, which at the time were supposed to have done great execution, but when the ground was examined immediately afterwards, a little blood and a wounded pony were all that was found.

It was now one o'clock, and the entrenchment was taken possession of. Like the first one, it contained a number of tents; some dead and wounded horses also were lying about. The Tartars themselves did not appear to have suffered, at least no indications remained of any casualties. Sir Hope Grant, with General Michel and a portion of the force, at once entered the village of Sinho, and passed through the main street, to effect a junction with Sir Robert Napier's division, which was advancing towards its rear. The street was in a very bad state from recent rains, and in many places the guns sank to the axles in mud. The houses seemed to be deserted, and the shops were closed. The village is about half-a-mile in length, and on emerging from it we came on a fine open plain, on which the second division and the cavalry were seen in the distance approaching.

On the outskirts of the village near this plain we passed a number of detached cottages, in some of the gardens of which I saw the peasants working as if nothing unusual had occurred. Poor people, in a short time they were deprived of everything edible to be found on their premises, and the contents of their poultry yards and gardens transferred to the camp kettles. On the road a little way beyond the village a blind man was standing leaning on his staff. He had a deep gash on the back and side portion of the neck, apparently a sword wound inflicted by some savage in wanton thirst for blood. The poor man seemed to dread moving, and stood statue-like as we passed. I examined his wound, and found there was no immediate danger from it. I could do nothing more for him at the time, having to follow in the line of march. On Dr. Telfer coming up with the hospital train, he humanely had him carried in, and his wound properly taken care of.

With the exception of some Tartar vedettes stationed amongst a clump of trees in the rear of this entrenchment, there were no signs of an enemy remaining. Vedettes of Probyn's horse were out watching their movements. I had a good view of them through my glass. They appeared to be eyeing each other with intense curiosity. The Tartars were dressed in the ordinary Chinese hat of black silk, with the brim turned up all round, and had two squirrels' tails projecting from the hat behind, which are decorations only worn by military men. They had on light-coloured jackets, over a long under garment of darker material, and blue trowsers tucked into black Tartar boots. They were armed with spears, having red horse-hair hanging from the end of the shaft where it joins the ironwork. They rode in short stirrups, and were mounted on stout hardy-looking ponies.

Sir Robert Napier's division gradually worked its way round. The infantry looked much exhausted, and the mud-stained limbs of both officers and men betokened the nature of the ground they had marched over. The appearance of the King's Dragoon Guards was a marvel. Their horses were covered with mud, but the men themselves, with the exception that they had on the Indian solar helmet, looked as if they had made a morning march from Hounslow to Hyde Park. The aspect of the Seiks was more rough-and-ready: they looked the type of irregular cavalry on active service.

We now heard the details of the action on the right, and the difficulties encountered by the second division in making its way towards Sinho.

About eleven o'clock Sir Robert Napier, having got within sight of the entrenchment, found a large cavalry force in its rear. Seeing at the same time the allied force advancing along the causeway to attack in front, he moved towards the position and took the Tartar cavalry in flank, Milward's guns opening fire at 1500 yards. Though their practice is stated to have been very good, it did not seem to have influenced the determination of the Tartars to attack, as they immediately afterwards issued in a long line from the rear of the entrenchment by a passage across a marsh which separated the two forces, and passing to the right surrounded the second division with a cloud of skirmishers.

Sir Robert Napier now ordered the cavalry brigade to charge. The King's Dragoon Guards led, followed by Probyn's Horse, with Fane's Horse in support. The ground, however, was not favourable for their advance. The Tartars rapidly retired, stopping when an opportunity offered and firing their matchlocks and bows and arrows.

While this was going on, Stirling's battery having been unable to follow the cavalry brigade through the heavy ground, had been left behind with an escort of thirty men of Fane's Horse, under Lieutenant Macgregor, and just at the moment that the guns of the first division were heard on the left, a body of about seventy Tartars, to the surprise of every one, galloped from their front, and charging down on Stirling's battery attempted to take the guns in flank. The attack was so unexpected that Captain Stirling had but time to fire two rounds before the Tartars were within 100 yards of the battery. There was no protection for the guns beyond the escort mentioned. Without a moment's hesitation Lieutenant Macgregor charged at the head of his Seiks and drove the Tartars back, in doing which he was severely wounded; also several of his men, one of whom I believe was killed.

About this time another body of Tartars appeared in considerable force to the left, and came on with great steadiness, notwithstanding the fire of two Armstrong guns and the advanced guard of the Buffs. A sharp fire was opened upon them and they soon withdrew, though apparently without any serious loss, attributable it is supposed to the infantry having sighted their rifles too high.

The Tartars being now driven back at every point into their entrenchments, and the fire from the first division and the French having rendered these untenable, the action of Sinho was over, gained after a trifling loss on our part.

The loss in killed of the enemy is variously estimated from 100 to 200—the former is probably the more correct estimate. The dead I saw lying on the field were fine stout muscular men, with the true Mongolian form of feature, their faces nearly as broad as they are long.

The troops were too much exhausted for any further operations to be undertaken to-day, and preparations were made for bivouacking on the plain. The French, a part of the infantry of the first division, and Barry's battery, had remained in the entrenchment fronting Sinho, and I returned through the village to rejoin the latter. As I passed along the main street, French soldiers were coming out of the houses laden with plunder, consisting principally of silk and fur dresses, similar to those found in such quantities at Peh-tang. The capture of poultry and pigs also appeared to receive an important share of attention from our gallant allies.

August 13*th*.—Slept in the open on some hay within the entrenchment, and was repeatedly awoke and nearly trodden on by baggage animals arriving during the night. They were some of those that, having broken down on the way, had been unable to reach Sinho until long after dark.

This morning for the first time I had leisure to look about the entrenchment, which is an earthwork of considerable extent, and might have been made a formidable obstacle to the advance of the allied columns, had it been defended by artillery and infantry, and not by a force apparently combining the duties of horsemen, gingal gunners, matchlockmen and archers. The place does not appear to have had a permanent garrison in it, as the Tartars were all living under canvas. Their tents in shape resemble those used in India, and are formed of light and very strong calico, which materially reduces their weight, an important advantage on the march.

The work is open in the rear, but in front and on the flanks is invested by a good-sized ditch, filled with water from a stream which runs past Sinho. I walked a little way along the ditch, and came on an old woman lying apparently dead near the edge of it. Finding, however, that she was still alive, I returned immediately to the entrenchment, where I got some of the coolie corps with a stretcher, and had her brought in. I placed her in one of the Tartar tents, where, under restoratives, in a short time she revived.

About an hour afterwards a wounded Mongolian found on the plain a little to the left of the work, was carried in, shot through the face by a rifle bullet. He was a fine powerful man, and seemed a good deal at a loss to understand what was going to be done with him. I placed him in one of the few Tartar tents now remaining (the soldiers having taken possession of the most of them), and after dressing his wound gave him some food. In a short time he appeared to comprehend our object in bringing him in, and gave unmistakeable signs of gratitude, but refused food, beyond a little rice-water that I got from the coolie corps encamped near us.

In the use of their weapons, such as they are, these Tartars and Mongolians displayed considerable dexterity in the action of yesterday. The matchlock-men were frequently seen, when retreating at full speed, to turn round, fire off their pieces, and reload as they galloped away. The bowmen also discharged their arrows when at full gallop. The gingals are long wall pieces, throwing balls from four ounces to a pound. They were used by them yesterday, as a substitute for field artillery; the gingal being carried on one horse and the stand on another. If, in place of carrying them about wherever they moved, they had concentrated their fire from behind the entrenchment, they probably would have caused some degree of damage, their range being considerable. After breakfast I rode through Sinho to the plain in its rear, where the troops bivouacked last night. A few of the Staff had got their tents, but the army had not yet received theirs, the anticipated break-down of the Horse Transport Corps having been complete, the whole line of road from Peh-tang to Sinho being reported to be strewed with baggage that has been cast off animals unable further to proceed. While here, I met Mr. Bowlby, of the *Times*, full of enthusiasm about the Armstrong guns he had seen in action yesterday on the right. He was anxious to hear from Colonel Barry how they had succeeded on the left, and accompanied me back to the entrenchment.

As we entered it, I observed the old woman that I had brought in a few hours previously, crawling away on her hands and knees, endeavouring to get out by the rear of the work on the causeway. Through the aid of a coolie, I managed to elicit from her that she wanted to reach Tang-koo. Mr. Bowlby being in the secrets of the cabinet shook his head ominously, saying—"She had better keep out of there," so I had her carried back to the tent, and ultimately into Sinho, where I made arrangements with one of the villagers, who had returned, to take care of her.

While in the village for this purpose, I observed in the stream from which the place takes its name an ingenious contrivance for catching fish, consisting of a labyrinth formed by a succession of zig-zags made of stout reeds, stuck into the bed of the stream, and so arranged that the fish when once in could not extricate themselves. The soil in the neighbourhood of Sinho is very rich, and cropped with luxuriant vegetation. With the exception of a considerable number of small-footed women and children, whose deformities interfered with their flight, the bulk of the inhabitants had fled to Tang-koo. These women and children took shelter on board some small junks moored in a creek that intersects the vegetable gardens on the outside of the village. As soon as it became known they were there, Sir Hope Grant ordered them to be carefully protected. Strings of cash were lying about, disregarded even by the coolies. I drew the attention of a passing coolie to two or three dollars' worth lying on the road. He shook his head, saying—"No good, too muchee heavy, dollar can do."

It appears that a sergeant of the 44th, a private of the Buffs, and eighteen coolies, were captured yesterday coming up in the rear of the second division with commissariat rum. They are supposed to have lost their way, and been cut off and taken prisoners by some cavalry that were seen in the distance yesterday afternoon, some hours after the action.

During the day numbers of baggage animals have been passing through the entrenchment, *en route* to head-quarters, while another set have been going back to bring in baggage that had to be abandoned yesterday on the line of march. It is stated that a large number of them have already had to be sent to the sick lines with sore backs, resulting from the injudicious construction of the pack saddles, which were made at Hong-Kong by Chinese tradesmen, from a pattern determined on by a board of military officers who did not take the opinion of a veterinary surgeon, and the result is now painfully manifest. A most pitiable sight certainly the poor animals now present.

Some very interesting and important papers have been found in the house of the Tartar general at Sinho, Teh by name, who commands the Chinese forces on the north bank of the Peiho, while Sang-ko-lin-sin commands on the south. Amongst these papers, there is a communication from the Great Council to Sang-ko-lin-sin and Hang-fuh, the Governor-General of Chili, enclosing the *ultimatum* and translations of extracts from the English newspapers, containing information respecting the allied preparations to avenge the defeat of Taku, cautioning them to beware and have the coast placed on the defensive.

In reply Hang-fuh and Sang-ko-lin-sin state, that the ground in the neighbourhood of Peh-tang being all salt flat, undefended as the place is the barbarians will not readily succeed in effecting a landing, but that should they be foolish enough to attempt it, and advance across these flats, there are camps of infantry and cavalry that will arrest their progress and drive them back. Then, should they still persist in their desire to take revenge for the chastisement they received last year at Taku, to that place must they go and there fight it out.

The correspondence also between Hang-fuh and the Tartar General Teh has been found, relating to events since the landing of the allies at Peh-tang. Teh gives an account of the reconnaissance of the 3rd of August, and states that he drove the barbarians back, with a loss of seven men on his own side, and an equal loss on the part of the allies. He goes on to state that he treated us thus leniently, knowing that the governor-general was anxious for peace, and therefore he did not wish to exasperate us. In reply, Hang-fuh cautions him against allowing diplomatic relations to influence him in his place of military commander, and that at all risks he must maintain his positions at Sin-ho and Tang-koo, these places being the key to the north forts of Taku.

Teh is also enjoined to take as many prisoners as possible, and forward them at once to Hang-fuh, who by promptly returning them, hopes to propitiate the barbarians, and thus secure good terms of peace. Lord Elgin is specially recommended to be taken, as in the event of his capture, the war would virtually be ended. A reward of a thousand taels is accordingly offered for his lordship, and one hundred taels for chiefs of lesser degree. In the event of the allies landing at Peh-tang, it is directed that no opposition be offered them.

The Engineers are busy to-day making bridges across a swampy plain, which the army will have to pass to attack Tang-koo, which report says is to be done to-morrow morning.

CHAPTER XI.

Advance of the army upon Tang-koo—The Artillery open fire—Capture of the fort—Apparent non-efficiency of our fire—Scenes inside Tang-koo—Cavalry enclosure—Captured guns—Prisoners—Camp flooded—Punishment parade—Samshu—Military bridge—Armstrong guns—Exaggerated statements respecting their success—Cholera—Return of the Sergeant and Coolies captured on the 12th—Flag of truce—Preparations for the attack on the Northern Forts.

August 14*th*.—At daybreak the force was under arms, and the coolie corps appeared with the scaling-ladders—light-hearted fellows and strongly built, the right men in the wrong place: for however valuable their services, it is difficult to lose sight of the fact that they are Chinese subjects, allured by the all-powerful attractions of the dollar to act against their government.

At 6 A.M. the army began to advance, crossing, by two narrow bridges, a large ditch separating the encamping ground from the plain.

Artillery and infantry were pushed on across the plain under a harassing fire from some batteries on the other side of the river—these were silenced by our artillery—and ground was taken up about 800 yards from Tang-koo. Upwards of forty English and French guns were now in line, pouring what seemed a tremendous fire into the fort, to which the Chinese replied with spirit from about an equal number of guns, but as usual firing at too great an elevation. After the firing had continued some time there was a short interval, during which the artillery advanced nearly half-way and re-opened. When the fire from the fort was nearly silenced, the infantry were ordered to the front, the 60th in advance, followed by the Royals and 31st. The 60th, on arriving at the ditch which invests the place, discovered a dam close to the river and an entry was effected, Lieutenant Shaw, of the 60th, being the first who got inside. Two guns from the angle of the work on the left still kept firing on the French, who had to construct a bridge to get across the ditch, which was quickly effected, Colonel Schmidtz, the chief of the staff, being the first on that side to enter. The Chinese on the right retired as the 60th rushed in, but those on the left continued firing on the French for some time afterwards. By the time these had crossed the ditch, the 60th had got some way round the interior of the earthwork.

Entering Tang-koo, I found it to be a small town surrounded by a very extensive earthwork.

It is difficult to account for the apparent inefficiency of our fire, unless by adopting the general belief that the mass of the dead and wounded had been removed by the Chinese prior to retreating. It is stated to have been ascertained from prisoners, that during the action a number of junks crossed over to the other side filled with killed and wounded. Several bodies, however, were found in the ditch in the rear of the place, and some in the houses of the town, but not in any number.

Immediately on the place being taken, I walked over the whole of the entrenchment, back and front, and did not see twenty dead Chinese. I heard in the afternoon of fourteen having been found killed round one gun; if so, they must have been buried by the person who found them before any one else had a chance of seeing them. On the whole line of ramparts, within an hour after the place was taken, I did not see more than a dozen corpses at the outside. Some of them I noticed had their port fires, in the shape of rope-yarn fastened round one wrist, which fact immediately afforded data to some imaginative individuals for setting the report in circulation, that to keep them from running away the artillerymen had been tethered to their guns.

A good many old men, women, and children were found in the houses. Several of the women attempted to destroy themselves and their infant children by rushing into the Peiho when the troops entered the town; some of them succeeded, others were prevented by the soldiers.

Inside the fort, generally in the rear of where guns were in position, there are huts with arched roofs, similar to those described in the cavalry camp in rear of Sin-ho. The garrison were apparently at breakfast when the attack commenced. At the door of each of the huts there was an earthen oven, and an iron pot containing rice; and inside, bedding for twelve men, chiefly rugs. The walls were here and there decorated with Chinese pictures; and playing cards were scattered about inside, as if they had been thrown down in a hurry. In an open shed, on the outskirts of the town, I found an old man, apparently a villager, dying from a wound in the chest by a rifle bullet—the vital spark was just flickering, and I could do nothing for him. Near this place, in a ditch that passes into the town, two women were lying, apparently drowned.

Leaving these painful sights, and returning to the battery, we ate our rations of biscuit and pork, and turned in for the night in Tartar tents, found in the enclosure near us.

August 15*th.*—This morning I went into the enclosure for cavalry, contained within the entrenchment. The Tartars had evidently retreated with precipitation, leaving the bulk of their property behind, the ground being covered with saddles, shields, swords, gingals, matchlocks, bows, arrows, and other munitions of war; also copper money to a considerable amount. The enclosure contained a large number of tents, inside of which quantities of soldiers' clothing were lying about, for the most part thickly padded. Suits of oiled cloth, oval-shaped fans made of basket work, and small brushes similar to those used for polishing plate, appeared to form a portion of the cavalry soldier's kit.

This cavalry enclosure occupies about ten acres, and is surrounded by a mud wall of some thickness, on the outside of which there is a broad trench filled with water, over which the enclosure is entered by a causeway on each side. This water I conclude is partly defensive, partly for the supply of the horses. The height of the enclosure wall is just sufficient to admit of gingals placed on their stands being fired over it.

Riding towards Sin-ho, I saw the brass guns captured in Tang-koo drawn up in line. They had been removed from the works with the view of being divided in due proportion with the French. They are all mounted on strong wooden carriages, some of them so constructed as to admit of two guns being placed on them side by side, after the fashion of double-barrelled fowling-pieces. In calibre these guns vary from four to twenty-four pounders.

Returning to the camp on the Peiho, I reached it about the time some Chinese civilians were brought in prisoners, under the supposition that they were soldiers. They were taken to the head-quarters of the first division, and interrogated by Mr. Gibson, the divisional interpreter. They went down on their knees, and were evidently in great alarm. One or two staff officers were indulging in the unfeeling pastime of aggravating their fears, by making signs to them that they were going to be strung up by the neck—an act of childish cruelty, against the continuance of which I took the liberty of protesting. The poor fellows were elderly men, and, according to their own statements, small merchants. They were ultimately released from apprehension, and allowed to go at large.

August 16*th.*—About four in the afternoon the Peiho suddenly overflowed, and before the 60th Rifles had time to strike their tents or remove their arms, the portion of the camp occupied by them was inundated. The men stripped and exerted themselves to the utmost, but were making such indifferent progress owing to the ditches they had to cross, and the rapid increase of the water, that General Michel ordered a fatigue party of a thousand men of the 31st Regiment to their aid, who coming down at the double, plunged up to their middles in water and mud, and rendered very effective assistance to the 60th in saving their kits and ammunition from submersion.

While this was going on, a scene of another kind was being enacted close by. Barry's and Desborough's batteries were formed at punishment parade, and three men were flogged for drunkenness—or as the coolies call it, "Samshu pigeon." *

August 17*th*.—Early this morning Sir Hope Grant and staff rode past the camp, going a short way up the river for the purpose of selecting the best place for forming a bridge of boats across the Peiho, the present intention being, that while the gun-boats attack in front, the first division cross over to the opposite side, and take the south forts in rear, the northern ones being attacked in like manner by the second division.

From a sick soldier brought into camp the night before last, some scraps of intelligence have been picked up; amongst others, that the garrison of Tang-koo originally amounted to two thousand five hundred men, commanded by a brigadier-general, who felt much perplexed what to do when the troops and inhabitants arrived in full flight from Sin-ho. At first a panic took place amongst the garrison, but ultimately he succeeded in re-establishing order, and got the troops formed into divisions for the defence of the works.

August 18*th*.—About two o'clock, two guns of Barry's battery and a company of the 31st Regiment were ordered

---

* Samshu is the intoxicating liquor most commonly used by the Chinese, and bears so close a resemblance to whisky, that our soldiers seldom allow it to escape when they come across it.

out to cover the advance up the river of a number of small junks, intended to be used in constructing the bridge across the Peiho. Sir John Michel commanded the party in person. The guns were placed in position on the bank, near the edge of the river. The 31st were ordered to lie down amongst some rushes in front of the guns. A Chinese battery opened fire at half-past two, which was immediately returned by the Armstrongs. The Chinese, however, continued to fire, sending their shot in excellent line, but at too great an elevation, the shot falling about fifty feet to the rear of the guns.

With my glass I could distinctly see the gunners at work, and a mounted officer, with two squirrel tails in his hat, riding about directing the operations, and apparently vociferating energetically. The batteries went on exchanging shots for about a quarter of an hour, when gradually appearing from amongst the rushes was seen one after another of the 31st getting up to have a look at what was going on. "Lie down, you red fellows! what are you doing there?—down every one of you," shouted Sir John Michel;—the scarlet tunics, or rather the red serge shirts which are worn in lieu of them, contrasting strongly with the bright green of the rushes, and presenting a most attractive mark to the enemy.

At this time, just as an Armstrong had been fired, the *Times* correspondent rode up and exclaimed, "What a magnificent shot! it has dismounted a gun." Sir John Michel turned round and said, "There has not a single shot gone near the battery. I have watched with my glass the effect of every one that has been fired." Captain Allgood, the Deputy Quartermaster-General of the division, who was standing with General Michel, and had also watched the course of the shot, said the same. The distance was about 1700 yards, and as the shot fell no doubt within the Chinese lines, though apparently not near the object fired at, it would almost seem as if length of range was incompatible with due precision of fire.

As the Armstrongs did not seem to be producing any effect where they were, Sir John Michel directed one of them to be moved down to the river side, and brought to bear from that point. At three o'clock the company of the 31st was ordered to retire from its advanced position in the rushes and move to the left. At half-past three the troops were withdrawn, the boats having passed up the river beyond reach of the Chinese guns, which, however, had been silent for about a quarter of an hour previously.*

* The following version of this affair appeared in the *Times* on the 3rd November, 1860, from the pen of its special correspondent, and painful as it is to me, under the circumstances attending the fate of this gentleman, to allude to it, I feel that I should shrink from a public duty, if I allowed statements attributing a success in the field to the Armstrong gun totally at variance with facts, to remain uncontradicted amongst the records of the Peiho campaign. The letter states :—

"The Chinamen opened fire from five guns in good line but about twenty feet too high. The first shot from the Armstrongs fell to the right and missed them; the second burst in their battery; the third dismounted a large gun, sending the carriage into the air in splinters; the fourth plumped in amongst the fugitive gunners, who never fired another shot. Every junk passed up in safety without the slightest accident, and the materials for the bridge were secured."

Now it appears to me, particularly at a period when the Armstrong gun was on its first trial, and the accounts of such trial would materially influence the Government in sanctioning its substitution for the old smoothbore artillery, that this style of "sensation" writing cannot be too strongly condemned; it also to my mind throws the shadow of exaggeration over all the other statements emanating from the same source, relating to the efficiency of the gun for the purposes of field artillery. The day after the affair, Brigadier Staveley carefully examined the Chinese battery. The guns were all in position; there was no sign of one of them having been struck, nor could he, on close search, find a fragment of an Armstrong shell nor an indication of one having burst in the neighbourhood—facts which, at the time, naturally produced an impression anything but favourable to the accuracy of the practice on the occasion in question. Where the Armstrong shells actually went, I happened to find out accidentally some months afterwards. One day in the winter of 1861 at Tien-tsin, happening to be talking to Assistant-Surgeon Heard, of the 67th Regiment, about the Armstrong gun, and questioning its efficiency at long ranges on active service, he cited, in opposition to my views, the affair of the 18th of August, describing the practice on that day as having been remarkably

A case of true Asiatic cholera occurred in the camp of the first division to-day. The subject of it was a soldier of Barry's battery, of feeble constitution, and who had been frequently under medical treatment. The disease proved fatal in a few hours.

The same day a soldier of the 67th was similarly attacked in Tang-koo, distant between two and three miles. The occurrence of these two cases out of some 10,000 men, would seem as if some very limited choleraic influence had passed over the neighbourhood, as there was no further spread of the disease, and all idea of its arrest by sanitary precautions a simple absurdity ; as the men in Tang-koo had been, and continued to reside, in an atmosphere supersaturated with the foulest of odours, while those in the first division camp revelled for days afterwards in unripe fruits and raw vegetables procured from the luxuriant orchards and well-stocked gardens in the neighbourhood.

August 19*th*.—Yesterday the sergeant of the 44th and the greater number of the coolies captured on the 12th inst., were sent into Tang-koo by the Governor-General of the province. The coolies look rather underfed and have been deprived of their tails—lucky fellows to have returned with their heads. The sergeant, who, by the way, is an Irishman, tells extraordinary stories of what he overheard the Chinese authorities saying ; and when questioned by Sir

good : he, along with others quartered in Tang-koo, had watched its effects, the position of the town enabling them to see where the shells fell and burst. They did so at a considerable distance in the rear of the battery, and right amongst the retreating Tartars who had been dislodged by the French. The practice seemed to be so good, viewed from Tang-koo, that a doubt never crossed the minds of the lookers-on but that the guns were specially directed against the fugitives—of whose existence in the rear of the battery, or any where near it, I may state with perfect confidence, not one of those who were with the Armstrong guns had the most remote idea, and further, that it was simply a matter of chance that the Armstrong shells had not dropped amongst our gallant allies, when in pursuit of the Tartars towards the village of Taku.

Robert Napier as to how he had picked up this information, seeing that he did not understand a single word of Chinese, except "weilo,"* he replied, "Sure, sir, thim fellows have no saecrets at all at all." The facts are, he and a private of the Buffs, named Moyse, coming up in charge of the grog on the 12th in rear of the second division, got drunk, mistook the road, and marched direct towards a party of Tartar cavalry on the Tien-tsin road, under the impression they were Seiks. The sergeant, who discovered his mistake by coming on one of the Tartar vedettes, gives the following description of their capture. "Whin I saw who he was, I cocked my pace and presinted it, but there was nothing in it. He retraited, and I retraited; thin says I to the coolies, 'Boys, you had better hook it,' and thin it was we were surrounded and made prisoners." Of his friend Moyse at this period he makes no mention, and the inference is that he was then in a state of happy oblivion. He however represents him at a later period of his captivity meeting his death for refusing to *kow-tow* before Sang-ko-lin-sin, a statement which, with great safety, may be placed in quarantine.†

That the Chinese intend to fight would seem beyond doubt. This morning Mr. Consul Parkes, in his capacity of interpreter to the Commander-in-Chief, accompanied by Major Graham, R.E., and some officers of the second division staff, went with a flag of truce to the fort nearest Tang-koo, and summoned it to surrender. The Commandant, however, ordered the party off, saying that if the English wanted the forts they must come and take them.

Looking over the parapet of the Tang-koo entrenchment we could see the rear of the Taku forts, with crowds of labourers

* *Weilo* is a corruption of the Cantonese *huelo*, to go, and is the term in common use by the English to promote locomotion amongst the southern Chinese.

† From inquiries made at a subsequent period, I ascertained from very good authority, that none of the prisoners taken on the 12th August met a violent death, but two or three died from disease during captivity; the result no doubt of ill-treatment.

moving about apparently busily engaged strengthening the defences in the direction of the expected attack. Our working parties were seen a mile or more to the left completing the approaches prior to the attack, which takes place to-morrow morning.

At nine P.M. the sky in the neighbourhood of the forts suddenly became brightly lit up by the explosion in rapid succession of a large number of fire-balls, which the Chinese threw up from the forts to see what the troops were about— a more brilliant pyrotechnic display I never witnessed.

This evening I was joined by my brother, who has landed from the "Sir William Peel" hospital ship, with the view of going off with the wounded to-morrow in the "Cooper," the steamer that has been detailed to convey them to the fleet, distant some nine or ten miles from the forts. When he left the anchorage, the gunboats were in course of taking up their positions in front of Taku.

CHAPTER XII.

Advance upon the Taku forts—Explosion of magazines—Upper North Fort taken—Aspect of the fort after its capture—A photographic group—The cavalier—The other forts hoist white flags—An armistice granted—Details of the capture of the upper North Fort—A Coolie in search of Sycee silver—Flags of truce arrive—A letter from the Governor-General—Mandarin conveying it speaks English—Termination of the armistice—The lower North Fort surrenders—Terrific thunder-storm—Return of the army through the mud.

August 21st.—As soon as daylight admitted of the guns being moved over the narrow and imperfect bridges by which the ditches intersecting the line of march to Tang-koo are crossed, Desborough's and Barry's batteries left the camp of the first division, and, in column of route extending over nearly two-thirds of a mile, crossed the plain towards the principal entrance of Tang-koo. The morning was still grey as we neared the outer defences. On our left front, looking dark and formidable, the tall cavaliers of the Taku forts were seen. All was then silent, and they showed no signs of activity. At ten minutes past five as we were riding slowly on, gazing on the forts and speculating as to whether they would resist or not, a bright flash shot forth from the summit of the fort nearest us, a cloud of smoke followed, and the report of a heavy gun fell on our ears: others followed in rapid succession. The allied columns were advancing from Tang-koo, and the Taku forts had opened fire upon them.

An interval elapsed before we heard our guns replying, but as we were passing through Tang-koo a pretty active fire commenced against the forts, though but a portion of the artillery had by that time got into position. On our way through the town, I observed on the roof of the house used as the head-quarters of the second division, the *Times* correspondent and a portion of the staff viewing the fight from a distance, Sir Hope Grant having interdicted any but those actually on duty with the troops engaged in the attack from passing the limits of Tang-koo. All over the town groups of soldiers were on the house-tops, every eye strained in the direction of the forts, from the whole of which a steady fire of heavy guns was now being kept up.

At this time the gunboats, having got into position within range, commenced bombarding the forts nearest the sea, while the fire of the allied artillery on shore became incessant and heavy.

At half-past six as we were watching the bombardment, our eyes at the moment diverted from the fort in front in the direction of the gunboats, a terrific noise as if some vast mine had exploded under our feet, for the moment almost deafened us. Its cause was in a second revealed. The upper northern fort had become shrouded from view, a massive cloud of dark smoke ascended high above the cavalier, and what seemed solid bodies were falling thickly about—the chief magazine of the fort had been exploded by one of our shells. There was now a lull in the bombardment, and the surrender of the fort might reasonably have been expected; on the contrary, to the surprise of every one, the Chinese, apparently unappalled by the tremendous explosion within their walls, still stood to their guns, and recommenced firing nearly as briskly as ever. About ten minutes after the first explosion, another equally severe occurred in the fort nearest the sea, the magazine of which had been exploded by a shell from one of the French gunboats. At this time the Chinese were still keeping up a steady, but ill-directed fire, the greater portion of the shot passing over the heads of the troops and falling in the rear.

The field-guns were now advanced to within five hundred yards of the gateway of the fort, and, under cover of their fire, a portion of the storming party (composed of the 44th and 67th Regiments) obtained an advanced position. The fire of the allied artillery now became, if anything, heavier than ever, while that of the Chinese was beginning gradually to decline. At seven o'clock, the infantry in front commenced a sharp and well-sustained rifle fire on the embrasures of the fort, the guns of which were not yet silenced : at the same time, the gunboats were seen in motion, apparently approaching closer to the forts on the seaboard : about this hour, also, Lieutenant Moorsom was sent to the rear to bring up the reserve ammunition of Barry's battery, that with which it went into action being nearly exhausted, so active had the fire been.

Immediately after the first explosion took place, a portion of the French force, consisting of three companies of the 102nd, was pushed forward to a position a good deal in advance. At a quarter to eight General Montauban and staff arrived on the ground and passed down to the front, where a heavy fire of musketry was now going on, with occasional salvoes from the mortars. The field-guns were employed making a breach, and a rather smart cannonade was being kept up between the guns in Tang-koo and those on the opposite side of the Peiho. A party of artillerymen also, under Lieutenant Anderson, were endeavouring to get to the front one of the large eight-inch siege guns. The ground was too heavy, the wheels of the carriage became imbedded in the mud, and though the men made every possible exertion, the attempt to get the gun forward had to be abandoned.

Professional duties now occupied my attention for some time, and my ideas with reference to occurrences in front are so confused and imperfect that I shall not attempt their description. Gradually the firing died away, and as such of the wounded as it had fallen to me to look after were got under way for Tang-koo, I rode forward to the fort, from the cavalier of which the flags of England and France were now fluttering in the breeze; the former represented by the Queen's colour of the 67th Regiment. The troops were massed by regiments and batteries close up to the outer defences. Sir Robert Napier was lying on the ground exhausted with fatigue and intermittent fever, from which he had been suffering during the whole attack. His glass had been knocked out of his hand by a matchlock bullet, and his boot cut open by another. His aide-de-camp also, Captain Broke, received a bullet through his helmet, and afterwards was wounded in the thigh. On my way to the fort I had met him being carried to the rear.

The number of casualties had so far exceeded what was expected, that a considerable proportion of those wounded during the storming had yet to be removed. A French soldier severely wounded was lying in the mud near the western angle where the French made their assault. There were no means of removing him at hand, and Colonel Foley came to me to see if I could give any aid. At this moment a party of men of the Buffs came up from Tang-koo with some stretchers, one of which I took and had the poor fellow brought in.

Having a brother in the 44th, I naturally looked first for that regiment, which I found in close column on the left in rear of the fort. The men looked weary, and were standing with their arms piled. Ten men of the 44th, who had been killed in the storming, were lying in a row, and a party of the coolie corps were digging one large grave for their interment near the outer ditch of the fort. On the extreme left on the top of an embankment some way in advance and commanding a portion of the river front of the fort, two companies of the 44th were drawn up under Major Hackett. They had been placed there to intercept the retreat of the Tartars as they escaped towards the lower northern fort during the storming.

I now went towards the entrance of the fort, and crossing

the formidable water defences by a pontoon bridge, laid down by the Royal Engineers, I came to the drawbridge which by this time had been lowered. Here some men of the 44th and 67th were employed with pickaxes widening a breach that the guns had partially made—through it I passed into the fort, and a distressing scene of carnage disclosed itself; frightful mutilations and groups of dead and dying meeting the eye in every direction.

I walked round the ramparts on the west side. They were thickly strewed with dead—in the north-west angle thirteen were lying in one group round a gun. Signor Beato was here in great excitement, characterising the group as "beautiful," and begging that it might not be interfered with until perpetuated by his photographic apparatus, which was done a few minutes afterwards. Not far from this group, a tall and very dignified-looking man of between fifty and sixty, stated to be the general who had conducted the defence, was lying dead, his lower jaw shattered by a rifle bullet.

Having walked round the western half of the ramparts, I ascended the cavalier by an inclined plane paved with brick-work, so arranged as to afford secure footing to men or horses dragging heavy weights up it, such as guns or their carriages. From the top of the cavalier—which mounted three large guns, two of them of brass, and one an English thirty-two pounder, supposed to have been taken out of the gunboats last year—I had a good view of the other forts. Though they had not surrendered, they had taken down their war flags and substituted white ones, of which the explanation given was that it was to enable their civil authorities to communicate with ours. Sir Hope Grant was sitting on one of the gun-carriages talking to General Montauban, and arranging ulterior proceedings, as the surrender of the remaining forts seemed uncertain; an equivocating answer having been returned to a summons to that effect which, under a flag of truce, had been conveyed to them by Mr. Parkes.

An armistice however was granted them until two o'clock, and in the meantime orders were issued for the Buffs and 8th Punjaubees to advance from Tang-koo and take the place of the 44th, Marines and 67th, now pretty well exhausted with the labours of the previous twelve hours, of which I now learned the following additional particulars :—

By a little after six A.M. the whole of the guns having opened fire, the bombardment continued nearly uninterruptedly until seven o'clock, by which time the guns of the upper northern fort had nearly ceased firing. A breach was then commenced near the gate, portions of the storming party being advanced near enough to open an effective fire on the embrasures. The Chinese, however, succeeded in bringing a heavy fire of small arms to bear on the troops, which occasioned some loss. The Sappers, with the Marines carrying the pontoons, were now advancing along a narrow causeway leading up to the gate, covered by two companies of the 44th. The fire, however, was so heavy that the attempt to get the pontoons forward failed, fifteen of the men carrying them being disabled within a few seconds. The two covering companies of the 44th, commanded by Captain Gregory and Lieutenant Rogers, had in the meantime gallantly rushed up to the edge of the outer ditch, and were endeavouring to keep down the heavy fire of gingals and matchlocks which was impeding the approach of the Marines. There being no cover for them, they in their turn became exposed to a fire which inflicted a rather heavy loss in killed and wounded upon them. The men of the 44th up to their middles in water were dropping fast, and no signs of the pontoons being forthcoming, Lieutenant Rogers, followed by a portion of the men, swam the ditches, and pulling up some of the bamboo stakes, succeeded in getting under the wall. At the same time the storming companies of the 67th, under Lieut.-Col. Thomas, left their cover, and advancing under a heavy fire endeavoured also to cross the ditches, which they ultimately did, partly by swimming, partly by joining the

French, who had pushed on to the angle of the fort nearest them, and, making bridges of their light bamboo scaling-ladders, under circumstances of no ordinary difficulty had succeeded in crossing the water defences and obtaining a position under the wall, which with their usual gallantry they at once attempted to escalade, but met with a resistance so determined that in the first instance they were repulsed.

While the infantry were thus employed, two of Govan's howitzers had been ordered up by Sir Robert Napier to within fifty yards of the gate, so as more effectually to form a breach; and an imperfect one had just been made, when the storming parties, reinforced by the head-quarter wing of the 67th, under Lieutenant-Colonel Knox, and three companies of the French Marine Infantry, succeeded in entering the fort—Lieutenant Rogers, of the 44th, and Drummer Fachard, of the 102nd, being the first who entered. The defence was continued for some time after the storming had been effected, and a free use of the bayonet had to be made before the remains of the garrison were placed *hors de combat*. Under cover of their casemates, they kept up a matchlock fire on the storming party as it entered, and in this way Ensign Chaplin, of the 67th, was severely wounded as he was ascending the cavalier, with the Queen's colour of his regiment. By nine o'clock the fort was completely in our possession after three and a half hours' fighting, the British loss being twenty-two officers wounded, seventeen men killed, and one hundred and sixty-two wounded; the French loss, two officers killed, eleven wounded—fifteen men killed, and one hundred and thirty wounded.

The Chinese coolies in the service of the French were employed bringing up the scaling-ladders, which exposed them to a severe fire, causing several casualties amongst them. They are reported to have behaved remarkably well, displaying great coolness under fire. The French made use of their scaling-ladders for bridging the ditches in the following manner:—They reduced the width of the ditch by placing a ladder in it, slanting from each bank, and then connected the two ladders by placing a third across.

Amongst those who particularly distinguished themselves may be mentioned Brigadier Reeves, who though wounded in three places remained in front until the capture of the fort was completed. Captain Gregory, of the 44th, also distinguished himself, rifle in hand, in aiding his men in keeping down the matchlock fire as the storming parties were advancing. Lieutenant Rogers, of the 44th, and Lieutenants Lenon and Burslem, and Ensign Chaplin, of the 67th, report says, are to be recommended for the Victoria Cross, in consequence of special services rendered during the storming.*

* These officers ultimately received the Victoria Cross, and in the *London Gazette* of the 13th August, 1861, their services, in common with those of some private soldiers on whom the decoration was also conferred, are thus mentioned :—

"The Queen has been graciously pleased to signify her intention to confer the decoration of the Victoria Cross on the undermentioned officers and soldiers, whose claims to the same have been submitted for her Majesty's approval, on account of acts of bravery performed by them in China on the occasion of the assault and capture of the North Taku Fort on the 21st of August, 1860, as recorded against their several names—viz. :—

"Lieutenant (now Captain) Robert Montresor Rogers, 44th Regiment (now of the 90th Regiment), Private John M'Dougall (No. 220), 44th Regiment, and Lieutenant Edmund Henry Lenon, 67th Regiment, for distinguished gallantry in swimming the ditches and entering the North Taku Fort by an embrasure during the assault. They were the first of the English established on the walls of the fort, which they entered in the order in which their names are here recorded, each one being assisted by the others to mount the embrasure.

"Lieutenant (now Captain) Nathaniel Burslem, 67th Regiment (now of the 60th Regiment), and Private Thomas Lane (No. 612), 67th Regiment, for distinguished gallantry in swimming the ditches of the North Taku Fort, and persevering in attempting during the assault, and before the entrance of the fort had been effected by any one, to enlarge an opening in the wall, through which they eventually entered, and, in doing so, were both severely wounded.

"Ensign (now Lieutenant) John Worthy Chaplin, 67th Regiment (now of the 100th Regiment), for distinguished gallantry at the North Taku Fort. This officer was carrying the Queen's colour of the regiment, and

During the armistice I availed myself of the opportunity of examining the rear defences of the fort. They consist of an inner lining of strong palisades supporting a thick and strong wall of unburnt brick, faced with mud and chopped straw, having casemates five feet apart, the embrasures externally being eight inches high and a foot in length, and intended to be used only for matchlocks or gingals. Immediately under the wall the ground is covered with sharp bamboo stakes; beyond this there is a moat, then another interval of staked ground, then a broad ditch; beyond these is a piece of ground covered with *aballis*, the branches of the trees being so arranged as to entangle men approaching from without, and by an arrangement of bells and wires an alarm would have been given in the event of a night attack. Beyond the *aballis* there is a deep ditch, which constitutes the outermost defence.

I walked under the parapet as well as I could, amongst the bamboo stakes, which were sharp-pointed, and arranged in lines alternately eight and eighteen inches high. In addition to these, crows'-feet of iron, presenting a sharp spike upwards whichever way they happened to be lying, were strewed thickly over the ground underneath the parapet. With a great deal of difficulty I was able to get round to the eastern side, where there are several large casemated embrasures, containing guns of considerable calibre. Underneath these casemates numbers of bodies were lying on the spikes impaled, having apparently been hurled from the embrasures by the storming party. In a casemate in the south-eastern angle, lying round a large gun, I counted three-and-twenty corpses; on the ground underneath the embrasure there were eight; and in the ditch immediately in front between twenty and thirty

first planted the colours on the breach made by the storming party, assisted by Private Lane, of the 67th Regiment, and subsequently on the cavalier of the fort, which he was the first to mount. In doing this he was severely wounded."

more—the latter, one of the coolie corps was poking about with a long bamboo pole trying to make out whether they had any sycee silver about them. While he was so engaged, a sergeant of the 44th came up and administered the following rebuke to him:—"What are you a-doing of? Can't you leave the poor dead alone? Surely they are not annoying of you." About this part of the fort the killed appeared to have been either bayoneted or shot while attempting to escape across the ditches.

At a quarter to one o'clock, I observed a boat arrive from the opposite side of the river. It bore a flag of truce, and two military mandarins landed. They wore long buff-coloured dresses, made of a light material resembling grass cloth, with waist-belts having precious stones set in the buckles. They had on conical-shaped straw hats, surmounted with the buttons of their ranks, from which red horse-hair hung down in the form of a tassel. Their boots were of black satin, and came half way to the knee. They were the bearers of a despatch, and had great difficulty in making their way across the various obstacles constituting the defences about here, their long skirts getting entangled in the bamboo stakes. From this cause one of them tripped and fell on the spikes, severely lacerating one of his fingers, which was bleeding profusely as he emerged on the clear ground where I was standing. Mr. Parkes received their communication, and said a few words to them. As the bleeding continued from the finger, I supplied some lint and had the wound dressed, which the Tartar acknowledged by politely bowing several times. At this moment another boat arrived, conveying a civil mandarin, accompanied by a soldier, bearing a flag of truce. The mandarin, a young man of delicate appearance, spoke very fair English. Mr. Parkes, Lieut.-Col. Crealoch, and Major Anson came down from the cavalier and met him. He seemed to be known to the former, who, on learning the nature of his mission, namely, that he was the bearer of a despatch from Hung, the Governor-General, to Lord Elgin, assumed what, to a looker-on, appeared a harsh and unnecessarily violent demeanour towards him, saying that such communications were now useless, as it was only with the commanders-in-chief that he could treat, as matters were now entirely in their hands. He, however, took the letter to Lord Elgin, who was on the cavalier, and left the mandarin standing below. He sat down on a piece of wood, and I went up and spoke to him, asking him where he had learnt to speak English so well. He said he had travelled both in England and America; he then, with much apparent feeling, said he could not understand why Mr. Parkes should treat him in the harsh manner he had done; that such usage of men, situated as he then was, was not customary amongst European nations; that current events were not his doing, nor was he responsible for the Governor-General having addressed himself to the ambassador in place of the general commanding the troops; that he was the mere envoy bearing it, and therefore ought to be treated with the courtesy common to civilisation. By the time he had thus expressed himself, a crowd had formed about him, and a young medical officer stretched his neck forwards, and remarked in a rather strong Irish accent, "Why, he is a very little fellow." "Yes," replied the mandarin, "I am a very small man, but I have a very large heart. Napoleon was a very little man, but that did not interfere with his being a very great one." I asked him if San-ko-lin-sin was in the forts opposite? He replied, "That is not my business; all I am here for is to deliver a letter from the Governor-General, and take back any reply that may be sent." I then asked him what office he held, and he told me that he was assistant magistrate of Pechili. He said that he did not know who the two military mandarins were, or what they had come about. Mr. Parkes now returned, and gave him an answer, with which he departed.*

* I have since ascertained that Wang is the name of this official, and

Preparations in the meantime were being made for recommencing the attack, and towards two o'clock the whole of the artillery that it was possible to bring forward was moving towards the remaining northern fort. By the hour appointed for the expiration of the armistice, the line of attack was formed; the English artillery on the left, the French on the right. The infantry, consisting of the 3rd Buffs, 8th Punjaubees, and a battalion of Infanterie de la Marine, had been brought up from Tang-koo; the troops engaged in the morning being retained in reserve. As there were no signs of resistance, the whole line of artillery advanced without firing a shot, and the storming parties pushed forward. In a few minutes, the Buffs, Punjaubees, and French were seen scaling the wall, and at half-past two the Union Jack and tricolor floated above the cavalier. About fifteen hundred soldiers, a good many of them wounded, were found inside. They threw down their arms, and quietly surrendered themselves as prisoners.

The day had been beautifully fine; but hardly had this fort been captured, when the sky suddenly became overcast, and a terrific thunder-storm burst over the place. The rain fell in torrents, and soon saturated the plain, converting it in a very brief space of time into one vast swamp. After an hour's exposure to this storm, drawn up in the rear of the fort, the artillery received orders to return to Tang-koo. The ground was in such a state that it was found impossible to move the heavier guns, and the lighter ones were got along with the greatest difficulty, and every now and then one had to be left in the mud. The army

that he was educated at Bishop Boone's American Mission School at Shanghai;—that he was employed by Mr. Wade in the Chinese Secretary's Office as a linguist for some time, and that in that capacity he accompanied Lord Elgin's mission to China in 1858. After the signing of the treaty at Tien-tsin that year, owing to his knowledge of barbarian affairs, the authorities put pressure upon him and made him remain in the government service near the capital. I was fortunate enough to have a very interesting conversation with him under very different circumstances, eighteen months afterwards at Tien-tsin.

returning looked one vast disorganised rabble. The English and French infantry were all in confusion and mixed up together, the men wading to their knees in mud. Struggling on through swamp and mud, sinking sometimes nearly to their thighs, I noticed a couple of the French coolie corps carrying back on a stretcher one of their dead comrades who had been killed at the assault. Here and there also horses were seen immersed and suffocating in the mud. We passed Milward's battery *hors de combat;* Desborough's howitzers had to be left behind ; and just as we were nearing Tang-koo, one of Barry's guns got so deep in the mud that it could not be moved on. By degrees the remainder of the battery got as far as the eastern side of Tang-koo, but there the streets were in such a state that its further progress for the night was arrested.

Having left one of the medical officers of the artillery and several men sick in camp at Sin-ho, I was anxious to reach there if practicable before dark. This, however, was not an easy matter, the plain intervening being now completely flooded, and what little daylight remained being nearly expended before I succeeded in extricating myself from the muddy intricacies of Tang-koo. Having taken a line as nearly as I could guess in the direction of the camp, all traces of road being obliterated, I had to go along at a slow pace through the water, and was overtaken by darkness before I had advanced more than half a mile from the intrenchment. It continued to rain at intervals, and every now and then the flooded plain was for a second revealed to view by flashes of lightning. After being out about three hours, I found myself in the vicinity of the camp; but owing to the intervening ditches and the difficulty of finding the bridges across them, nearly another hour elapsed before I reached the tents, which were at this time about a foot deep in water. The Peiho also had overflowed, and in the imperfect light it was impossible to distinguish between the river and the flooded plain, rendering it unsafe to approach too near the bank.

CHAPTER XIII.

Surrender and occupation of the South Taku Forts—Gallantry of the Chinese defence—The Chinese coolie corps—Capacity of the Chinaman to make an efficient infantry soldier—Defects in the Armstrong gun—Revisit the North Taku Fort—Burial scene—Admiral Hope proceeds to Tien-tsin—Visit opposite bank of river—Embark for Tien-tsin—Accident to the gun-boat.

August 22nd.—Yesterday afternoon, on the second north fort being surrendered, Mr. Parkes, Major Anson, and Mr. Loch crossed the river and had an interview with the Governor-General, which ended, after a great deal of discussion, in the unconditional surrender of the remaining forts, and all the munitions of war therein contained; the Governor-General expressing the conviction that the course he had consented to adopt was one which would bring ruin on himself, but that the necessities of the people forced it upon him.

There appears to be little doubt that the pressure caused by the population of Peh-tang, Sin-ho, and Tang-koo, having been driven in on Taku, must have had considerable influence in bringing about so speedy a termination of hostilities. Peh-tang by itself had a population of between twenty and thirty thousand, and a grievous amount of distress must have followed our somewhat ruthless but unavoidable occupation of it.

During the night the southern forts have been completely evacuated, and are now in the possession of our troops. Upwards of five hundred guns have been captured, amongst them a number of brass cannon, worth from eight to twelve hundred pounds each. The value of the gun metal taken must amount to a considerable sum, which, it is presumed, will go to the allied forces as prize-money. In the great south fort an immense quantity of war stores of all kinds has been found, also the hut occupied by San-ko-lin-sin, which is described as being very comfortably furnished, and the walls decorated with military plans. San-ko-lin-sin, accompanied by an escort of about a hundred and fifty cavalry, left the forts yesterday afternoon for Tien-tsin, *en route*, it is supposed, for Pekin, where he will arrive, like Sir John Cope, the bearer of the news of his own defeat.

The loss of the Chinese in defending the northern forts must have been heavy, judging from the numbers of dead lying about yesterday. Though some of the bodies were fearfully mutilated by cannon shot, yet the majority of the dead seemed to have been either shot by rifle bullets or bayoneted in resisting the storming. No men could have behaved better than they did, and certainly on this occasion they proved themselves "foemen worthy of our steel." The forts are stated to have been garrisoned chiefly by Manchu Tartars,* and while bearing testimony to the determined gallantry they displayed, I must not forget a word for true old John Chinaman himself, as represented by the French and English coolie corps; their coolness under fire and apparent indifference to danger having called forth the admiration of both armies. The French employed their coolies in the dangerous duty of carrying the scaling-ladders to the assault, which they did with remarkable steadiness and alacrity.

Though we did not employ our coolies at the same dangerous work, still their duties were not unattended with risk, as they were constantly under fire removing the wounded and bringing up ammunition to the front, and

* I have since ascertained that the garrison was a mixed one of Chinese and Tartars, the former probably the more numerous.

very well they behaved. They seemed to take great interest in the bombardment, and when the place was taken displayed genuine delight.

At a period when the reorganisation of our Indian army is occupying so large a share of attention on the part of the Legislature, and the difficulty found to be so great in replacing the old sepoy army of Bengal, is it not worth while entertaining the possibility of making China an enlisting field for a force for service in India? The experience of this campaign has demonstrated the great physical endurance of the Chinese, their docility and amenability to discipline, combined with intelligence and courage. Between 3000 and 4000 of these men will return to Hong-Kong with the expedition, accustomed to British military rule and to association with British soldiers, and, above all, with a full confidence in the honour and financial integrity of the British service, the all-important point in securing a good and faithful servant in a Chinaman. As far as I am qualified to judge, it appears to me that, in place of disbanding them, an effort might be made to form those who may be willing to take service as soldiers into an experimental Anglo-Chinese corps, which might be called the Hong-Kong Regiment. The opinion of Major Temple and the other officers who are now connected with the coolie corps is highly favourable to the capacity of the coolie for making an efficient infantry soldier. They are now all partially drilled, and have shown a ready aptitude in picking up the few military manœuvres that it has been necessary to teach them.

This question of coolie enlistment is of peculiar interest at a time when we have a prospect of having to expend annually some thousand English soldiers in garrisoning a country, to the climate of which, from their constitutions and habits, they are to a great extent unequal. The tastes of the English soldier in the mass are those pre-eminently unsuited to a climate like India: he eats largely of animal food, consumes freely intoxicating liquors, frequently of the worst kind, and narcotises himself with the strongest forms of tobacco. He is taught to dread the sun and to take no exercise during the day; he consequently swelters during the greater portion of it in his barrack-room, in a state of drowsy inactivity, the practical results of which are in no way conducive to his health or physical capacity for prolonged Indian service. The English soldier as a general rule saves money only when he cannot find an opportunity to spend it, and when the opportunity comes, what has been thus saved too frequently all goes in one grand bout of excess: with Chinamen, enlisted as soldiers and serving in India, the chief thing they would think of would be the saving of money, partly to remit to their relatives, partly looking forward to the time when their agreements would expire, and they would be able to revisit their native villages with the accumulated proceeds of their frugality. This propensity on the part of the lower orders of the Chinese to save money operates powerfully against their giving way to those habits which act so injuriously on the constitutions of our soldiers in India. I do not mean to say that the Chinese in the mass are less vicious than English soldiers in the East; I simply say that when earning dollars, from whatever source they come, they have a greater capacity for taking care of them than English soldiers have, and this chiefly results from the faculty of self-denial which they seem to be more capable of exercising.

The Armstrong guns returned to camp this forenoon, men and horses looking dirty and jaded; the result of having spent the night in the mud where I left them in Tang-koo. One of the guns in the subdivision of the battery commanded by Lieutenant Philpots is disabled in the breach, owing to a concussion shell having burst in it at the moment of loading. It would seem as if the gunner in the excitement of the moment had not used sufficient care in the introduction of the shell, the slight jar it then received causing its explosion. This tends to show that the gun possibly requires more deliberate handling than can always be secured in the excitement of a general action. The Armstrong guns have certainly shown capacity for firing at long ranges, and possibly are capable of doing so with considerable precision, should the range be accurately known (which in the case of moving objects must always be difficult to ascertain), but to suppose, as very probably some will assert, that the campaign on the Peiho has been in any way abbreviated by them is a mistake; the very satisfactory results which have been attained are mainly due to our tremendous force of artillery generally, and the cautious and judicious use made of it; and in saying that these results would have been equally readily attained had the Armstrong batteries been common field artillery, I am writing the unprejudiced opinion of one who has had opportunities for tolerably close observation, without having a bias one way or the other. In the different operations connected with the advance on the Peiho and capture of the Taku forts, the Armstrong guns have been invariably in action alongside the ordinary field batteries, and this seems to me to be hardly their proper place; an amount of rapid firing being thus entailed upon them, possibly more than they are equal to, owing to the tendency they have to become speedily heated. Slow and careful firing at long ranges, with a specific object to carry out, most probably will be found to be the true position of the Armstrong gun as a novel form of field ordnance.*

* Further experience in the north of China has brought under my notice other defects in the gun, one of which is a tendency the vertical vent-piece has to fly out; attributable, I believe, to repeated firing causing it to fit too loosely, in consequence of the wearing down of the copper facing, and which interferes with the breech being properly screwed up. This copper is stated to require "bushing" about every hundred rounds, an easy operation, but one which necessitates a field forge accompanying the guns.

That care and deliberation are necessary in loading was also illustrated

This afternoon I revisited with Dr. Telfer the scene of yesterday's events. On entering the gate of the upper northern fort, I observed on each side of it, two large thirty-pounder carronades with piles of canister-shot close by. I was surprised to see how closely the Chinese have copied our method of manufacturing this destructive munition of war. In a hut near the entrance, a number of wounded Chinese were collected, and what little could be done on the spot to mitigate their sufferings seemed to have been attempted, but a good deal remained to be done, and Dr. Telfer humanely brought the subject under the notice of the principal medical officer on returning to camp.

I ascended the cavalier overlooking the river front of the fort: a strange scene was going on underneath. A large shallow pit had been dug, which a fatigue party of soldiers were filling with the dead who had been shot on the outside of the fort, and whose bodies yesterday pretty thickly strewed the ground. They were brought in by ropes attached to their heads or heels, according as they had lain most conveniently. A couple of soldiers harnessed thereto dragged them in through the mud, as merrily, to all appearance, as if they were engaged at a harvest home. Dead dogs and cats were thrown into the same pit amidst laughter and jokes—mirth presiding over the grim scene; to such an extent do the finer feelings of human nature become blunted by war

at Tien-tsin, a breech explosion and severe injury to the man loading resulting from the neglect of it. It appears that sponging out the gun is not sufficient to ensure the extinction of any sparks remaining in the grooves, and that it is necessary after each sponging for the man loading to look up the breech prior to introducing the cartridge. On the occasion in question the man neglected to do so, and a spark remaining in one of the rifle grooves ignited the cartridge. That field batteries entirely composed of Armstrong guns will at no distant period be recognised as a mistake, I think exceedingly probable; as far as my very limited means of observation enable me to judge, I have formed the opinion that the most efficient field battery for general service would be one composed of two howitzers, two field pieces, and two Armstrong guns.

and its attendant circumstances, a very brief experience with which had rendered young soldiers indifferent to scenes that perhaps a few weeks before would have filled them with horror.

August 23rd.—This morning, the obstacles having been removed from the river, the "Coromandel," bearing the flag of Admiral Hope, entered the Peiho, and about eleven o'clock steamed past the camp of the first division, on her way towards Tien-tsin. Mr. Parkes accompanies the Admiral, and we hear that peace negotiations may be expected shortly to commence.

The Engineers, French and English, are still working at the bridge of boats, which is now approaching completion. This afternoon, partly through its aid, partly by a boat, I succeeded, along with the Rev. Mr. Mahé, in getting over to the opposite side of the Peiho, and was much struck with the magnificence of the orchards, which seemed to extend for miles into the country, the road in fact lying between a perfect jungle of fruit trees and vines. In one of these orchards we found the Royals encamped, a portion of the first brigade under Brigadier Staveley having been sent across this forenoon. The soil on this side of the river appears to be a rich brown clay.

It was dark before we succeeded in re-crossing the river, and then, owing to the rise of the tide, it was impossible to return by the way we came, a broad ditch which intervened being now flooded. In our difficulty, some sappers undertook to guide us in the dark to a part of the canal not far from the camp, where some means existed for getting across. With a good deal of difficulty we reached the place, and with still more, succeeded in crossing; the means by which we effected it being a few loose poles floating in the water, over which we had to crawl on our hands and knees, the darkness preventing us seeing where to put our feet.

August 24th.—Early this morning I was awoke by Colonel

Barry, with the information that in three hours the battery was to start for Tien-tsin.

The battery had to wait some time before the bridge was sufficiently finished to admit of the horses and guns being taken to the opposite bank, where gun-boats were waiting to receive them. I embarked with the first portion of the battery in the "Leven," and it was six o'clock before we fairly got under way.

We had got but a short distance up the river when we grounded near the left bank. As the tide was coming in we had hopes of soon getting off. Perfect stillness prevailed around until seven o'clock, when the bugles of the Royals were heard in the distance.

At eight o'clock the tide was well in, and just as we seemed to have a prospect of getting again under way, the screw got foul of a boat's hawser. We were now at a complete stand-still, and in a fair way of being left with so little water that, from the great weight on board and unsteady nature of the cargo, it was not improbable that when the tide receded the vessel would heel over and serious loss ensue. It was an anxious moment for the Commander, who did all that possibly could be done to get the boat clear, and just as the last effort had proved unsuccessful, the "Coromandel" hove in sight on her way back from Tien-tsin. Admiral Hope learning the state of matters, sent the "Snap" gun-boat to our assistance, which came alongside about midnight, just as the "Leven" had commenced to settle down.

CHAPTER XIV.

Steam up the Peiho—Vessels get aground—Obliging disposition of the villagers—Arrival at the Forts of Tien-tsin. Their appearance and construction—Occupation of Tien-tsin by Admiral Hope—Visit to the walled city—Civility of the inhabitants—A village deputation— Assault on a villager by a sailor—Sang-ko-lin-sin's commissariat arrangements—Appointment of Imperial Commissioners—Lord Elgin's arrival at Tien-tsin—Reinforcements sent to defend Shanghai— Departure from Tien-tsin.

August 25th.—After great exertion and a good deal of difficulty, the horses and guns were transferred to the "Snap," and at six A.M. we got once more under steam for Tien-tsin, which gave us the advantage of daylight during our whole progress up the river. It is difficult to convey an idea of the multitude of villages which crowd the banks of the Peiho.

Numerous groups of villagers were watching the steamer pass, while others were going along the banks with their nets to fish. In dress and general appearance, no difference could be recognised between them and the peasantry of the south. The river for a considerable distance presents no variety, either in width or aspect of its banks,—a dense jungle of reeds on the right or southern side, and a low, sloping mud bank on the left, surmounted with a bright surface of green vegetation, constitute the scenery,—its sameness here and there being broken by a cluster of richly clad trees. Judging from the number of people seen on the banks, the population about here would seem considerable.

We passed two towns exactly opposite each other, the one

K

on the left bank being of some size and apparent commercial importance, twenty-three junks being at anchor, with several others in docks cut in the bank of the river. This town extends nearly a mile up the river-side, and the houses are built so close to its edge as hardly to leave room for a foot path between them. Crowds of inhabitants flocked down to the banks as we passed, and from their dress and general appearance seemed well to do.

The "Grenada," with the English ensign at the main, was now close a-stern, and at half-past eight she passed us, Lord Elgin standing on the bridge. General Grant and his staff were also on board. One of the small Indian river steamers followed as tender to the "Grenada."

We continued to pass numerous villages and towns on either side of the river, separated from each other in several instances by an interval of only a few hundred yards.

Presently we reached a portion of the river where the banks are lower and the country more open, exposing to view a vast alluvial plain in cultivation, and intersected by a good road, along which covered carts and donkeys with pack saddles were travelling. Near this point the river seemed to be rather shallow, as our screw commenced to turn up mud every now and then. We passed on the left bank a maritime town, with a number of large junks anchored opposite it, and on the right bank a village of some size. The sailors in the junks seemed taller than the average of Chinamen generally. They looked on silently, but attentively, as we passed, without gesticulation or any manifestations of surprise. About here, the number of boats, junks and fishing punts, indicate a considerable maritime population. The punts are fitted with large nets suspended from a sort of spider-shaped bamboo frame. At this part the river is not over a hundred yards wide, and we passed within twenty yards of the bank, which was crowded with villagers watching the progress of the Western Barbarians, and amongst them several women, the first we have seen since leaving Sinho. Business here seemed to be going on undisturbed; the troubles of war apparently not having as yet reached so far inland. No dread of us was shown, as boats laden with merchandise were quietly pursuing their way up the river, without making any effort to elude us by passing up the creeks that branch off the river at short intervals. All about here a number of small villages are dotted about, some close to the river bank, others a little inland.

On coming to a sharp turning opposite a village we found a French gunboat aground, and a crowd of villagers vigorously pulling at a hawser under the direction of a few French sailors. Here we met the "Woodcock" gunboat returning from Tien-tsin. In passing she threw us a little too near the bank, and we also got aground. Crowds of peasants soon came about us; the poor people seemed friendly in the extreme, and, judging from their manner, by no means sorry to see us. The devastation of war had not reached them, and their recollections of foreigners were probably those only of the year before last when our temporary residence at Tien-tsin had opened up a new market for their supplies.

We sent a hawser on shore to the side opposite where the French were at work, and here we likewise met with plenty of volunteers, who set to work and pulled our head round, in five minutes getting us afloat. As we steamed slowly along close to the bank, our friends, who were dark-complexioned with true Chinese features, accompanied us some little way, seemingly pleased at having rendered us a service, and ready to do it again if necessary. Here, for the first time, I observed a variety in the marine architecture of China, namely, boats formed of two conical-shaped punts lashed stern to stern, the front one having a long thin mast and calico sail on it run up on numerous strips of bamboo. These boats are guided by steer oars, and a considerable number of them were moving about at this part of the river.

Presently two new looking forts came in view, from which, with the glass, the flags of England and France were made out to be flying. As the forts are neared, indications of Tien-tsin begin to appear; a large pagoda-shaped building being seen in the distance. About four we were abreast of the forts, and dropped anchor a little way inside of them, near the " Opossum" gunboat.

At five o'clock Sir Hope Grant and his staff arrived in the Indian steamer; the " Grenada" having got aground. The General immediately landed and inspected the forts on both sides of the river, the 67th Regiment being in occupation of them, having arrived a few hours before us.

The forts appear to have been hardly completed. In construction and material they are much superior to those at Peh-tang. They are more closed in behind, though the upper battery or cavalier is approached in the same way by an incline or ramp. A crenellated wall is some distance in front of the cavalier, and fitted with an extensive series of casemates; the embrasures being fitted with traversing platforms *à la Chinoise*, in the form of massive wooden carriages, revolving on a central axis. All the guns have been removed, and are believed to be buried in the neighbourhood.

In the distance, flying from the top of a pagoda-like building, which rises above a mass of low-roofed houses, the union jack and tricolor were distinguished, showing the occupation of the gate of Tien-tsin by an advanced portion of the allied force.

Near the fort on the left bank, there is a small village, with a temple having a burying ground in front of it, with the graves rounded over, and arranged exactly in European fashion, most of them having tomb-stones at their head. There are also several regularly constructed brick sarcophagi in the vicinity of this temple. Altogether, I have seen nothing in China so closely resembling an English graveyard as this does.

While I was looking up the river with my glass, a crowd of natives came round me and seemed very anxious to have a peep through it. I allowed them to do so, and their awkward manipulation showed that the telescope is not yet an instrument in general use in the Celestial Empire. One of them, however, seemed more at home with it than the others, and, to my surprise, looking in the direction of some trees in the distance, he remarked "*voilà les bois.*" On interrogating him as well as I could, I made out that he was a Christian, and had at a former period received tuition from the French missionaries.

The circumstances attending the occupation of the city are the following:—On the evening of the 23rd instant, Admiral Hope, with his small squadron of gunboats, anchored about seven miles below the forts, where he was met by a deputation of citizens who informed him that the authorities had no intention of defending the works, which have just been completed on a very extended scale by Sang-ko-lin-sin, for the protection of Tien-tsin, the guns and garrisons having been withdrawn; also, that Sang-ko-lin-sin himself had passed the previous day, accompanied, as stated above, by about 150 horsemen. He is represented as having been so depressed in spirits as not to enter the city, preferring going on direct to Peking.

Such being the state of matters, Admiral Hope determined at once to occupy Tien-tsin, and pushing on yesterday morning, he landed marines at the forts, and went right up to Tien-tsin in the "Coromandel," arriving there about nine o'clock. The Viceroy (Hang-fuh), who also had arrived from Taku, came off and had an interview with the Admiral, who informed him that Tien-tsin must be considered in the possession of the allies, but that the people would be protected and the civil authorities allowed to remain in the exercise of their judicial functions. The east gate of the city was then taken possession of, and the English and French flags hoisted on it. A proclamation at the same time was posted up on it by direction of Admiral Hope, informing the people of the circumstances under which they are now placed. The Admiral then returned to Taku, leaving Captain M'Cleverty as senior naval officer, and Mr. Parkes to act in conjunction with him.

August 26th.—This morning, at a quarter to six, I left the camp for the purpose of visiting Tien-tsin. The road, which passes between fields of tall millet on the left, and vegetable gardens on the right, is of good breadth, and at present in fair order, the weather being very fine. In wet, however, I should say it becomes an indifferent one. Peasants in considerable numbers, laden with market supplies, were going in the direction of the forts. The attire and mode of dressing the hair adopted by the women, seem the same as at the south; their feet, however, in some instances, looked as if they had been exposed to a more modified form of contraction than is the rule there.

After proceeding along this road for about a mile, I reached the suburbs of Tien-tsin, and entered a long, narrow irregular street, lined with shops of a common description. This street led down to the river bank, and terminated in a bridge crossing a small creek or canal. Hereabouts the river was full of junks, and the left bank crowded with houses. On the opposite side houses occurred only here and there, the vacant spaces being occupied by large and lengthy mounds, covered with matting, which I have since learned are enormous stores of salt.

The people seeing me puzzled when I came to turnings, and guessing where I wished to go to, were very civil in directing me, and I succeeded in reaching the east gate of the walled city. Here I found a company of the 67th, and some French sailors on guard. The gateway is of considerable strength, and seems a sort of citadel or fortified yamun, ascended by a ramp on each side from without the city wall, and defended in front by a crenellated bastion, having a gateway at its side. From the top of the east gate it is readily made out that the city is invested by a strong brick wall, about twenty feet thick; that its shape is quadrilateral, and that there is a similar gateway at the centre of each of the three other faces of the city; also, that there is a small pagoda-shaped tower at each angle, with a large one in the centre of the town. With the exception of the temples, the houses are all single storied, and over-topped by the wall, which is about thirty feet high.

On entering the town, the stranger forms the impression that the streets are paved; this, however, is not the case, the pavement extending only some fifty yards from the gateway. The streets then become like those at Peh-tang or Sinho, and in wet weather must be equally bad. Happening to use my note-book inside the city, a crowd immediately surrounded me, and appeared to take the most lively interest in English calligraphy. I made a rough sketch of a Tartar soldier who happened to pass at the time, which seemed to please them so much, that they immediately drew my attention to several other objects, as being worthy my most indifferent of pencils. At the particular request, however, of one of the crowd, I made a sketch of a fish that was exposed for sale at a stall near where I was standing, and presented it to him, which seemed to please him amazingly. I then walked straight up to the pagoda in the centre of the town, and found it to be the point of intersection of the main streets traversing the town from east to west, and north to south, and communicating directly with each of the four gates. Articles of food seemed abundant, the butchers' shops being particularly well supplied, and the meat cut up and exposed for sale on swivel hooks as in England. The sheep appear all to have the large fatty tail similar to those at the Cape of Good Hope. Vegetables and fish were also plentiful in the market. Perambulating barbers' establishments seemed as numerous as at the south, and equally busily employed. Judging from the time it took me to walk briskly back from the central pagoda to the east gate, I should say the walled town from east to west measures about a mile and a quarter.

The houses of Tien-tsin are for the most part built of slate-coloured brick, the windows being formed by wooden trellis-work, covered with paper. In a few instances I observed large panes of glass introduced into the centre of the trellis and paper-work. After leaving the walled city, it took me a quarter of an hour's quick walking to emerge from the suburb which has grown up on its south-eastern aspect, and another quarter of an hour brought me back to the forts, their distance from the walled city being a little over two miles. These forts, I have ascertained, form the southern extremes of a connected series of earthworks, fronted by a deep and wide ditch, that invests the whole of Tien-tsin and its suburbs on both sides of the river. These defences are supposed to be over fifteen miles in extent, and are the works referred to as recently constructed by Sang-ko-lin-sin. Two guns have been dug up this morning under the wall of the fort, where they seem to have been buried within the last two or three days. One is a short, heavy gun, having "12-pounder carronade" marked on the trunnion; the other, a 24-pounder carronade marked with a crown and E. C.

At one P.M. the King's Dragoon Guards, the Seik Cavalry, and Stirling's battery appeared on the opposite bank of the river, having just arrived from Sinho by land. About this time, while I was standing at the gate of the fort with Major Hague of the 67th and Colonel Barry, several respectable looking villagers collected round us, and one old gentleman with a moustache and fan commenced to talk and gesticulate with energy, and after some little delay we made out, at last, what he wanted. Perceiving that Major Hague had a binocular glass, he wished to have a look at the Dragoon Guards and Probyn's Horse on the opposite side of the river. The glass was given to him, and after he had satisfied himself, it was handed from one to another, until at least thirty had made their observations with it. By this time the crowd had considerably increased. The old gentleman with the moustache then suddenly assumed an official attitude, and dropping on one knee presented an address written on red paper, which Colonel Barry, as the senior officer, received. The rest of the crowd then went down on both knees, and made the usual salutation of the country, by clasping both hands and shaking them in front. They then got up and dispersed. They were a deputation of villagers accompanying the head man of the village to present the address. At two o'clock, the second division of Barry's Battery arrived in the "Woodcock," and at half-past three the "Leven" came up with a portion of the Royals and Brigadier Staveley, who assumes the command at Tien-tsin.

At half-past four, a second deputation of villagers came to the fort, accompanying an old man, whose face was bruised and bleeding. He had been assaulted by a sailor from one of the gunboats, and in the scuffle had managed to secure the sailor's cap, which he produced. I took him to Captain M'Cleverty, who had the cap identified as belonging to a man of the name of Boodey. Finding on inquiry that the assault was one of an altogether unprovoked character, he took the sailor off to the "Opossum" accompanied by the old man, and in his presence and that of the crowd who accompanied them, had forty-eight lashes administered to him, which he richly deserved; the assault having been the result of mere wanton brutality.

At five o'clock the "Bantam" gunboat arrived with the head-quarters of the Royals. The regiment was disembarked at once, and at six o'clock marched off to an encamping ground a little to the left of the fort. Prior to moving Colonel Urquhart addressed the men, telling them that they were to behave to the Chinese exactly as if they were at Hong Kong—that they were to treat them in every way as friends—that no man was to take anything without paying for it, nor were they to enter dwelling-houses without permission.

The commissariat arrangements made by Mr. Parkes have resulted from its having come to his knowledge that a committee of supply, composed of the gentry of the neighbourhood, had been formed by Sang-ko-lin-sin, to assist him in rationing his army. He has accordingly arranged with the authorities that this committee shall continue in operation for the procuring of supplies for the allied forces, and this we hear has been readily agreed to. To-day an edict is stated to have arrived from Peking, degrading Sang-ko-lin-sin for the loss of the Taku forts, characterising the punishment as light, which consists of his being deprived of his three-eyed peacock's feather, his command in the Manchu banner force, and honorary position in the Imperial Body Guard. It is also reported that Kweiliang and Hang-fuh have been appointed Imperial Commissioners to enter at once on negotiations for peace, and that the former is now on his way from Peking.

The "Grenada," with Lord Elgin on board, arrived this morning, and is now anchored off the town of Tien-tsin. The general impression now is that hostilities are completely over, and that the force will not move beyond Tien-tsin, with the exception of a cavalry escort that will accompany the ambassadors to Peking. Already the break-up of the force may be said to have commenced, the 44th Regiment having been sent off in haste yesterday to Shanghai, in consequence of the threatening aspect of the Taeping rebels in the neighbourhood, and their apparently fixed determination to capture the native or walled city of Shanghai, the fall of which would seriously endanger the European settlement. Under these circumstances, the English and French Ministers have determined to aid the Imperial forces in defending Shanghai, and thus we are about to act in the paradoxical capacity of enemies and allies of his Celestial Majesty at the same time.

To-morrow morning I start for Shanghai *en route* to Hong Kong, in conformity with instructions I have just received to proceed there and take over the Provisional Battalion again, in consequence of the medical officer in charge of it having been invalided.

August 27th.—At half-past four this morning I left Tien-tsin in the river steamer that came up with the "Grenada," and which returns with Lord Elgin's mail. Five hours after starting we passed through the bridge of boats at Sinho; after which, on the way to Tang-koo, I had an opportunity of seeing the battery referred to on the 18th instant. Five good guns were still in position, and I could detect no indications of their having suffered from the fire of the Armstrongs, on either of the occasions on which the battery was the object of their fire.

CHAPTER XV.

Arrive at Shanghai—State of affairs—Visit the European settlement and the Chinese city—Brigadier Jephson's interview with the Tautai—Tea-gardens—Baby Tower—Sail for Hong Kong—Chinese festival—Return to Shanghai—Chinese soldier's devotions—Chinese petition to Mr. Bruce—English shooting party—Sickness on board ship—Malaria and ague—The English in Japan—Arrive at Tien-tsin—News from Peking.

ON the 2nd of September we reached Shanghai, and dropped anchor off the European settlement. We learnt that during the last fortnight the greatest excitement had prevailed. The Taepings had assaulted the city in vast numbers; but had been gallantly repulsed by the British and French troops, with volunteers of the foreign residents. As the return of the rebels is not improbable, the state of defence is carefully maintained, and the Volunteer Guards do duty at the various posts with energy and caution. Colonel Neale, commanding the volunteers, goes round every night, and convinces himself that all is safe.

I landed in the afternoon and walked through the European settlement, which is laid out in streets intersecting each other at right angles. The houses are all substantially built, and, on the whole, rather elegantly designed: for the most part they stand within enclosures, or compounds as they are called in the East. In the rear of the settlement is the race-course, and on it, at the present time is encamped the left wing of the 44th Regiment, which arrived two days ago. Strong wooden barriers, with loop-holed defences, have been erected in the main avenues of the settlement, and a party of marine artillerymen are quartered near the race-course.

The reinforcements, with the Loodiannah Regiment and Marines, are distributed in and about the native city. The head-quarters of the former occupy a large temple outside the wall, known as the Ningpo Joss House, which in reality is an extensive funereal establishment, wherein natives of Ningpo have been in the habit of depositing the coffins containing their deceased relatives until freights became low, and other circumstances propitious for their removal to their native spots. The rebels are now twenty miles off, and no immediate apprehension appears to be entertained of their resuming the attack.

September 3rd.—This afternoon I visited the Chinese city, which is situated to the south of the European settlement, and immediately adjoining the French quarter. It is of nearly circular shape and invested by a brick wall about twenty-five feet high, supported inside by an earthen embankment sloping up to the base of the parapet, where it forms a rampart from six to ten feet wide. The parapet is seven feet high and upwards of two feet thick. It has embrasures for large gingals or wall-pieces at intervals of a few feet. Between each of them there is a small aperture in the wall, containing an earthen vessel filled with slacked lime; so as to be ready to be thrown in the faces of the rebels in the event of an attempt to escalade.

Chinese troops are disposed all round the walls and live in tents on the rampart. Flags of various colours and designs fly in every direction from the wall. In some places groups of them, similar in pattern, are planted and indicate the positions respectively of the corps serving under them; the colours of their uniforms corresponding with their banners.

The various posts round the walls are defended in the rear by sand-bag batteries; the guns being placed so as to sweep the streets of the city—a precaution deemed necessary owing to the uncertainty which exists in respect to the presence of a considerable number of rebels amongst the intramural population: it having been pretty well ascertained that several thousand Canton and Chan-chew men were in league with the rebels.

September 4th.—Having slept inside the city at the quarters of the Royal Marines, I availed myself of the opportunity of going round the walls at midnight, and seeing how the Chinese sentinels performed their duty. Opposite each guard tent a number of loaded matchlocks were ranged against the wall. The sentries were walking about, every now and then beating a piece of hollow bamboo. The guards were asleep, but the petty officers were on the alert. In the tents lighted lanterns were hung up, and the soldiers to the number of six in each tent were sleeping, two on a mat, neck and heels. This morning, in the course of a walk round the walls, I looked into some of the tents by daylight. They are all floored with loose bricks, and in most cases the mats are spread on bed boards. Small lamps were burning inside for the soldiers to light their pipes at. Their arms consist of matchlocks and long spears with light bamboo shafts. The matchlocks are fitted with sights in the form of a raised plate of brass with a small hole in it corresponding with a raised point near the muzzle. As I passed one of the gates, some soldiers of the Loodiannah regiment were about to kill a sheep. It was led outside the wall, and the wool being removed from the upper part of the neck, the head was severed by one blow of a tulwar.

In the forenoon I accompanied Brigadier Jephson, on the occasion of his paying an official visit to the Tautai, or governor of Shanghai. Mr. Forrest, the interpreter, in an open chair, preceded by a few Chinese soldiers, led the way through the narrow and intricate streets of the city. One hundred men of the 44th accompanied the brigadier as a guard of honour, and a detachment of marines, under Lieutenant Pritchett, closed the procession, which after passing through a number of paved streets reached the

VISIT TO THE TAUTAI.

Tautai's Yamun—the Mansion House of Shanghai. On entering the court the brigadier was received with a salute of three guns and a Chinese air performed by a band of musicians perched up in an orchestra some distance from the ground. The 44th formed up in front of the Yamun and presented arms. After passing through two outer courts, we reached the inner entrance where the Tautai was waiting to receive the brigadier. He came forward and saluted first after the custom of his country by shaking his own hands, after which he shook hands "English fashion" with all who were introduced to him by the interpreter. He played the host with great ease and grace, and conducted us to his reception hall, a handsomely furnished room carpeted with red cloth, and having chairs with small tables between them for tea ranged down each side. As soon as we were seated, tea was brought in with little saucers over the cups to keep it warm.

Conversation then commenced, the brigadier, through Mr. Forrest, informing the Tautai, that he had just arrived from Taku, having been sent down to take command of the English troops at Shanghai, and that he wished to have his assistance in reference to lodging the force. The Tautai replied that he had only to select whatever accommodation he wanted, and he would at once give the order for its being handed over—adding, that he had learned that the foreign troops liked to keep separate, at the same time to be near the walls, and recommending the Confucian temple as a building that would be found suited for the purpose in view.

Before leaving we were conducted to a dining-room, where a déjeûner was laid out *à l'Anglaise*, the table being spread with a white cloth, and furnished with knives, forks, and wine-glasses. Fruits and cakes were handed round by a large staff of servants, and the glasses kept well supplied with champagne. At the close of the entertainment, a species of thin custard strongly flavoured with almonds was brought in, and the glasses filled with hot Chinese wine poured from a kettle. The custards were handed round in handsome English tea-cups. The Tantai entered freely into conversation about affairs on the Peiho, and congratulated the brigadier on the victory of Taku, which he said, now that it was over, he had no doubt would be to the benefit of both parties, and end in our becoming better friends than we have ever been before ; as the whole war had originated in a misunderstanding and positive unacquaintance on the part of the government with our true character and intentions. He also said he was very glad to hear that the Chinese troops had behaved so well at Taku, for he was sorry to say those he had at Shanghai were of very little use. On our leaving he shook hands most cordially with us all, and accompanied the brigadier to the door—strange contrast, I could not help thinking, to the scene I was an eye-witness of, about the same hour this day fortnight under the blood-stained cavalier of the Taku fort.

The Tautai's name is Wu ; he is a tall gentlemanly-looking man and a Tartar by birth. In addition to being Governor of Shanghai, he holds the appointments of intendant of circuit and chief superintendent of customs and trade. He wears the blue button of the second class, and peacock's feather. His dress, which consisted of a richly-embroidered blue silk jacket, over a robe of brocaded blue silk, was not an official one—that costume only being put on when he receives the Governor-general of the province, and on the Emperor's birthday. He has upwards of 200 servants and retainers about his Yamun, and is reputed to be one of the richest Mandarins in China ; report alleging him to be worth about a million sterling.

Returning from the Tautai's, we visited the tea-gardens, which are places of public amusement, neatly laid out, containing artificial rocks and grottoes, with ponds, canals, bridges, &c. Various entertainments were going on—one old gentleman in particular, seemed to be a special centre of attraction ; he was telling ribald tales, and amongst his audience several young ladies of dubious respectability were sitting. Near the tea gardens we went into a Chinese carver and gilder's shop. The proprietor was busy tracing out with ink elaborate designs on a long piece of wood, which a lad cut out with astonishing rapidity, with the simplest form of saw, consisting of a piece of brass wire about the thickness of common whip-cord, one side being slightly notched by cuts with a chisel. This wire was made tense by stretching it from the two extremes of a piece of split bamboo bent like a bow. With this instrument, as perfect action and efficiency seemed to be attained as if it had been made of the finest steel—so much for the effects of tension.

The Baby Tower of Shanghai is a small pagoda-shaped building, about twenty feet high, situated in the country a little way from the west gate of the native city. In it are deposited the remains of infants whose parents are too poor to bear the expenses of an ordinary funeral. When a child dies, it is wrapt round with bamboo straw and deposited in the Tower, which when full is cleared out by the municipal authorities.

On September 5th I embarked in H.M.S. "Urgent," for Hong-Kong, and arrived there on the 10th. The following day I resumed medical charge of the provisional battalion. About a month afterwards six staff-surgeons landed from England, and the option was given me of remaining with the battalion or rejoining the expeditionary force in the North, where, by the last accounts, hostilities had recommenced. I chose the latter, and on the 11th of October re-embarked for the Peiho.

I cannot forbear describing, as illustrative of the traditionary pageants of the Chinese, a grand festival, which, under the name of a "Joss pigeon," was carried on during the greater portion of the time I was at Hong-Kong.

A procession traversed the streets daily, composed of about 3000 people (including the Chinese merchants and tradesmen of the place, dressed in the gaudiest attire) and covering over a mile in length. It embraced a large number of bands of music, allegorical groups, formed by *tableaux vivans*, arranged on wheeled platforms or carried in palanquins. Three huge dragons, each 100 feet long and supported by thirty men, were amongst the prominent features of the procession.

Every evening a grand entertainment was open to the public, without charge, in a building that had been got up specially for the occasion. It was a vast structure of bamboo framework covered with matting, and elegantly fitted up with richly gilt altar-pieces and sacerdotal figures. Many of the decorations were fitted with automaton groups, and the building was lighted up by hundreds of glass chandeliers, producing a brilliant and striking effect. Concerts of vocal and instrumental music were going on in various parts of the building—refreshment rooms were also provided, where tea, cakes, and fruit were furnished free of charge. All classes of Chinese and foreigners were admitted, and the utmost decorum prevailed. A singular want of unity of decoration, however, was observable, such as gorgeous lustres suspended by common rope—richly-carved and gilded altars, having round them a common bamboo fence, tied with rope, over which might be seen hanging some gorgeous drapery. Here and there conservatories were arranged within the building, containing flowering plants, shrubs, &c., tastefully arranged. Outside the building there were refreshment stalls and eating-booths for such of the visitors as required more substantial support than that afforded by the tea and cakes inside; parties coming in and taking their refreshments at tables, and paying their bills according to their consumption.

The following particulars respecting the origin of this festival appeared in the *Hong-Kong Register* at the time it was going on :—

"There is a legend that a certain young man, Muh-leen

by name, to which the title of 'honourable' is now attached, was so unfortunate as to have a very wicked mother who died, and then went from Tartary to Tartarus or Tophet. Muh-leen was a very virtuous person, and knowing that his mother was in torment, he went on the 15th day of the seventh moon to the place of punishment, and succeeded in rescuing his mother. His kind offices did not rest here, for being in no hurry to shut the infernal door after him, a great number of the spirits of darkness took advantage of the circumstance and escaped also from prison. It is upon this impromptu jail delivery that the observances of this period are founded, and the Chinese name of the festival 'Shaoa-e-tsee" is derived from the custom of making garments of parti-coloured paper and burning them, that they may pass to the invisible world. Benevolent and rich men invite priests of Fuh and Taou to religious and gastronomic exercises, prayers and eatables being freely offered to elevate and cause to pass over from abodes of darkness and woe, the disconsolate or orphan spirits who have no relations to pay honour to their manes or to intercede for them. The Chinese also go on the water in boats to scatter prayers and burn clothing on behalf of the spirits of those who have been drowned."

Probably not one in ten of the Chinese who take part in the festival can state their reasons for so doing, but having originally been established on the basis stated, it is now kept up through habit, and the Chinese reverence for anything which has antiquity to recommend it, or as they style it in pigeon English, the "Olo (old) custom." I had no idea that spectacles of such magnificence could be got up in China, and I learned that the large sum of 32,000 dollars, raised by subscription amongst the Chinese merchants of Hong-Kong, had been expended upon the procession, affording a strong proof of the commercial prosperity of the settlement.

On the 11th of October, along with the Rev. Mr. Halpin, Chaplain to the Forces, Staff-Surgeon Dr. Bindon, and

Deputy-Assistant Commissary-General Ross, I embarked in the Peninsular and Oriental Steam Company's ship "Aden," specially chartered at Hong-Kong to convey to Shanghai a draft of 180 French soldiers of the 102nd Regiment that had just arrived by the ordinary mail steamer, *viâ* Suez. They seemed gay, light-hearted fellows, laughing, chatting, and skylarking with one another, and having apparently but little respect for their officer, a sub-lieutenant, who had risen from the ranks, and with whom they appeared to be on terms of considerable familiarity.

The following day there was considerable sea on, and with the view of getting into smoother water, we kept pretty close to the land, which was lofty and picturesque. At sun-down we began to ship a good deal of water amidships, and the French soldiers in that part of the vessel, came up and located themselves on the poop. The Captain was frantic, and ordered them down, but they declined going, quietly remarking (and with a good deal of truth), that they were not ducks. His personal exertions failing to dislodge them, he appealed to their officer, who very wisely declined to interfere; as there was no doubt that, however at variance with the rules of the Peninsular and Oriental service such an intrusion on the poop might be, the soldiers could not reasonably have remained where they were amidships, and the place to which they might have retired between decks was so intensely hot that the men said they could hardly breathe in it. They, therefore, despite the Captain's ruffled feelings, retained possession of a dry berth in the fresh air.

As we passed the "Great Chusan," and the numerous islands of the group, numbers of small craft were sailing about—pirates, when the vessels they meet are weaker than themselves, and inoffensive fishermen, when they happen to be of a contrary kind. We took a pilot* on board near the

---

* The river pilots at Shanghai are chiefly Americans, and have formed themselves into a pilot company, keeping as nearly as practicable a regular roster. The charge for piloting a vessel to Shanghai is five taels (about

"light-ship," and came to anchor a little below the English settlement on the afternoon of the 17th.

It was dark by the time I was able to get on shore, and having ascertained that my brother, with a portion of the 44th, was quartered in a small joss-house on the wall of the Chinese city, I went in search of the North Gate, which I was informed constituted the nearest point of approach. The night was very dark, and I made but slow progress up the side of the Yan-kin-pan creek (which runs between the English settlement and the native city), as I was afraid of walking over the bank. Coming upon the city wall, I followed it until I reached a bastion, from the top of which I was challenged by an English sentry. This proved to be the West Gate, in charge of a party of the 44th. The sergeant of the guard provided me with a lantern, and after a ten minutes' walk round the ramparts, I reached the joss-house I was in quest of, the upper story of which had been converted into a barrack. After spending a short time there I returned to the English settlement, and learned that we were to continue our voyage northward the next day, and embark in the "Australian," with the left wing of the Marine battalion, orders for which had been sent by the Commander-in-Chief.

My *compagnons de voyage* not having visited Shanghai before, were anxious to see as much of the place as possible; so early next morning I took them along the top of the wall of the native city, as the best means of enabling them to see the surrounding country. On looking at the cultivation which met the eye in every direction, one could not but feel regret that we should be involved in a war with a people who had attained such excellence in agriculture, and whose chief characteristic seemed that of peaceful industry, combined with an amount of civilization greater perhaps, than

thirty-three shillings sterling) for each foot of water the vessel is at the time drawing.

can be found amongst the corresponding class of the lower orders in our own land.

On reaching the temple, where I was the previous evening, we went into the lower portion of it, which was still available for religious exercises, not having been converted into barracks. A Chinese soldier was kneeling on a cushion before an altar and shaking a piece of hollow bamboo, containing a number of bamboo slips, each one having an inscription on it. He went on bowing to the altar, and shaking the bamboo case until one of the slips fell out. He then picked it up and took it to a priest, who was sitting behind a species of counter. The priest examined it, and having interpreted its meaning, the soldier went and put some money through a slit into a long bamboo tube hanging up by the side of the altar, and recommenced his devotions, whilst the priest weighed some roots, which after pounding up in an iron mortar, he divided the whole into six parts, made them up in little paper parcels, and gave them to the soldier on completing his devotions.

I learned from Colonel Neale that the province of Shensi, adjoining that of Chili, was in a state of revolt against the Imperial authority, owing to an attempt having been made to "squeeze" an influential nobleman out of a quarter of a million of taels, as a contribution towards defraying the expenses of the war. This he refused, but offered to pay 200,000, which was not accepted, the full amount being insisted on. He then raised the standard of rebellion, and proclaimed himself Governor of the Province and of some twenty towns within it.*

At Shanghai itself at this time everything was going on quietly, the rebels having made no further attack on the city since that of August, though the surrounding country was pretty well in their possession; notwithstanding which

* The name of the nobleman referred to was Chang-lo-sing. The rebellion he headed continued for some time afterwards, but was only of a purely local character.

silk was then coming down from the interior in unusually large quantities, sometimes having to pay a tax to the rebels, sometimes passing without any exaction, opium, arms and ammunition being supplied them in return; with these exceptions the trade in staple imports was represented to be completely at a stand-still, the consumers being either ruined or afraid to buy. The rebels were moving about from place to place committing great havoc, and inspiring wide-spread terror amongst the population of the province. A petition had been presented to Mr. Bruce by a number of respectable Chinese residents of Shanghai, begging him to have compassion on their people, and to cause English vessels of war to be stationed at different points to protect the routes and to prevent the incursions of the rebels.

On the afternoon of the 18th of October, our party embarked in the "Australian" with 260 men of the Royal Marine battalion, under the command of Lieutenant-Colonel March. These men, with about 250 more effective at the time at the Peiho, constituted the wreck of two battalions of Royal Marines, numbering 1900 men, that came out to China in 1857; the remainder, with the exception of 200 sent over to British Columbia, having for the most part either died or been invalided.

October 19*th*.—Prior to weighing anchor this morning, a fleet of about fifty Chinese gunboats was seen coming up the river from a cruise in the Yang-tse, where it had been watching the movements of the rebels. At noon we got under steam. We soon saw in the distance the town of Pow-shun, the head-quarters at the present time of the Taepings, near Shanghai. Woosung being the advanced post of the Imperialists, we observed a number of tents pitched and Chinese troops loitering about.

Of Wu, the Tautai, report speaks very favourably. He would appear to have been most liberal in his disbursements for the defence of the European settlement, in illustration of which, a day or two before our sailing, a bill came in to the Defence Committee from an English shipwright amounting to about £2000 sterling, for erecting barricades in the settlement, which Wu paid without demur. This, however, I hear is but a trifling example of the sums he has had to pay out, connected with recent protective measures. His payments are not likely to cease soon, as by the last mail from the Peiho orders were received that the whole of the expenses of the British troops in Shanghai were to be defrayed by him.

October 20th.—In conversation with Lieutenant Godfrey of the Royal Marines, I learned that recently he formed one of a party of four Englishmen who made an excursion fifty miles up the Yang-tse-Kiang, as far as the town of Lun-Shan, a large military post of the Imperialists, situated on the north bank of the river. The country in its neighbourhood is hilly, and abounds with excellent game, consisting chiefly of deer, woodcock, quail, and pheasants. On landing they were challenged by the local authorities, and their object in coming demanded. On explaining who they were, and what they wanted, they were told by the authorities that they were very good men, and that they were very glad to see them, but that they had come a month too soon to get any sport. They, however, supplied them with guides to the hills, and sent a party of soldiers with them as an escort. They remained on shore three days, but failed to find any game, the statement of the officials that they were in advance of the shooting season being evidently correct.

October 22nd.—Out of the 260 marines that embarked four days ago, there are now thirty on the sick list, suffering from ailments such as are usually referred to malaria. The medical officer in charge informs me that the men are now much more sickly than they were while on shore at Shanghai. This apparently injurious result of a change from a malarious locality and comparatively unhealthy atmosphere to conditions of an opposite kind, is quite in accordance with what I have frequently observed, and tends to confirm me in an impression I have formed since returning to China, to the effect, that exposure to emanations from badly drained soils, decaying vegetable matter, &c., is not the actual excitant of the train of symptoms familiar to us under the name of an ague fit, the exciting atmospheric cause being generally one of a contrary nature, namely, free currents of fresh air.

This statement, no doubt, will seem at first sight paradoxical in the extreme, but it is not the less in accordance with actual facts, and, I believe, admits of the following explanation—namely, that a residence in malarious localities, though not the special exciting cause of the paroxysms of ague, still produces in particular constitutions a lowering of the vital power, characterised by organic changes of an obscure and frequently non-overt kind, which renders the individuals peculiarly susceptible of certain atmospheric influences, which, in constitutions thus predisposed, possess the power of generating paroxysmal febrile action—the most patent of such atmospheric agents that I have observed being ordinary fresh breezes. This fact has been noticed particularly in Hong-Kong, where invalids sent over from the extreme heat of Victoria to the sea breezes at Stanley, on the opposite side of the island, have suffered more from ague and general sickness than they did at the less salubrious locality. Another illustration came under my notice lately. The men of the 67th Regiment, while in occupation of the city of Canton, had good apparent health, and freedom from ague, so long as they were quartered in the lower portion of the city, where they were a good deal shut in from the fresh air, but they were no sooner removed to the heights above the city, where they were freely exposed to the breeze, than they commenced to suffer from ague, which was attributed to the malaria arising from the rice fields outside the city. The case of the Marines is another illustration. The men are now suffering severely from malarious diseases, where there is no generating agent but that of the pure atmosphere which now surrounds them. Hence, I think it not unreasonable to infer, that a residence in certain atmospheres, whether of the nature usually referred to malaria or not, developes a constitutional predisposition to intermittent fever and other diseases of a periodic type, which predisposition is brought into activity by meteorological conditions, which, to those in actual health, are not only quite innocuous, but in reality invigorating.*

Notwithstanding all we hear about the progress which sanitary science has made in the public service of late, a singular illustration to the contrary came to my knowledge this day. It appears that during the last summer, at Shanghai, the Marines, and particularly the Artillery section of the corps, suffered a good deal from sickness. No provision was made for the occurrence of fatal cases; and when a death took place, the corpse was removed to one of the punishment cells, and the prisoner taken out until the funeral was over. One man thus taken out refused to sleep on the bed board that a corpse had been placed on, and during the remainder of his confinement slept on the ground with a log of wood for a pillow.

The weather being very fine as we neared Talien-whan bay, its general aspect was much more inviting than on the stormy day I last entered it. We left the bay for the Peiho at four P.M.; previous to which numbers of native boats came off from the shore with fruit, vegetables, eggs, and the usual bum-boat stores. Quail seem very plentiful in the neigh-

---

* An account by a Mr. Gougher has lately been published of an imprisonment he underwent a good many years ago in Burmah. He gives a frightful account of the disgusting nature of the atmosphere which he, in common with the other prisoners, had to reside in, and yet he describes his own health as having continued what seemed to him very good, until he was removed to a cell where he was exposed to the fresh breeze blowing on the banks of the Irrawaddy. Immediately he began to suffer from malarious disease, which naturally was referred by him to emanations from the banks of the river; the more so, as the symptoms disappeared as soon as he was replaced in the pestilential air of the interior of the prison.

bourhood, an officer of the "Magicienne" having yesterday shot twenty-seven brace.

October 25th.—A conversation with Captain Boon regarding the ill treatment which the natives of India too frequently receive at the hands of Englishmen, and the insults which the higher class natives are exposed to by hearing themselves called "niggers" and "suars" (pork eaters), the latter the most offensive term that can fall on the Oriental ear, led to our discussing our prospects in Japan. It is his opinion that, ere long, the insulting, unamiable, and overbearing conduct generally of the English in Japan will give rise to a general massacre of the European residents. This belief is strictly in accordance with what I have heard repeatedly expressed of late by those who have visited the Japanese ports, and have thus had opportunities of becoming acquainted with the sentiments of the natives, and the impression formed by them of the English character.

The Americans, it would seem, from all I can learn, get on much better with the Japanese authorities than we do—frequently gaining by a little quiet perseverance what we entirely fail to accomplish by bluster and attempts to ride rough-shod over their prejudices. This is a sad defect in our national character abroad, and one that, until in some way or other it is checked, will be the means, as it has already too often been, of embroiling us from time to time in wars with the semi-civilised races with whom our commercial interests as a nation bring us into intercourse.

October 26th.—At daylight the masts of the fleet at anchor off the Peiho began to appear. Though reduced in number nearly one-half since I last saw it, the fleet still presents an imposing aspect. At nine A.M., we dropped anchor close by H. M. S. "Impérieuse," still flying the flag of Rear-Admiral Jones, who now commands at the Peiho, Admiral Hope having his head-quarters at Tien-tsin.

Immediately on anchoring, Captain Boon proceeded to the Admiral's ship for instructions: and, on his return, we learned, that as there was every prospect of peace being concluded, orders had been received from Peking, where the headquarters of the allied forces are now established, that all troops arriving from the south were to be detained on shipboard off the Peiho.

Our party not strictly coming under the denomination of troops, we went on board the "Impericuse," and saw Admiral Jones, who recognised our right to proceed as far as Tien-tsin at least, and gave us permission to go up in a gunboat, about to start with the mail. We accordingly embarked in the "Banterer," and at half-past twelve she steamed off, towing a large junk filled with government stores. The deck of the "Banterer" was crowded with all sorts of miscellaneous stores; boxes, barrels, rolls of matting, firewood, &c., removed indiscriminately from transports, and shipped for Tien-tsin, without reference to their being actually wanted or not, the object being to clear out the transports, so as to enable them to be paid off as speedily as possible.

We soon came up to Tang-koo, with its miles of crenellated wall. The inhabitants seemed all to have returned, and but little trace remained of its having been in our occupation, or exposed to the storm of shot and shell which fell about it, a little over two months ago. At five P.M., the tide running strong against us, we anchored near a brickwork on the north bank of the river, a little above Sinho. After dark, native boats in considerable numbers passed down towards Taku, availing themselves of the tide. They were laden chiefly with firewood and forage.

Through the kindness of the sailors, we were given the deck-house of the junk to sleep in, they themselves having a dormitory underneath, totally destitute of ventilation, with the exception of the little hatchway, through which they got into it,—the warmth afforded by the absence of fresh air being, in a sailor's opinion, infinitely preferable to any of the sanitary benefits which are believed to result from adequate cubical space.

Approaching Tien-tsin, we passed through the bridge of boats which extends across the river, the centre one being so arranged as to be quickly removed when vessels require to pass; bridge-keepers being stationed there for the purpose. On landing, we learnt that despatches had, a few minutes before, been received from Peking, conveying the news that a treaty of peace had been signed at a reception hall three miles within the city of Peking on the 24th instant,—the Emperor being represented by the Prince of Kung. The affair was described by those who were present as by no means cordial. The French treaty was to be signed the following day.

CHAPTER XVI.

Summary of Occurrences on the Peiho—Communications between the Commissioners and Lord Elgin—Negotiations broken off—Advance towards Tung-chow—The Prince of I—Mr. Parkes' interview—18th September—Endeavours to recover the prisoners—The Prince of Kung—Advance towards Peking—Imperial Palace plundered—Prisoners returned—Anting Gate surrendered—Funeral of the murdered English—Destruction of Yuen-Ming-Yuen—Entry into Peking—Treaty signed—Character of the Chinese negotiations—Conduct of the Chinese on the 18th September—Opinion of Lord Elgin.

THE occurrences on the Peiho subsequent to my departure in the latter part of August, have been of the highest interest, and a summary of them seems necessary here. At that time there seemed every prospect of peace. Sang-ko-lin-sin's commissariat had undertaken to continue its functions for the supply of the allied troops. Lord Elgin and Baron Gros were awaiting the arrival from Peking of Kweiliang and the other commissioners nominated for the ratification of peace.

On the 25th of August, Kweiliang addressed a communication to Lord Elgin, stating that he had been sent by the Emperor with full powers to make the necessary arrangements for the exchange of the ratifications,—that he had brought with him the seal of Imperial Commissioner—and that, of the propositions of the British Government, there was not one which it was not in his power to discuss and dispose of.

Lord Elgin replied on the 29th, to the effect that the action of the allied forces had been rendered necessary by the failure of the Chinese Government to receive the British envoy peaceably—and had resulted in the capture of the Taku forts and the city of Tien-tsin, which the allied armies now held; that the increased war expenses resulting from the conduct of the Emperor's Government, made it necessary that the contribution required should be raised from four to eight millions of taels; that if these demands were evaded or postponed, the Commanders-in-Chief would advance from Tien-tsin.

On the arrival of the commissioners, to whom Hang-ki, previously collector of customs at Canton, had been added as assistant, Messrs. Wade and Parkes waited upon them on the 6th September, with a draft of the convention which it had been arranged should be signed on the 8th. On their return they reported to Lord Elgin that the commissioners had declared that they had no power to sign any convention until it had been submitted to the Emperor, and were also unable to produce any decree investing them with the powers implied by certain words in their official title. On the commissioners then requesting an interview with Lord Elgin, he declined to grant it, alleging this failure of the powers which they had claimed, their assumption of which alone had induced him to regard them as competent to sign the ratification of peace. His lordship concluded his despatch by stating:—"The undersigned will not dwell on the want of good faith indicated by this proceeding. It is enough for him to observe that the alleged necessity of reference to Peking from a point so distant as this, involves delays to which he will not submit. He has accordingly called upon his Excellency the General Commanding her Britannic Majesty's Army in China, to provide him with such a force as will enable him to proceed without loss of time to Tung-chow, and he has further to intimate to the Imperial Commissioners that he can neither receive their visit nor enter into any convention with them for the re-establishment of peace till he shall have reached that city."

The commissioners then begged for a delay of three days, till they obtained powers from Peking. Lord Elgin refused to accede to their request: they then made a second appeal for delay, representing that the march of the British force northwards would have most unhappy results in alarming the people. Lord Elgin persisted in his decision, and stated that a proclamation was being issued to assure the people that they should still be protected from molestation.

Instructions were at once issued to the allied commanders to move a sufficient force on to Tung-chow—a walled town, about twelve miles from Peking—as negotiations would not be resumed until that place was reached.

On the 9th September, the first portion of the force started under the command of Brigadier Reeves. The next day General Montauban marched with 3000 French. Lord Elgin reached Yang-tsun, twenty miles from Tien-tsin, on the 11th. The next day he received a communication from two of the highest functionaries in the empire, the Prince of I (a near relative of the Emperor), and Muh-yin, stating that Kweiliang had received full power to discuss and dispose of "the forms or rules" in which the articles were to be arranged—that now the journey of Lord Elgin to Tung-chow would be a waste of time, and too probably would create distrust and alarm in the minds of the army and the people; that they had received commands to proceed to Tien-tsin to consider all matters.

The seal appended to this document was to all appearance new, and bore the characters "Prince Imperial Commissioner."

The same day Lord Elgin replied, detailing what had occurred at Tien-tsin, and expressing his determination to adhere to his original decision to sign no treaty prior to reaching Tung-chow.

The next day the commissioners replied to the effect that they had reached Matan, and that, therefore, instead of wasting the time by going back to Tung-chow, they thought it better that the British force should return to Tien-tsin, and a conference be held at some intermediate place, either at Hoo-se-woo or Ngan-ping, as Lord Elgin should decide, when they would conclude a treaty, seal and sign it.

Before replying, Lord Elgin wrote to Sir Hope Grant, to ascertain whether the army was in a position to continue its march to Tung-chow without interruption. He stated in reply that for seven or eight days at least it would be inexpedient for the army to advance beyond the point it had by this time reached, namely, Hoo-se-woo, a town on the Peiho, forty miles from Tien-tsin, as the smallness of the force made reinforcements necessary, and a depôt for the supplies coming up the river in boats, would require to be formed at Hoo-se-woo.

Under these circumstances, Lord Elgin determined to entertain to a certain extent the proposition of the commissioners, and addressed a letter to them to the effect that the force would continue to advance on Tung-chow, but that if the Chinese authorities gave such securities for their good conduct as would be required, he would cause the force to be halted at an easy stage from that city, and proceed from there with an escort of one thousand men to Tung-chow, for the signature of the convention, and then go on to Peking for the exchange of the ratifications of the treaty of Tientsin. This letter Lord Elgin entrusted to Messrs. Wade and Parkes for delivery, recommending them at the same time to obtain, if possible, a personal interview with the Prince and his colleague; thinking it possible that a verbal explanation of our real views and objects in China might have more weight with such high functionaries on the occasion of their first coming in contact with foreigners, than an expression of them in writing.

At this interview at Tung-chow, the commissioners, after some hesitation, agreed to meet the plenipotentiaries in that town, the main allied force being halted at a distance of five li from Chang-kia-wan.

Mr. Parkes, after reporting this arrangement to Lord Elgin, returned to Tung-chow to make preparations for the reception of the embassy, accompanied by Lieutenant-Colonel Walker, Mr. Thomson, Mr. Loch, Mr. de Norman, and Mr. Bowlby, with an escort of five Dragoon Guards, and twenty men of Fane's Horse, under Lieutenant Anderson. Similar steps were taken by the French. The allied armies moved on towards the proposed encamping ground.

Mr. Parkes was admitted to an audience with the Prince of I, and was courteously received. In the course of discussion, the greatest difficulty was made about the presentation of the autograph letter of the Queen to the Emperor, which the commissioners pressed Mr. Parkes to agree should not be personally delivered. This Mr. Parkes was not authorised to decide, but replied that he would refer it to Lord Elgin. The French secretary of embassy also had an interview. A proclamation was agreed upon to be issued by the imperial commissioners, and Mr. Parkes parted from them at 8 P.M., impressed with the satisfaction they seemed to feel on the conclusion of the preliminaries of peace.

The events of the 18th September are too well known to require a detailed narrative. A large Chinese force had during the previous day taken up a strong and extended position, commanding the proposed encamping ground, which had been marked out by the commissioners themselves for the use of the allied armies. The return of the English and French parties from Tung-chow lay through these lines. Some passed safely, but a *mêlée* having arisen around a French officer who was mobbed and ill-treated by the Chinese soldiers, fire was opened by the Chinese army, and an engagement ensued, during which Mr. Parkes and others of his party were arrested within the lines, in spite of the flag of truce which they carried. The prisoners thus treacherously seized by the Chinese numbered twenty-six British and twelve French subjects. The circumstances of their horrible treatment, and of the consequent death of twenty of the number, are known to all from the interesting narratives of Messrs. Parkes and Loch.

Every endeavour was made by the allies to recover the prisoners. The enemy, defeated at Chang-kia-wan, were followed to Palee-chow, where another severe defeat was inflicted upon them, and forty-three guns captured. Tung-chow was now taken possession of. At this place a communication was received from the Prince of Kung, a brother of the Emperor's, stating that he was come with full powers to supersede the Prince of I, who "had not managed matters satisfactorily." Negotiations were opened between the Prince of Kung and Lord Elgin. The surrender of the prisoners was demanded, but was delayed from time to time, the Prince stating that they could not be restored till the allied forces had fallen back, but that on the conclusion of peace they should be sent back with all proper attention. This answer could only be regarded as a rejection of the demand made. Lord Elgin accordingly called upon the commanders of the forces to march upon Peking, to the north of which the Chinese army was encamped under Sang-ko-lin-sin.

On the morning of the 5th of October the allied armies advanced towards Peking, and halted about five miles from the city. The French soldiers, owing to every man carrying a portion of his tent, got under canvas, while the British force, in consequence of the tents and baggage having been left behind, had to bivouack in the open air. The next day the armies continued their advance, and reached a point to the north-east of Peking, whence the gates of the city could be seen. From this point, a short march brought the French to the imperial palace, Yuen-ming-Yuen, which they at once plundered. On the 8th, the prisoners detained within the city were delivered up by the orders of the Prince of Kung. On the 9th the English siege artillery arrived, and a demand was made that the

Anting Gate should be given up to be held by the allies, as a security for the good faith of the Chinese, while the ambassadors entered Peking for the purpose of ratifying the treaties. The hour of noon of the 13th of October, was fixed as the latest hour that the city would be spared if this demand was not complied with. Every preparation was made for breaching the wall: the French had no siege guns, but placed their field pieces at a short distance.

On the morning of the 13th October, Mr. Parkes had an interview outside the city with Hang-ki, who made strenuous efforts to postpone the giving up of the gate. As noon approached the gate continued to be held by the Chinese. " The artillery officers in charge of the batteries commenced getting everything ready for opening fire ; the guns were sponged out, and run back for loading, with the gunners standing to their guns, waiting for the orders to commence. A few minutes before twelve o'clock the Anting Mun was thrown open, and its defences surrendered to Major-General Sir Robert Napier, whose division was on duty close by. Our troops took immediate possession, the French marching in after us." The English took possession of the portion of wall extending between the Anting Gate and the Tch-sheng Gate ;* the French occupying the wall between the Anting Gate and the north-east angle of the city,—upwards of two miles of wall, over fifty feet broad on the top, being thus held by the allied forces. Field guns were mounted on the wall, so as to command the inner approaches to the Anting Gate, and the position was speedily placed in a state of defence so as to resist any attack from within the city.

At noon on the 17th of October, the remains of Messrs. Anderson, de Norman, Bowlby, and Private Phipps, were buried in one grave in the Russian cemetery, outside the

---

* The north-west gate, out of which a broad road leads towards the Great Wall and Je-ho.

walls of Peking, which had been most considerately placed at the disposal of the Commander-in-Chief by General Ignatieff, the Russian minister. The coffins were placed on separate gun-carriages, and were accompanied by detachments of cavalry and infantry, with the band playing the Dead March. Lord Elgin and Sir Hope Grant were the chief mourners; the pall-bearers being the members of the embassy, and the Commander-in-Chief's staff. A considerable number of officers from both armies, including General Montauban, attended the funeral. The service was performed by the Rev. Mr. M'Ghee, chaplain to the forces, and one of the most striking occurrences of the ceremony is stated to have been the presence of a Roman Catholic priest, and a priest of the Greek Church, in their vestments, joining in prayer over the grave.

On the 18th of October, a portion of the first division marched from the camp in front of Peking to Yuen-ming-Yuen, where two days were occupied by the force in carrying out the destruction of the various buildings, scattered as they were over an area of several miles. By the afternoon of the 19th the chief palaces had been pretty well destroyed, though a good many of the buildings escaped demolition. The following description from an eye-witness conveys some idea of its extent :—"Two days were required effectually to set fire to and destroy all the buildings and walls. Much valuable property that it was impossible to remove was destroyed. It is said that it exceeded two millions sterling, exclusive of the buildings. From the place at which it was first entered by the French on the 6th of October, it was at least six or seven miles before the last building was reached. This was at the foot of the first range of hills that bound the plain to the north of Peking. Over this large extent of ground were gardens, palaces, temples, and pagodas on artificial hills, some of them three or four hundred feet in height, with forest trees of all kinds covering their sides, through the green foliage of which were seen the yellow-tiled roofs of the various imperial residences. A large lake lay buried in the midst of these wooded hills, with two or three islands on it, with picturesque buildings joined to the mainland by quaint but beautiful stone bridges. On one side of the lake, extending upwards of two miles, winding in and out, among grottoes and through flower-gardens, roofed in by flowering creepers, was the favourite walk of the Emperor and his court; in some places, where the palaces came to the water's edge, the walk was carried past them on a light and beautiful stone terrace overhanging the lake. The high mountains of Tartary forming the background made it, while it certainly was one of the most curious, also one of the most beautiful scenes I had ever beheld. During the process of destruction the soldiers came upon two presents that had been sent out to the Emperor of China by Lord Macartney from George III.— a state coach and two 12-pounder howitzers, complete in every way and in very good condition and repair, great care having evidently been taken of them; yet, strange to say, with these guns in their possession, they have never made any endeavour to improve their own field artillery carriages. Shot and shell were piled close to the guns, in the kind of coach-house in which they were found.") I may here remark that whatever property the troops employed in destroying the palace were able to pick up, they were allowed to keep, a permission, however, that was not of much use to them, as the articles of value remaining were not of the most portable character. Such of the officers, however, who could command means of transport removed property to a considerable amount.

All loot taken prior to the burning of the palace had been, by order of Sir Hope Grant, sold by auction, and the proceeds formed into a prize fund for general distribution in sums proportionate to rank—a private soldier's share amounting to seventeen dollars, equal to about seventy-two shillings sterling. Sir Hope Grant, whose share would have been a large one, generously relinquished his claim—an act of liberality which was followed by Sir John Michel and Sir Robert Napier—the sum falling to the subordinate ranks being thereby considerably increased. The total proceeds of the sale amounted to 123,000 dollars, one-third of which went to the officers, and the rest to the noncommissioned officers and men.

Arrangements were now made for signing the treaty at the Board of Ceremonies, within the Tartar city of Peking.

On the 24th of October, Lord Elgin entered the city in state, with an escort of 500 men. The Prince of Kung attached the great seal of the Empire to the document, and the treaties were then signed and exchanged.

On the 25th of October the signing of the French convention took place; the same formalities being gone through as on the previous day. On this occasion the Prince of Kung seemed rather more at ease, or probably less alarmed than he did on the signing of the English convention.

On the 26th of October the treaty was dispatched for England in charge of Mr. Loch; and Major the Hon. A. Anson, V.C., was sent at the same time with the Commander-in-Chief's despatches.

On the 27th of October Lord Elgin took up his residence inside Peking; the Palace of the Prince of I, situated within the Tartar city, near the south-eastern gate, having been fitted up for his reception.

With regard to the negotiations for peace thus at last brought to a successful issue, an opinion has been entertained that the intentions of the Chinese Government in opening them were not *bonâ-fide*. It has been thought that "it was never intended that Kweiliang's negotiations should be any more than a sham to gain time, and so if possible prolong operations into the cold season, which they considered too inclement for our constitutions to bear up against." I am rather inclined to believe that the attempt to negotiate was a *bonâ-fide* one; but undertaken in ignorance of the more extended character which our demands had assumed, and that when Kweiliang and his colleagues became cognisant of their exact nature, they found that their powers were unequal to their disposal, and applied to Peking for further instructions. I think that the apparent bad faith which characterised their conduct, arose from a want of straightforwardness on their part in not stating at the outset the restricted authority they possessed. Evasion of fact, where telling the truth is disagreeable or inexpedient, is in accordance with all we know of Chinese, in common with Oriental diplomacy generally. The commissioners were empowered to accept the treaty of 1858, and the opening of Tien-tsin to trade, in lieu of residence at the capital. Further than this they could not go. It appears certain from documents found in the palace of Yuen-ming-Yuen, that while the Emperor was willing to sanction the cession of these the most important points at issue, he was determined to resist by a fresh appeal to arms those of minor consequence—namely, the payment of an indemnity, military occupation of certain ports until it should be paid, the presence of the ambassadors in Peking with military escort, and permanent residence of ministers there.

I am also of opinion that a wrong estimate has been formed of the conduct of the Chinese in regard to the events of the 18th September. That there was the characteristic want of straightforwardness on the part of the Princes of I and Muh-yin in their communication with Mr. Parkes, and that the flag of truce was shamefully violated, I freely admit; but I do not think that there was any deliberate treachery intended, either with reference to capturing those who were ultimately made prisoners, or in respect to the position at Chang-kia-wan being designed as an ambuscade into which the allied force should be led as it advanced to the appointed encamping ground.

And this was the opinion formed by Lord Elgin, and expressed in his despatch to the Secretary of State, under date 23rd September.

His lordship states :—" I may be expected to say something respecting the origin and cause of the renewal of hostilities which took place on the 18th instant. To hazard conjectures as to the motives by which Chinese are actuated is not a very safe undertaking ; and it is very possible that further information may modify the views which I now entertain on this point. I am, however, disposed at present to doubt there having been a deliberate intention of treachery on the part of Prince Tsai and his colleague ; but I apprehend that the General-in-Chief, Sang-ko-lin-sin, thought that they had compromised his military position by allowing our army to establish itself so near his lines at Chang-kia-wan. He sought to counteract the evil effect of this by making a great swagger of parade and preparation to resist, when the allied armies approached the camping ground allotted to them. Several of our people —Colonel Walker, with his escort, my private secretary, Mr. Loch, Baron Gros's Secretary of Embassy, Comte de Bastard, and others—passed through the Tartar army during the course of the morning on their way from Tung-chow without encountering any rudeness or ill-treatment whatsoever. At about a quarter to ten, however, a French commissariat officer was assaulted by some Tartar soldiers, under circumstances which are not very clearly ascertained ; and this incident gave rise to an engagement which soon became general. On the whole, I come to the conclusion that, in the proceedings of the Chinese plenipotentiaries and commander-in-chief in this instance, there was that mixture of stupidity, want of straightforwardness, suspicion, and bluster, which characterises so generally the conduct of affairs in this country ; but I cannot believe that after the experience which Sang-ko-lin-sin had already had of our superiority in the field, either he or his civil colleagues could have intended to bring on a conflict, in which, as the event has proved, he was sure to be worsted. At the same time the facts that he covered by his guns, and with a portion of his troops, the ground assigned to us, and that a French officer returning from Tung-chow with the knowledge and consent of the Chinese plenipotentiaries was assaulted and killed on his lines, entirely justify both the charge of bad faith which has been brought against the Chinese authorities in this instance, and the proceedings of the allied commanders-in-chief which have ensued therefrom."

CHAPTER XVII.

Tien-tsin—Housing of the Troops—Chinese shot by sentries—The sponge-cake man—Temple of the Oceanic Influences—City wall—Heavy rain—Seizure of houses—The Caugue—Committee of British Supply—Imperial decree—Chinese entertainment—Wounded Chinese soldiers—Magistrate—Return of Lord Elgin—Occurrences at Peking—Return of Troops—Reappearance of Trade—Chinese dinner—Indian followers—Departure of Baron Gros—Comte de Bastard—Departure of Lord Elgin—The mess-room of the 31st—The Peiho frozen—Sir Hope Grant—Arrival of the Indemnity Money.

October 28*th*.—Tien-tsin is to be occupied by an allied force during the winter. The British troops are to be commanded by Brigadier Staveley. Preparations for the housing of the force are to commence immediately. An extensive range of buildings was taken into use yesterday as a general hospital, and is being rapidly filled with sick that are arriving daily from Peking en route to the hospital ships off the Peiho. A considerable number of sick are also collected at the Tien-tsin forts waiting for conveyance to the fleet.

The general hospital range of buildings is situated close to the bank of the river, and consists of a series of one-storied houses built in the form of three sides of a square, the usual mode of constructing private residences in China. Each house contains one suite of apartments, a central one facing the door and having a single room on each side of it.* They are separated from each other by wide folding

* A Chinese gentleman's house, such as the building in question was, consists of a series of these squares. The central apartment is used as a sitting or refreshment room, and the side rooms are usually occupied as bed-rooms.

doors, the upper two-thirds of which consist of elegant designs in trellis work covered over with ordinary white paper, which seems to be in general use in the north of China as a substitute for glass. The window-frames are large and extend from each side of the door-way the whole length of the house fronts. They consist of ornamental trellis-work covered with paper, like the inner doors separating the apartments. The outer doors are the same. The walls and ceilings are covered with glazed white paper of a satin pattern similar to that used for papering rooms in England. In the bed-rooms the dormitory is in a recess formed by a screen of wood and trellis work, the sleeping place consisting of brick work raised about two feet above the ground, and heated in cold weather by a flue which passes through it, communicating with a furnace outside. A ledge of wood faces the upper portion of the brick work, over which thick matting is spread.

The interior of a better class Chinese dwelling, such as the one under description, is neat, cleanly, and very pleasing to the eye. The building belongs to Chang, the principal salt merchant of Tien-tsin, by repute enormously wealthy and very kind to the poor.

Yesterday a Chinese lad about fourteen years of age was brought into hospital mortally wounded in the chest. He had been detected in the act of taking away two or three old iron hoops from amongst some government stores, over which there was a sentry of the Royal Marines, who, in place of attempting to make a prisoner of the boy, as he might have done, deliberately loaded his rifle and shot him. Recently, also, a Chinaman was killed by one of the Seiks on sentry. The man was approaching a bridge that Chinese were not allowed to cross, and was challenged in Hindoostanee, which, of course, not understanding, and continuing to advance, he was shot dead. Another instance of the unavoidable evil of entrusting to undiscriminating brains the power of taking human life in the form of "Orders to

Sentries" during military occupation, occurred lately in the case of a sentinel of the Royals placed over a bridge across the Peiho, beyond which point his orders were not to allow native boats to pass. A boat attempted to do so after being warned off, and the sentry shot the steersman dead. By the slightest exercise of judgment or reflection this could have been avoided, and the progress of the boat arrested by other means. The men were mere villagers anxious to get their boat beyond the restricted point, and utterly unacquainted with the meaning of the words addressed to them as a caution not to proceed.

Notwithstanding these distressing occurrences a very brisk commercial intercourse seems to have sprung up between the soldiers and the petty traders. A confectioner, who has become celebrated amongst the troops for his sponge cakes, is picking up English, and addresses every one of a respectable exterior who goes into his shop, "How do you do, good morning, sit down and eat a sponge cake." He keeps a book in which he requests the various naval and military officers who visit his premises to enter their names, of which advantage has been taken by several to inscribe, instead, epithets and sentiments not calculated to redound to the good taste or refinement of their authors, but which "Sponge cakes," as he is called, exhibits in happy ignorance of their meaning, though, apparently, puzzled to understand why some people's names seem to attract so much more notice than do others.

October 29*th*.—This morning while at breakfast, in the quarters within the general hospital which have been allotted to the Medical Staff, the sound of the lash fell on our ears. In the court-yard adjoining the room in which we were sitting a sailor was tied up to the triangles, receiving corporal punishment under the superintendence of the Provost-Marshal. Then followed the administering of "forty-eight" to a Marine. The former had been found lying in a state of helpless intoxication, and the latter had been ill-using a Chinaman. Temporary pressure for quarters appears to have caused this somewhat singular amalgamation of the Provost-Marshal's establishment with that of the general hospital.

In the afternoon I rode out to the temple dedicated to the "oceanic influences," where the treaty of 1858 was signed. It is a somewhat extensive building situated on the plain to the south of the walled city, about a mile distant from it, and not far from the outer works which communicate with the forts already described. This temple, under the name of the "Treaty Joss-House," has been until three days ago, in use as a general hospital, and its sacerdotal equipment is now in a state of complete disorganisation, the interior presenting one vast scene of general destruction of property and confusion. Immense numbers of books are scattered about the various rooms. In that in which the treaty was signed, there is a cabinet nearly as high as the roof still containing thousands of volumes. Some of the sacred figures are of large size and still in good preservation. At the entrance of the chief temple there is a very fine bell suspended; its size is considerable, and the outside is covered with thousands of characters in relief. The bell has no tongue, and is sounded by being struck like a gong. Beside it there is a large drum and a gong of peculiar construction, consisting of a thick plate of metal bearing an inscription.

I went on as far as the outer earthworks, which I find have a broad and deep ditch in front of them, extending, apparently, the whole way round Tien-tsin and its suburbs on both sides of the river.

Returning to the city, I rode round the walls. In many places they are in a dilapidated condition, portions having slid down in consequence of the loose nature of the foundation, and, in place of being removed and properly rebuilt, the municipal authorities in their veneration for everything that is old, have allowed the displaced portions to remain, and have built up the gaps in the upper parts that the settlements in the lower have caused.

Mr. Loch arrived last night from Peking with the treaty, and started this morning for England. Peking is distant eighty miles from Tien-tsin, and it takes two days to reach it by land. By water the distance is considerably greater (about 120 miles), and it generally takes the boats from five to seven days to reach Tung-chow, which is the nearest point they can go to Peking by the Peiho. A depôt for stores has been established there under a guard of the Royal Marines. By the last accounts from Peking the departure of the army is to commence about the 2nd of November. Lord Elgin now waits at Peking the arrival from Je-ho of the Imperial decree approving of the treaty, and the arrival also of Mr. Bruce, daily expected from Shanghai.

October 30*th.*—During the night it rained heavily, and the depth of mud in the streets this morning is such as to render it a matter of no ordinary discomfort to have to move about out of doors. In the course of the day two drunken soldiers were found rolling over one another in the mud which nearly submerged them, affording extreme amusement to a crowd of Chinamen who were looking on. Prior to tumbling in the mud from which they could not extricate themselves, they had been insulting a guard of the 19th Punjaubees. On being brought to the Provost-Marshal's establishment, their clothes were so mud-begrimed that it was impossible to make out what corps they belonged to. On washing the mud off their buttons they were ascertained to be Royal Artillerymen.

October 31*st.*—This morning while at breakfast we again heard the sound of the "cats." The two artillerymen, now sober, were receiving the regulated allowance of fifty lashes.

Much distress is now being occasioned by the necessity of providing quarters for the army of occupation shortly expected from Peking. Lieutenant Currie, Adjutant of the

19th Punjaubees, mentioned to me this afternoon a disagreeable duty which had occupied him the whole day, and which he had just completed, namely, turning between forty and fifty females of the better class out of a large house required for the use of the head-quarter staff. The outer doors were found barricaded, but ultimately were opened. The soldiers were met in the passage by some men, who pulled their ears to indicate that the rooms contained women. There was no help for it; the orders had to be carried out; the Punjaubees entered the rooms and proceeded to put the ejection in force. Some of the women were composed, others screamed and became hysterical. Several were suckling children. Mr. Currie was as considerate as he possibly could be, and it took him from eleven in the morning until half-past four P.M. to carry his orders out, and turn them cold and houseless into the streets ankle deep in mud. They were allowed to remove their personal property with the exception of household furniture, which was retained for the use of the military occupants. The women's rooms were neatly furnished, and their toilet tables were supplied with looking-glasses and rouge pots.

It appears that after the break-down of Kweiliang's negotiations, the Tien-tsin authorities stopped the supplies which had hitherto been furnished to the troops. Sir Robert Napier, on assuming the command at Tien-tsin, sent a military guard and made a prisoner of the Tautai, until supplies were forthcoming. This functionary is stated to have conducted himself like a wayward child when the escort removed him from his Ya-mun: refusing to be seated in his chair in the ordinary way, but squatting on the floor and kicking at the sides of the sedan. He was taken to the camp near the Tien-tsin forts and placed in a tent next to Sir Robert Napier's, with a sentry over him. After two days confinement he undertook that supplies should be forthcoming, and was released. He sent a present of forty dollars to the sentries who had been over him remarking, "The difference between your soldiers and ours is that when you give them an order they carry it out, ours do not." At first he was very desponding, and sent a message to Sir Robert Napier requesting that he would send him a bottle of sam-shu and a knife, as he wished to commit suicide. Sir Robert complied with the first portion of his request in the shape of a bottle of sherry, the latter he declined complying with. This Tautai appears to have been held in affectionate regard by the population of Tien-tsin, as a very large concourse of people followed his chair when he was arrested, and seemed to be in a state of anxious solicitude for his safety.

November 1st.—The streets are beginning to have English designations painted on them; that which contains the confectioner's shop, mentioned above, is now known as "Pastry Cook Street." I went into it again to day; both the shop and back premises were crowded with soldiers and sailors. Some half-dozen assistants were busily engaged putting up sponge cakes in paper parcels for the numerous customers that were waiting. He continues to invite his patrons to come in and take a cup of tea and a sponge cake, and refuses to make any charge for anything consumed on the premises; adding another to the many contrasts of the Chinese character with the customs of the West.

November 2nd.—Saw a man with a caugue on, walking about very unconcernedly in front of what seemed a magisterial residence. The caugue consists of four boards fitted round the neck, two on each side, and secured by two cross boards, the joinings being covered with strips of paper bearing the official seal, as a check against their removal from the neck before the expiration of the sentence.

November 3rd.—Visited a temple outside the north-western angle of the city, of which a part is devoted to the representation by figures of every sort of physical torture and horrible mode of death. This is supposed to convey an idea of what the hell of Buddha is; and from the frequency with which women are represented as the victims, it seems that the future life is thought to have most sorrow in store for them. Temples of this kind exist in all Chinese cities, and this portion is known among foreigners as the "Chamber of Horrors."

The "Committee of British Supply," composed of several of the most influential merchants of the place, meet daily at their office, and transact all the business connected with keeping up supplies for the troops. The prices are fixed by them, and they receive the money, paying it over to the contractors.

November 5th.—News received from Peking, under date of the 3rd. The Imperial decree approving of the treaty arrived from Je-ho on the 2nd, and everything may be looked upon now as settled. The decree, of which the following is a translation, has appeared in the *Peking Gazette.*

"On the 15th of the 9th moon (October 28th), the Grand Secretariat had the honour to receive the following Imperial Decree:—

"In the matter of the exchange of treaties reported to us by Yih-sin, Prince of Kung : Yih-sin, Prince of Kung, having, on the 11th and 12th of this moon, exchanged with the English and French the treaties concluded in the 8th year (of our reign, 1858), together with the treaties in continuance thereof (the conventions) of the present year, we command that it be known that we promise and authorise the operation for ever more of each and every article in the treaties and conventions, that there may be henceforth no more war between us (that the shield and spear may for ever more rest), but that both may contribute to the consolidation of a good understanding, peaceful relations reposing on good faith, without doubt or suspicion on either side.

"And let the high provincial authorities be directed by circular, one and all, to carry out everything that by the treaty it is essential should be done in accordance therewith. Respect this."

November 6th.—Mr. Bruce reached Tien-tsin last night at eleven o'clock, and at one o'clock this morning started on horseback with a small escort of Scik cavalry for Peking.

Walking through the town this afternoon, I noticed on the outside of a building, written up in chalk, and signed by Brigadier Staveley, " Foundling Hospital, not to be interfered with." I looked in at the door; it seemed an establishment of some extent, and is, I believe, supported by voluntary contributions.

The Confucian temple is now occupied by a portion of the Military Train; and Chinese workmen are at present busy constructing stables in its court-yard; the walls being built of sun-dried bricks faced with the usual mixture of mud and chopped straw.

November 7th.—Yesterday the officers of the Commissariat, accompanied by Messrs. Mongan and Davonport as interpreters, were entertained by the " Committee of British Supply" at an hotel about two miles out of town; an equal number of Chinamen were present. These are stated to have kept up a lively conversation amongst themselves, and to have eaten enormously. The remarks which passed between the hosts and their guests, through the aid of the interpreters, referred chiefly to the viands; politics and business being carefully eschewed. The dishes were eighty in number, and the order of their consumption the reverse of our practice; tea and sweetmeats being eaten first, fish and soup last.

During September, within the city of Tien-tsin alone, the sum of seven thousand pounds sterling was disbursed from the military chest to Chinese contractors; this expenditure being exclusive of the large sums also disbursed at the Tien-tsin forts and at Taku.

November 8th.—This afternoon Surgeon-Major Denny

was buried on the plain to the south of the city wall. He died yesterday, having arrived two days previously in a hopeless state from Hoo-see-woo, where he had been stationed. Death has been active within the last three days amongst the medical staff; news reached Tien-tsin this forenoon of the sudden death at Peking, on the 5th instant, of Surgeon-Major Thomson, the principal medical officer of the second division, who has been buried alongside the remains of the prisoners in the Russian cemetery.

November 9th.—Some officers of the 67th Regiment arrived this evening from Peking. Sir Robert Napier left with the second division on the morning of the 7th. Mr. Bruce had reached Peking, and arrangements were being made for his introduction to the Prince of Kung by Lord Elgin, who was still residing in the Palace of the Prince of I, in the Tartar city, with the Royals as a guard of honour.

November 10th.—The 67th Regiment marched in this forenoon, looking very dirty and ragged. The 10th company of Royal Engineers came in shortly afterwards. A considerable number of sick are now accumulated at Tien-tsin, and the yard of the general hospital for some time this morning was crowded with invalids of different corps lying about, waiting the arrival of a steamer opposite the hospital to convey them to the fleet,—King's Dragoon Guards, Military Train men, Riflemen, Marines, Artillerymen, Sappers, and Infantry soldiers, forming a confused mass, whose contracted cheeks and sunken eyes showed the presence of serious chronic disease. While they were thus lying clustered about, a sight the contrary of cheering was brought prominently before them—the funeral, rough and ready, of two soldiers who had just died.

November 11th.—This morning I visited with Mr. Mongan some wounded Chinese soldiers that are under medical treatment in the hospital. They are six in number, three having been wounded at Taku, and three at Pa-lee-chow; of the latter, one was an ensign, one a horseman, and one a bowman. According to their statement, the Tartar cavalry receive five-and-a-half taels per month, out of which they have to clothe and feed themselves and horse. The bowmen receive three taels, and the matchlock men two taels per month. They are paid every fourteen days, and have also to provide their own food and clothing. They expressed themselves as being unwilling to leave us at the present time, as they have no medical department in connection with the military service. When men are wounded government affords them no regular aid. If they are disabled any where near their homes, they are always conveyed to them. But if at a distance, they are left to manage as best they can.

Of the three men wounded at Taku, one is from the village near the southern forts, the other two are from Pow-ting-too, a large town, 100 miles to the west of Tientsin. In addition to these six men, there is a seventh, who, having recovered, acts as attendant upon the others. He was a pedlar, and happened to be in the village of Pa-lee-chow on the day of the action, where he got mixed up with the fugitives, and received a severe sabre wound on the head, the marks of which he still bears. He says that he has no recollection whatever of receiving the injury, illustrating the remarkable tendency which exists in the human brain to lose all knowledge of the occurrences immediately preceding deprivation of sense, caused by injuries' to the head.*

Orders having been issued by Brigadier Staveley for the handing over of these men to the Chinese authorities, the police magistrate of the city came to-day and saw them, and it was while waiting for him that the foregoing facts were

---

* This man, some months afterwards, accompanied the horse soldier to his home in Mongolia, as his wound prevented him travelling without an attendant. Having performed this kind office, he returned to Peking, and was appointed gatekeeper to Her Majesty's Legation there.

ascertained. He arrived in a sedan chair, covered with blue cloth, and having glass windows on each side; four attendants accompanied him. His appearance was gentlemanly, and his dress consisted of a blue satin jacket lined and trimmed with fur, over a light brown coloured robe of figured silk, yellow silk trousers, and black satin boots. He inquired into each of the men's histories, and seemed much affected when he saw the care we had taken of them; and when one of them showed him his broken leg, carefully put up in splints, he turned round and seized Dr. Nicolson's hand with both of his and shook it warmly—he being the medical officer under whose care the men immediately were. He requested that we would be good enough to keep them in the meantime, and he would send them some warm clothing, as they complained of feeling cold when they sat up in bed.

One of the members of the committee of British supply was present also at the interview and conversed with the soldiers in what Mr. Mongan said was very bad "Mandarin," while the Manchu bowman spoke the dialect fluently.*

We invited the magistrate to take some refreshment, such as we had to offer. He sat down and took some biscuit and sherry—pulling out his pipe and making himself quite at home. He tried beer and brandy also, but seemed to prefer the sherry—his friend, however, of the committee of supply, appeared to take to the brandy very kindly. We gave some ration rum to the attendants, which they did not seem to object to.

On leaving the hospital and before getting into his chair, our magisterial friend stood for a short time looking at a company of the 67th Regiment preparing to march to the south Tien-tsin forts. He inquired as to what they were about to do, and laughed heartily at a trio of drunken Frenchmen who were rolling arm-in-arm along the street.

* The "Mandarin" is the court dialect, and is that in general use at Peking and the country around it.

Seeing a Punjaubee soldier approach with a piece of yellow silk in his hand, which he was offering for sale, he at once recognised it as taken from the Yuen-ming-yuen, and drew our attention to the four-clawed Imperial dragon, embroidered on it in gold.

Lord Elgin, Mr. Bruce and Sir Hope Grant arrived to-day from Peking, having come down by the Peiho, and Her Majesty's legation is therefore now established at Tien-tsin, where it will remain for the winter. Sir Hope Grant proceeded on board the "Grenada," where Lady Grant, who arrived a few days ago from Hong Kong, has been waiting his return.

November 12th.—The streets this forenoon presented a scene of more than usual bustle and excitement—coolies carrying about baggage, fatigue parties of Punjaubees conveying stores, carts laden with loot, mounted men and waggons of the Military Train forming a confused mass, rendered more confused by the arrival of the Royals and the 8th Punjaubees, who, as soon as they could be extricated from the living stream that thronged the narrow streets, were embarked in gunboats for the anchorage.

Lord Elgin and Mr. Bruce have taken up their residence in a large house on the river-bank, where the members of the permanent legation recently arrived from Shanghai are residing.* In the same house (late the private abode of a Tien-tsin merchant) Baron Gros, General Montauban, and their respective staffs are staying; quarters are also provided for Sir Hope Grant and his staff, the accommodation afforded by this mansion being considerable.

We now learnt the following details of occurrences at Peking :—

On the 2nd of November Prince Kung paid a friendly visit to the Earl of Elgin at his residence in Peking. He

---

* Mr. Bruce's suite at this period consisted of Lieutenant-Colonel Neale, Secretary of Legation, Messrs. St. Clair and Wyndham, Attachés of Legation, with Mr. Wade as Chinese secretary.

came in a sedan chair accompanied by a numerous retinue, mounted and on foot. He was dressed in a puce-coloured satin robe with the Imperial dragon within a circle about eight inches in diameter embroidered in gold on the breast, shoulders and back. He wore the ordinary turned-up hat without any ornament beyond a twisted knob of red silk at the top, where the Mandarin button is worn. He was received with the full honours due to his rank and position; the entrance and courts of the embassy being lined by detachments of the King's Dragoon Guards and the Royals; the band of the 67th Regiment also being in attendance. He remained about two hours, and a good deal of conversation took place with Lord Elgin, in the course of which he repeatedly admitted the advantages which would accrue from more direct intercourse between foreign ministers and the government at Peking, inaugurated under the new treaties. He is also stated to have remarked in the course of conversation after lunch, that it was not until the expedition of 1860 that the Chinese government was aware that India was a province only of the British empire, their impression formerly having been that Great Britain was a very small island, the population of which was so large that the greater half of the people were compelled to reside afloat. The following day Lord Elgin returned the Prince's visit, and in the evening dined at the Russian minister's.

On the 7th of November Mr. Bruce arrived at Peking, and without hesitation offered at once to enter on his duties as resident minister there. Lord Elgin, however, on consultation with Baron Gros and General Ignatieff, found that the latter was about to depart immediately for St. Petersburgh, and that the former was of opinion that it was not advisable that Monsieur de Bourboulon should establish himself as Minister of France at Peking until spring. Under these circumstances Lord Elgin advised Mr. Bruce to return to Tien-tsin and remain there until such time as a suitable residence could be provided for him at the capital.

In order, however, to prevent any misapprehension on the part of the Chinese Government with reference to residence at the capital being carried out, a house in the immediate vicinity of the Russian Mission was selected as capable of being adapted to the purpose, and Mr. Adkins, one of the student interpreters, placed in charge of it; he having volunteered to remain at Peking for the winter, and superintend the alterations required.

Having made these arrangements, Lord Elgin wrote to the Prince of Kung expressing his sense of the good faith evinced by him in regard to the publication of the treaty, informing him that the British force would at once retire to Tien-tsin, and proposing an interview to take leave, and also to introduce Mr. Bruce. At this interview Lord Elgin was particularly anxious to show that Mr. Bruce's rank was in no degree inferior to his own. He accordingly, after a prolonged and friendly conversation with the Prince, requested the interpreter to inform him that as the person representing the Sovereign always holds the highest rank, and that peace being happily restored, his own functions were at an end, and that those of Mr. Bruce recommenced as the representative of Her Britannic Majesty in China, therefore with the permission of the Prince he would cede to Mr. Bruce the seat of honour (on the left) which he was at the time occupying.

The next morning (November 9th) Prince Kung returned the visit, and Lord Elgin purposely absented himself, in order that Mr. Bruce might receive him alone. They had a long and interesting conversation, in which, as in the interviews he had previously had with Lord Elgin, the Prince showed much less reserve than is usual with Chinese diplomatists in the discussion of delicate questions. In the course of the interview Mr. Bruce pressed strongly on the consideration of the Prince the situation of the province of Keang-soo, coupled with the fact of Shanghai being at the time prevented from falling into the hands of the

Taepings only by the presence of a protecting allied force. Mr. Bruce pointed out to the Prince the improbability of the allied occupation being indefinitely prolonged, and the necessity which therefore existed for immediate steps being taken to restore the Imperial authority in the province. The Prince listened with great attention, and expressed himself as much indebted for information much of which was new to him; his general tone conveying the impression that he now seemed fully to recognise the benefit his government would derive from direct personal intercourse with foreign ministers.

Mr. Bruce also informed the Prince of his resolution not to accept any provincial authority as Imperial commissioner during his stay at Tien-tsin, but that his correspondence would be carried on with himself or the minister for foreign affairs at Peking, also that he would come up from Tien-tsin at any amount of inconvenience, should business of importance call for his presence in the capital.

Before the interview closed Lord Elgin entered the room, and after thanking the Prince for having paid him a visit of adieu, took a friendly farewell of him. The same afternoon Lord Elgin and Mr. Bruce left for Tien-tsin.

On the 28th of October the remains of the French prisoners were interred in the burying-ground formerly used by the Jesuits, situated outside the north-west gate of Peking, and known as the Portuguese cemetery. The Roman Catholic Bishop of Peking, Monseigneur Mouly, and his coadjutor bishop officiated. Almost all the English officers off duty were present. The following day the ceremony of re-opening the Roman Catholic church in the Tartar city was performed by the two bishops—Baron Gros, General de Montauban, with their staffs and a numerous assemblage of French officers attending. Bishop Mouly in his discourse expressed in grateful terms his acknowledgments to Her Majesty Queen Victoria and the English army for the assistance thus rendered to the cause of

Christianity in the North of China. The ceremony was a good deal marred by rain ; the roof of the cathedral being in a very dilapidated state.

On the 1st of November General de Montauban declined to prolong his stay at Peking beyond that date, in consequence of the uncertainty of the weather, and started with his force, leaving one battalion of the 101st Regiment and two guns as an escort for Baron Gros, whose departure was deferred until such time as Lord Elgin saw it expedient to leave.

On the 7th of November, Baron Gros forwarded to Paris the following summary of the conclusion of negotiations :—

"Peace was signed on the 25th of October between the brother of the Emperor and myself.

"The ultimatum of Shanghai has been accepted.[*] The exchange of the ratifications of the treaty of Tien-tsin has taken place ; 60,000,000 francs will be paid as an indemnity to France ; 3,750,000 francs will be paid in cash on the 30th of the present month.

"The emigration of coolies is authorised by the Chinese Government.

"The churches and cemeteries, with their dependencies, belonging formerly to Christians throughout the whole empire, will be restored to them through the medium of the minister of France. Prince Kung sent to me yesterday (6th November) an official document containing the statement of handing over to me (already done) of the Catholic cathedral of Peking ; he adds, that he knows that in the Imperial city there was formerly another church, now destroyed, but that the ground and dependencies will be

---

[*] The terms of this ultimatum were :—1st. Formal excuses for the attack on the allied forces at Taku ; 2nd. Exchange at Peking of the ratifications of the treaty concluded before at Tien-tsin ; 3rd. Declaration that the French Government reassumed the right of establishing a permanent diplomatic mission at Peking ; 4th. Payment of an indemnity of 60,000,000 francs.

handed over to me. This day I have given passports to missionaries.

"On the 28th of October, nearly the whole of the army, headed by the embassy, took the six victims of the ambuscade of the 18th of September to the Catholic burying ground, already handed over to Monseigneur Mouly, Bishop of Petcheli, and where repose the remains of Fathers Gerbillon, Ricci, and Shaal. General Grant and his staff joined us; M. Ignatieff, the minister of Russia, whose frank support has been of great use to me on all occasions, awaited us at the burial ground. On the following day mass was performed in the cathedral, which has also been given up to M. Mouly.

"The iron cross has been replaced on the summit of the edifice, and the *Domine, salvum fac Imperatorem* has inaugurated the public re-establishment of the Catholic faith in China.

"Moreover, there has been remitted to me, as a special indemnity for the outrage of the 18th of September, the sum of 1,500,000 francs.

"Everything is progressing admirably, and encourages the hope that this success will be lasting. I shall probably leave Peking in two or three days to return to Tien-tsin, to concert with Lord Elgin as regards what remains to be done." "BARON GROS."

November 13*th*.—The French Legation is now established at Tien-tsin, M. de Bourboulon having arrived to-day from Shanghai.

The streets again present an extraordinary scene of confusion, being blocked up in all directions with baggage and stores, also horses and carts looted from the unfortunate peasantry. Here and there Chinese might be seen bargaining with coolies, and buying from them the rich vestments of silk and fur, in which many of them were attired, as the simplest mode of carrying their shares of the plunder.

November 14*th.*—A communication was received to day from Mr. Adkins at Peking, dated the 12th inst., to the effect, that after Lord Elgin's departure on the 9th, he took possession of the building selected for the Legation, and that he received every aid from the local authorities; one of the magistrates of the city having accompanied him to the spot. The disposition of the people is friendly, and he is as free from molestation in his rides and walks as he would have been had the allied forces still been before the city. The gates are now open, and the inhabitants who had fled while hostilities were impending, are now returning in large numbers. On the 11th, a memorial was despatched from Peking to the Emperor at Je-ho, informing him of the final adjustment of the foreign troubles.

November 15*th.*—The suburb of Tien-tsin, on the opposite side of the river, is to be held by a French force under General Collineau. The rest of the French army is embarking as fast as practicable for Shanghai, where it will remain for the winter, and await further orders from the Minister at War with reference to, its destination, which it is expected will be Cochin-China.

Trade is increasing in Tien-tsin. Street stalls are reappearing, and money-changers, with portable bureaus, are becoming numerous. The inhabitants also are returning, and the streets are getting English and French designations painted on them in the respective quarters of the two forces. A large yamun, in a central position of the English suburb, now figures as "Charing Cross."

In General Orders of to-night, I find myself detailed to take medical charge of the 31st Regiment, which is still at Hoo-see-woo, where it has been stationed during the operations before Peking. It returns to Tien-tsin the day after to-morrow, and remains there for the winter as a portion of the occupying force.

November 16*th.*—The town is now placarded with our version of the treaty in the Chinese character. Mr. Wade, it is stated, has detected some Chinese editions of it in circulation, wherein the Emperor is represented as having, in his extreme kindness, been pleased to extend permission to barbarians to enter into trade with this portion of the celestial empire.

Trade continues to increase; the streets in many districts being converted into lines of bazaars, and "how much" in the English, and "combien" in the French quarter, being heard from one end to the other, the venders endeavouring to attract attention by using the only foreign words they are as yet acquainted with.

November 17th.—A sale by auction took place this forenoon of Military Train horses, a considerable number of which were bought by Chinamen at two and three dollars a head.

November 18th.—The 31st Regiment marched in this afternoon, over 1000 strong, including officers. The Chinese coolies attached to it have been placed in quarters opposite the general hospital. They seem in excellent spirits, and are busy cooking and preparing firewood, using Tartar swords they have brought with them for choppers, and making somewhat free with the wood work of the houses they are occupying.*

November 19th.—Great as has been the bustle and confusion prevailing in the streets of Tien-tsin within the last eight or ten days, I have seen nothing equal to the scene they present to day. The last portion of the army has just marched in, and in all directions the avenues are blocked up by lines of horse transport, mules, and Peking carts, laden with plunder and baggage, the interstices filled with masses of the coolie corps, staggering under loads of baggage, and extra weight, in the shape of loot, belonging to themselves. Amidst all this confusion, lines of dhoolies,

---

* A few days afterwards when these men were embarked for the fleet, many of them wept bitterly at being separated from the regiment, to which they seemed to have become much attached.

containing sick, were struggling on endeavouring to reach the general hospital. From many of the Peking carts small pug-nosed dogs were peeping out, numbers of which had been taken at the sacking of the Yuen-ming-Yuen. At one place might be seen a complete stoppage, in consequence of a troop of Fane's horse having got jammed at the corner of a street amidst a line of carts; at another, progress arrested by a load having tumbled off a camel.

In the afternoon, a dinner and theatrical entertainment was given to the English officers by a number of Chinese gentlemen who have been associated with the authorities in connection with the question of supplies. It took place in a theatre in a suburb, near the north gate. The guests were seated at separate tables in front of the stage. The play commenced at half-past four, and continued till nine o'clock, during which period a succession of dishes, to the number of about eighty, had been placed on each of the tables.

November 20*th.*—Snow fell nearly an inch deep during the night, but by morning had begun to thaw. Dr. Telfer came to the hospital to-day to see the wounded Tartars, it having been through his kind exertions that the men were originally taken care of. They recognised him at once, and the old pedlar rushed forward and seized his hand, shaking it with much earnestness and affection. The Mongolian horseman Dr. Telfer mentioned to me, had lain on the field of Chang-kia-wan for five days with his wound unattended to, during which period the only sustenance he had was one apple. Mr. Morrison, I believe it was, who found him, and brought him to Dr. Telfer's notice.

November 21*st.*—Sleet continues to fall, and the streets are at best ankle, and in many places knee deep in mud. Sir Hope Grant visited the hospital in the afternoon, and put a kind interrogatory to each of the sick men in succession.

November 22*nd.*—To-day realises our worst recollections of the mud of Peh-tang, with a piercing cold temperature on the verge of freezing superadded. In the evening I dined with Sir Hope Grant at the house already alluded to, where the whole of the diplomatic and military staffs are quartered. On my way in I met Mr. Parkes and asked him a few hurried questions about Sang-ko-lin-sin, who, it appears, is a burly-looking personage, rather short and thick-set, with a red, pimply face, as if he indulged in strong waters—a practice by no means uncommon amongst his countrymen, the Mongolians.

November 23rd.—Cold and slush continue ; pitiable sight to see the Indian followers of Fane's Horse with their bleeding feet and naked limbs, shivering in the cold, half-way up to their knees in mud, and frequently losing their footing and coming down their whole length in it.

November 24th.—Cold very severe during the night. Thermometer down to 21 degrees at nine A.M., and water frozen in the sleeping-rooms.

Baron Gros left to-day for Shanghai. His secretary of legation, the Comte de Bastard, has become insane. He received a severe mental shock at the sight of the remains of the prisoners, and has been living ever since in constant apprehension of some impending evil, especially treachery, until at last his mind has completely revolted from control, and he has been removed to ship-board a raving lunatic under mechanical restraint.

November 25th.—This morning the thermometer at six o'clock was 15 degrees. Towards the afternoon the day cleared up to one of bright sunshine, and, notwithstanding the extreme cold of the morning, the temperature during the greater portion of the day was very pleasant. Masses of ice are now floating down the Peiho, which may soon be expected to be frozen over.

Lord Elgin took his departure from Tien-tsin at eight o'clock this morning, and when last heard of at six P.M., had only got a third of the way down the river, the steamer having got aground.

Two soldiers died in hospital to-day, also one of the

Chinese coolie corps. The remains of the latter having been placed in the ordinary dead-house, were taken by mistake for those of a soldier of the 60th Rifles, and buried with military honours by a funeral party of the 31st Regiment.

November 26th.—This forenoon I met Mr. Parkes on his way to Taku by land, accompanied by a couple of sowars of Fane's Horse. I asked him his opinion with reference to the probable time that the force would be detained at Tien-tsin. He said we might make up our minds for a whole year, and by no means improbably two.*

November 27th.—The mess of the 31st Regiment is now established in the portion of a gentleman's house set apart for religious exercises, in other words a private "joss-house." There are three altars in the room, each containing a large deity. The centre one had to be removed to make room for a fire-place. The owner of the house came and superintended the removal of the figure, paying it great deference as the displacement was being effected. He begged as a special favour that the two remaining figures might be taken good care of.

November 28th.—The Peiho is now completely frozen over. The "Slaney" gunboat has got aground seven miles below Tien-tsin, and is being roofed in for the winter, it being impracticable to extricate her before spring. The "Atalanta" steamer has got on the bar at Taku, and is also in a fair way for being frozen in. Five Indian followers going off to the fleet in a junk have died from cold.

Staff-Surgeon Dr. Galbraith arrived this evening from Taku, where he reports the weather as very rough, and ice beginning to form on the shore of the gulf. All the troops have embarked, and the infantry transports sailed yesterday. The cavalry and artillery were to leave to-day. Dr. Galbraith had started from Taku in the steamer "Cooper," but

* This estimate proved a correct one, the occupation of Tien-tsin having extended over one year and a half.

it had stuck opposite the village of Ko-koo, the mandarins and inhabitants of which had shown every attention to those who had to get out and find their way to Tien-tsin by road, supplying carts and doing everything in their power to assist. Dr. Galbraith met on his way up 500 Indian followers walking down to Taku, the vessel in which they had been despatched from Tien-tsin having grounded. All their clothing was concentrated about their heads and shoulders, and, for the most part, they were either walking on their stocking soles, or barefooted.

November 29th.—The last of the staff of the expeditionary force left to-day, Colonel Ross, the Assistant Quartermaster-General, and Dr. Muir, leaving at half-past ten, followed shortly afterwards by Sir Hope Grant on horseback, looking very cold, with his hands in his pockets, and the reins loose on the horse's neck. Lady Grant accompanied him in a sedan chair, carried by Chinese coolies.

November 30th.—The portion of the indemnity money arranged to be paid to-day, has come in.

CHAPTER XVIII.

A Chinese druggist's shop—The remains of the prisoners—Quarters of the garrison—Soldiers' barrack-rooms at night—Ozone and its influence on health—Population and revenue of China—The Chinese candle—French soldiers' inscriptions—Parental grief—Opium smoking—Peking—Cruelty to dogs—Chivalrous sports of officers—Visits to Chinese officials—Acts of violence—Insecurity of property entrusted to military guards—Chinese hawking—State of affairs at Peking and Je-ho—The Tien-tsin Fire Brigade—Chinese funeral obsequies—Public baths—Marriage procession—Effects of the looting of Yuen-ming-yuen on the French army.

December 1st.—Visited the shop of a Chinese apothecary, in which a large staff of assistants were busy dispensing prescriptions. The drawers were all labelled, and everything seemed to be conducted with as much regularity as in our own country. A few days ago Dr. Nicolson went into one of these shops and found a prescription being made up containing camphor reduced to a fine powder, a pharmaceutical process that we ourselves have not yet been able to arrive at. I went also into a Chinese cook-shop, filled with fat, sleek-looking cooks and waiters. Sitting at one of the tables were several soldiers of the 67th Regiment and the Military Train; a really excellent, and what in many places would be viewed as rather a *recherché* meal, was being placed before them, and the charge for this they informed me was one shilling per head; the viands embracing mutton, fowl, duck and quail, cooked in a variety of ways.

December 2nd.—To-day my connection with Her Majesty's Legation commenced—Colonel Neale having conveyed to me Mr. Bruce's request that I would undertake its medical care.

December 3rd.—I learned this evening from Mr. Wade that when the bodies of the prisoners of the 18th of September were brought in, their names were written in Chinese characters on their coffins, with their ages and dates of death. Mr. Wade had to interpret the writing. The characters on Mr. Bowlby's coffin gave the sound in English of Bo-bee. The clothes had evidently been removed after death, but replaced prior to the bodies being brought in, as portions of wearing apparel were found on the deceased not belonging to them. Mr. Bowlby's socks, for instance, had been put on a sowar, and a pair of boots placed on him which he never possessed. He died four days after capture at a place called Cham-ping-chow, about thirty miles from Peking, where those prisoners were taken who were so unfortunate as not to be detained within the capital.

December 4th.—The following is the disposition of the Tien-tsin force. The Royal Artillery occupy an extensive series of buildings known as the Prefect's Yamun, near the centre of the walled city. In a street near it the headquarters of the 31st are located in a number of separate houses, the remainder of the regiment being quartered in a large joss-house, called the "Temple of the Moon," situated in a partly open space, a little way inside the south gate. The 60th Rifles occupy the "Hall of Literary Examinations," and a number of houses in the neighbourhood of the east gate. The Military Train occupy the Confucian Temple. In the suburbs to the north and east of the city, the 67th Regiment and Fane's Horse are quartered, the former occupying houses on the bank of the grand canal, the latter, the "Devil's Temple," and a street near it, both of them between the east gate and the bank of the river.

The arrangements which time and circumstances permitted to be made for the reception of the army of occupation, were unavoidably very defective. The men are seriously overcrowded and a good deal of disease is prevailing, there being about 200 under treatment in hospital. Deaths continue also of frequent occurrence, hardly a day passing that the melancholy strains of the dead march are not heard in the streets, two and three funerals a day not being uncommon. The sickness amongst the troops there is some difficulty in assigning to climatic causes, as the officers of the garrison and civilians who have taken up their residence at Tien-tsin are enjoying excellent health, the climate to all appearance being a fine one. Various representations have been made by the regimental medical officers respecting the sanitary defects to which the troops are exposed, and Brigadier Stavely is doing all he can to improve the state of matters, a work of very considerable difficulty. It is to be hoped, however, that the efforts which are now being made to improve the barrack accommodation may prove successful before spring sets in, otherwise serious results it is to be feared will be produced by a continuance, during higher temperature, of the close packing which at present exists in the barrack-rooms, the amount of space being so small and the men so close together, that they have been unable as yet to use the bed boards which have been issued them to keep their Indian beds off the cold and damp floors of their dormitories.

December 6th.—Walked with Dr. Galbraith on the opposite bank of the river, as far as the south forts. On our way we passed a very elegant and characteristic Chinese residence with ornamental gardens, a good deal out of repair, but still giving an excellent idea of the national taste in the laying out of grounds, and in the construction of the higher class of houses. . In the course of our walk we saw the peasantry engaged preserving cabbage for the winter by a process similar to that adopted by ourselves in reference to the potato. A square pit or cellar is dug out of the clay soil to the depth of about six feet, walls of clay to the height of about six feet more are then built round and the whole roofed in, the entrance to it being by a small hatch-way just large enough to allow a man to pass. The interior is fitted up with wooden racks on which the cabbage is placed in rows one above the other, all the outer leaves and partially decayed portions being removed and the leaves cut square at the end. The cabbages are arranged in symmetrical lines, and are carefully kept from touching the walls of the pit. The peasants were sturdy, good-humoured fellows, who seemed to enjoy seeing us descend through the hatch-way by the ladder inside and examine the interior arrangements. There were seven of them on the top of the pit round the hatch-way, and we were altogether unarmed and totally isolated from Europeans by a couple of miles; had they been actuated by those feelings of treachery, deceit, and revenge, that it is too much the custom to identify with the Chinese character, to the exclusion of a great deal that is amiable and estimable, we need not have been heard of more.

December 7th.—Last night about twelve o'clock I visited the barrack-rooms of the 31st Regiment, with a view of ascertaining their state after the men have been a few hours asleep in them. The atmosphere I found so hot and mephitic that I felt an immediate sensation of relief on emerging from it; nevertheless, the soldiers had no complaint to make, their sensations being those of warmth and comfort. In one instance only was a complaint made, and that was with reference to a current of fresh air which came through a flaw in the wall of a room in a joss-house, and which tended somewhat to reduce the temperature inside.

December 8th.—During the last few days the quantity of ozone in the atmosphere has been observed by Dr. Lamprey to be very deficient, and coincident with this I have noticed a more than usual prevalence of neuralgic ailments, not only in the form of acute attacks in those previously healthy, but also appearing as a complication in connection with pre-existing disease. Ague has likewise been of frequent occurrence lately.

December 9th.—On going out this morning the air seemed to me to have a more than usually exhilarating effect; not that I had previously felt unwell, but there was an indescribable something that seemed to have been hanging about me for some two or three days before. The patients also who had been suffering from neuralgia have become much better, and, in some instances, the ailment has suddenly disappeared. During the night a great increase of ozone is shown by the ozonometer, and this occurring together with a decrease in a prevalent form of disease, warrants, in my opinion, the conclusion that they are connected as cause and effect.

Baron de Meritens, the interpreter to the French Legation, has proceeded to Peking to make arrangements respecting the preparation of a house for the reception of M. de Bourboulon in spring.

December 10th.—When at the Legation this forenoon, I learned that amongst other records which had come into Mr. Wade's possession from the Imperial library at Yuenming-yuen, there is a series of Imperial edicts extending over the last thirty years, containing a great deal of most valuable information with reference to the statistics, trade, finance and population of the country, constituting, in fact, a modern history of China. The series is very nearly complete, a few edicts only being wanting, probably destroyed during the sacking of the palace. From these papers an interesting statistical fact has been ascertained regarding which great doubt has always existed, namely, the actual population of China; the papers in question making it 413,000,000 in China proper and Manchuria, exclusive of Formosa and some other outlying possessions; including them, it is calculated that in the aggregate the population cannot be under 450,000,000.

In reference to this it would be interesting to make a

calculation founded on that of Stephenson, which went to show that the steam power of England in manufactures was equal to a population of 400,000,000; therefore, if we with our 40,000,000 can effect by steam power the manual labour of 400,000,000, what would be the amount of labour procured by the introduction of steam power amongst a population stated to be about half that of the whole human race?

It appears to be difficult to get at the exact revenue of China, but from some documents that have fallen into our hands it has been ascertained that until lately, after paying the various government expenses in the different provinces, there was a surplus of 8,000,000 of taels (about £3,000,000 sterling). Amongst the papers referred to, a memorandum from Canton has been found relating to some years ago. It states, "Pottinger has gone, Davis has succeeded him. This latter barbarian has been selected on account of some rude knowledge he has of our language acquired during his service with the trading company (East India Company). Up to the present time he has not been obstreperous or otherwise troublesome."

My attention was called to-day to the ingenuity with which the Chinese tallow candle is constructed, so as to prevent guttering;—the outer coat being a thin envelope of wax, which, dissolving more slowly than the tallow, forms a ledge about the fourth of an inch round the tallow in solution, and thus its running down the sides is completely prevented. While our candle is placed in the candlestick, the Chinese candlestick is placed in the candle on the principle of a "save-all;" an improvement which, in combination with the wax envelope to the tallow candle, might be introduced for the benefit of the poorer classes in our own country.

December 11*th*.—Walked to the south fort on the opposite bank of the river—found it quite deserted, and the villagers in the neighbourhood unroofing the casemates and carrying away the timber. This fort is nearly the counterpart of the one on the opposite side of the river. Here and there on the walls of the houses within the enclosure were personal memoirs of several of the French soldiers, in the form chiefly of annotations of the dates of their leaving France and arriving at various places on their way out—also guesses at the probable period of their return, and solicitous expressions in reference to the health and general welfare of their "maîtresses." One soldier in particular, "Grougon, Sappeur, 1er Génie," is very minute in detailing his feelings, and seems to have been more anxious than his companions that his name should stand forth pre-eminent, having inscribed it in large letters, as I have quoted it, on the most prominent portion of the cavalier; and with the view of furthering his desire I am thus particular in noting it.

Returning to Tien-tsin, I met two men carrying a small coffin—a respectable-looking man, walking a little way behind it, came up, and with an expression of grief pointed to the coffin and then to himself, and holding up his fingers indicated that the child was five years old, then holding up his hand a little way from the ground to show its height, he burst into tears and continued his course home with the coffin, which he had apparently been into Tien-tsin to purchase. This little incident conveys a practical contradiction to a statement I heard confidently made last night, to the effect that the Chinese are without any true feelings of affection, and that their regard for their relations is principally confined to respect for their remains, an impression which, on whatever data it has been formed, is altogether unsupported by experience in the north of China, manifestations of affection for offspring every day coming under our notice. Did disregard for offspring prevail to the extent it is represented, the population could hardly keep up to the huge number shown in the Imperial statistics.

December 12*th*.—Talking of the injurious consequences of opium smoking this evening at the Legation, from the account Mr. Wade gives, its baneful influence would not seem to be exaggerated by those who have written on the subject. The reason why it does not overtly come under our eyes in China is, that it is not a common vice of the labouring and other classes of the Chinese with whom foreigners are most familiar, but of the higher classes, who in a great measure are excluded from our observation. Mr. Wade describes its effects as far outdoing our worst ideas of alcoholic intemperance, and he makes mention of a somewhat singular and interesting fact, namely, that while opium smoking seems to produce comparatively little effect on Europeans, alcohol is equally inoperative on the Chinese, as they can consume large quantities of it without becoming intoxicated. He mentions as an illustration the case of a Chinese teacher of his at Shanghai, who told him that a brother from the country had been in to see him, and that being anxious to taste some of the foreign wines that he had heard a good deal about, he sent out for two bottles, which they drank between them in an hour without being in any way injuriously affected. On being asked the name of the wine, he said Pa-lan-ti, the nearest approximation he could make to the pronunciation of the word brandy, which the so-called wine turned out to have been.

In this peculiar unsusceptibility to alcoholic influences and proneness to be affected by the narcotic vapour of opium, a very interesting question is involved, as it implies a more active condition of the respiratory functions in the Chinese than in our own countrymen, and may possibly throw some light on the remarkable prevalence of intemperance amongst our lower orders, amongst whom impaired conditions of the pulmonary organs are the most common cause of physical disability, while, on the contrary, the lungs of the Chinese enjoy remarkable immunity from disease. The stronger the lungs, the more opium is inhaled and the more alcohol is evaporated.

Conversation turning on the desire which our merchants

have to be permitted to carry on a coasting trade in grain in China, there would appear to have been no point in arranging the details of the Treaty of Tien-tsin in 1858, that the Commissioners so stoutly resisted as this; more especially from Mu-che-wang, in the gulf of Lian-tung, and from Tang-chow, the chief port in the province of Shan-tung. One Shanghai merchant alone is known to have 500 junks employed trading in beans and grain from Mu-che-wang.

December 13th.—News was received to-day from Mr. Adkins, that everything is progressing satisfactorily at Peking, of which place the following is a general description:—

Peking is distinguished from other Chinese cities by its great extent, the width of its streets, and the grandeur of its wall. It contains numbers of shops with elaborately carved and gilded fronts, but on the whole the general appearance of the houses presents nothing remarkable, being for the most part one-storied, with little variation of architecture beyond that which we have been long accustomed to see on the willow-pattern plate. The temples and yamuns, however, are on a very large scale, and altogether Peking quite realises the anticipations which one who has acquired some previous acquaintance with the north of China would be inclined to form of it; though, no doubt, in some respects it falls short of what Canton now is and what Nanking formerly was, owing chiefly to the fact that no manufactures whatever are carried on in it. The city consists of two divisions, a Chinese and a Tartar one, enclosed by upwards of twenty miles of wall, averaging about fifty feet high and over forty feet thick. These two cities are separated from each other by four miles of wall of similar dimensions, making a total of twenty-four miles of investing wall.

Within the Tartar city there is a third, or Imperial city, likewise enclosed by a high wall. The Imperial Palace is in the centre of this third city. The Tartar quarter is occupied chiefly by the bannermen or hereditary soldiers of the Manchu dynasty. The tradesmen and the principal shop-keepers reside in the Chinese city, while the Imperial one is occupied by a somewhat mixed class. The palace itself is a very extensive range of buildings, covering a large number of acres, and surrounded by a crenellated wall and deep ditch. The Emperor has not resided in it for many years, having preferred the Yuen-ming-yuen, but since its destruction repairs have been commenced in the city palace, so as to have it in a fit state for the reception of the Emperor when he returns from Je-ho, which is distant from Peking about 150 miles, or nearly 100 miles on the Tartary side of the Great Wall.

December 14*th*.—At the recent sale of military horses it appears that a Chinese official was present, and that all Chinamen who were purchasers had to pay to their own government 10 per cent. on the cost of the horses bought, as an import tax. Not a very serious "squeeze," as in many instances the horses went for a few dollars.

December 15*th*.—Called on Captain Govan, commanding the Royal Artillery, to bring under his notice the brutal conduct of a gunner employed in the military police whom I observed yesterday sauntering along the streets with a heavy whip in his hand amusing himself with lashing every unoffending dog that came within his reach, whether they happened to be quietly walking along or sitting at the doors of the shops they belonged to. Captain Govan, while concurring in the necessity for checking such unnecessary cruelty, regretted that the man had anything but a good example set him by his betters, dog-spearing on the plain outside the city having been one of the favourite amusements of the officers of the garrison for some time back, the unfortunate animals being hunted down by mounted spearmen until they sank exhausted, when they were subjected to a lingering and painful death in consequence of the unskilfulness of their tormentors in dispatching them with the spear. These dogs are the property of the neighbouring villagers, and the cruel scenes which take place in connection with these hunts, from all accounts, would seem to be but little calculated to dispel from the Chinese mind the term barbarian.

December 16*th*.—Admiral Hope arrived last night on horseback from Taku, having come up in a gunboat from the Miatan Islands. He proceeds immediately to Hong-Kong, having arranged that a mail will be run fortnightly during the winter between Shanghai and Che-foo, and from thence be conveyed by land to Tien-tsin.

It is reported that the "Committee of British Supply" have been found out squeezing the coolies employed by the commissariat, who are paid 200 cash per diem, while in reality it is alleged they receive only about fifty.

December 17*th*.—Riding out on the plain this forenoon, I found a group of officers collected about the Oceanic Temple preparing for what is known as a "paper hunt;" a fox being represented by a piece of paper wafted about by the wind over the perfect level which characterises the country as far as the eye can reach; the plain is dotted with villages, and little clusters of trees around them, now destitute of foliage, but beautiful in summer.

Walking in the afternoon with Colonel Neale, he mentioned to me, that yesterday he accompanied Mr. Wade to return the visits of several of the local officials who had called on Mr. Bruce, amongst others, the salt commissioner, who is one of the chief salt directors in the empire, Tien-tsin being the centre of the great saline district. This official farms the trade from the government. Hang-ki also was one of those whose visit was returned. He is here at present as an envoy from the Prince of Kung for the dispatch of business. Colonel Neale in these interviews was much struck with the resemblance of many of the Chinese customs to those of the Turks; such as the eating of sweetmeats prior to departure, and the crowds of attendants that form round the door, and listen to all that passes,—the officials, strange to say, seeming quite indifferent to it; Hang-ki, for instance, talking in a loud tone about certain delicate matters, the subject of present negotiation. In the course of conversation, he stated that since their amalgamation with the Chinese, the Tartars have lost many of their best customs. Mr. Wade having some business in detail to settle with Hang-ki, stayed to dinner with him, taking pot-luck; and I hear a very good dinner he got.

A point that has been mooted lately by the local authorities, has reference to a muster of their troops, which it is customary, as a financial measure, to have at Tien-tsin about the present period; and they desire to know whether any objection will be raised by us to its taking place as usual. An opinion, I am informed, has been expressed, that, under existing circumstances, it will be better that this muster of militia should not take place at Tien-tsin for the present.

An illustration of the gambling propensities of the Chinese in petty matters was observed this morning at the Legation. A carpenter, who has been working there for some weeks, a steady respectable man, was seen to go out to one of the gambling street venders of eatables to have his breakfast. He tried his luck, once, twice, and thrice, and losing each time, he went back to his work without his breakfast.

December 18*th*.—Charges and counter-charges are becoming the order of the day. While some Seiks were employed yesterday carrying ration wood from the bank of the river, one of them left his greatcoat lying on the ground, which a Chinaman, passing by, took possession of. A European sergeant, however, happened to notice it, and securing the Chinaman by his tail, waited until some Seiks came up, when he handed the man and greatcoat over to them. Summary punishment was then dealt him,— one of the Seiks, taking his tail and rolling it round his sinewy arm, amused the others by making him go down on

his knees and be pulled up by his tail over and over again.
This went on until the owner of the greatcoat appeared,
when the man was handed over to him, to be disposed of
according to his discretion; so he secured him by the tail,
and commenced to kick him on the abdomen; as he was
doing this, an English sergeant came up, and, by pantomime, gave him to understand that the other aspect of the
Chinaman's body was the orthodox one to apply the foot to,
at the same time giving him some practical instruction as
to the mode of proceeding. At this moment my informant,
who had been watching the scene, interfered, and had the
man released.

A Chinawoman is stated to be dying from a stab in the
temple, alleged to have been received from a soldier of the
31st; and another soldier of the same regiment is accused
of robbing one of the street beggars,—while a counter-
charge is brought against the Chinamen of having stolen
200 blankets from Fane's Horse, who, by the way, are believed to be generally capable of looking after themselves.

A complaint has been made to Mr. Mongan, the acting-
consul, by a Chinese brazier, against two officers of the garrison, who, it appears, went into his shop and purchased a
couple of brass kettles, ordering them to be brought to their
quarters, when they would be paid for. The man accordingly brought the kettles, and a dollar was sent to him in
payment, which he refused to receive, and requested that
his property might be given back to him. A second dollar
was then sent in lieu of the six he demanded, failing to get
which or his kettles, he went to the consul, who has
brought the matter under the notice of Brigadier Staveley,
who, I believe, has adopted such measures as will not only
secure the Chinaman having justice done him, but check a
repetition of attempts at unfair dealing with the native
tradesmen.*

* At a subsequent period of the occupation of Tien-tsin an officer mentioned to me that he was present in a curiosity shop in the chief street in

December 19th.—Last night Dr. Gordon, Deputy-Inspector-General of Hospitals, arrived from Hong-Kong to assume the duties of Principal Medical Officer of the Tien-tsin force. According to the last news from Shanghai, Lord Elgin was still there, waiting to hear from Admiral Hope in reference to the projected expedition up the Yang-tse-kiang in spring; the object of which is to visit the treaty ports, and also to give the rebels to understand that they are not to interfere with English trade on the river. Sir Hope and Lady Grant were also at Shanghai, and were about to proceed to Japan.

From Taku, we hear that a quantity of stores, belonging to Mr. Bruce, landed there for transmission by land to Tien-tsin, have been broken open by a guard of the 31st Regiment, placed in charge of them, and liquor and other articles made free with. I may here remark, that on the march to Peking both Lord Elgin and Sir Hope Grant were looted of nearly the whole of their wine by the escort of the 60th Rifles that accompanied it: the loss of each, I am informed, amounting to about sixty dozen.

This morning a soldier of the 60th was found dead in bed. Medical examination went to show that his death was the result of insensibility caused by excess of alcohol.

December 20th.—A court-martial has been ordered to assemble on the soldiers of the 31st who broke open Mr. Bruce's stores. It is not safe to entrust property to the care of soldiers; so demoralised has the army become by the constant looting which has been going on during the expedition, that the Legations at Tien-tsin have determined

the suburb, when an English officer was bargaining for an article. Failing to get it at the price he wanted he took it up and threw down its money value according to his own estimate. The shopkeeper, an old man with grey hair, objected to the amount, and came forward, putting out his hand at the same time to take back the article. The officer struck him a severe blow between the eyes, which knocked him down; and he then, after having performed this ruffianly feat, walked deliberately off with the poor man's property.

to establish a Chinese agent at Taku, and thus for the future prevent property being entrusted to soldiers.

An American missionary, the Rev. Mr. Blodgett, came to me to-day, with the view of seeing the wounded Tartars. I took him accordingly to see them, and through his knowledge of the language, ascertained that the second in command to Sang-ko-lin-sin at Taku, was a lieutenant-general, named Lao. He was sent over to the north fort shortly before the attack, to take the command, and was killed. They adhere to a statement they made the other day, that in the fort taken by storm the garrison amounted to only 700 men, while in the north fort that surrendered there were about a thousand. They do not appear to know the exact strengths of the garrisons in the forts on the south side of the river. If there were only 700 men in the stormed fort, 400 of them were killed, that being the number of bodies buried after its capture. From what I personally observed, I am inclined to believe their statement to be tolerably correct.

Hawking is one of the amusements of the north of China. This forenoon Dr. Lamprey, of the 67th Regiment, who has some knowledge of the language, went out with about a dozen Chinamen on the plain beyond Sang-ko-lin-sin's Folly, as the fourteen miles of earthwork investing the walled city are now called. They extended themselves in line at certain distances from each other, and as soon as the Chinese greyhound started a hare, the hood was removed from the hawk, which one of the men carried on his wrist, and it shot off after the hare—soon hovered over it, and descending with force, fixed its talons in its back. The sportsmen then made all haste up, otherwise the hare would soon have been picked to pieces. As an illustration of the unacquaintance of the Chinese with the use of firearms for the purposes of sport, Dr. Lamprey could not persuade them to take a shot at anything with his gun, and he describes their astonishment as something intense, when

P

he managed to bring down a quail flying, and the impression made was so great that they mentioned the occurrence to every one they met, and drew attention to the wonderful weapon by which the feat had been effected.

December 21*st.*—The thermometer fell during the night to 8°. At 9 A.M. it stood at 12°. The weather is fine, clear, and bracing, but the cold is rather severe; especially as affecting the feet. The river this morning is completely frozen over above the bridge of boats, but not altogether so immediately underneath it; owing to the force of the current passing between the boats.

I went to-day into a Chinese shoemaker's shop, with an officer who wanted to purchase for warmth's sake a pair of native fur-lined shoes. His foot, however, was too large for the stock of ready-mades on hand. The shopmen seemed much amused at the size of the foot, and laughed heartily at their want of success in finding a fit. The proprietor of the shop then placed his head in an attitude of repose, to indicate that by to-morrow he would have a pair of shoes ready. He also indicated by signs that in consequence of the unusual size of the foot, the charge would be one dollar and a half, or one third more than the usual charge.

Baron de Meritens returned to-day from Peking, much charmed with the Prince of Kung, whom he describes as being all that can be desired. Matters, however, are not proceeding quite so *couleur de rose*, he states, with the Emperor, who is represented as much disgusted with the present state of affairs—especially so with the destruction of Yuen-ming-yuen, and with the foreign residency at Peking. It is therefore difficult to predict what the results may be; Prince Kung, however, has declared in the most unequivocal manner his intention faithfully to act up to all that he has contracted to do, so long as he is allowed to remain at the head of foreign affairs. It is the opinion of M. De Meritens that the Ministers should go as early as possible to Peking, and it has been determined that Mr.

Wade and Count Kleiskousky shall proceed there in advance of their respective Legations.

One important fact has been established by our visit to Peking, namely, that the Emperor has been fully cognizant of all that has been going on in respect to Anglo-Chinese intercourse for years (with the exception of our recent defence of Shanghai). This is a curious and interesting fact, being so opposed to the generally received opinion respecting his Celestial Majesty, and it shows the small amount of confidence that is to be placed in rumour and assertion, even when emanating from apparently good authority.

To-day we met a Chinaman with a sort of hand-drum, beaten after the fashion of a child's toy. With this he was making a great noise, and while we were speculating what it meant, some flames were seen on the opposite side of the canal near the French quarter, and a number of men coming down the opposite bank in line, with white flags and black letters on them. We concluded that they were connected with the police, and that the flags were to indicate the direction of the fire, which the beating of the drum was intended to announce to the neighbourhood. We accordingly followed the direction of the flags and soon reached the fire, which had settled on a cluster of houses up a narrow lane, in which, fortunately close to the burning houses, there was a vacant space. We had hardly got into it, before a number of men bearing gaudy flags and standards arrived, followed in rapid succession by eight fire engines—odd-looking machines with gilt inscriptions on them, each carried on the shoulders of four men by a pole passing through the upper part. These engines consist of forcing pumps worked by a double lever, the jet of water being projected through a brass nozzle about six feet long, working on a swivel from the upper portion of the pump. They have no hose, yet a very effective jet was projected some distance. The great fault seemed to be the rapidity with which the supply of water was exhausted. In a short time the enclosure was filled with flags of all colours and devices, drums, tom-toms, gongs, &c., the noise and general confusion which prevailed baffling description. Some sailors from a Russian gunboat, frozen in not far off, and a number of French soldiers, were actively employed on the roofs of the houses, detaching the thatching and other combustible material. Fresh engines continued to arrive, and without heeding the direction, the moment they got into the open space, they commenced discharging their contents towards the flames. One engine I saw playing right on the Russians and the Frenchmen, with the thermometer 20° below freezing. They seemed, however, not to mind it, but continued to work away with right good will. As darkness began to creep on, the effect of the lines of flags and lanterns was very picturesque—taken altogether it was one of the gayest sights I have seen in China, and not unlike a gigantic teetotal procession at home. The Tien-tsin Fire Brigade appears to consist of several sections, each of which has a distinctive uniform and distinctive coloured flags. The engines were supplied with water from the Grand Canal close to its junction with the Peiho, carried in buckets slung in the ordinary way from the ends of a bamboo supported across the shoulder. In this way it was brought up from different parts of the canal, where the ice had to be broken for the purpose. The system of lighting by lanterns was very perfect, and altogether the arrangements gave us the idea of being wonderfully complete; more especially the rapidity with which the different sections of the fire brigade were on the ground with their engines.

December 22nd.—During the night the cold was intense; the thermometer having fallen to 5°. At eight A.M. it was 10°, and inside the bedrooms 25°; the barometer standing at 30·50, the sky continuing clear and the weather very fine.

On the bank of the canal there is an elegant country house, with two showy-looking lions carved in stone in front of it, presenting the usual grotesque attitude of all Chinese lions. *Apropos* of lions, I may mention that about the thirteenth century of our era, a present of lions was made by some foreign power to the Emperor of China, who after due deliberation determined not to receive them, for the following truly Chinese reasons :—" We have no animals like them, therefore we do not know that they are lions; supposing we accept them and they turn out not to be lions, then we shall become the laughing-stock of the whole world." Near the house referred to, a number of junks from the south were lying ice-bound in the canal. The Peiho itself is now completely frozen over, and people are walking over it in all directions.

December 25*th*.—The Peiho is now covered with small wooden sleighs. They are propelled by a man standing at the stern pushing the sleigh along by a pole with an iron point, at a pace varying from five to eight miles an hour, according to the loads upon them. They take the place of boat traffic during winter. Already they have become a source of great amusement to the soldiers, who for a few cash are taking trips several miles up and down the river.

An inquest was held to-day on Private Holt of the 31st Regiment, who was found dead in his bed yesterday morning, after marching up from Taku, where he had just landed from the "White Star." He was, to all appearance, a fine healthy young man, and no other cause could be assigned for his death than the extreme cold to which his system had become suddenly exposed.

December 26*th*.—Learned this morning from Lieutenant de Saisset, who now commands a French gunboat frozen in at Taku, that the ice at present extends over six miles out into the Gulf of Pe-chi-li, and that communication with the shipping is quite impracticable until spring. The captain of a vessel lying in the anchorage had offered the Chinese boatmen at Taku one hundred dollars to put him on board his vessel, but none would undertake it, and he had started for Che-foo by land, in hopes of being able to come round by sea from that place.

According to Hang-ki, the cold will steadily increase for the next twenty days, at the expiration of which the strength of the ice on the river, as compared to what it now is, will, he says, be as that of a piece of timber placed vertically to support a weight, compared with its strength when similarly employed horizontally.*

December 28th.—Met a funeral procession coming out of one of the cross lanes. On reaching the centre of the street some "joss paper" was placed on the ground, and burned. The procession consisted of one priest and six musicians, followed by mourners in white. After burning the paper they returned by a cross street to the residence of the deceased, near the south gate. The Reverend Mr. Mahé here joined us, and he went to the door of the house and made signs to be allowed to enter, which was at once accorded. The master of the house, a polite gentlemanly man, came forward and met us, and ushered us in through a courtyard filled with white funeral trappings: the whole having a rather ghostly and very singular appearance. We were then taken into a chamber fitted up with peculiar tapestry, which by signs we were given to understand was connected with mourning, also that the deceased was the father of the owner of the house, and that his age was eighty-five—a fact speaking well for the climate. Tea was brought in, and with it sugar, the latter specially provided for us; the Chinese never using it with tea themselves. Mr. Mahé exchanged snuff with one of the mourners, and before we left, paper was brought in, and we were requested to write down our names, which we did, and explained to them as well as we could our respective callings. They seemed interested with the fact that Dr. Galbraith and myself were "esungs" (professors of the healing art), and

---

* This comparison turned out to be somewhat exaggerated.

particularly so that Mr. Mahé belonged to the "chin-chin joss" order.

Mentioning this occurrence to Mr. Wade, I learnt from him that the funerals in this part of China are much more elaborate and ceremonious than in the south of China, also that the obsequies have no necessary connection with the period of actual burial, as that is frequently deferred until a lucky day can be selected. White is the mourning colour.

December 29th.—Visited one of the public bathing establishments. Several men were performing their ablutions, and everything seemed conducted with much order and propriety. A man stands at the door behind a small counter, having a slit in it, through which he slips the cash which the bathers pay on leaving. The tubs are oval shaped and the walls are fitted with boxes for the clothes of those bathing. The temperature is very high, and of this advantage is taken for the forcing of bulbous plants, a large number of which, in saucers, were ranged on the floor. The cost of a bath at this establishment is less than one farthing. Baths are also furnished from it to private houses, a tub, hot water and other appliances, including the services of a man as a scrubber, being furnished for 100 cash, about fivepence of English money. In these public baths we have an evidence of one thing at least in which the Chinese would seem to have kept ahead of us, as it is only of recent years that we have begun to recognise the sanitary importance of providing the poor with cheap means of ablution, whereas the Chinese appear to have done so for centuries; the same also being the case in Japan.

December 30th.—This forenoon the strains of Chinese music heard near the hospital attracted our attention—a wedding procession was passing. At the head of it walked half a-dozen men carrying large globular-shaped lanterns, made of fine diaphanous horn, hanging from the ends of poles. A couple of men beating gongs came next, followed by men bearing gaudy flags. These were followed by others carrying boards painted red, with gilt inscriptions on them. Following these came flags, banners, and a number of boys, with axes and spears made of wood and showily painted and gilded. Then a line of men with gaudily decorated horn lanterns, suspended from poles amidst a quantity of ornamental silk work. A full band of music ; the musicians clad in robes of the most showy kind. A kettle-drum, a pair of gongs, and a carved and gilded pagoda carried on poles closed the procession.

This evening at dinner, at the French Legation, I had an interesting conversation with an officer of French Engineers, who described the consequences of the army coming in contact with the Yuen-ming-yuen, as having been very demoralizing. The first day the French army got to the summer palace everything went on very well, the men merely taking away trifles as mementoes of the place, but the next day matters were very different—temptation could no longer be withstood, and officers and men were seen rushing off wholesale to plunder—discipline was completely annihilated, and had the Tartars been able to profit by the general disorganization which prevailed, the results might have been disastrous.

CHAPTER XIX.

Frozen porter—Statistical fallacies—Indifference of local officials in respect to hostilities against the Government—Dead beggar—New Year pictures—Chinese hawking party—Scarcity of copper—Occasional resistance of the Chinese to extortion—Self sacrifice—Distribution of money to indigent Chinese—Its disastrous results—Extreme cold—Serious illness and death of General Collineau—Procession to propitiate a weather divinity—Funeral of General Collineau—Sketch of his career—Outrage by English soldiers at Taku—Private of 67th in trouble.

January 1st.—The day has been one of intense cold, the frost so severe that the men of the 60th Rifles carried their ration porter from the commissariat in sacks and baskets, it having been issued to them in a frozen state.

Brigadier Staveley visited the hospital to-day, and in the course of his inspection an illustration occurred showing the fallacious character which medical statistical returns frequently assume. The " Daily State of Hospital Sick " showed the 31st to be the most sickly of the three infantry regiments in garrison, when in reality it is by far the most healthy. This attracted the brigadier's attention, and it was explained to him that it arose from the fact of all non-effectives of the 31st being treated in hospital, whereas in the other two regiments there were a large number of sick men in barracks under medical treatment and relieved from duty in consequence, but who, from not being in hospital, did not appear on the daily sick state of the garrison.

A Chinaman called Cha-low-ya, who has been employed for a few weeks back about the hospital as a teacher by some of the medical officers, hearing that this was the English new-year, dressed himself in his best clothes and left his card (a large red one with his name in black letters) in the mess-room, in accordance with the Chinese custom on their own new-year, which will be in between five and six weeks.

January 2nd.—The river presents a very animated spectacle from the number of sleighs that are running up and down, conveying passengers and merchandise.

As an illustration of the vagaries of the Chinese character and diplomacy, Mr. Bruce mentioned to me that shortly after the insolent reply to the British ultimatum was received from Peking, Soo-chow fell into the hands of the rebels. Immediately afterwards Ho, the Governor-General of the two Kwang, a high Chinese official whose name I forget, and Wu, the Tautai of Shanghai, called on Mr. Bruce and tried to persuade him to march troops against Soo-chow and retake it. Mr. Bruce hinted to them that we were on the eve of going to war, and asked them how they were to get us out of Soo-chow supposing we retook it for them. They all three jumped up from their seats and said they knew us and had perfect confidence in us, and that the cause of all our misunderstandings was that they did not know us at Peking; in their own words, that the taoli (ideas) of the south respecting the English were different from the taoli of the north.

January 6th.—Passing out of the south gate, in the centre of the road a dead beggar was lying. He had apparently dropped from exhaustion and cold, and had been allowed to die without any effort being made to relieve or remove him to a place of shelter. The Chinese, as a general rule, will never interfere with dying people who may be lying about outside, or with their remains afterwards, because if they do, they are held responsible by the local authorities for all the funeral expenses.

January 9th.—To-day, for the first time, I observed stuck up at stalls in various parts of the chief streets, numbers of highly-coloured gaudy paintings on paper, round which were large crowds of admiring Chinese. The scene reminded me forcibly of the valentine season at home. These pictures are connected with the approaching new-year festivities; the present being the twenty-ninth day of the eleventh month, there being thirty days in each month, and twelve months in the year.

January 10*th.*—Mr. Bruce being desirous of seeing the Chinese mode of hawking, Dr. Lamprey of the 67th Regiment arranged with the chief sportsman to get up a party, which rendezvoused this morning at the hospital gate. Three Chinamen, bearing on their wrists hooded hawks of large size, resembling falcons, first arrived. They were accompanied by two Chinese hounds of the true greyhound build, but with rather short shaggy tails. They are said to resemble closely the Persian hound, and probably are of the same breed. A mounted huntsman next arrived, having a hare's head hanging from his girdle. The head man of the party, a tall military looking Manchu, came next, accompanied by several attendants, in all about a dozen: the party being larger than usual, attracted by the novelty of the English Chin-si (ambassador) going out to witness one of their national sports.

We crossed several fields in stubble and fallow; the party being extended in line. After we had gone about two miles, a hare suddenly started out of the fallow quite close to us. In an instant the hounds and hawks were after it. After a run of about a quarter of a mile one of the hawks pounced down on the hare, and plunging its talons into its back, overturned it, the dogs coming up and securing it. Being on horseback we were up almost at the same time; also the mounted huntsman on his China pony at full gallop. It suddenly pulled up at the spot, and he went over its head, but was on his feet so instantaneously, that one felt uncertain at the moment whether this eccentric mode of dismounting was not intentional, and as such, a further illustration of the contrarieties of the Chinese character. The use of the hare's head attached to his waistbelt now became apparent; he unloosened it and threw it on the ground to the hawks, to save them from disappointment, and to attract their attention, while the hare was saved from being torn to pieces.

We proceeded on in the same direction, towards a village about four miles beyond the outer fortifications, and started a second hare, which gave the party a good chase of over a mile; baffling its pursuers a good deal, from taking a course through a number of funereal tumuli, at the base of which it managed to burrow itself at the moment it was overtaken —apparently being now safe from hawks, hounds, or other pursuers. Not so, however, for as soon as the head man came up, the unfortunate hare was speedily dug out and secured. The sport continued for a short time afterwards; two more hares being killed.

Talking during the ride home of the special fitness of the coin known as a cash (of which twenty go to a penny), for a poor and numerous population like the Chinese, Mr. Bruce told me that one of the great financial difficulties of the country at the present time is the scarcity of cash from the want of copper wherewith to make it—so much so, that lately the government at Peking have been obliged to issue iron cash, which has caused great dissatisfaction amongst the people. Hence, it is not improbable, that should the extensive copper mines which exist in the provinces of Honan and Hu-peh not soon be restored to working order, copper will become an extensive article of import.

Referring to the question of public dissatisfaction amongst the Chinese, and to the fact of their not hesitating under certain circumstances to give vent to it in a violent manner, Mr. Bruce mentioned that not long ago a disturbance took place near Ning-po, connected with the land tax, which is one of the great sources of revenue in China. It is usually paid in copper cash annually, and remitted in silver to

Peking. It seems that the mandarin collecting it in the district referred to, had added on a higher per-centage for himself than had been heretofore the custom; in other words, increased the amount of the ordinary official squeeze. The people of one of the villages subjected to this imposition determined to resist the increased taxation, as far as it referred to the mandarin himself, though they were willing to meet the fair demands of government, and even would not have demurred at paying the squeeze to which they had hitherto been accustomed. They therefore determined to respect all public and private property, and confine their attacks solely to what belonged to the extortionate mandarin. Ultimately the local authorities sent to Hang-chow for troops, and a number arrived sufficient to quell the petty insurrection.

At this juncture, as the easiest mode of settling the difficulty, and saving the villagers from the calamity of a conflict with the troops, the leader of the movement made a proposition to his brother insurgents, that on condition of their subscribing a sum of money sufficient for the future support of his family, and also sufficient to erect a monument to his memory, he would deliver himself up for the public weal. The conditions were agreed to, and he surrendered himself to the authorities, and was beheaded in due course. No further steps were adopted against the villagers, the movement having subsided on the surrender of its leader. This incident affords a very remarkable illustration of one of the most striking characteristics on the bright side of the Chinese character—a total absence of feeling for self, where, by personal sacrifice, the welfare of those nearest and dearest to them can be secured.

The land that is to be given up to the English and French as a settlement for commercial purposes, is situated on the river bank, about a mile below the walled city of Tientsin. The greater portion of it belongs to Chang, the great salt merchant. It has been determined that when bought by foreigners (English, French, Americans, Germans, &c.) for the purposes of trade, forty per cent. on the market price per mow* is to be paid for it. At the present rate of garden land, it is calculated that an acre of ground will cost 30*l.*, exclusive of the forty per cent., which will make it 42*l.* per acre.

11th January.—This is the first day of the Chinese twelfth month, which is said to be very cold, high and cutting winds prevailing during the greater portion of it. A steady fall of snow commenced early in the morning, and continued all day.

Shortly before Christmas a subscription was started to relieve indigent Chinese, by the Rev. Mr. M'Ghee, garrison chaplain, 867 dollars being collected.

It was resolved by the managers of the fund to intimate to the Chinese by placards, that on a certain day a sum of money would be divided amongst such as applied. I urged that this mode of distribution would not be attended with the least practical benefit, owing to the numbers that were certain to come for it, begging being to a certain extent a regular trade in China. I recommended the establishment of a soup kitchen, as a *bonâ fide* means of relieving distress, where actual want of food existed. A soup kitchen once set on foot, the expense of supporting it would have been materially modified by making use of the *débris* of the soldiers' dinners, which amounted daily to a considerable quantity of wholesome food, waiting for which there were always crowds of beggars round the barracks of the respective corps. The Seiks of Fane's Horse, in particular, were remarkable for their charity and kindness to poor Chinese; charity being a principle inculcated on them by their religion. This proposition of a soup kitchen was not entertained. Dr. Gordon, again, was for employing the money

---

* In this part of China (Tien-tsin) about three mow go to an English acre. At Shanghai, the land measurement is different, about six mow going to the acre.

in support of an hospital, that we are trying to set up for the cure of Chinese cases requiring surgical treatment. This was also overruled, and this day was fixed for the distribution of the 867 dollars at the yamun of the Literary Chancellor, at present used partly as the garrison church, partly as barracks for a portion of the 60th Rifles—an open space extending between it and the city wall.

The distribution commenced at ten in the morning, the day being unpropitious for the gathering of so many people in the open air; snow falling steadily, accompanied by a severe frost.

At two in the afternoon, as I was crossing the open space from the Temple of the Moon, I had to pass near the yamun of the Literary Chancellor, and my attention was drawn to the spot by cries and groans, which I found to come from a number of women lying about in the snow, apparently suffering great pain. On inquiring into the cause I learned, from some soldiers of the 60th who were standing about, that a crowd of some five thousand people had assembled to share in the distribution of the money, and that the rush for admission had been so great that nine people had been trodden to death. Besides the women lying about in the snow a large number had been injured and removed by their friends.

I asked what had been done with the bodies, and was told that they were inside. I went in and looked at them lying in one of the detached buildings of the yamun, where, by some unaccountable want of sense on the part of the British soldier, the dead were carefully ranged side by side on a raised caugue,* in a well covered and closed-in building, while sixteen suffering and crippled women were left lying out in the open air with the snow falling upon them for full three hours.

I found as stated by the soldiers nine corpses, six of them elderly females, one young woman, a lad about fifteen, and

* Stone bed place.

an infant; a sorry sight they presented; all their countenances showed that they had died from suffocation. It was grievous to see the poor people coming in to identify their deceased relatives. One respectable looking old woman was sitting over the body of the girl—her grand-daughter, weeping bitterly.

The arrangements for the preservation of order must have been very defective; as the gate of the yamun was forced and thrown from its hinges by the impetuous rush of the crowd. The Chinese police, sent down by the municipal authorities to aid the military in keeping order, are stated to have been of no use. The wounded persons were taken care of in a temporary hospital, but their relatives fetched them away within twenty-four hours, preferring to have them under their own care.

January 12*th*.—In the course of the night the thermometer fell as low as 5° below zero. During the day slight snow has been falling at intervals. Towards noon the cold became excessive, and between that and three in the afternoon the thermometer fell to 4°. This extreme cold was attended in some instances with serious results. Two soldiers, apparently in the enjoyment of perfect health, were suddenly seized with symptoms of ordinary ague. They were conveyed to hospital, and almost immediately afterwards died; death resulting from some abnormal susceptibility to the depressing effects of extreme cold.

The commander of the French troops also, the gallant General Collineau, who has survived so many fights, fell a victim to this day's cold. He was convalescing favourably from small pox, and in the earlier part of the day issued his "brigade orders" with his usual clearness and energy. His nervous system then seemed in a state of perfect integrity. In the afternoon symptoms of palsy of the lower limbs suddenly set in; in a short time the symptoms indicated the disease to be of a serious nature.

January 13*th*.—To-day is Sunday, and the town, for the

first time since we have been in Tien-tsin, resembles a Sunday at home; the shops being all closed, the streets usually so crowded, deserted by the Chinese, and business completely suspended—so bitter is the cold, so cutting the wind, and so destructive to their wares is the dust that is flying about in dense clouds.

January 14*th*.—Cold continues very severe, though not attended with such disagreeable sensations as yesterday. The bread at breakfast this morning was so hardened by the frost that it had to be sawn into slices.

The present is the seventh day of the third period of nine periods each of nine days, into which the Chinese divide the cold weather in this part of the country. This is stated to be the coldest of the nine periods.

General Collineau's case has assumed an almost hopeless character, the palsy having extended from the limbs to the upper portion of the body. He has made his will, and declares himself now to be merely a living corpse; the only portion of his organism that he feels alive being his head. He received the announcement of the very serious nature of his disease with the utmost fortitude, and at once ordered pen and paper to make his will. It was suggested to him that he had better wait until the next day. He said no; that it was better it should be done at once. The only regret he expressed was, that after being repeatedly wounded, and his life exposed in thirty general actions, he should have survived to die in so helpless a state in China.

January 15*th*.—At noon a communication was sent from the French head-quarters to the effect that the medical attendants of General Collineau would feel obliged if Dr. Gordon and myself would meet them in consultation; also, that it was the wish of the General himself that we should see him. Three in the afternoon was fixed as the hour. We went over accompanied by Messrs. de Fontblanc and Wingfield of the commissariat, who, having a thorough

Q

colloquial knowledge of French, had kindly offered to interpret if necessary.

We met at the General's quarters, in the street known as "Rue, 102." Dr. Jerrier, "Médecin en chef" of the army, and Dr. La Rivière, chief of the hospital, were there. The latter, who is the General's ordinary medical attendant, entered into a full and clear exposition of the case, and from what he stated little doubt could exist that the symptoms indicated a hopeless form of the disease. We accompanied Dr. La Rivière to the General's bedroom, where we found him lying on a humble bedstead placed on the top of a caugue, attended by two men of the Infirmary corps. He was sadly altered since I last saw him on the 21st of August, standing on the top of the cavalier of the North Taku Fort, flushed with victory, talking to an English staff-officer, and pointing out the part of his epaulette that had been struck by a ball during the assault, and discoursing with animation regarding the circumstances under which medals and clasps are issued in the British service. Now consciousness was annihilated; the breathing had become stertorous, and his face was assuming a livid hue from imperfect respiration. I felt his pulse; it was still beating with tolerable force, and his heart seemed to be all that was alive within him. The hand of the grim Serjeant was upon him, and escape from his grip impossible. Two hours after our visit the gallant General breathed his last.

January 16th.—When out this morning early, I met a grand procession with the usual amount of music, flags, banners and gilded paraphernalia. This procession I ascertained was of a religious character, and intended to propitiate a deity supposed to exercise an influence over the weather, the present severity of which it was desired should be modified.

Going through some of the curiosity-shops with Colonel Neale, a good deal of very fine jade and enamel work was shown us in a stealthy manner in the back rooms, evidently the product of the looting of Yuen-ming-yuen, which it is well-known was extensively indulged in by the Chinese villagers in the neighbourhood. They carried off a class of articles that were too bulky for the French or English to burden themselves with; more especially enamels, which they concealed until opportunities offered of getting them into the curiosity market at Tien-tsin, where they have met with a ready sale, at very high prices.

January 17*th*.—Received a message from Baron de Meritens asking me if it were practicable to procure a little nitric acid to enable a soldier who had been a copper-plate worker to engrave General Collineau's name on his coffin-plate, there being none of the acid in question amongst the French medical stores. As we had plenty, there was no difficulty in complying with this request.

January 18*th*.—General Collineau's funeral took place to-day, the *cortège* leaving his quarters at half-past eleven, in the following order:—Drummers and buglers of the 102nd Regiment, six Roman Catholic priests, including two missionary bishops and one Chinese priest, a gun-carriage drawn by six black Japanese ponies. On the carriage rested the coffin, covered with a black velvet pall—on it lay the coat, orders, epaulettes, sword and cap of the deceased. In the rear of the coffin walked the chief mourner, Colonel O'Malley, of the 102nd Regiment, M. de Bourboulon, Mr. Bruce, Brigadier Staveley, and staff. The English officers followed according to regiments. The Commissariat and Medical Staffs accompanied the Brigadier. In the rear of the English officers followed the three principal municipal dignitaries of Tien-tsin, accompanied by a numerous body of retainers. Behind them walked such French officers as were not on duty with the troops lining the streets along which the funeral passed. These afterwards assembled at the grave and formed the firing-party.

Detachments of gendarmerie and artillerymen on foot, the

sedan chairs of the Chinese officials and those of the French Legation closed the procession, which went at a slow pace along the bank of the river until it reached the temporary chapel that has been fitted up by the French. The coffin was removed from the gun-carriage and taken into the church. Mass was said and the Host elevated : the troops within the church presenting arms.

The service occupied about an hour ; all the priests, including the Chinese one, officiating. One of the missionary bishops wears a tail, and is said to have been fifteen years in captivity among the Chinese in the interior.

The coffin having been replaced on the carriage, the procession was re-formed and proceeded across the river by a bridge of boats to the peninsula above Tien-tsin, and passing through the Temple of Supreme Felicity reached the French burial-ground near the bank of the river, about half-a-mile beyond Tien-tsin. All the French troops were drawn up there, three battalions of infantry forming three sides of a square. As the body was being lowered into the grave, each battalion faced about to the outside and fired two volleys. The Almoner of the French army then came forward and made an address over the grave. Colonel O'Malley followed, and entered in detail into the career of the deceased, concluding his address by extending his hand to the grave, saying, "Adieu, my General, adieu, in the name of the army I bid you adieu." Captain D'Hendecourt, aide-de-camp to the late General, then came forward, and made a short and very appropriate speech, expressive of his personal feelings at the loss he had sustained.

Holy water was next sprinkled on the coffin by the officiating priest, after which the same ceremony was gone through by Colonel O'Malley, M. de Bourboulon, Mr. Bruce, Brigadier Staveley, and the senior officers of the English army. After this the *élite* of the army, including the artillery, engineers, and gendarmerie, marched past the grave, each soldier discharging his musket into the grave as he passed. The troops then marched home, the funeral ceremonies being concluded.

General Collineau was born in 1810, and entered the army in 1831, as a private in the "Légion d'Étrangers," a corps raised specially for service in Algeria. After being six years in the ranks he became sub-Lieutenant, and gradually rose to be Colonel of Zouaves, in which capacity he proceeded to the Crimea and, as is well known, commanded the regiment that was the first to enter the Malakoff. Collineau was the first man in and the first man out, having been knocked on the head by the butt end of a musket as he got on the parapet, and thrown back into the ditch. On the conclusion of the Crimean war he returned to Algeria, and from thence proceeded on active service to Italy, being present at Magenta and Solferino. On the conclusion of the Italian campaign, he returned to France, for the first time since he left it as a private soldier, returning a General of Brigade. He died a General of Division—having been promoted to that rank for his recent services in China.

Colonel O'Malley, as the next senior officer, succeeds him in the command of the French troops.

This evening, at the Legation, I heard of a most deliberate and murderous outrage that has just been committed at Taku by some soldiers of the 31st Regiment stationed there. It appears that a party of them went down to the village and endeavoured to procure sam-shu. Failing to do so, they returned to their barracks, procured their rifles and loaded them. They then returned to the place where they had been refused the sam-shu, and opened fire upon the establishment, killing one man and wounding several others. Up to the latest date all attempts to identify the ruffians have failed.

Late in the evening a soldier of the 67th Regiment was, according to his own statement, caught in one of the narrow back lanes near the 31st head-quarter barracks by some Chinese, bound hand and foot, and signs made to him that he was going to have his head cut off. He hollowed lustily, and was heard by some soldiers of the 31st, who came and rescued him. Whether this was going to be an act of retaliation for the recent murders, as feared by the Prefect, or the soldier had been misconducting himself in one of the houses in the neighbourhood, and the Chinese were conveying him to the authorities, it is difficult to say; the latter is the most probable, because if murder had been their object, that would have been done in a summary manner, and not by a formal decapitation.

CHAPTER XX.

An opium smoking-shop—The kow-tow—Small-pox and rude inoculation—The Foundling Hospital—Chinaman executed—Funeral procession—Demolition of a house for sam-shu dealing—Pawnbroker's establishment—News from Peking—Juvenile gambling—Garrison theatre opens—Approach of the Chinese New Year—Mortality amongst the troops—A Foreign Office to be established at Peking—Severe cold—Preserved fish—A Chinese joke—Old furniture shops—The silver pheasant—A dying Mandarin—The Audience question—Lord Macartney and the kow-tow—Ushering in of the New Year—Chinese compliments of the season—The ancestral tablet.

January 19th.—We visited an opium smoking-shop,—some were lying down, just getting under the influence of the drug, others were filling their pipes, preparatory to narcotising themselves. The place was comfortably heated, and the smokers reclined on a good caugue, nicely covered with matting, and provided with head stools (or, as we should call them, pillows) for the smokers. The first victim that Mr. Blodgett interrogated was a young man, pale and dissipated looking. He was twenty-five years of age, and had smoked opium for the last two years, commencing the habit originally as a cure for diarrhœa, and ultimately finding himself unable to give it up. He said he was very anxious to do so, and would be ready to subject himself to any restrictions in an asylum or hospital which would be likely to cure him. He expended thirty cash daily on opium, an allowance he had from his father as pocket-money. He followed no occupation, neither did his father. On being asked from what source his father derived his means, he said that he lived on his relatives, who were well to do,—

this being a mode of livelihood by no means uncommon, I may remark, in China.

An old man about fifty came in while we were in the shop, and recognised Mr. Blodgett, who had previously had some conversation with him about the baneful practice he was indulging in. He kow-towed* to him in proof of his anxiety to follow his advice and give up opium. He had smoked for the last twenty years, having commenced the habit for the cure of an affection of the bowels. He is a hawker by trade, and earns from 150 to 200 cash a day, spending 100 of the amount on opium. He pointed to the poverty of his attire in further proof of the desirableness of his relinquishing the habit, and said that if his family could be secured support while he was undergoing treatment to break him of the habit, he would readily submit to any restraint that might be necessary.†

Noticing one of the smokers marked with small-pox, we asked him what the disease is called that had caused his disfigurement. He answered "chu-toad-tso," meaning "the issuing forth of the bean disease." ‡ The Chinese in this part of the country generally have the disease when they are about five years of age. A singular and rude mode of inoculation appears to be in vogue, namely, during lactation impregnating the maternal milk as it issues from the breast with small-pox matter, which in this way is supposed to be conveyed into the system of the child; though the probabilities are, that it undergoes decomposition by the gastric juice, and thus proves inert.

We afterwards visited the Foundling Hospital. At the

---

* The kow-tow is the Chinese obeisance indicating extreme respect. It is performed by going down on the knees and bowing the head until it touches the ground—the motion being repeated several times.

† I may observe, that after the Chinese hospital was established, several cases of opium smoking were cured by medical treatment carried out by Dr. Lamprey, who conducted the hospital.

‡ This expression is similar to the name exanthemata, which we give to the class of eruptive diseases to which small-pox belongs.

entrance a board, with the regulations of the institution, is hung up. The superintendent, a respectable looking old gentleman, received us very politely. The hospital is divided into four squares according to the points of the compass. Each square is presided over by a matron. At present eighty children are being reared under the care of forty nurses, who are hired at a monthly wage of 2500 cash (two-and-a-half dollars) and their board. The children seemed all warmly clad and tolerably clean. The rooms are not overburdened with interior fittings; the chief ones being caugues, warmed to a comfortable heat. The male infants in arms have all rudimentary tails under cultivation; the hair, in most instances, though not an inch long, is, nevertheless, carefully tied up with braid. Some of the female children have contracted feet, but the greater portion have not.

The institution has an endowment, and is further supported by voluntary subscriptions. Over the outer door there is a board, having on it "I beseech you to rescue the naked;" and over the inner door is one bearing the inscription "Hall for the Nourishment of Infants." The children are kept until they are fourteen. The boys are then apprenticed to tradesmen. The girls are married off at once, and are prohibited from being taken as concubines. Each boy on discharge receives ten taels, which goes to his master as an apprentice fee, and acts as an inducement to tradesmen to take them. Fifteen taels are given to each girl as a marriage portion. There are several deaf, dumb, and idiotic children at present in the institution,—these are never discharged, but are taken care of for life.

On my way home, as I was passing the store kept by Douglas Frazer & Co., I saw lying in the street a human head just cut off. It was the head of a Chinaman who had been detected selling sam-shu to some English soldiers. The crime being proven, he was taken to the execution ground outside the west gate, and decapitated in accordance with Chinese martial-law. The head was sent down to the scene of his offence, to show the rigidity of the law, and to operate as a caution to others who may be engaged in the same traffic.

January 20th.—One of the wounded Chinamen took his departure to-day from the hospital provided with a new suit of clothes and five dollars kindly given him by some of the medical officers. He was anxious to get home before the new year, having to go to Pan-ting-foo, a town about 100 miles to the westward of Tien-tsin. Another cause of anxiety to get home was a fear that his wife might marry again, as he had had no means of communicating with her since he was wounded at the capture of the Taku forts, and she may not unreasonably infer that he was amongst the 500 that were killed on that occasion.

January 21st.—The Chinese commenced to-day breaking up portions of the river into square blocks of ice, which are conveyed to deep pits and there stored until required for use in summer. The ice is of the purest quality, the process of freezing having precipitated all the muddy particles from the water—squeezed them out as it were.

Going along the road outside the southern face of the city wall, I overtook an unusually grand funeral procession, in which there were at least 200 of the gaudiest flags and banners displayed. The coffin was very large, being composed of massive slabs of wood elaborately carved. It rested on a species of palanquin temple, borne by the aid of a complicated arrangement of bars on the shoulders of fifty-six men dressed in a sort of livery, with black felt hats of a conical shape, surmounted by a blue feather. Several bands of music were performing. A considerable number of Chinese of the better class, handsomely dressed in winter garments of fur, accompanied the procession on foot, while their chairs formed a part of the *cortège* behind. Immediately in front of the coffin the chief mourners walked. They were all attired in white, with head-dresses of the same colour. The procession moved at a slow pace, frequently halting, owing to the weight of the coffin and its bier. It went into the country in the direction of the Oceanic Temple.

In the afternoon I took a walk down the river on the ice, and on reaching the first bridge of boats my attention was attracted by a crowd of Chinese standing on the bank; I found they were watching the Provost-Marshal's men, in other words, the military police, levelling with the ground a house in which it had been ascertained that sam-shu had been sold to English soldiers. Really the position of the unfortunate Chinese in respect to sam-shu is a most critical one; if they sell it to soldiers their heads are cut off should the case fall to the legislation of their own authorities, or their houses are pulled down should they fall into the hands of the English Provost-Marshal; if they refuse, they are poniarded and shot. Such are the curses entailed on the inhabitants through the insatiable passion of British soldiers for any form of spirit that is sufficiently strong to produce intoxication—the property in liquor most appreciated by them.

January 22nd.—Visited one of the large pawnbrokers' establishments of the city. Everything seemed conducted in the most orderly and business-like manner; several clerks were engaged making out pawn-tickets and duplicates to be attached to the articles pawned. The store-houses where the pledges are deposited are situated in the rear of the receiving office. They are spacious and clean, the doors being fitted with alarm bells. We were conducted with much readiness and civility through several court-yards into which the establishment is divided, each containing stores filled with pawned goods. Wearing apparel and domestic articles, such as metal kettles and candlesticks, appeared to be the most common form of pledge. The clothing, carefully rolled up and ticketed, is arranged in most perfect order on wooden racks extending from a few feet above the floor to the lofty ceiling, the various tiers being reached by long bamboo ladders.

In the neighbourhood of this establishment were several juvenile gaming tables at work, consisting of boards divided into different coloured compartments, each having a certain number of balls of various colours painted on it. The young gamesters put their money down on one or more of these compartments, four dice were then shaken underneath a bowl, and according as the upper surfaces on the bowl being lifted up corresponded or not with the number of balls painted on the compartment in which the money was placed, did they win or lose. The tables were all kept by boys, and numbers of urchins were staking their cash, the most of whom, during the time we were looking on, seemed to have a run of luck, as they were winning each time.

January 23*rd.*—This afternoon news was received at the Legation from Mr. Wade, at Peking, the chief items being that the authorities at the capital are getting rather uneasy about Sang-ko-lin-sin, who, it would appear, is hemmed in and shut up in a town on the borders of the Honan province. Jui-lin, his lieutenant-general, has been degraded in consequence of his having reported him to Peking for incapacity and misconduct. The Prince of Kung has been displaying an unquestionable desire that we should interfere, by asking if it would not be possible to afford them some aid in officers or men. Mr. Wade explained the circumstances that rendered it impossible for us to interfere in domestic strife of the kind, on which Hang-ki, who was present at the time, made the remark, " Ah ! I perceive the difference ; suppose you see a riot in the street, and are brought accidentally in contact with it, then you can interfere, but you cannot go into a man's house and interfere, supposing you know a disturbance is going on there." The Prince asked Mr. Wade some questions about our religion. Wan-see-ang, one of the remaining members of the Imperial senate in Peking, joined in the conversation, and showed by his remarks that he was not only acquainted with the general principles of Christianity (a sketch of which he gave), but also that he had read translations of both the Old and the New Testament; but Mr. Wade observes that the knowledge thus acquired seemed to have made no greater impression on him than a general sketch of Buddhism, or the perusal of the Koran would make on us.

This evening the garrison amateur theatre opened in a temple situated in the main street running east and west, within the premises where the head-quarters of the 60th Rifles are stationed. The scenic decorations are the handiwork of Captain Fane, and reflect great credit on his artistic skill and taste. The fitting up of the theatre and the mechanical arrangements are very complete, and owe their success to the care that has been bestowed on them by Lieutenant Clements of the Royal Engineers, who undertook this important part of the preliminary arrangements. The band of the 60th Rifles formed the orchestra, and a clever prologue written by Assistant Commissary-General de Fontblanc was spoken by its author. General O'Malley and a number of French officers were present, and were afterwards entertained at supper by the officers of the 60th Rifles.

January 29th.—Visited the French cemetery. A large sarcophagus of a pyramidal shape has been already erected over the grave of General.Collineau.

January 30th. — Thermometer fell to 2° during the night, and three deaths took place in hospital. It fell again in the course of the day to 4° with a cold wind blowing.

News from Peking is to the effect that Mr. H. N. Lay has been appointed Inspector-General of Customs by the Chinese Government, and that it is intended to establish a Foreign Office at Peking, and Hang-ki, it is supposed, will be one of the ministers for the conducting of foreign affairs from his long experience as collector of customs at Canton.

January 31st.—The cold was intense during the night, the thermometer having stood at 0°. Two more deaths occurred in our hospital this forenoon, and four took place yesterday in the French.

Large fish are now for sale in the streets preserved in a coating of ice three inches thick, forming a complete transparent case round them. The Chinese say that when the ice is thawed these fish will recover their vitality. The correctness of the statement however has not yet been subjected to the test of experiment by any of our garrison naturalists.

February 1st.—Connected with the gaities of the approaching new year, a number of soldiers had letters presented to them in various parts of the town by Chinamen, in which a few words were written inside. These, on being submitted to an interpreter, were found to be " You're a devil." It is curious that this joke should be played at our Valentine season, and that a certain analogy should exist between it and our least refined forms of Valentine, which usually contain sentiments as little complimentary to the recipients as that conveyed in the epistles of the Chinamen.

Immediately under the north-eastern portion of the city wall there is a line of shops occupied chiefly by carpenters and dealers in second-hand furniture, the latter generally having fat old women sitting at the door, reminding one strongly of like emporiums at home.

New Year's Day is an important one in a financial point of view, as, on it, every solvent Chinaman is supposed to liquidate his debts; with this exception, business is said to be completely suspended for the first ten days of the year.

February 3rd.—I had an opportunity this morning of seeing the silver pheasant of Tartary, Dr. Lamprey having purchased one in the market, where he found it offered for sale in a frozen state. The bird is of large size, with a plume-shaped tail, the feathers not being unlike those of the ostrich. It had evidently been sent from a considerable distance, the entrails and eyes having been removed to facilitate its preservation by the frost.

Dr. Lamprey was sent for this morning to visit professionally an old mandarin dying of apoplexy. On arrival he found the case to be of a totally hopeless nature. The old man was lying on a satin couch, dressed out in his full mandarin robes and decorations, that he might die with the dignity due to his position. He was surrounded by his family, several of whom were daughters. They were good-looking and nicely dressed. They appeared to be in great distress, and were wailing loudly. They ceased their lamentations, however, as soon as they observed that Dr. Lamprey had entered the room.

To-day is the first of the sixth division of the nine cold periods which, allowing nine days for each, will bring the termination of the cold season to about the 11th of March. To-day also is said to be the first of the Chinese spring. In the afternoon there was a grand municipal procession to the "Temple of the Oceanic Influences," in which all the chief civic authorities of the city took part. A number of mounted archers accompanied it. The object of the procession and of the ceremonies connected with it was, I believe, propitiatory, connected with the advent of spring, and the approach of the period when agricultural operations will commence.

February 5th.—With reference to the probabilities of an audience being granted to the ministers should the Emperor return to Peking, I am given to understand that the same obeisance will be paid his Celestial Majesty, as would be paid the Emperor of the French under similar circumstances, namely, making three bows and retiring backwards.

Lord Macartney, at his audience with Kien-lung, the great grandfather of the present Emperor, went down on one knee arrayed in his robes of the Bath, on a flight of steps and made three bows; his head consequently coming unduly near the upper steps, hence the Chinese misconstrued the obeisance into the kow-tow, which to the present day they maintain Lord Macartney performed, and cite it as a precedent for the same being gone through at any future interview; hence out of this misconception has arisen a difficulty that seems insurmountable in respect to the granting of an Imperial audience to the foreign ministers. Mr. Ward, the late American minister, whose journey to Peking in one of the country carts has so often been made the subject of discussion and ridicule, might have had an interview with the Emperor, if he had consented to perform the kow-tow.

February 6th.—The temperature is now much milder, the lowest range of the thermometer during the night having been 20°. A considerable amount of snow was on the ground at daylight, and it continued to fall during the remainder of the day, having by the afternoon reached a depth of over four inches. There is a total absence of wind, and a large increase of ozone in the atmosphere.*

This evening the amateurs from amongst the soldiers of the 60th Rifles perform at the garrison theatre, the farces being "Slasher and Crasher," "Hunting a Turtle," and "Boots at the Swan."

February 7th.—News received at the Legation from Mr. Wade, dated the 4th inst. Everything continues to go on satisfactorily. The arrangements for the establishment of the foreign office progress, and Kwei-liang is named as one of the members. The Emperor continues to reside at Je-ho. The streets of Peking were in a sad state of mud and slush, from a thaw that had succeeded the intense frost that has prevailed for the last two months.

The French mail arrived at Che-foo, having travelled at the rate of over forty miles a-day. Snow continues on the ground, and the weather is fine and clear. Ozone is still on the increase, the ozonometer showing five, while the day before yesterday it only showed one.

* Ozone may be briefly described as a recently discovered ingredient in the atmosphere, always present in it, though frequently in proportions too small to be detected by the ozonometer. It is believed to be most abundant in winter, and after the air has been purified by storms. Amongst other useful properties attributed to it may be mentioned the neutralising of noxious substances in the atmosphere.

February 8th.—In the course of the forenoon the streets and country around Tien-tsin rapidly thawed, rendering walking both difficult and disagreeable from the depth of the mud that invariably ensues on such changes in the weather.

The mail received yesterday brought instructions for the immediate reduction of the French force occupying Tien-tsin. The 102nd Regiment has therefore been placed under orders for France, viâ Suez, and will leave as soon as the ice clears away and navigation is re-opened.

February 9th.—The present is the thirtieth day of the Chinese twelfth month, consequently the last day of their year. It has again become very cold.

The streets of the city and suburbs have presented during the whole day an appearance very like that seen during the corresponding period in Scotland or the day preceding Christmas in England. The streets were densely crowded, streams of people proceeding in all directions laden with provisions and tinsel decorations for the interior of their houses. Lanterns of various grotesque shapes and designs were being hawked about in large quantities, shaped like crabs, dragons, fish, wild beasts and the like. They are made of wire-work covered over with gaudily-painted gauze. Gold fish, in glass globes, formed also prominent articles for sale in the streets.

February 10th.—The sleep of the inmates of the hospital was disturbed the whole night by the almost incessant discharges of crackers, welcoming the new year. In fact one might as well have attempted to sleep through a general action as close the eyes for half-an-hour continuously, owing to the successive explosions, accompanied by the clashing of gongs, chimes of musical bells, and shouting of voices. The seeing of the old year out and the new year in, for demonstrative effect kept up for a succession of hours, by far exceeds any effort of a like kind that the most enthusiastic of my own countrymen would be likely to find themselves equal to, considering the important part which strong waters play in their annual festival: whereas the demonstrative Chinamen carry on their rejoicings under no stronger stimulant, as a general rule, than tea; hence their capacity to prolong them.

By the morning all was quiet. On going into the town, the streets were deserted and the shops all closed. From the interior, however, of many of them the hum of voices combined with the jingling of money could be heard; indicating that the customary settling of accounts was not neglected in the general hilarity of the period.

In the afternoon, being curious to see if any of the shopkeepers were able to resist the temptation of the barbarian dollar, I made a circuit of the streets most frequented by Europeans, and the only shops found open, were three of the curiosity shops that have been doing an extensive trade with the officers of the garrison in enamels[*] and jade ornaments, their owners foregoing the national attachment to the "olo custom," in hopes of their self-denial meeting with a profitable return.

Yesterday Colonel Neale found in one of these shops a white porcelain vessel resembling a soup tureen, having gilt margins, and the lid bearing an inscription in Roman letters round it, wide apart, showing it to be of undoubted European origin. He bought it for a few dollars, and after spending some time over it, he made out that the letters meant Maria Juliana. This gave little or no clue to its origin; but as there was a large F and V on the side of the vessel, the colonel set about looking up all the Ferdinands and Fredericks to be found in history, and at last his perseverance was rewarded by finding that Frederick V. of

---

[*] The composition of the enamel, the art of making which the Chinese are said to have lost, was, according to one of the Jesuit missionaries, oxide of lead and tin, salt of tartar, pounded glass, and colouring matter. Copper appears to have been the material most commonly selected for the enamelling process.

Denmark, in the year 1736 took for his wife Maria Juliana, daughter of the Duke of Brunswick. It is not easy to say how it found its way into China.

The makers of figures of painted clay are beginning to mould English soldiers very well. One of these artists drew my attention to a pair, saying—" Inglice very brave;" he then went through the motion of firing a gun, adding—" Ping pung Tartar weillo;" meaning that the Tartars bolted as soon as our soldiers fired on them—a statement not strictly in accordance with fact, as one of our regiments fired a volley from their " Enfields " at four hundred yards, with so little effect that the Tartar cavalry did not move, but complacently looked on ; the amount of damage done to them being about the same as if the volley had been one with blank ammunition. So much for weapons of precision.

The government at Peking would seem to have heard of the doings of the curiosity dealers at Tien-tsin, as a decree has been received by the local authorities, directing all articles in the possession of Chinese that have belonged to Yuen-ming-yuen, to be given up by the tenth of the month —an order likely to be "more honoured in the breach than the observance."

February 11th.—In the streets mandarins are met going in state to pay official visits accompanied by all their retainers. The higher orders are going about all day in their chairs, paying their new-year calls, and the middle classes are similarly engaged on foot, remarkably well dressed in fur robes, black satin boots, with soles about an inch thick, and black silk hats, the turned-up portion sometimes lined with fur. In the streets, every few yards you see them exchanging new year's salutations with each other. Nothing can exceed their politeness. They first make a profound bow, at the same time clasping their hands and lowering them towards their knees. As they raise themselves from the bow profound, they shake their clasped hands towards one another, accompanying the movement by several short bows. At first the proceeding looks rather ridiculous, and reminds one of a couple of game cocks going through the preliminary motions with their heads before commencing actual hostilities. After a little time the eye gets accustomed to it, and the apparent absurdity wears off.

Yesterday a large number of the inhabitants went to the temples to worship the tablets of their ancestors. This is one of their most cherished annual customs, the ancestral tablet being of all things in China the most revered.

February 12*th*.—Notwithstanding the advanced period of the winter, and the alleged commencement of the Chinese spring, there is no permanent modification of the cold, which to-day is intense; the thermometer during the night having been 2° below zero in the hospital, and 6° below zero on board the "Slaney" gunboat, frozen in seven miles down the river.

In the streets all day beggars were going about in small organised mobs, extorting charity from the dwelling-houses and shops; refusing to move until money was given to them, keeping up while they were waiting a monotonous noise by the knocking together of pieces of hard wood. This proceeding reminded me of the custom which prevails at the new year in Scotland, of bands of songsters going about in disguise, under the name of "Guisers," from house to house, extorting money much after the fashion of the Tien-tsin beggars, by continued singing and noise.

A story is in circulation at present, stated to have come from a reliable source, that on the allied forces withdrawing from Peking after the signing of the treaty, all the Chinese troops within the city were turned out, cannon discharged, and an imaginary pursuit gone through. Immediately afterwards reports were circulated of the defeat and flight of the barbarians. Mr. Adkins, however, who remained in Peking after the troops were withdrawn, and who has been there ever since, has made no mention of such an occurrence, which could hardly have taken place without his knowledge, therefore I am inclined to believe that the story has no more truthful origin than the report which, by a mail lately received, appears to have found its way into the English newspapers relative to Mr. Adkins himself—his assassination at Peking, immediately on the departure of the army, being detailed with all the confidence of an undoubted authenticity. Mr. Adkins, up to the period of Mr. Wade's proceeding to Peking early last month, resided alone in the large building called the Lee-ang-kung-foo, or palace of the Duke of Lee-ang, which is to be the future British Legation, and during the two months he was thus alone, received neither insult nor molestation from the Chinese, beyond being occasionally shouted at by children, and called some non-complimentary Chinese name commonly applied to foreigners.

CHAPTER XXI.

New Year's Visit from Chang—Injudicious snowballing—Ingenious toymaker—Robberies—Literary examinations—Peking Foreign Office—Seal of the late Emperor for sale—French loot—Rent dispute—Funeral obsequies—Visit to Chang—Chinese theatre—Restaurants—Feast of Lanterns—Presentation of the Victoria Cross—Brigade drill—Chinese opinions thereon—Ice commences to break up—News from Mr. Morrison—Chinese General reduced to the ranks—Sang-ko-lin-sin—Effect of electrical changes on the sick—Health of the Seiks compared with that of Europeans—Legation Guards detailed for Peking—Break-up of the ice—Prussian Diplomatic Mission—Commercial prospects of Tien-tsin—The Legations proceed to Peking—Evacuation of Tien-tsin.

February 13*th*.—Chang, the great salt merchant, and proprietor of the buildings applied to hospital purposes, called on the medical officers this afternoon, and left his card in accordance with the custom of the season. The visit being one of ceremony, he came in full mandarin state, wearing his pink button * and peacock's feather; also his official silk robe, embroidered with devices in gold, worn over an under dress of fur. His conveyance was a sedan chair of goodly size, covered with blue cloth, the interior lined with fur, and carried by four bearers. A white-buttoned mandarin preceded the chair on horseback, and three

* The pink coral is the highest class button, and is generally only attained through distinguished literary, political, or military services; Chang, however, has had the button conferred upon him as a reward for his great benevolence and for the pecuniary aid he has been able to lend in troubled times to the government at Tien-tsin. He is stated to be illiterate, and to have been originally a coolie (porter) in a pastrycook's shop.

mounted attendants followed it. Chang expressed a desire to look at the alterations that had been made on his property to render it suited to English tastes during the cold weather, but he was speedily satisfied. He held up his hands when he saw the metamorphosis which had taken place, and said that he would not look at any more, as the sight was by no means a pleasant one to him; the destruction of his property having been wholesale, and in many respects most wanton; an enormous quantity of elaborate and valuable carving having been recklessly pulled down, made away with in various ways, and no small portion of it used as firewood.

The weather being fine and clear, with a good deal of snow on the ground, some officers of the garrison amused themselves for a considerable portion of the day by snowballing Chinamen. They took up positions on the ramparts over the gates, and had little boys employed bringing them up relays of snowballs in baskets. Every Chinaman that passed was thus pelted, and the more respectable he was, the greater was the shower of snowballs sent at him. Amongst others subjected to this not very manly or considerate treatment (which a Chinaman cannot be expected to view as a joke), was one of the chief civic officials, who went immediately to the English consul, and made an indignant protest against the proceeding.

February 14th.—Last night Mr. Bruce received his first English mail since the river has closed, by the French courier from Che-foo. No letters for the army have arrived, nor does there seem to be much prospect of any until the navigation re-opens at Taku early next month.

February 15th.—The Chinese are engaged at present making preparations for the feast of lanterns. The streets are crowded with men going about with every species of grotesque design that it is possible to make answer the purposes of a lantern.

A report is in circulation in Peking, that the Emperor is

dead. This report has been officially contradicted; at the same time, there is reason to believe that the Emperor is seriously ill at Je-ho. The Prince of Kung also is indisposed, and obliged in consequence to defer giving an audience to Count Kleiskousky; his ailment, however, is not serious, being only an eruption on the face.

Referring to the injudicious and somewhat unfeeling amusement of certain British officers noticed yesterday, the following Brigade Order has been issued:—

"GARRISON OFFICE,
"15th *February*, 1861.

"GARRISON ORDER.

"It having been brought to the notice of the Brigadier that some young officers have occasionally ill-used Chinamen, by striking them or pushing them in the street, and snowballing respectable people;

"Commanding officers will be good enough to caution their officers against such conduct in future.

"It is highly desirable that the Chinese should have no reason to complain of their treatment by the British, now that peace is established, and the Brigadier will take the most serious notice of any complaint brought before him."

This order attributes the general ill-treatment of Chinamen to young officers; but I regret to say that they have had the example too frequently set them by their seniors, more than one of whom were engaged in the recent snowballing.

February 16th.—Fatigue parties are now employed filling up "stink ditch," where it borders on the barracks of the 67th Regiment, the material for the purpose being procured in a manner hardly fair to the Chinese; namely, by dismantling the ramparts of the neighbouring portion of the city wall which previously were in very good order. While the soldiers were thus employed yesterday, they came on a human skeleton in perfect preservation, some feet from the surface.

The discovery occasioned considerable excitement amongst the men, and they were with difficulty restrained from commencing a series of excavations in the vicinity, in hopes of finding treasure concealed in the wall.

February 17th.—Count Kleiskousky was presented to the Prince of Kung on the 15th instant. The Count proceeds about Peking in a sedan chair borne by eight bearers, to which objections have been raised by the authorities, on the ground that that number of bearers is a privilege only of those belonging to the Imperial family. The French Legation, however, as representing an imperial power, are determined to push the eight-bearer question, and of course, under the pressure of compulsion, the Chinese will have no resource but to yield; in fact, not only in this, but in a great many other questions likely to arise, to adopt the adage of " what cannot be cured must be endured."

This afternoon I met Tsung-how, the Commissioner of Customs at Tien-tsin, proceeding on an official visit, accompanied by several mounted attendants, and preceded by the beating of gongs, and by a score of men carrying flags and red boards bearing in gilt characters the various titles possessed by Tsung-how, and the various offices he has filled under the state. In front of the procession some of his retainers were clearing the way, and calling out " Ta-jin" (great man). I met also several carts coming into town from the country laden with sacks of flour. The carts, which are two-wheeled, are drawn by a large bullock in the shaft, with three other bullocks harnessed a-breast in front.

Last night Dr. Lamprey was called upon to visit an old Chinese gentleman suffering from dysentery. His family having heard of the skill of the English physicians, applied to the consul (Mr. Mongan) to aid them in procuring the services of one of them, and he gave them a note to Dr. Lamprey, who has some knowledge now of the northern dialect.

February 18th.—Walking on the city wall with Dr. Galbraith, we found near the tower over the east gate, a quantity of old Chinese munitions of war lying on the rampart, consisting of iron helmets, rude scale armour, formed of wadded calico, with thin plates of iron arranged after the manner of scales between the layers of the calico; large wall pieces loading at the breech, but now out of repair; bamboo tubes, with a coating of rope, intended for the projection of stones by gunpowder; quivers for arrows, and small very antique-looking cannon. These constituted the remains of some old armoury in the upper story of the tower over the gate, which has lately been turned out to make room for some ammunition of our own. The Chinese, like European nations, seem to have given up the use of armour, as we came across no indications of its being worn on the field during the late war.

February 19th.—In one of the streets near the river, I was much amused at the ingenuity and dexterity displayed by a manufacturer of toys. He was sitting behind a portable counter, having a soft composition like putty before him, of various colours, which he made into toy figures wearing dresses of brilliant hue, with astonishing rapidity. The figures represented men or women blowing through a glass trumpet, from which, by pulling a reed that communicated with it, an abrupt musical sound was produced. Each figure took about three minutes to make, and I never witnessed such delicacy and rapidity of touch—the figures being perfect models of what they were meant to represent.

Several robberies have occurred of late at the Military Train barracks in the Confucian temple, which appears to offer peculiar facilities for the operations of light-fingered Celestials. Last night Lieutenant Bruce had nearly the whole of his personal effects stolen, including Crimean medals and the Legion of Honour. This makes the eighth robbery from the quarters of officers of the Military Train during the winter. In connection with these robberies, some amusing incidents have occurred. Captain Williams, in the middle of the night hearing a noise in the room, jumped out of bed, struck a light, and drew his sword, upon which a Chinaman popped his head out from beneath the bed, and with most perfect self-possession gave him the customary salutation of "Chin-chin;" his politeness, however, I believe, did not save him from being handed over to the police. Mr. Fleming, the veterinary surgeon, and his servant, were for some days unable to understand how it was, that when charcoal was placed on the fire, it disappeared as soon as the room was unoccupied, before it could have been burned. The mystery was at last solved: the Chinamen had made a hole from the outside into the chimney, and as soon as they knew there was nobody in the room, they put their hands down and removed whatever fuel was worth taking. Lieutenant Aplin, lying in bed one morning, happened to glance at his brass Chinese kettle, which was on the fire at the time; suddenly he saw the laws of gravity reversed, and his kettle, like Mr. Home, the spiritualist, floating in the air, and then disappear up the chimney—a like expedient having been adopted for its abstraction as for Mr. Fleming's fuel. The Chinese police magistrate (the Chee-hee-en) is endeavouring to find the thieves who have been engaged in these robberies, especially those concerned in the last one, which is the most serious of the lot, and he declares that if he succeeds in bringing the offender to justice he will take his head off. He has his staff of detectives now on the look out. The Chinese name for this class of police rendered into English, means swift horse.

The annual examinations for literary honours have commenced in Tien-tsin, and the Chinese municipal authorities are very anxious that we should give them up this same Confucian temple, as it is necessary for the graduates, after passing, to go there and worship. It is not practicable, however, at the present time to comply with their request, owing to the difficulty and expense connected with the finding and fitting up of new quarters for the officers, men, and horses of the Military Train.

February 20th.—The Prince of Kung has sent a communication to Mr. Bruce, calling his attention to the disturbed state of affairs on the Yang-tse-kiang, and leaving it to him to decide whether, under the circumstances represented, he will at present carry out the settlement of the consulates at the new treaty ports of Chin-kiang-foo, Ku-kiang, and Han-kow, as already has been determined shall be done in spring. The Emperor is expected to return to Peking on the 18th of next month (28th March), and orders have been issued for the restoration of Yuen-ming-yuen.*

The establishment of a foreign office at Peking has been completed under the name of "The Court for the administration of the affairs of foreign nations." The members are the Prince of Kung, Kwei, and Wan.

February 21st.—The seal of the late Emperor, Tan-kwang, was brought to the French Legation to-day by Baron de Meritens. It is formed out of a piece of massive green jade, of oblong shape, measuring six inches by four. The handle is in the form of an animal of fabulous configuration. The face of the seal bears the inscription "Tan-kwang, Emperor, his seal," and on each of its four sides are comments in gilt characters, on the duties of an emperor, and maxims relating thereto, taken chiefly from Kien-lung, his grandfather. Tan-kwang was the reigning Emperor during the first Chinese war in 1840. The seal belongs to a French artillery soldier, and was taken by him from the Yuen-ming-yuen. He wishes to sell it, and asks twelve hundred taels for it, or about four hundred pounds sterling.†

* When I was last in Peking (April, 1862), no steps had been taken up to that time to carry out this order; the buildings remaining as the conflagration left them.

† This seal became the property of Mr. Bruce, who purchased it a few days afterwards for five hundred dollars.

Another artillery soldier has the seal of the late Empress, which is of solid gold.

The plunder of the French army is said to be a good deal exaggerated as regards the mass of the army, though there is no doubt that a large amount of very valuable property fell into the hands of two companies of marine infantry and a battery of artillery, that were the first to enter the palace.

A Chinaman who happened to be about the hospital to-day was offered by some one a silk dress for sale, having the Imperial dragon on it in gold embroidery. He twisted his tail round his head, and indicated by pantomime and the few words of English he knew, that should he purchase it, and the article be found in his possession, he would be sent to Peking and his head taken off.

A small rent being paid to the owners of the houses occupied by the troops, a dispute has arisen respecting the right to receive this rent, between the proprietors respectively of the ground and the houses where the head-quarters of Fane's Horse are. Both of them claim the rent, but declare their willingness to be satisfied provided that neither is paid, and the quarters considered free.

February 22*nd*.—A thaw is gradually becoming established, but as yet no marked effect has been produced on the river. Some officers of the 31st, who came up from Taku to-day, report that the ice there is not yet beginning to break up.

I met another very large funeral procession which crossed the river and passed through the suburbs on the opposite side. I followed, in hopes of seeing the mode of interment. On arriving at the outskirts of the suburb, the men bearing the flags and other paraphernalia* of the procession, along with the bands of music, drew up on each side of the road until the coffin, borne on a gaily decorated palanquin carried

---

* These appear to the western eye to be much the same whether the nature of the procession be funereal or matrimonial.

by thirty men, passed between them. The bier was then placed on the ground, and the coffin removed from it by red ropes placed under it and suspended from shoulder poles, also painted red. On the lid there was a long inscription in white characters, with the exception of the upper ones, which were red. The massive lid was removed, an inner boarding concealing the corpse. This inner lid was covered over with cement to make it air-tight, and the outer lid was then fitted on. Large nails were now introduced into holes previously made for them in the lid. One of the nails was of peculiar shape, and had several pieces of red, black and blue calico hanging from it. The chief mourner came forward, and taking a hammer in his hand gave a few knocks on the nail; and thus, as it is with us the last sad office of relatives to close the eyes of those near and dear to them, so with the Chinese would it seem to be to knock the first nail into the coffin. On the chief mourner retiring from the side of the coffin, the carpenters set to work and quickly knocked the other nails in. By this time the component parts of the procession, and all those who had attended the funeral, had left, the two chief mourners only remaining. The coffin apparently was going to be taken some little distance, as they got into a cart and drove into the country, the coffin being carried after them by eight coolies. It continued to be suspended by red ropes from red shoulder poles. This colour is the "happy" one in China.

February 23rd.—In the afternoon Dr. Galbraith, Dr. Lieberhman, of the French army, Mr. Moffitt, and myself, paid a visit to Chang at his residence, near the north-west angle of the city. The way lay through a series of narrow streets and tortuous lanes. On arriving at the entrance to Chang's house, our attention was attracted by something unusual going on in the house on the opposite side of the street, which proved to be funeral obsequies. The outer court-yard was matted over and a temporary altar erected, before which six Buddhist priests were chanting service in the presence of a number of white-clad mourners. The coffin, with the corpse in it, was in a room in an inner courtyard, and in front of the door a table was placed, having candles burning on it, and a quantity of food laid out. In another room in the same court, a number of females in the mourning garb were seen. Returning to the street, we saw about twenty little boys in gay dresses, with circular lanterns in their hands. They went through a variety of dancing evolutions, but whether they were in connection with the funeral service going on in the neighbouring house or with the feast of lanterns, which commences to-morrow, we could not ascertain.

Having sent our cards in to Chang, we were ushered into a large room handsomely decorated, and furnished with armchairs provided with cushions, and having small tables between them. A large brass stove, in which charcoal was burning, stood in the centre of the floor, which is of stone. In a few minutes Chang came in, and welcomed us with great cordiality, conveying through Mr. Moffitt (who has already acquired some colloquial knowledge of Chinese) the pleasure it gave him to see us at his house. He was dressed in a fur lined silk robe, and wore a small skull cap of embroidered silk. Tea, fruit, and sweetmeats were immediately brought in ; after we had partaken of which, Chang conducted us over the numerous buildings constituting his family establishment, consisting of two sets of courts, separated from each other by a passage between. These courts, or small squares, are eight in number, there being four in each set, arranged one behind the other. On this principle all houses of the better classes in China are built. Each court contains three houses. We were shown the kitchen, a large and well-appointed one, in which a number of cooks were busily employed. We also inspected the larder, which is well-stored, and contains a good supply of preserved hams. The various courts are at present fitted-up all round with oblong lanterns, made like picture frames, only deeper, and the front covered with tastefully-painted gauze, intended to be illuminated during the feast of lanterns.

Chang has about fifty relatives, who live on the premises, and are entirely supported by him. One of these dependents was sick, and Chang asked Mr. Moffitt to look at him. He was labouring under bronchitis, and on Mr. Moffitt's undertaking to relieve him, Chang sent one of his servants to the hospital to get the medicine prescribed. On taking our departure Chang, in accordance with Chinese courtesy, insisted on accompanying us to the outer door.

After leaving Chang's we walked through the suburb bordering on the grand canal, and went into a large theatre that is a good deal frequented. The outside was placarded with red play-bills, but no performance was going on, in consequence of to-day being the anniversary of the death of one of the Emperors. The *corps dramatique* were found behind the scenes playing Chinese cards, which are 124 in the pack. The game seemed to us a most complicated one, and proved a long way beyond our western comprehensions. The audience portion of the theatre is fitted-up with tables and chairs, refreshments being furnished during the performance, after the manner of the *cafés chantants* of the French.

In the neighbourhood of the theatre we went into several Chinese restaurants, with the completeness of the arrangements of which and the good style of the cookery we were much pleased. In one of these establishments, suited to the middle classes, we had the curiosity to wait and see what a man paid for a liberal meal that he was eating, consisting of a bowl of rice, a vegetable stew with Chinese macaroni in it, two meat pasties, tea and pickles. For the whole of this, which was more than he was able to consume, he paid only thirty cash, or three half-pence sterling. He gave the waiter five cash, which increased the expense of dinner one farthing.

February 24*th*.—This morning, at daylight, three guns

were fired by the Chinese, which turned out to be a salute for a new Tautai who had just arrived from Peking, and was then entering the town.

The feast of lanterns has commenced, but the municipal authorities have decided that this year there shall be no night procession, as disturbances might arise from the number of foreign soldiers going about the streets. They have therefore prudently determined to restrict the lantern festivities to the illumination of the interior of their premises and reciprocal hospitality, of which there is a great deal at the present season.

February 25th.—Last night we were a good deal disturbed by frequent loud reports like the firing of cannon. They were caused by the explosion of large crackers about the size and shape of a twelve-pounder Armstrong shell, composed of hardened clay filled with gunpowder, and ignited by a slow match passing down a narrow opening like a touch-hole.

February 27th.—The weather having again become fine, a parade took place this afternoon. The troops having been formed into three sides of a square on the plain facing the south, between the city wall and Sang-ko-lin-sin's Folly, Lieutenant Heathcote was called out from the ranks of the 60th, and Brigadier Staveley read the *Gazette* conferring the Victoria Cross upon him for gallant conduct at the siege of Delhi, for which decoration he had been selected by the officers of his regiment. The Brigadier also read the official communication from the War-office, and made a short address to the troops prior to fastening the Cross on Lieutenant Heathcote's breast.

The principal Chinese officials of Tien-tsin having been invited to attend, were present, and included the new Tautai, a remarkably gentlemanly and intelligent looking man of middle age, Tsung-how (Commissioner of Customs), Chung (the Chee-hee-en, or district magistrate), the Salt Commissioner, and the Brigadier-General Ching-lung, who commanded the great northern fort that bore the brunt of the naval attack on the 21st of August, and had its magazine exploded by a shell from one of the French gunboats. He is a fine massive-looking, elderly man, wearing a pink button and high-class peacock's feather.* His head-dress, the ordinary silk hat turned up in front and lined with light brown fur. He was dressed in a dark blue satin jacket over a rich light blue silk robe, both of them lined with white fur. The Brigadier-General and the other Chinese officials arrived on the ground in sedan chairs, each accompanied by a number of followers, both mounted and on foot. They then got out of their chairs and mounted ponies they had sent on before.

After the presentation of the Victoria Cross, Brigadier Staveley put the troops through a series of brigade movements, in which the Chinese visitors seemed to be much interested. When the nature of the manœuvre of forming square to receive cavalry was explained to them, they characterised it as "a most excellent idea," and admitted it to be one that had not occurred to themselves. Brigadier-General Ching-lung expressed himself as much struck with the artillery and Seik cavalry; the rapid movements of the former, so different from the pace at which the ponderous field-guns of the Chinese move, astonished him much. The Chee-hee-en appeared to be specially interested, and in conversation with one of the interpreters, without committing himself to any admission of moral superiority on our part, he candidly admitted that we had the advantage of them physically, and that it was folly their having entertained the idea that they were equal to a contest of arms with us.

The charge of the Seik cavalry was very picturesque, and

---

* The grades of the Order of the Peacock's Feather are indicated by the number of "eyes," which are formed by an arrangement of two or more feathers. A single feather is the lowest grade in the Order, as it has only one "eye."

excited great admiration amongst all classes of the Chinese—the wild yell of the Seiks and their irregular mode of advance being more in accordance with their preconceived notions of military effect than the more regular and precise movements of the infantry. Tsung-how was a good deal puzzled to understand how the Armstrong guns, from being open at both ends, could form efficient machines of projection, until the mechanism by which the breach is closed after loading was explained to him.

Immense crowds of the Chinese population were present; every one of the large funereal tumuli with which the plain is dotted that commanded a view of the troops being crowded with dense masses, looking on with the most intense interest at the different evolutions.

February 28th.—At the French Legation this evening I made the acquaintance of M. Pecheroff, the astronomer to the Russian Mission at Peking, and talking with him about the probabilities of the Emperor's return, he told me that during a three years' residence at Peking he has only been able to get a glance at the Emperor once, and that was a very imperfect one, obtained by looking through the key-hole of a shop as he passed. No one is allowed to be in the street except the troops lining it, and all the windows and shops are closed as the Imperial procession passes—the punishment being severe for any one who ventures to play "Peeping Tom," and look at the sacred person of his majesty.

March 1st.—At Taku, outside the bar, the ice has broken up, and it is hardly safe now to walk across the river between the forts. The "Clown" gunboat, however, cannot yet get out from where she has been frozen in since December.

Letters were received to-day from Mr. Morrison and Captain Harcourt, who left for Che-foo early in January. They appear to have had a very interesting journey, having visited numerous parts of the country where Europeans had never been seen before. They were on the whole treated with great civility, though frequently (and very naturally) followed by immense crowds, numbering sometimes as many as fifteen hundred people. On one or two occasions they were taken up before the local authorities, on suspicion of being connected with rebels; but as soon as it was understood that they were Englishmen they were at once released and kindly treated. The people in many parts of the country they passed through were impressed with the belief that the English were coming to their assistance against the rebels, and had a *canard* that Sang-ko-lin-sin had in the first instance refused their aid, but had latterly been soliciting it. Mr. Morrison and Captain Harcourt had a near chance of meeting Sang-ko-lin-sin, as they arrived at a town that he had left only three hours previously.

We learn from Peking that everything continues to go on satisfactorily, with the exception of the Emperor's return, which appears to be very uncertain.

Sang-ko-lin-sin has been again defeated in Shan-tung, and report says handed over to the Board of Punishments to explain the causes of his want of success. Jui-lin, his lieutenant-general, has returned to Peking in disgrace, and has been degraded by the Board of Punishments to the position of a common bannerman, at three taels a month —in other words, reduced to the ranks on a rate of pay of about 7½d. a day. He left Peking in September last, a Secretary of State for War.

Of Sang-ko-lin-sin, Mr. Adkins says report speaks very favourably. He is said to be an honest, upright man, and much respected by his army, as he does not peculate in their pay or rations, thereby differing widely from other Chinese generals, to whom commissariat peculation is a regular source of emolument. Sang-ko-lin-sin went down early in the winter to Shan-tung with about five thousand men, the remnant of his army, and was there joined by militia which increased his force to about fifteen thousand men; but the latter being in great part a rabble indifferently armed, he has been unable successfully as yet to cope with the rebels, who are represented as existing in formidable numbers. It is also stated that their advance on Peking is only prevented by the knowledge that there is an English and French force occupying Tien-tsin, which, judging from what has occurred at Shanghai in the case of the Taepings, would in all probability oppose them also should they attack the capital.

Shung-pow, who has already been referred to as the general who commanded the Chinese army at the action of Pa-lee-chow, and to whom on that occasion Jui-lin was second in command, is now at Peking with a force of some four thousand men, and he is chiefly employed hunting up plunder in the neighbouring villages that has been taken from the Yuen-ming-yuen. It is stated that he has found a considerable quantity concealed in the houses of villagers, and that a good many heads have been forfeited in consequence.

March 7th.—The morning, which was remarkably fine, became suddenly overcast about ten o'clock, becoming dark and lurid. The electrometer was greatly disturbed; the electricity coming down in one continued stream, and the sand rose into the air as if drawn up by magnetic influence, being in much greater quantities than the amount of wind could account for.

March 8th.—Though the air is now clear and the weather fine, the same disturbed state of the atmospheric electricity continues as prevailed the whole of yesterday, and it would appear to have exercised an injurious influence on several cases of sickness, judging from the sudden aggravation of symptoms which set in concurrently with it. In two cases that have come under my observation, a very remarkable effect has been produced on the nervous system; in one of them a sensation as if the blood was circulating backwards, accompanied by spasmodic startings, and inability to remain in the recumbent posture for any length of time, without the desire to spring up.*

March 9th.—It is worthy of observation, that while the sickness and mortality amongst the European troops are very considerable, the Seiks are wonderfully healthy. Under ordinary circumstances, they have only half a pound of meat allowed them per week, but since the cold weather set in the allowance has been increased to a whole pound. The bulk of their diet consists of wheaten flour baked into unleavened bread. Dr. Daly, the surgeon of the corps, informs me that the men have enjoyed total immunity from pulmonary complaints, their chief ailment being slight attacks of ephemeral fever. They have also been perfectly free from small-pox. About one-half of them have been inoculated, the remainder are unprotected. They do not believe in vaccination, and are averse to submitting themselves to the operation. They cannot understand sitting round an ordinary fire-place, but must have the full benefit of the fire, smoke included, consequently they sit round an open fire in the centre of the room.

Some of the Indian followers of Fane's Horse (of whom there are 300) are suffering severely from frost bite; one man has lost both his feet. No proper provision was made at the commencement of the winter for keeping their feet warm, by giving them long boots like those of the troops, and such a delay occurred before Tartar boots were procured for them, that the mischief was done before their feet received adequate protection.

March 10th.—Preparations have commenced for the journey of the English and French Legations to Peking, there to be permanently established. An embassy guard of twelve men of the 31st, under Lieutenant Gow, has been detailed in garrison orders for Mr. Bruce, and the men are now

---

* The case referred to was one of a chronic and serious nature, and the disturbed state of the nervous system disappeared when the atmosphere recovered its normal electrical condition.

undergoing instruction in riding at the Artillery Barracks. A similar number of gendarmes have been told off to be stationed with the French Legation.

March 11*th.*—The weather is now clear and mild. A change is beginning to take place on the ice. People are still crossing on it above the bridge of boats, but about three quarters of a mile lower down a fracture has taken place in the ice, and the river got the better of it so quickly, that by the afternoon that portion was clear of ice; a general break-up may soon follow. This is the last day of the nine periods into which the cold weather is divided, and the Chinese calculation, judging from the present season, would seem a very accurate one.

March 12*th.*—At noon a slight movement was observed on the ice opposite the town, when all at once, like the transformation scene in a pantomime, the whole mass began to break up and move away. In a short time the river was clear, and by three o'clock, though large masses of ice came floating down from above, yet the river was covered with boats and all the ferries at work—so little time was there lost in re-establishing water communication.

March 16*th.*—Some information being required with reference to the question of water transport to Peking, it has been ascertained that the Peiho will be very shallow in the neighbourhood of Tung-chow (twelve miles from Peking) for a month to come, as the snow has not yet begun to melt on the hills to the north of Peking.

Herr Von Brandt, secretary to the Prussian diplomatic mission, which has lately been negociating a treaty in Japan, arrived to-day, to prepare the Chinese Government for the arrival of an envoy from the King of Prussia, for the purpose of opening up diplomatic relations. As M. de Brandt has no interpreter, Mr. Bruce has allowed Mr. Gibson to go to Tsung-how, and request him to grant M. de Brandt an interview. Tsung-how, on hearing of Prussia, said, " Pollucia qua" (Prussia country), where is that?" and on being told that it is an important European country, he asked if it was one having any ships, and also, if it was a country that we had any interest in, or connection with; evidently fishing for information to aid him in deciding whether it would be desirable or not to be civil to the envoy's representative. The information he received from Mr. Gibson convinced him that it would be desirable.

March 17*th*.—Met M. de Brandt at the French Legation. He has just come from Shanghai, where the Prussian mission now is. It left Yeddo after the murder of Mr. Enskin (secretary to the American Legation), who was assassinated by the Japanese as he was returning home from dining with Count Eulenberg, the Prussian envoy.

March 19*th*.—Mr. Wade arrived this morning from Peking, to accompany Mr. Bruce to the capital. Sang-ko-lin-sin, up to the latest dates from Shan-tung, continued unequal to making head against the rebels. He has no artillery, it seems—and this fact accounts for an application which the authorities here made a few days ago to Brigadier Staveley, that they might be allowed to dig up and remove some guns that, prior to our taking possession of Tien-tsin, had been buried in the court of the Tautai's Yamun, at present occupied by the Royal Artillery.

Some fears are entertained of a famine at Peking, as all the ordinary supplies are getting used up. As soon as their exhaustion is officially announced, the Emperor orders the government granaries to be thrown open, and the people supplied with rice and other grains at a cheap rate; then it is that the famine is feared, because it is more than probable that the granaries will be found empty, owing to the notorious corruptness of the mandarins charged with the care of them.

March 21*st*.—Prior to leaving Tien-tsin, I made some inquiries amongst the mercantile community regarding the commercial prospects of the place in connection with the opening of the port to foreign trade. From what I can learn, calico goods, chiefly in the form known as "shirtings" (piece cotton), will be the chief article of import. The exports, again, will be for the most part peas, beans and other grains that come up the Peiho in junks from Nu-che-wang. At Tien-tsin they will be trans-shipped in foreign vessels to the south of China, the direct export trade in "foreign bottoms" being contrary to the recent treaty, this provision having been introduced into it for the protection of the junk trade, as Chinese merchants now much prefer shipping goods in foreign vessels to trusting them in their own. They are also beginning to realize the advantages of marine insurance, which they cannot avail themselves of when they ship in junks. It is also probable that a small amount of tallow and wool will be exported annually, and there is little doubt that a considerable export trade in ice with the south of China, and possibly with Singapore and India, will gradually be developed. The Chinese merchants at Tien-tsin are represented as having been a little shy at first in entering into commercial transactions with foreigners. They are doing so however more readily now, and as their confidence increases a very considerable trade is anticipated.

At noon on the 22nd of March, 1861, their Excellencies the Honourable Sir Frederick Bruce, K.C.B., and M. de Bourboulon, along with Mr. Wade, C.B., and the writer of this narrative as surgeon to Her Majesty's Legation, left Tien-tsin for Peking. A party of gendarmerie and mounted French Artillerymen formed the escort. Madame de Bourboulon, who had but partially recovered from a severe and dangerous illness, accompanied her husband to Peking, performing the journey (to an invalid a very fatiguing one) in a sedan chair. Four days afterwards, the flags of England and France were peacefully flying in Peking ; the entry of the envoys and their escorts had been accomplished without the slightest indications of a hostile feeling either from the populace or the Government.

Tien-tsin remained in the occupation of the English and

French forces during the summer of 1861. The hot season was a very unhealthy one, and the allied troops suffered severely, the mortality amongst the English troops being, at the end of the year 1861, at the rate of between sixty and seventy in the 1000. Everything was done that sanitary science could suggest to improve the condition of the men and render them as resistant as possible to the morbific influences prevailing. Sanitary science, however, proved totally unequal to coping with an epidemic constitution of the atmosphere which was not confined to Tien-tsin, but was equally active at Peking, and which it is not unreasonable to suppose was in some way connected with the large comet that made its appearance in July, the more so as it was shortly after its advent that the serious sickness commenced.

At the end of the summer of 1861, everything having gone on satisfactorily at Peking, the occupying force was greatly reduced, and Tien-tsin was held during the winter by Govan's battery, the 31st and 67th Regiments, and the company of Engineers. The whole of the French troops were withdrawn prior to the commencement of the winter, with the exception of a detachment of Marine Infantry left in the north Taku fort to represent the French occupation.

In the spring of 1862, Sir Frederick Bruce decided that Tien-tsin should be evacuated, and the British occupation on the Peiho reduced to holding the south Taku fort with a small force.

In March of the same year Sir John Michel sailed for England, giving up the command of the troops in China to Brigadier-General Staveley, C.B. At this time the Taepings had recommenced their incursions in the neighbourhood of Shanghai, and as the city and foreign settlement were considered in danger, Admiral Hope, from motives of pure philanthropy, lent his aid to the disciplined Chinese force that had recently been organized by the American adventurer known as General Ward, and commenced active operations against the Taepings, pending a reference to Sir Frederick Bruce, who, taking into consideration all the circumstances of the case, sanctioned such aggressive measures being adopted as would clear the country of Taepings for a radius of thirty miles round Shanghai. The occupation of Taku has continued up to the present time (August, 1863), more to oblige the Chinese Government than as a political necessity, the Chinese being now as averse to our withdrawing our protecting influence from the mouth of the Peiho, as they were three years ago that we should approach it. This desire that our occupation should continue, arises from a dread entertained by the Imperial Government of a combination between the pirates on the coast and the Taepings, and of their making a descent by water on Peking. As Ning-po has been retaken from the latter this is not now a probable occurrence, though it was so at one time. It is therefore not likely that any British troops will be exposed to the cold and dreariness of a fourth winter, ice-bound at Taku.

JAPAN.

INTRODUCTION.

An appointment on special service under the Government of India, which it pleased the Secretary-at-War, on the recommendation of the Earl of Elgin, to authorise my accepting, led to my remaining in China after the embarkation for England, in July, 1863, of the 31st Regiment, of which I was then surgeon. An opportunity having been offered me while thus in China of visiting Japan, I obtained leave to defer my departure for India, and to avail myself of the only chance I should probably ever have of seeing this beautiful, and comparatively little known, country. Of this visit, the following narrative is the record. It is a mere Journal of what I saw and heard during a sojourn in the country so brief that, at the time I left it, the thought never occurred to me of publishing the information I had acquired. Everything, however, relating to Japan and its people has now become so interesting, that I am induced to give even these imperfect notes to the public.

The following summary of the events which immediately preceded my visit is necessary for the right understanding of the state of affairs.

Early in January, 1862, a Japanese embassy embarked at Yeddo on board Her Majesty's steam-ship "Odin," flying the broad pendant of Commodore Lord John Hay, C.B. The purpose of this embassy was to visit the different European Courts having diplomatic relations with Japan, and to request their consent to certain treaty obligations being deferred, which the Tycoon had entered into with them; the most important of these being the opening to foreign trade of Osaca, the chief town on the shores of the inland sea; and of the port of Miaco, the capital of the empire, and the residence of the Mikado, or spiritual ruler.

The ambassadors having reached Europe *viâ* Suez, succeeded in the object of their mission. While they were receiving every mark of kindness and attention from the European Powers, the Ministers of England, France, and America were residing at Yeddo, under the protection of the Japanese Government, in apparent security. The British Legation, however, had a small guard attached to it, consisting of a few Marines and a dozen mounted men of the Military Train; the latter as an escort for the Minister, a precaution which had been adopted since the attempted assassination of Sir Rutherford Alcock in June, 1861.

At midnight, on the 26th of June, 1862, the anniversary of the attack the previous year, Colonel Neale, who had been but a few weeks previously transferred from the post of Secretary of Legation at Peking to be Her Majesty's Chargé d'Affaires in Japan, was lying in his bed in the temple used as the British Legation at Yeddo. By some fortuitous coincidence, he felt an unusual indisposition to fall asleep,—a sort of unconscious presentiment, as it were, of approaching danger. A window and door of lattice-work, covered with paper, separated him from the verandah in which a sailor from Her Majesty's ship "Reynard" was walking up and down as a sentry. Colonel Neale heard the ordinary challenge "Who goes there?" which was followed by the words "What is that you say?" and immediately afterwards by groans. Colonel Neale had the guard under arms in a few seconds, but before it had time to leave the house, the unfortunate sentry crawled to the door, mangled and bleeding to death, his right hand hanging by a shred of skin. The non-commissioned officer of the watch, Corporal

Crimp, of the Marines, was found lying dead at the corner of the verandah, where he had been attacked and cut down as he was going his rounds. His body had sixteen wounds on it. The sailor, Charles Sweet by name, lived for an hour afterwards, and had strength sufficient to state,—that seeing a suspicious-looking Japanese approaching on all-fours without a lantern, he challenged and received the right parole, but not feeling satisfied, he went forward quickly. When he had reached within a short distance, the man jumped up, and gave him a severe wound in the neck with a spear. The Japanese guard, who ought to have assisted him, ran away, and he was left in the dark. He then tried to get at his revolver, but before he could do so, he was disabled by sword cuts, and left on the ground for dead; his consciousness, however, remained, and he managed to crawl to the guard-room door.

The murderer was never discovered; but he is believed to have been one of the Japanese soldiers on guard,* as he was acquainted with the correct countersign. His intention, no doubt, was, after killing the sentry, to have burst into Colonel Neale's room, and to have assassinated him. It is probable, however, that his arrangements were thrown out by the appearance of the corporal of Marines before he had succeeded in dispatching the sentry. The guard at the Legation on the night of the murders was furnished from the retainers of the Daimio Matz Dairo Taubano Kami, a connection by marriage of the Prince of Satsuma.

These repeated attacks on the British Legation and attempts on the lives of the Ministers have been attributed to public dissatisfaction at the giving up of a portion of Yeddo, called Gotenyama, as a place of residence for the foreign Ministers, the feeling of annoyance, it is stated, being shared in by all classes, from the Daimios downwards

---

* The Japanese Government at this time furnished guards to the foreign Legations at Yeddo, as a protection against attacks from Loonins, or political desperados.

—hence the adoption of extreme measures to render Yeddo so uncomfortable a residence to foreigners as to necessitate their withdrawing from it. This result was obtained on both occasions: Sir Rutherford Alcock retired to Yokohama after the first attack; and after the second the British and French Legations withdrew on the 16th of July, 1862, from Yeddo, and re-established themselves at Yokohama, which they had left but a month or five weeks previously. Why the British Minister has been on both occasions selected for assassination has not been satisfactorily explained. Personal dislike to Sir Rutherford Alcock has been assigned as a reason, but such a supposition would not account for the second attack, Colonel Neale having been too short a time in the country to have given rise to personal feelings one way or another;—unless his re-establishing the Legation at Yeddo after it had been removed to Yokohama by Sir Rutherford Alcock was the cause of his attempted assassination, which I am inclined to think very probable.

In the month of August following, a notification was issued by command of the Tycoon, recommending the purchase of foreign steamers and sailing vessels by the Daimios.* This was the means of bringing to Yokohama, in the beginning of September, Shimadzo Saburo, the father of the Prince of Satsuma. He entered into friendly commercial intercourse there, which terminated in his purchasing the steamer "Fiery Cross," from the firm of Jardine and Matheson, for 125,000 dollars, having first made a trial trip in her. At this time complaints were stated to be numerous on the part of the population of Yeddo, respecting the savage dispositions of some of the retainers of the

---

* The Tycoon set the example by buying three steamers and two sailing vessels, and his recommendation resulted in the purchase, by Daimios, of thirteen steamers and four sailing vessels; the whole of them being bought at high prices from English and American merchants, with the exception of one small steamer that was bought by the Prince of Sendai from a Dutch firm.

Prince of Satsuma, who formed a part of Shimadzo Saburo's train, and who were represented as using their swords on repeated occasions, with little or no provocation.

A week after his visit to Yokohama, Shimadzo Saburo was on his way from Yeddo to Miako, and when about seven miles from Yokohama, on the Tokaido or great seaboard road, his retainers met a mounted party from Yokohama taking an afternoon ride; the party consisted of Mrs. Borrodaile, her brother-in-law Mr. Marshall, a merchant in Yokohama, Mr. Clark, of the house of Heard and Co., and Mr. Charles Lennox Richardson, of Shanghai, who had just retired from business, and was on a visit to Japan prior to returning to England. This unfortunate rencounter ended in one of those tragic scenes which of late have been so common in Japan, having their origin in the hatred which seems to be cherished towards foreigners generally, by a certain section of the feudal population. The facts are briefly the following:—

On the afternoon of Sunday, the 14th of September, the party left Yokohama about 2 o'clock in a boat, and proceeded across the harbour to the town of Kanagawa, where they met their horses, previously sent round by land. They rode on towards Kawasaki, with the intention of visiting a fine temple there. Proceeding along the road (the Tokaido) they passed several noromons,* each having a few two-sworded attendants. These noromons formed a long train broken at short intervals, and as they passed, the party walked their horses, cantering in the intervening spaces. This continued for between three and four miles along the Tokaido, beyond Kanagawa, when a regular procession was met, preceded by about 100 men in single file on each side of the road. The party kept on one side of the road, going at a walking pace, until arriving at the main body which was then occupying the whole road. Mr. Richardson and

* Noromons are box-like conveyances, carried on men's shoulders like palanquins, in which the better classes of the Japanese travel.

T

Mrs. Borrodaile were riding in front, and almost immediately they were ordered to halt by a man of large stature, who came out of the ranks and divesting himself of his upper clothing sprang forward, and with the same sweep of the sword which removed it from the scabbard, brought it across Mr. Richardson's loins, inflicting a fearful wound, following it up by others which proved speedily fatal, as he fell dead almost immediately from his horse. The remainder of the party made their escape, Messrs. Clark and Marshall being both wounded in getting clear of the train. Mrs. Borrodaile had a blow aimed at her head which she escaped by stooping.

No reason has been assigned for this savage murder beyond the statement that if any Japanese, through being mounted on a highway, had interfered with the progress of a noble of the same calibre as Shimadzo Saburo, they would have been similarly attacked. It would seem that the Yeddo authorities had some misgivings respecting the probable results of a meeting between Satsuma's retainers and foreigners on the high road, as they intimated to the ministers that on the 15th of September a Daimio's train would be on the Tokaido, in the neighbourhood of Yokohama, and specially requested that foreigners would on that particular day refrain from going on the road in question. Shimadzo Saburo and his train passed the night at a village no great distance from where Mr. Richardson was murdered; and the Yeddo authorities, in notifying the 15th as the day on which it was desirable that foreigners should keep off the Tokaido, probably had not calculated on any of them being so far from Yokohama on the afternoon of the 14th as to come in contact with Shimadzo Saburo before he had completed that day's journey.

The murder of Mr. Richardson was followed by much excitement amongst the foreign residents, and desire for the adoption of immediate retributive steps. Efforts, in the shape of public meetings and the like, were made to force

Colonel Neale to adopt this view, and request Admiral Kuper (who had the same day arrived from England in the "Euryalus" frigate) to commence hostilities. Colonel Neale was placed in a position of great difficulty, the press and the public being alike clamorous for revenge, but he adhered to his decision to abstain from taking immediate action; and in doing so, I may add, he was fully supported by Admiral Kuper, who was of opinion that even had it been desirable to adopt retributive measures at that time, he had no adequate force at his command to do so. Colonel Neale, therefore, made a strong representation to the Japanese Government, who admitted itself to be powerless in the affair, and he referred the whole question to Her Majesty's Government, who in the fullest manner approved of the course he had adopted in avoiding precipitate hostilities.

After this tragedy, no event of importance relating to foreigners occurred until the 2nd of January, 1863, when a Governor of Foreign Affairs came at a late hour to Colonel Neale, and communicated to him that reports had reached the Gorogio,* which were occasioning it much anxiety, to the effect that a band of Loonins† were meditating disturbances in Yokohama, which it was their intention to inaugurate by the assassination of the foreign representatives. The Japanese Government in making this communication declared that it was occupied in tracing the threatened danger to its source, and in adopting every means to avert mischief. In the meantime the members of the Gorogio begged that great caution and discretion should be exercised by the foreign community in respect to exposing themselves on the Tokaido or in its neighbourhood. Colonel Neale issued a notification to the residents apprising them of the

* The Tycoon's Council of State at Yeddo.
† Loonins are outlaws, who have thrown off their allegiance to their respective Daimios, as well as to authority generally, and constituted themselves the free-thinkers and free-doers of Japan—patriots, according to their own ideas.

nature of the communication he had received, and informing them that he was occupied in remonstrating with the Japanese Government against the then existing condition of affairs, as well as adopting in concert with the naval and military authorities the necessary measures of precaution. About three weeks afterwards the following communication was sent to the foreign ministers by Assano-Yega-no-Kami, the Governor of Kanagawa:—"As some of the Great Daimios are now passing along the Tokaido, which will be the cause of great confusion on the road, and as there are besides reports in circulation that some barbarians (Loonins) are walking round, and for all that I know may be now in Yokohama, it is desirable that your countrymen should not go out of Yokohama during one week from to-day until you receive another communication from me." Exactly a week after this warning was given, a new building which had just been completed at Gotenyama, in Yeddo, for the British Legation, was totally destroyed by fire; no doubt an act of deliberate incendiarism, as several explosions of gunpowder took place in different parts of the building during the progress of the fire. The building for the French Legation not being completed no harm was done to it, which strictly accorded with a threat which had been made, that the residences would be destroyed as soon as they were completed. This threat was further verified by the burning of the American Legation three months afterwards.

Matters continued in the same unsettled and insecure state until the end of March, 1863, when the instructions of the British Government, relative to the reparation to be demanded for the murder of Mr. Richardson, were received by Colonel Neale. At the same time Admiral Kuper arrived from Hong-Kong with the China squadron, prepared if necessary to enforce compliance.

On the 6th of April, Colonel Neale forwarded to the Japanese Ministers of Foreign Affairs at Yeddo, an ultimatum. Four months previously he had called on the Japanese Government to pay the sum of £10,000 for the families of Corporal Crimp of the Royal Marines, and of the sailor, Charles Sweet, which demand up to that time had been evaded. He now further demanded an ample and formal apology for the offence of permitting a murderous attack on British subjects passing on a road open by treaty to them, and the payment of £100,000 as a penalty on Japan for this offence, assigning twenty days for the answer of the Japanese Government, in failure of which the Admiral would be called upon to take measures to secure the reparation demanded. He also informed the Government that as they had openly avowed their inability to arrest malefactors within the domains of the Daimio, Prince Satsuma, the British authorities were constrained themselves to demand satisfaction and redress from that Prince. That a naval force would therefore proceed to a port pertaining to him, and would demand of him the immediate trial of the murderers, and the payment of £25,000 to be distributed to the relatives of the murdered man and to those who escaped the swords of the assassins. In reply to this communication the Japanese Government urgently requested an extension of time, which was granted for a fortnight longer, to the 11th of May.

Colonel Neale advised the foreign residents to adopt precautionary measures for their security, in the event of coercive measures being adopted.

The 11th of May passed without any satisfactory answer from the Japanese Government, further delay being requested, which, in the hope of averting hostilities, was again conceded them. In the meantime the position of affairs at Yokohama began to wear so threatening an aspect, that Colonel Neale requested Admiral Kuper to send a steam-vessel to Shanghai without delay, conveying an application to Major-General Brown, commanding in China, that he would divert to Japan the portion of the North of China force that was then about to embark for India and England, namely, Govan's battery of Royal Artillery, the 31st Regiment, and the 5th Bombay Native Infantry. This request the Commander of the Forces did not feel himself warranted in complying with.

On the night of the 23rd of May, the temple at Yeddo, in which the United States Legation resided, was burned to the ground. Shortly after this event a member of the Japanese Government waited on General Pruyn, the American Minister, and urged him to leave Yeddo without delay, as the Government had just ascertained the existence of very imminent danger to the lives of foreigners residing there. In the face of this warning, and with his residence destroyed, the American Minister could not with any prudence remain longer in Yeddo, and he accordingly withdrew his Legation to Yokohama. A similar warning was given to the United States Consul (Colonel Fisher), and some American missionaries who up to this time had resided at Kanagawa. They immediately proceeded, under an escort from the United States sloop of war "Wyoming," to Yokohama, and thus was accomplished the complete expulsion of foreigners from Yeddo and Kanagawa, and their confinement within the limits of the settlement of Yokohama.

During the ensuing three weeks, delay after delay, at the earnest solicitation of the Japanese authorities, was conceded by Colonel Neale in the humane hope of averting an appeal to arms and the suffering which such a course would entail on the industrious and non-offending portion of the Japanese community; at last, on the 20th of June, it became necessary to resort to coercive measures, and the matter was put into the hands of Admiral Kuper. On the 21st the Admiral notified to the foreign residents that the force at his command was unequal to the double duty of carrying out coercive measures and protecting also life and property in Yokohama. Upon this, Admiral Jaurais, the French naval commander-in-chief, came forward and undertook to guarantee the safety of the settlement, which produced a re-assuring effect upon the foreign community generally, the more so as he at the same time sent his Imperial Majesty's steamer "Monge" over to Shanghai, with instructions to return with the head-quarters of the regiment of French infantry (3rd Zephyrs) stationed there. This she did, landing the troops at Yokohama fourteen days afterwards.

Matters continued stationary until midnight of the 23rd of June, when one of the governors of Kanagawa* (these officials being now cut off from direct communication with Her Majesty's Chargé d'Affaires in consequence of his having for the time suspended diplomatic relations with them) waited on Monsieur de Bellecourt, the French Minister, and informed him that they were ready now to pay the money. This was immediately communicated to Colonel Neale, who replied, that as the Japanese Government had, by repeated acts of procrastination, allowed matters to assume their present form, the arrangement previously entered into for the payment of the money by instalments was cancelled, and that if they wished the money to be received, the full amount of the one hundred and ten thousand pounds must be paid down, in the form of four hundred and forty-thousand Mexican dollars of good quality, by seven o'clock the following morning.

In their anxiety that no further delay should occur, long before the appointed hour the money arrived at the Legation—its payment, I am of opinion, having been materially expedited by the appearance the previous day before Yeddo of her Majesty's ship "Pearl," commanded by Captain John Borlase, C.B., who had been sent up by Admiral Kuper to take observations, and give the Japanese Government an idea of the direction the fleet was about to take, if the terms were not at once complied with.

By a singular inconsistency of action, immediately after the money was paid, a notification was received from the

* About this time a second governor had been appointed, in consequence of the existing difficulties.

Gorogio, informing the foreign ministers that instructions had been received from the Tycoon, then at Miako, to put in force without further delay the Mikado's commands, that the treaty ports were to be closed forthwith, and all foreigners expelled from Japan. The officials, in making this communication, gave it clearly to be understood that they in no way indorsed it, nor were at all sanguine that any attention would be paid to it by the foreign representatives; they merely discharged their duty in serving the notification.

At the very time that this notice to quit was served on the foreign ministers, the first indications of its being practically enforced occurred at the opposite end of the island, some five or six hundred miles distant.

On the 24th of June, the "Pembroke," with the American ensign flying, passed an European-built barque without colours, but full of armed Japanese, and shortly afterwards anchored for the night near the eastern entrance to the Straits of Semonosaki or Vander Capellan. The same afternoon the barque came up with a fair wind, and the Japanese man-of-war flag flying. She passed the "Pembroke," and anchored between her and the entrance to the straits, about a quarter of a mile off. As the barque was approaching her anchorage, a gun was fired from a headland about four miles distant, and the signal was repeated for some distance along the coast. Nothing took place in the evening, but it would seem that after dark the barque warped up and got springs on her cable, since, at the time she opened fire, she was much nearer than at sundown. The barque opened fire on the "Pembroke" at a quarter to one on the morning of the 25th, and after she had fired about a dozen shots, one of which cut away the topmast backstay, a brig, recognised to be the "Laurick," * passed within forty yards of the "Pembroke," and anchored close to the barque. Both vessels

---

* This vessel, a brig of 280 tons, had shortly before been purchased by the Prince of Negato, from Jardine and Mattheson, for 35,000 dollars.

then commenced firing as rapidly as they could, but the "Pembroke" having got her steam up, soon got out of range, and made her escape from the straits by the Bungo channel. Her guns being lashed, and all hands busily engaged in getting her under way, no attempt was made to return the fire.

I have thus entered into a brief summary of the principal occurrences relating to the foreign community in Japan during the twelve months preceding my short visit to that country. The further progress of events arising out of the Mikado's order for the expulsion of foreigners, and the demand of the British Government for the indemnity of twenty-five thousand pounds from the Prince of Satsuma for the murder of Mr. Richardson, will be found in the following narrative.

CHAPTER I.

Embark at Shanghai for Japan—Cholera in the Yang-tse-kiang—Aspect of the coast—First impressions of the European settlement—The French and Dutch flags fired on—Aspect of affairs at Yokohama—Rural scenery—The peasantry and their habitations—Position of the foreign settlement—The British Legation—A Japanese garden and gardener—H.M.S. "Centaur" expected.

On the morning of the 12th of July, 1863, I embarked at Shanghai on board Her Majesty's ship "Racehorse," commanded by Captain Charles Boxer, about to start with the English mail for the China fleet, then lying at Yokohama Harbour, Japan. We made good speed down the Shanghai river (properly called the Wang-po), and were soon on the wide waters of the Yang-tse-kiang. From the pilot we had on board I learnt that he had taken the "West Derby" out, and that three cases of cholera had occurred amongst the soldiers after she entered the Yang-tse-kiang, and that two of them had terminated fatally before he left the vessel; the third one being in a dying state as he came away.

We had hardly well got into the Yang-tse-kiang, before one of the sailors was attacked with cholera and died in a few hours, and at daybreak of the 13th another fatal case occurred.

July 18*th*.—By degrees the coast of Niphon discloses itself, and first impressions are decidedly favourable—a bold, well-defined outline covered with pastoral vegetation coming down nearly to the water's edge, here and there only bald patches of rock being visible. As we continued our course several little bays with villages on their shores came successively into view ; also large patches of cultivation on the slopes facing the sea. The country all along the coast line hereabouts looked thickly wooded.

After rounding the two principal points indicating the southern entrance to the Bay of Yeddo, one called " Treaty Point" came in sight, and shortly afterwards the fleet in Yokohama anchorage was seen ; two French men-of-war, the Dutch steam-frigate, and about twenty merchant vessels and steamers were also in the anchorage. In a short time the European settlement of Yokohama came into view, and the first glimpse of it was certainly disappointing, to one, at least, who had just come from Shanghai, with its palatial Hongs.* The houses seemed comparatively few in number and of insignificant construction ; but as we came closer in, this impression began to wear off, as it became apparent that the architecture was more or less an adaptation of the Japanese style to European wants. The bungalow style seemed to be that chiefly adopted—here and there only, houses on the European model being seen. The ground on which the settlement is built is a perfect flat, surrounded by several miles of wooded hills in the form of a horseshoe.

On anchoring, an officer from the "Euryalus" (the flag-ship) came on board for the mails, and from him we heard that news had lately reached Yokohama of the flags of three nations having been fired on in the straits of Semonosaki ; namely, the American, the French, and the Dutch. Of the first case (that of the " Pembroke" already narrated) we had heard before leaving Shanghai. The second case was the French gunboat " Kein-chang," on her way from Yokohama to Shanghai, *viâ* Nagasaki. On the morning of the 8th of July, while she was at anchor† near the entrance to

---

* "Hong," in Chinese, signifies an extensive mercantile establishment.
† Vessels making the passage to Nagasaki from Yokohama, through the

the Straits of Semonosaki, two Japanese officials came on board, apparently to make inquiries where the ship was from and where she was going to. No objections were raised by them to her proceeding through the straits. Two hours afterwards some shots were fired from the forts on the north side of the straits; but as they did not come near the ship, it was supposed that the Japanese were only practising with their guns and no attention was paid to this; the "Kein-chang" continued her course up the straits. As she passed a second battery, however, a heavy fire was opened on her, but at too great an elevation, the shots passing overhead. Captain Lafont then ordered a boat to be lowered, with the intention of sending on shore to demand an explanation. Before the boat, however, could be manned she was struck by a shot and sunk. The "Kein-chang" then steamed on, the forts continuing to fire on her. After she had got about one-fourth of the way through the channel, two armed vessels, a sailing barque and brig, were observed leaving a small bay. They both joined in the attack, and the brig before opening fire partly hoisted the Japanese Imperial flag, but hauled it down again before it was fully run up. The barque, however, hoisted it, and kept it flying during the whole time she was firing. The forts on the southern side of the straits remained silent, which was fortunate, as the "Kein-chang" had to go within a few hundred yards of them, and made her escape from the straits by taking a passage hitherto unknown to European vessels, through which she was conducted safely by the Japanese pilot, who had been brought from Yokohama for the navigation of the inland sea.

The third vessel fired on was the Dutch frigate "Medusa," on her way from Nagasaki to Yokohama by the inland sea. As she passed through the Straits of Semonosaki she was exposed to the fire of the batteries for upwards of an hour,

inland sea, usually anchor at night, owing to the difficulties connected with the navigation after dark.

and received thirty-one shots in her hull, suffering a loss of four men killed and five wounded. This act of aggression, like the others, was confined to batteries on the Niphonese side of the straits, the property of Matz-daira Daizen no Daiboo, Prince of Negato. Had both sides of the straits been hostile, it is improbable that either the "Kein-chang" or the "Medusa" would have escaped.

In consequence of these outrages the United States steam sloop of war, the "Wyoming," commanded by Captain Macdougall, left Yokohama on the 13th instant for the Straits of Semonosaki, with the intention of demanding an explanation of the attack on the "Pembroke," and two days ago Admiral Jaurais, with his flag-ship the "Semiramis" and "Tancrede" gunboat, followed, his intention being to destroy the batteries and capture the vessels that fired on the "Kein-chang," should they still be in the straits.

On landing I went to the British Legation, and gladly accepted Colonel Neale's kind invitation to take up my quarters with him during my stay in Japan.

Amongst the events of the last few days has been the hiring of two English merchant steamers, the "Elgin" and the "Rajah," by the Tycoon's government, for the conveyance of troops to Osaca, by way of making a demonstration in aid of the Tycoon, who is supposed to be in difficulties with the Mikado at Miako, where he is at present, having been ordered there from Yeddo some months ago. Taking into consideration the partly feudal, partly federal, system of government prevailing in Japan, and the civil war which would seem to be on the point of breaking out, it appears to me that existing relations with the Tycoon's government are quite as satisfactory as could reasonably be expected. It is evidently the wish of the Tycoon to remain on friendly terms with foreigners, and especially with the English, if circumstances will possibly allow him; he, on the other hand, is pressed by the Mikado and various hostile Daimios to adopt coercive measures, for at once giving effect to the order for the expulsion of foreigners generally. He has, therefore, as already stated, gone through the form of giving the notice, but no act of hostility towards foreigners has yet been committed either on his own territories, or on those of Daimios known to be friendly to him, which explains the fact of the batteries on one side of the straits only having fired on foreign vessels passing through; the Daimio on the Kinsin side being an ally of the Tycoon.

In the afternoon, Admiral Kuper, with Captains Borlase and Josling, called at the Legation, on their way to take a ramble over the hills in the vicinity of the settlement. Colonel Neale and myself accompanied them, and I had thus an early opportunity of seeing Japanese inland scenery and rural life. Much as I had heard of the former, I hardly expected the reality to be equal to the description, and found myself agreeably disappointed, as nothing could be more pleasing than the richly wooded hill and dale scenery which met the eye as we descended inland from the hills overlooking the settlement. The country we passed through was very fertile. We saw rice and a species of vetch, and later cereal crops in various stages of growth. At short intervals, in the course of our walk, we came to cottages, sometimes two or three together; and as we approached them, the little children flocked out with boxes and bottles in their hands, containing insects, to show Admiral Kuper, who is an accomplished entomologist, the additional specimens they had procured for him since his last visit. It was pleasing in the extreme to observe the amiable good-humoured bearing of the peasantry, who, in their general appearance, closely resemble the Chinese rural population, with the exception that they shave the front and whole top part of the head, and tie the hair into a little knot, which they bring forward on the back part of the shaven crown.

The cottages are very clean inside, and in this respect

they contrast favourably with those of the Chinese, though the latter, on the whole, are more substantially built, and have a better exterior. The Japanese do not use tables or chairs, but sit on the floor, which is raised about two feet from the ground, and covered with matting, having some soft material between it and the floor, rendering it suitable for sitting or lying on without causing fatigue. The matting is kept very clean, as neither men nor women ever walk on it with their shoes, always taking them off before stepping from the ground. The wooden utensils employed for domestic purposes are beautifully kept, being scrubbed to the highest degree of perfection. The fires used by the lower orders are contained in small boxes, placed on the raised floor, and the fuel in common use seems to be charcoal. The Japanese would appear to be fond of strong waters,—as we passed several road-side houses devoted to the sale of saki, which is the national spirit, the gin or whiskey of Japan. It is made from bad rice, and possesses highly intoxicating properties.

Yokohama has been for three years a foreign settlement. The swamp, on a reclaimed portion of which the houses have been built, was previously occupied by a few rude fishing huts. Originally, that is to say, in 1859, after the treaty, the European merchants took up their residences under the protection of their respective consular flags at Kanagawa, a native town, on the road to Yeddo, and two and a-half miles from Yokohama. It is built on much higher ground, and the houses stand on each side of the Tokaido. The foreign merchants, however, did not find Kanagawa well adapted to commercial purposes, difficulties existing connected with the erection of jetties, wharves, &c., and gradually they removed to the swamp of Yokohama, where, by reclaiming ground, they were enabled to erect places of business, and thus by degrees has sprung up an European settlement of considerable size on land which, in its natural state, was only fit for the culture of rice. The portion of the swamp which has been allotted to foreigners has a defined limit; a canal having been dug round it, as well as round the Japanese town that has sprung up in connection with the European settlement, and which immediately adjoins its northern extremity. The extent of land separated from the swamp by the canal has a water frontage of over a mile, and proceeds back for about three quarters of a mile. A large extent of swamp still exists between the settlement and the canal boundary, and any extension of its present limits involves first the reclaiming of the swamp. On the rising ground overlooking Yokohama, on the Kanagawa side, is Tobay, the residence of the Japanese governor, whose jurisdiction extends over both Kanagawa and Yokohama.

Bluffs of high land exist at each extreme of the swamp, and from these extend right round, in the form of a horseshoe, a range of low and picturesquely wooded hills, averaging about a hundred feet in height. Behind these hills, Fusiama Mountain is seen, some fifty miles distant, rearing its summit in the form of a truncated cone, some fourteen thousand feet above the level of the sea.

The building at present used as the British Legation, a long two-storied bungalow, is situated at the southern extreme of the settlement on the bund, and faces the sea.

Within the last fortnight, Colonel Neale has had a small piece of ground in front of the Legation converted into a Japanese garden, the execution of which has been carried out with great taste by native talent. Its general outline is not dissimilar to the gardens that are attached to the domains of the wealthier classes in China. Artificial rocks, forests, miniature waterfalls, caverns, and fountains, have been introduced into it; also a picturesque little lake, filled with gold fish, and crossed by a miniature bridge. The formation of the garden was undertaken by contract by a Japanese, and a celebrated artist was brought down from Yeddo to execute the work. He is an old man, well known for his skill and taste in such work. On the completion of the job, which occupied only fourteen days, Colonel Neale suggested to him that he should remain as permanent gardener, and supervise and keep in order what he had so skilfully made. The proposition was accepted, and the old man is now at work the greater portion of the day, watering-pot in hand, refreshing his groves and forests. He seems to be absorbed in his work, and to be of a silent and sedate disposition. His working dress consists of a single upper garment of dark blue calico, fastened round the waist by a girdle, and coming down as far as the knee, like the kilt of the Highlander. On the back of this, a large circular design, in white, is worked, which indicates the particular section of the Yeddo fire brigade that he belongs to.

As regards the movements of the British fleet in reference to matters in the Straits of Semonosaki, Admiral Kuper will do nothing until he hears what happens to H.M.S. "Centaur," which left Shanghai on the 10th instant for Yokohama, *viâ* Nagasaki and the inland sea. There is every probability that she will be fired into if she passes through the Straits. In this case, Admiral Kuper will proceed at once with a squadron, and bombard the hostile forts. The Admiral, however, is of opinion that as the news of the attacks on the "Pembroke" and "Kein-chang," have reached Nagasaki, it is not improbable that Captain Leckie, of H.M.S. "Leopard," the senior naval officer there, will order the commander of the "Centaur" to avoid placing his ship in unnecessary danger, and direct him to take the outside passage by Van Dieman's Straits. Supposing, therefore, that all has gone well with the "Centaur," she ought to be here the day after to-morrow.

CHAPTER II.

The steamers "Elgin" and "Rajah"—Fire at Yeddo—Visit to the native town—Curiosity shops—Reconnaissance along the Tokaido—Kanagawa—Scene of Mr. Richardson's murder—Japanese grooms—A teahouse beauty—Japanese disciplined troops—Arrival of H. M. S. "Centaur" from Nagasaki—Action of the "Wyoming" with the vessels and forts of the Prince of Negato—Extreme heat and its fatal effects—An earthquake.

July 19*th.*—This morning, Mr. Fletcher, one of the interpreters attached to the Legation, returned to Yokohama, from a trip he has made to the inland sea, in the "Rajah" steamer, while she was under charter to the Tycoon's Government for the conveyance of troops to Osaca. Mr. Fletcher had been sent by Colonel Neale, with the view of his picking up what information he could regarding the present state of Japanese internal affairs. He sailed from Yokohama on the 13th instant in the "Rajah," which was filled with well-equipped troops, armed with revolvers, and evidently intended to act as a body of cavalry for the special protection of the Tycoon. In place, however, of going direct to Osaca, the port of Miako, or more properly speaking, Kioto,* the "Rajah" was taken to a bay forty miles from Osaca, on the east side of the Kino Channel, in the territory of the Prince of Kew-shew. The "Elgin" steamer had arrived there the previous day, also with troops on board. On her arrival being notified by telegraph to Osaca, two steamers came from that port, and took the troops out

* "Miako," in Japanese, signifies the capital. "Kioto" is the name proper of the city, which is the capital, and the residence of the Mikado.

of the chartered vessels, so that they could return at once to Yokohama. The commander of the troops expressed the wish that no Europeans from the "Elgin" or "Rajah" would land, which was complied with. Several villagers, however, came off, who showed a friendly disposition, and represented the people on shore as being delighted at the prospect of foreign trade. One man in particular, a doctor, who came off to see if his professional services were required, was very intelligent and communicative, speaking with an absence of reserve which seemed to entitle his statements to credence. He spoke with great respect of the power and influence of England. He said that the Tycoon was in trouble, and on bad terms with the Mikado, and had been residing at Osaca, but had lately gone back to Kioto. This statement was at variance with what the Japanese officers had told Mr. Fletcher on the way from Yokohama. In their general conversation they had seemed anxious to convey to him the impression that the Mikado and Tycoon were on excellent terms. Privately, however, one of the officers informed him that their friendly relations were more apparent than real, as the Mikado was much influenced by evil advice tendered him by Daimios hostile to the Tycoon; that he was in want of money, and therefore inclined to lend a ready ear to the overtures made by certain Daimios, who were offering a higher price for the temporal throne on the part of the Prince of Mito, than the Tycoon, who held it by law and prescriptive right, was inclined to give. Also, that the Daimios as yet were not declared enemies of the Tycoon, only enemies to foreigners, and that nominally; as he believed they had no real objection to them, and were merely pretending an animosity towards them, as the most probable and speedy means of embroiling the Tycoon, and facilitating the downfall of his government. Mr. Fletcher is of opinion that the "Elgin" and the "Rajah" were not hired from any want of steam transport of their own, but merely as a sort of demonstration, to impress the plotting Daimios with the belief that the sympathies of the British Government were on the side of the Tycoon, and hence that it was vain continuing their efforts for his overthrow. This seems very probable; as I am informed by Colonel Neale that, in the first instance, the Tycoon's Government applied for the aid of English vessels of war to convey the troops, and on being told that that was not practicable, they then asked if there would be any objection to the hiring of English merchant steamers for the same purpose. The Japanese officers had no hesitation in stating that if the Prince of Mito succeeded in dislodging the Tycoon, he would in all probability pursue exactly the same course in reference to foreigners that the latter has done, and throw open the ports to European commerce—jealousy of the advantages which the Tycoon is gaining from his recent treaties with foreign powers being one of the chief causes of their desire for his dethronement.

News arrived this morning from Yeddo, that a portion of the Tycoon's palace, called the outer castle, was yesterday destroyed by an extensive conflagration. The principal castle was at one time on fire, and has suffered some damage. Three of the Daimios' palaces, and several of the Government officials' residences have also been destroyed. Whether this fire originated from accident or design, has not transpired.

I visited to-day the Japanese town adjoining the foreign settlement. Some of the streets are wide, not unlike the main avenues of the Tartar city of Peking, while others are narrow and dirty looking. The houses are all built of wood, and those in the main street, where the principal shops are, have a new and cleanly appearance, this part of the town having been recently rebuilt, after having been swept away by an extensive fire. With the exception that the Japanese use neither tables, chairs, nor counters, I saw nothing in the general appearance of the interior of the shops, that struck my eye as being very novel, accustomed as it has been for some years back to things Chinese, and I was on the whole surprised that the scene should seem one by no means unfamiliar to me, though it was the first occasion of my having been in a Japanese street. The shops in the main street are chiefly devoted to the sale of lacquer ware, bronzes, carvings in ivory, charms, toys, and porcelain. The latter is very beautiful, being superior to the modern porcelain of China. The colours, however, are deficient in that remarkable brilliancy for which the older porcelains of China are noted, which now are difficult to procure.* In the selection of toys and ivory carvings, great care requires to be exercised, owing to the gross designs which are very frequently introduced into them. The same applies to the Japanese toys, paintings, and books, which are usually of the most indecent description.

In the afternoon, Captain Brine, of the Royal Engineers, whose services have been temporarily placed at the disposal of Admiral Kuper, called on Colonel Neale to say, that as it has been reported that the Japanese are placing guns on a height commanding the settlement, it was thought desirable to make a reconnaissance in that direction, and ascertain whether such was the case or not. He, therefore, requested that the Military Train escort might be allowed to go out, along with the mounted escort attached to the French Legation, which had been placed at his disposal by M. de Bellecourt. Colonel Neale gave his sanction for the escort to go out at daybreak, and I was invited to accompany it, which I was very glad to have the opportunity of doing.

July 20*th*.—This morning at half-past five I started with the reconnoitering party. It was thought advisable to defer

---

* China, of late years, has retrograded in the manufacture of porcelain, owing to the pottery districts having been ravaged by the Taepings, and their trade destroyed.

visiting the heights,* and to make in the first place a reconnaissance along the Tokaido to Kanagawa, and if possible ascertain what condition the fort is in, on a point there, commanding the Yokohama anchorage. A demonstration in this direction also was thought the more expedient, as some time had elapsed since any foreigners had ventured on the Tokaido, owing to the threatening aspect of affairs around, and the repeated warnings of the Tycoon's Government, cautioning them to keep within the limits of the settlement. After passing through the Japanese town of Yokohama, we crossed by a wooden bridge the canal which runs round the settlement, and got on a road passing over a wooded headland jutting out into the bay, on the top of which is Tobay, the governor's residence. Descending on the opposite side of the hill, we came to a bund constructed across a small bay formed by the prominence we had just passed over, and having a swamp of considerable size near it, similiar to the one in the rear of Yokohama. On leaving this bund we found ourselves on the Tokaido, and in a short time entered the town of Kanagawa, which is about three miles by road from Yokohama and fourteen miles from Yeddo.

The town of Kanagawa is upwards of two miles in length, and consists of a continuous line of wooden houses and shops, for the most part two storied, along each side of the Tokaido, the breadth of which is here about thirty feet. The people seemed inoffensive, and we did not encounter any indications of hostility. As we passed through the town two temples were pointed out, on a thickly wooded

* An examination of the heights was made the following day, but no guns were seen in position, though some temples were found to be occupied by a considerable number of disciplined Japanese troops. Whether this occupation of the heights was a precautionary measure on the part of the Tycoon's Government against any attack from that direction by the anti-foreign party on the settlement, or a preparation made with an opposite intention, was a matter of uncertainty—though I think the former supposition much the more probable.

ascent close to the road. In these the English and American Consulates were originally established.

After being clear of Kanagawa, we continued our course along the Tokaido for upwards of a mile, when we came to the scene of Mr. Richardson's murder, which occurred a little way beyond one of the road-side tea-houses. Mr. Aplin, who went out with the escort on the evening of the murder to recover the body, pointed out the spot where the first blow was struck, having traced it back from where the body was found by the tracks of blood on the road. At this part of the Tokaido, which is narrower than usual, a small vegetable garden intervenes between it and the bay, and on the other side there is a field under cultivation enclosed within a small amphitheatre of low hills. Passing this spot fraught with painful recollections, we continued our ride about two miles further along the Tokaido, until we reached a large village called Namamoogie, at a tea-house near the centre of which we halted, so as to give the horses a rest and the men some refreshment after their early ride.

We had hardly time to pull up our horses at the tea-house door, before a number of grooms rushed out, and, seizing the horses by the bridles, commenced refreshing them by throwing into their mouths, with wooden ladles, water taken from buckets they brought out with them.

Apropos of horses in this country, observing several men running along the road and keeping pace with us, except when we went very fast, and soon catching us up on the pace being slackened, I inquired who they were, and found them to be the bettoes or native horsekeepers. It appears they always go out with the horses they have charge of, and that they will run as they did this morning the whole way to Yeddo. They denude themselves of all clothing except a piece of calico round their middles, another piece bound round their foreheads (which they wet from time to time in cold water) and a pair of white calico stockings coming just over the ankles. These bettoes are remarkably fine muscular men, perfect models of strength, and capable of undergoing an amount of fatigue considerably in excess, I should say, of what the syces* of India are equal to.

We dismounted and went into the tea-house, which is kept by a Japanese beauty, who in less troubled times appears to have been known amongst the English by the sobriquet of "Jenny," by which she was addressed by some of the party who had known her formerly. She seemed very glad to see them, and did the honours of the tea-house with charming *naïveté*. Jenny, however, was evidently a bit of a flirt, and not disregardful of personal appearance, as she availed herself of an early opportunity of slipping away and changing her ordinary working dress, reappearing in one of a better and more showy description, and bringing with her the *carte de visite* of an English gentleman in Yokohama, well known for his admiration of the fair sex in Japan, and who, in days when the Tokaido could be ridden with safety, was, I am informed, a frequent visitor at Jenny's tea-house. After resting half an hour, during which we had some tea and melons, we started homewards. The tea, I may remark, is served in smaller cups than the Chinese use, but its preparation is the same, and, like the Chinese, no sugar is used. The interior of the tea-house was very clean; the raised floor, which serves both for sitting and sleeping on, was covered with white matting.

On our way back we halted for a short time in the rear of the Kanagawa fort, which is star-shaped, projecting out into the sea, and constructed on regular principles of fortification, evidently under European guidance. Captain Brine made an attempt to see into the interior and ascertain the nature and extent of its armament, but having a narrow causeway to ride along to reach the gate, his approach was observed

---

* The native grooms employed by Europeans in India; they generally follow the horses they have care of, in the same way as the bettoes of Japan.

by the Japanese guard, who turned out and closed the gate, thus preventing his obtaining the information he wanted. As we approached the Governor's house at Tobay, bayonets were seen glancing through the trees accompanied by the sound of European drums. As we got nearer we met three parties of Japanese infantry, each thirty strong, marching down from Tobay, where they seemed to have been mounting guard. They looked as if they were independent companies, each one being under the command of an officer, who marched at the head on the right hand side in European style. Two other officers and a drummer were attached to each company, the latter marching in front, dressed in alternate stripes of blue and white, with conical hats on their heads, beating their drums and looking the pictures of mountebanks. The soldiers had no covering on their heads, and were dressed in uniforms of light blue calico striped with white, consisting of a short jacket and loosely-fitting pantaloons, tied at the ankle. In place of the ordinary loose slipper that is in common use amongst the Japanese, they wear straw sandals, like those worn by the Chinese foot soldiers when they have long marches to make. The men were armed with muskets and bayonets, the former having polished barrels, and apparently of Dutch manufacture. Their belts and cartridge-boxes, however, looked as if they had been made in Japan. In marching they rest the musket as high as possible on the shoulder and carry it nearly vertically, seemingly with the object of giving it an imposing appearance from the length of polished metal shining above the heads of the soldiers. This they effect by resting the hammer portion of the lock on the back part of the shoulder.

The officers wore a modification of the ordinary Yaconin* dress, with two swords stuck in the sashes round their waists. They carried, in the same way as an English officer

---

* Yaconins are Government officials of a certain class, and are authorised by law to carry two swords.

carries his drawn sword when marching with men, what looked at first sight like sharp rapiers, but which proved to be ramrods with black braid round their butt ends to answer the purposes of a handle. The explanation of their carrying such a peculiar weapon is, that it is the custom of the country never to draw the sword unless it is to be used, and the act of drawing it generally carries with it the blow, both being effected with one sweep of the arm. The officers wore the Japanese military hat, which is of a somewhat singular and not very becoming shape. It is formed of a piece of round basket-work painted black, and worn doubled over the top of the head, being secured underneath the chin by strings of green silk ribbon.

One of the commanders of companies went in for being the smart officer, and seemed anxious to impress us favourably with his proficiency in drill. As he advanced towards us he formed his men from fours into twos, and thence into Indian (single) file, in which order he passed us as we were drawn up on the road to look at his men, it being the first time that any of the party had seen Japanese troops disciplined or armed according to the European system.* After the companies had all passed we continued our way to Yokohama and overtook the smart officer's company, who, as soon as he saw us coming, halted his men, drew them up on one side of the road and presented arms as the escort passed —the compliment being paid as correctly as if they had been English troops.

On returning to the Legation, I found that the "Centaur" had just arrived from Nagasaki, and the "Wyoming" from the Straits of Semonosaki, the latter with her rigging looking a good deal cut up. With reference to the "Centaur," Admiral Kuper's conjecture had proved correct, she had avoided the inland sea by taking the outward passage by

* The disciplining of Japanese troops has heretofore been conducted by Dutch officers at Nagasaki, from which place, most probably, these men came.

Van Dieman's Straits, having been ordered to do so by Captain Leckie at Nagasaki, who very judiciously thought it was inexpedient unnecessarily to embarrass the Admiral at that particular time with an affair in the Straits while matters continued in an unsettled and critical state at Yokohama. Consequently, much to the disappointment of Commander Creasy, his officers and crew, they had to forego the encounter, which, from the news they had received at Nagasaki, they had made up their minds they were going to have with the batteries of the Prince of Negato. Mr. Morrison, Her Majesty's Consul at Nagasaki, arrived in the "Centaur," having left his post in consequence of daily apprehension of assassination, repeated threats of which had been conveyed to him from Japanese sources. He had been obliged to sleep on board ship in the harbour for some days before leaving, it being unsafe for him to remain on shore during the night. Lieutenant Lyster of the Royal Engineers also arrived in the "Centaur," having been sent over by Major-General Brown to make a report for his information respecting Yokohama as a military position, in the event of troops having to be sent there.

The "Wyoming" entering the inland sea by the Bungo Channel, had proceeded on the 16th to the Straits of Semonosaki. As she was nearing them a signal-gun was fired from a masked battery on the northern shore, which was repeated by two others on the same side but further up the Straits. On rounding a point on the southern side of the entrance to the Straits, a steamer, brig and barque were seen lying at anchor close to the northern shore. The two former were recognised as the "Lancefield" and "Laurick." The name of the barque was not known. The three vessels were flying the Japanese ensign (white with a red ball in the centre) at the peak, and the private flag of the Prince of Negato at the main. The "Wyoming" was steaming directly for the vessels, when a battery of three guns on the north side, about fifty feet above the sea, opened fire upon her, doing considerable damage to the rigging. She then hoisted the American flag and continued steaming on, when a second battery of four guns opened on her from the same direction, to which she replied with a broadside. By this time she was rapidly approaching the vessels. The barque was close in shore, the brig was about fifty yards outside of her, and a little way ahead of the brig, about fifty yards also outside was the "Lancefield." Though the vessels were between the land and the main channel, Captain Macdougall gave the orders for the "Wyoming" to run between the steamer and brig, in doing which, as she got abreast of the barque, the latter fired a broadside of three guns. In about two minutes the "Wyoming" was abreast of the "Laurick" and received a broadside from her of four brass thirty-two pounders. At this period the "Wyoming" had the steamer on her left side and the brig on her right. As she passed between them she gave them each a broadside, which hulled them, and then, keeping close round the bows of the steamer, stood over towards the southern shore, receiving a constant fire from six batteries and the three vessels. In performing this manœuvre the "Wyoming" got aground, but by backing the screw she was able to get afloat again without much difficulty. By this time the "Lancefield" had got her steam up and had slipped her cable and was keeping close along the northern shore, either with the intention of escaping or of running on shore, owing to the damage she had received from the broadside. The "Wyoming" then worked up into a favourable position and sent an eleven-inch shell from one of her large Dahlgren guns right amidships into the "Lancefield," about a foot above the water line. Instantaneously volumes of steam and smoke issued out of her, fore and aft, her boiler evidently having exploded. After giving her two more eleven-inch shells, the "Wyoming" directed her fire on the batteries, the brig and the barque, all of which were firing as quickly as they could load. By this time the "Wyoming" had had four men killed and seven wounded, and as her armament consisted of only four thirty-two pounders and two eleven-inch pivot Dahlgren guns, Captain Macdougall prudently determined to withdraw from a contest to the continuance of which he was unequal, the more so, as any damage to the machinery, unsupported as he was, would in all probability have involved the loss of his vessel and the sacrifice of the lives of every one on board. The "Wyoming" was an hour and ten minutes under fire, being hulled eleven times and having received about thirty shots through her rigging. As she passed out of the Straits she sent a few shots into the "Laurick," which, when last seen, was settling down by the stern and apparently sinking. The batteries continued firing on the "Wyoming" as she repassed the entrance to the Straits, but the fire was not so brisk as when they first opened, the ardour of the gunners having been no doubt a little cooled by a few of the "Wyoming's" shells that were seen to explode in the batteries. Captain Macdougall is represented by his officers as having behaved with remarkable coolness and bravery during the whole of the trying period his vessel was under fire. One shell fell immediately below the tackles of one of the forward broadside guns, and exploding, killed or wounded five men.

The heat to-day was 92° in the shade, with hardly a breath of wind stirring, the day being one unusually sultry for Yokohama, where there is generally a refreshing sea-breeze. In the afternoon, about three o'clock, I went to the Japanese town with Captain Boxer and one of the foreign residents to look at some of the curiosity shops—the latter before leaving his house girded on a revolver, an exercise of the law of self-preservation that seemed to me somewhat in excess of the actual necessities of the period. The custom of the place, however, seems to be not to move out without fire-arms on the person, nor to go to sleep without them under the pillow.

I had been in the Japanese town but a few minutes when

a messenger came to me from Colonel Neale, asking me to return to the Legation as quickly as I could, as one of the Military Train escort had been seized with sun-stroke. By the time I reached the barracks the man was dead, notwithstanding the prompt attention which his case had received from Dr. Willis, the medical officer attached to the Legation. This soldier, who looked the picture of rude health, had been out with us in the morning along the Tokaido and returned apparently quite well, as he went out on some other duty on foot afterwards. At 1 o'clock he seemed in his ordinary health, ate a hearty dinner, and then lay down on his bed and fell asleep. He had not been exposed to the sun for upwards of two hours prior to the symptoms of heat apoplexy showing themselves, which is in accordance with what I have repeatedly observed in China; the worst cases of what is ordinarily called sun-stroke frequently occurring in men who have not been at all exposed to solar influence for several hours previously. This man was attacked shortly after 3 o'clock, and was dead by 4. This is the first death that has taken place amongst the military in Yokohama. The man had never suffered from any previous sickness in Japan. This I happened accidentally to know, from having the day before interrogated him regarding his own health and that of his comrades since they left Tien-tsin in the latter part of 1861.

The heat continued oppressive in the extreme during the remainder of the day, and an ominous stillness pervaded the atmosphere. About half-past eleven o'clock at night, as I was sitting with Colonel Neale in the verandah of the upper story, talking over recent events, the house suddenly began to shake, and the supports of the verandah vibrated backwards and forwards for about a minute. We at once recognised that it was an earthquake, and a tolerably smart shock of one, though unattended by any damage. Earthquakes are of frequent occurrence in Japan, and occasionally very severe; one in 1855 nearly destroyed Yeddo. Thus, taken altogether, what between political troubles, impending assassinations, revolvers under the pillow at night, and terrestrial convulsions, Japan, notwithstanding its many attractions, would not seem to be the most delectable of foreign residences.

CHAPTER III.

The Japanese custom-house system—Objections to the exposing of the sword blade—The Gaukiro—A Japanese entertainment—A Japanese game—Public baths—Freak of two French soldiers—Visit to the "Medusa"—Japanese shot and shell, whence obtained—Visit to the "Wyoming"—Terms of construction of Legation residences—H. M. S. "Coquette" sent to communicate with the French Admiral in the Straits.

July 21*st.*—The Japanese Government appear to have adopted such careful precautions against smuggling as to render contraband trade almost impossible. Their custom-house system is a very perfect one, and the strictness with which it is carried out is a frequent source of grievance to some of the foreign merchants, compelling them to confine speculation within the limits of legitimate trade—in other words, to articles on which import duties have been paid.

The length of the bund in front of the European settlement is a little over half-a-mile, and all along its front, stout stakes are driven into the sea, at intervals of about a foot, to prevent boats landing passengers or cargo at any but recognised places, where the custom-house authorities are on the look-out. In addition to these fixed precautions, a line of the Tycoon's "preventive-service" boats are moored at short intervals off the bund in front of the stakes, and also at the entrances to the canal investing the settlement.

There is a custom-house station, with an armed guard, on the bank of the canal close to the British Legation. It is quite open in front and the men on guard, generally three at a time, sit with their legs crossed, motionless, like a row of idols in a temple. This morning I went into it, having first by signs obtained the permission of the guard to enter. On showing a desire to look at their arms, which are ranged with military regularity in wooden racks, they readily showed me their muskets, bayonets, and the contents of their cartridge-boxes; but on my attempting to examine one of their native swords, they civilly stopped me, being afraid apparently that I might remove it from its scabbard, and thus break through the national custom, which I have already referred to, of never drawing the sword except for use.

In the course of our walk I was shown the "Gaukiro," or section of the native town set apart for the residences of the "social evil" class of the community. It consists of a collection of wooden houses and tea-shops at the back of the Japanese town, built on a portion of reclaimed ground in the midst of the swamp. A long narrow street passes down to it, and at its entrance a strong wooden barrier separates it from the respectable portion of the town. At the end of the "Gaukiro" there is a small temple built on the margin of the swamp, and specially intended, I presume, for the inhabitants of this noted locality.

The principal establishment in the "Gaukiro" is known amongst the English under the name of the "Crystal Palace," owing to its extent and light framework-looking exterior, as well as the remarkable neatness and simplicity with which the interior is fitted up. The building is situated just within the barrier-gate, and is under government supervision, its receipts forming a source of state revenue. It contains a theatre and two or three large rooms where dinner parties take place; the dinners being provided by the establishment at so much per head. As it was open day, we thought that, without detriment to our characters, we might venture to inspect the interior. The officer in charge received us with much politeness, no restrictions as yet apparently

x

having been placed on the admission of "Tojins"* into this particular state institution. The official conducted us to one of the dining-rooms. My friend, who understood a little of the language, made out that he was under the impression we had come to make the preliminary arrangements for an evening entertainment of a semi-musical—semi, it is difficult to say what—character, that is a good deal patronised by the resident foreign community, as well as by casual visitors to Japan. At Yokohama it is known as a "jon-ki-no," from the first words of a song which is sung by a number of dancing-girls. This national entertainment, so far as I understand it from the descriptions I have heard, is a game of forfeits accompanied by singing and dancing—the forfeits consisting of the girls divesting themselves one by one of their different habiliments, until they are gyrating in a state of perfect nudity before the audience who have furnished the funds for the organisation of the entertainment. At Naga-saki the same thing is known amongst the English as a "jon-no-ge," owing to the difference of the dialect. Notwithstanding their total disregard of what we have been accustomed to consider decency, these dancing-girls are said to be perfectly moral characters, and to belong to a class altogether distinct from the frail inmates of the "Gaukiro" generally.

We walked through the establishment, which appears to be kept in a state of most perfect order and cleanliness. Nothing whatever approaching to levity or obscenity was seen. Some of the female inmates were at their meals, others were sitting before looking-glasses performing their toilets; some were dressing their hair; others were cleaning their teeth, using rose-coloured tooth-powder, made of pounded coral, flavoured with some aromatic powder, and applied by a piece of wood divided at one end into a sort of brush by repeated splitting-up of the fibre. The Japanese

* Tojin is the name usually applied by the Japanese to Europeans, and means, I believe, simply "foreigner."

unmarried girls, or "moosmees," as they are called, have beautifully white teeth; these, however, they dye black immediately on marriage, which, with the shaving of the eyebrows, done at the same time, tends in so marked a manner to diminish their personal attractions, as to materially lessen the risk of their getting involved in troubles likely to lead them into the divorce court. One of the girls I observed on her knees with her hands closed in front of her, saying her prayers with great apparent devoutness.

The social position of this class of females in Japan is very different to what it is in most other parts of the world. No disgrace seems to attach to their calling, and I am told that they almost invariably marry well. Children of tender years are taken care of and reared within the walls of this establishment until they attain an age suited to its purposes. I noticed several little girls of three and four years of age playing about, and I am told that it is not uncommon for parents in poor circumstances to make over their children, even when infants, to government institutions of the nature under description.

On leaving the "Gaukiro" my attention was drawn to a shop where a sort of gambling game is kept. The player takes a tube containing a dart, and blowing through it aims at any one of a number of knobs of wood ranged in a line on a board within the shop, at a short distance from the window. According to the particular knob the dart strikes, some grotesque representation falls down from above, suspended by a cord, the designs for the most part being more original than chaste; and upon the particular oddity thus liberated the player's chances of a prize or a blank depend. The game was under the supervision of a man and a woman, both of whom looked the pictures of squalid debauchery.

In a respectable portion of the town, outside the "Gaukiro," I saw one of the public bathing-houses, where men and women perform their ablutions promiscuously. There were about twenty of both sexes bathing themselves at the time we stopped at the door, which was wide open, and the interior patent to all passers-by on the public street. The bathers appeared to be as little put about by our presence as by that of one another, and proceeded with their ablutions in the most matter-of-fact manner. They do not use tubs or baths, but sit on a wooden floor with small buckets of hot water before them, which they throw over themselves, procuring fresh supplies from a reservoir in the form of a wooden trough, which is fed from a boiler in a sort of back kitchen. The Japanese do not use soap as we do, but I believe they have an alkaline preparation, enclosed within calico bags, which seems to act as a substitute, with which they occasionally rub themselves over.

Two privates of the "Zephyrs" (Algerine Light Infantry), who have been missing for the last six days, returned to their corps this forenoon. They represent themselves as having been thirty miles into the interior, and to have been well treated at the different villages they went to, excepting that as soon as they came to one village they were recommended by the inhabitants by signs to go on to the next one; no village apparently being desirous of being saddled with the responsibility of having them in it. The one soldier it appears had induced the other to accompany him, and in explanation the man states that every five years an uncontrollable desire seizes him to wander into the interior of the country wherever he may happen to be stationed at the time. The desire subsides in the course of a few days after the impulse has been gratified.

July 22*nd*.—This forenoon Colonel Neale proceeded afloat to pay visits to the Commanders of the "Medusa" and the "Wyoming," and congratulate them on their escapes from the dangers to which they had been lately exposed; his private secretary, Mr. Alexander Von Siebold, and myself accompanied him. We went first to the "Medusa," and were shown by Captain Casambroodt the various injuries she had received during her passage through the straits. Some of the shot that had lodged on board were thirty-two pounders, others were twenty-four pounders. The fragments of shell that I saw looked as if they belonged to the five-and-a-half inch diameter. The Captain mentioned a rather singular accident that occurred, which might have been attended with untoward consequences. During the action, the concussion caused by a shot striking the vessel broke a large bottle of muriatic acid in the dispensary, where the surgeon was at the moment operating on one of the wounded seamen.

The Captain also mentioned to us that he was so surprised at the Dutch flag being fired at, considering their long and friendly intercourse with Japan, that he was under the impression, in the first instance, that it had been mistaken on shore for the French flag. The projectiles, I may remark, which told with such effect on the "Medusa," are stated to have been supplied to the Japanese by the Dutch, who naturally looked upon their nation as the one least likely to be the recipients of them back in so uncommercial a manner.

On leaving the "Medusa" we went to the "Wyoming," which, like the former, has suffered chiefly in her rigging and smoke-stack. Captain Macdougall was not on board, and Colonel Neale was received in his absence by Lieutenant-Commander Young. The damage to the hull of the "Wyoming" seemed to be pretty well repaired, but a good deal still remained to be done to her rigging. It appears that, when the "Wyoming" entered the straits, it was not anticipated that she would be fired at from the batteries on shore, news of the affair of the "Kein-chang" not having reached Yokohama at the time she sailed. The batteries opened fire before the "Wyoming" hoisted her ensign, which proves that the hostilities are directed against foreign vessels generally, and no nation or nations in particular.

In the afternoon I went with Colonel Neale to call on the Dutch Consul-General, who resides in a very nice house in the native town, that has been built by the Japanese

Government for the Netherlands Consular Residence. As rent for it, the Dutch Government pay a certain rate of interest on the amount the building of it cost. The British Legation Residence at Yeddo was to have been paid for on the same principle by Her Majesty's Government, had it not, immediately on its completion, been destroyed by fire; with reference to which I may mention, that the day before the event occurred, a high officer of the Tycoon's Government called on Colonel Neale, and endeavoured to get him, on the part of the British Government, to abandon the claim to the building, on the plea that it had been erected on sacred ground set apart for the amusement of the people. Whether the burning of the building, which took place the following day, was an act of the Tycoon's Government in consequence of the unsatisfactory issue of this interview, or an act of the anti-foreign party, which it had no power to avert, is not known; the latter is the more likely, as the Government would hardly wilfully destroy an edifice the erection of which had just been completed at a considerable cost. The interview was probably an effort to avert the fate which the Gorogio knew to be impending the building at the hands of those whom it had no power to restrain.

In consequence of the reports given by the "Wyoming" of the formidable character of the batteries in the straits, M. de Bellecourt has become very uneasy about Admiral Jaurais being supported only by a small gunboat, and at his urgent request, Admiral Kuper has despatched H.M.S. "Coquette," under Commander Alexander, with instructions to communicate with the French Admiral should he be in the straits on his arrival, and to place himself under his orders,—at the same time, giving him strict injunctions not to undertake any operations on his own account, in the event of his failing to communicate with Admiral Jaurais.

CHAPTER IV.

Seamen and marines land for battalion drill—The armament of the "Euryalus"—Remarks on the Armstrong gun—Arrival of a member of the Gorogio from Yeddo—His interview with the Foreign Ministers—Sanitary paradox at Yokohama—Japanese washermen—The Chinese in Yokohama—Comparison between the Japanese and the Chinese—Question of the descent of the former from the latter.

July 23*rd.*—At five o'clock this morning, the seamen and marines from the fleet, to the number of about 800, were landed for drill on the race-course. The blue jackets, headed by the band of the flag-ship, were formed into a regular battalion of eight companies. The marines were drilled separately.

In the forenoon I went on board the "Euryalus." Her spar-deck is now armed entirely with Armstrong guns, and the main deck with the ordinary 68-pounders and two large Armstrongs on each side. How the larger-sized Armstrong guns will answer in naval warfare remains to be seen; but I cannot say that the unfavourable impression I formed of the 12-pounder gun and its projectile in the North of China campaign has been removed by anything that I have been able to observe connected with them during the recent operations against the Taepings in the province of Kiang-soo. The chief defects noticed on the Peiho referred to the flying out of the vent-piece, and the stripping of the lead coating from the projectiles, both of them undoubted sources of danger; more especially the latter to infantry lying down in front, as I have myself personally witnessed.

During the Taeping campaign, the Armstrong guns were not subjected to any very rapid firing, and I am not aware of any accident having happened to them. The defects which came under my notice related to the imperfect explosion and occasional non-explosion of the shell.) I have frequently seen it, in place of exploding into the thirty-nine segments of which it is built, burst only into two or three pieces, and apparently without any great force. Again, I have seen the shell picked up entire, except that the bursting charge had blown out the metal fuse, the segments being in no way detached. As far as I, as a layman, am capable of forming an opinion, the performances of the Armstrong guns in the North of China have been much overrated and, I may add, that the spirit of exaggeration in reference thereto seemed to me at one time to be carried to an almost puerile extent; inasmuch as, whenever any marked damage was observed to have been done by artillery fire, it was invariably attributed to the Armstrong guns; whereas, if reduced to a matter of fact, at the ranges they were for the most part used at, I believe that they were not nearly so destructive as the ordinary field-battery howitzers of the Royal Artillery that were in action at the same time. I do not think that for general purposes, whether in the field or on ship-board, the Armstrong or any other form of breech-loading gun will in the end be found equal to guns of improved construction loading at the muzzle.

While I was on board the "Euryalus," a steamer, under Japanese colours, made out to be the "Lyemoon," was reported to the Admiral to be coming into the anchorage from Yeddo. On returning to the Legation, I found that one of the members of the Gorogio, named Sa-ki-oko-nos-ki, had landed from the "Lyemoon," and had requested an interview with the Foreign Ministers. It appears, however, that Sa-ki-oko-nos-ki has been recently promoted, and that in accordance with what is customary in Japan on acquiring an accession of rank, he has changed his name to Saki-he-ka-no-kami, by which designation he is now officially known.

The interview took place at the French Legation, M. de Bellecourt being the senior member of the foreign diplomatic body at present in Japan. The two Governors of Kanagawa and Yokohama accompanied Saki-he-ka-no-kami, who, it turned out, had nothing whatever to say beyond wishing to mention that he was on his way to Osaca, and that he could not think of passing Yokohama without calling to make inquiries after the health and well-being of the Foreign Ministers. He avoided altogether the question of the hostilities in the Straits of Semonosaki; but when pressed on the subject, he said that the Gorogio would inquire into the matter, adding that they were very sorry that the ships had been fired into, the more so as the Dutch were such old and good friends of theirs. On being asked for an opinion as to what the Mikado would be likely to think of the proceedings of the Prince of Negato, he said that he thought he would approve of them, as they were in reality the putting into effect of his order with reference to the expulsion of foreigners. He said also that the Tycoon would in all probability be compelled to approve of them in public, but that he would secretly disapprove of them. When told by Colonel Neale that the result of these proceedings would be, that we should have to seize all their vessels that had guns on board, it seemed to take him rather by surprise, and he immediately said, "Then, I suppose, you will seize the steamer in which I have now come." "No," replied Colonel Neale, "we will let you go, that you may give warning to the others what a continuance of their present course is about to bring upon them."

He was then, as representing the Gorogio, taken to task with respect to their having lent the "Victoria," one of the steamers recently purchased by the Tycoon's Government, to the Prince of Satsuma for the purpose of carrying guns.

This he at once denied, but immediately turned round to the two Governors, and, audibly to the interpreter, the three discussed the matter among themselves, and were heard to say that they did not think it could possibly be the case that the "Victoria" had been lent, but that it must be the "Shanghai;" thereby admitting the fact that the Government had lent Satsuma a steamer for war purposes, but whether to be employed against foreigners or not, does not appear. It is merely of interest as a proof that the conduct of Satsuma's followers in connection with Mr. Richardson's murder has not in any way interfered with overt friendly intercourse continuing between him and the Tycoon.

One of the facts which transpired at this interview was the admission on the part of Saki-he-ka-no-kami, that orders had been issued by the Tycoon's Government to certain Daimios to invest Yokohama and carry out the expulsion of foreigners; but in making this admission, he qualified it by saying that it was previous to the payment of the indemnity money that the order had been issued. Such would appear to be the anomalous state of matters at the present time—the Tycoon's Government secretly keeping up friendly communication with foreigners, and in public going with the stream against them. That it is really averse to the rupture of negotiations, I think there can be little doubt, otherwise it would never have thrown away the £110,000 indemnity money.

Rumours have been afloat all day of news having gone on to Yeddo that the French Admiral has attacked the forts at Semonosaki, and has been beaten off. Another rumour is going about of an opposite kind, namely, that he has taken the forts, but with a loss of fifty men. Neither report is believed to have any truthful origin.

In the afternoon I walked to the back of the foreign settlement, which is as nearly as possible half a mile from the bund, and found the houses to be in immediate contiguity with what sanitary science would characterise as a pestilential swamp, and which, certainly, as far as the eye is capable of judging, ought to be a hotbed of malaria, and a focus for the generation of ague and other fevers; nevertheless, opposed as the fact is to a generally received belief, they are almost unknown in the place. On this point I have been particular to obtain information, and am assured by the two resident medical officers (Dr. Jenkins, late of the Royal Navy, and Dr. Willis of Her Majesty's Legation), that, with the exception of an occasional case of ague occurring in some one who has suffered from the disease formerly in China, the inhabitants generally of Yokohama enjoy a remarkable immunity from it as well as from other malarious fevers. Both of these medical officers readily admit that the contrary ought to be the case, judging from the local conditions under which the inhabitants live; but, to make use of their own words, "however strong the theory may be in favour of ague prevailing at Yokohama, the fact is, that it does not."

I confess, that though many facts have come under my observation in China calculated to throw doubts on the accuracy of the aphorisms of sanitary science as promulgated at home in reference to the operation of foul smells, collections of filth, &c., as exciting causes of disease, I still clung to the belief that a liability to contract ague was inseparable from a residence in the immediate vicinity of swampy land and extensive surfaces of decaying vegetable matter, with a powerful sun playing upon them. That such however is not necessarily the case admits of no doubt; and it is therefore clear that other conditions enter into the causation of malarious fevers than those to which it has been customary heretofore almost solely to attribute them. Viewed with the eye of a sanitarian, Yokohama ought to be generally unhealthy. In addition to marshy land and decaying vegetable matter, huge accumulations of filth and garbage exist in the immediate vicinity of the native houses; for notwithstanding the attention of the Japanese to interior cleanliness, as regards exterior cleanliness I cannot say that I recognise any very marked difference between them and the Chinese, if, that is to say, the back portion of the native town of Yokohama is a fair specimen of Japanese sanatation. On the contrary, however, far from the place in any way having acquired a reputation for sickness, the remarkable salubrity of the climate has led to its being extensively adopted as the sanatarium of China.

Though its natural climate is healthy in the extreme, Yokohama, like most other places however salubrious they may be under ordinary circumstances, is subject to occasional epidemic visitations, amongst others to cholera. Last year, in common with the whole of Japan, it was visited by a severe epidemic of measles, which caused a considerable mortality. There are no facts however to show that its swampy locality confers upon it any special predisposition to become the seat of epidemic disease; because Nagasaki, which is altogether free from malarious soil, and distant from Yokohama about 600 miles, is also subject to similar visitations. The epidemic of measles, for instance, appeared there some weeks before it showed itself at Yokohama. Nagasaki, I may add, is equally liable to visitations of cholera, and suffered very severely from that disease during the summer of 1862. The great epidemic of cholera, which first appeared at Shanghai in the end of May of that year, ultimately took the following course to Japan. From Shanghai the cholera travelled up the north coast of China, and on the 16th of June appeared at Taku, where it committed great ravages, the place having been up to that time noted for its salubrity. Leaving Taku, it took a course up the Peiho, and at Tien-tsin it is stated to have destroyed in a few weeks 20,000 of the inhabitants. From Tien-tsin it went on to Peking, where it fell likewise with very fatal effect. From that city it travelled eastward over to Manchuria, and thence turned southward again, settling on Japan, where it seemed to expend itself, as we have no further trace of it; Hong Kong and the other Chinese ports to the south of

Shanghai having apparently been beyond the line of its operation. At Shanghai the disease seemed to fall with peculiar severity on those living afloat, the proportion of deaths on ship-board considerably exceeding that of the shore population : a fact tending still further to disconnect choleraic visitations with specific local impurities. As far as my opportunities for observation have enabled me to form an opinion, it is to the operation of certain electro-chemical changes in the atmosphere on certain constitutions, and not to special local defects of sanatation, that we must look for an explanation of this dire and mysterious disease.

In the course of my walk this afternoon, I visited the consular prison, where the detachment of the 67th Regiment is at present quartered, and had an opportunity of practically verifying the apparent innocuousness under certain collateral conditions, as yet unknown to us, of a residence in the midst of malarious soil, exposed to the decomposing influence of solar heat of tropical power. The local disadvantages under which this detachment, consisting of thirty men, has been living for some time back are very marked; in addition to the mass of swamp and vegetable *débris* to which the building is immediately contiguous, the chief drain of the settlement empties itself into a semi-stagnant pool close to the house ; yet the men do not seem to suffer from these sanitary defects in any appreciable manner. I made a careful inspection of them, and found them all looking the picture of robust health, very different indeed to what their aspects were when I saw them embark for Japan eleven months previously at Shanghai. I inquired particularly with reference to the occurrence of ague amongst them, and found that attacks took place very rarely, and usually on certain changes in the weather in men who had contracted the disease originally in China.

In the rear of the foreign settlement, beyond the ordinary limits of the native town, I found a street inhabited by

Japanese tradesmen, apparently chiefly in European employment; amongst others, I observed some washermen at work getting up linen. For ironing purposes they use a conical-shaped copper box, with a handle over the top like the European hand-iron. The interior of the box is filled with lighted charcoal, which keeps the copper at a uniform heat. This ironing machine is probably borrowed from the Chinese, who use one of a similar kind, only round in shape and having the handle stuck into the side like that of a warming-pan.

Strolling down this street with an independent swagger, evidently looking upon themselves as "first chop,"* were several Chinamen, dressed in light-coloured silks, with feather fans in their hands, and smoking cigars with an air of cool confidence. John Chinaman, of whom there are about 200 representatives in Yokohama, is said to be inclined to give himself airs here, and to look upon himself as much superior to the Japanese of the corresponding class, that he is brought into contact with in the course of business; and I am told that to a certain extent he is looked up to by the natives as belonging to the nation from which Japan has derived its literature. With respect to the relative merits of the two people, from all I can gather it seems to me that the Japanese, though more prone to adopt European improvements, are commercially a long way behind the Chinese—also less industrious, more licentious and intemperate, and in the main their inferiors, though on a superficial view the Japanese are much the more attractive nation. In Europe the opinion is generally entertained that the two nations are of common origin. Kœmpfer, however, who was the medical officer of the Dutch Factory at Nagasaki for several years during the latter part of the seventeenth century, and is, perhaps, the best authority we have on Japan, holds a contrary belief, supporting his opinion by a very learned

* The Canton English for the superlative degree.

disquisition on the differences of language, religion, and customs which exist between them.

Yet, irrespective altogether of the question of the descent of the one from the other, there is no doubt that a physical resemblance exists between the two people sufficient to identify them as belonging to the same race. The Chinese differ in many essential points from the natives of Mongolia, physically as well as morally, nevertheless these differences do not throw any doubt on the Chinese belonging to the Mongolian race. As far as I have been able to observe, the physical difference between the Japanese and the Chinese is not so great as between the latter and the Mongolians; and I do not think that the most acute ethnologist could tell which was a Chinaman and which a Japanese, provided they were dressed alike, and their heads shaved in a similar manner. However dissimilar also the two languages may be, it has been practically ascertained that a knowledge of the Chinese characters constitutes an important preliminary step to acquiring a knowledge of those of the Japanese language; and on this account the student interpreters sent out by Her Majesty's Government for the Japan diplomatic service, go first to Peking, and under the tuition of a literary superintendent, learn the Chinese characters along with the student interpreters sent out to Her Majesty's Legation in China.

CHAPTER V.

Return of the French Admiral—His proceedings in the Straits of Semonosaki—Daimios' retainers—Military character of the Japanese—A Chinaman's views regarding the hostilities—Captain Macdougall—The Governor of Kanagawa—Conference of Foreign Ministers—Visit to the barracks of the disciplined Japanese—Barrack-room drill—Disregard of national prejudices.

July 24th.—This morning, about five o'clock, I was awoke by the news that the "Semiramis," the flag-ship of the French Admiral, was in the offing. I rose at once to have a sight of her, and a noble vessel she appeared, with her long black hull and thirty guns aside, as she steamed into the anchorage. I have gathered the following particulars of what Admiral Jaurais has done in the straits.

On the 20th instant the "Semiramis" entered the Straits of Semonosaki and took up a position opposite a fort on the northern side. The fort did not open fire upon her, which forbearance the French attribute to the position the "Semiramis" had taken up, as they seem to think that it was impossible for the fort to have fired at them without the risk of firing also on a town on the opposite shore, with a number of junks anchored in front of it. The "Tancred" gunboat however, having gone farther in, was fired at from another battery, receiving one shot in her hull, and two or three through her rigging. The "Semiramis" then opened fire upon this latter battery from her rifled cannon, at a range of 3000 yards, with considerable effect. After this, a landing was ordered, the force consisting of 180 sailors and 70 Zephyrs, who took the fort in the rear, the Japanese escaping

as they advanced. The battery consisted of seven twenty-four pounder brass guns which were dismounted, spiked, and their carriages burnt. The party then crossed a rice field towards a village, which they set on fire, and on breaking open the door of a house of better construction than the others, found it to be a large powder magazine. Twenty-five minutes afterwards the flames extended to it, and it exploded with a terrific noise. Having effected this the party re-embarked; three men were wounded, one of them since dead. About forty Japanese are believed to have been killed. The number of Japanese troops seen on shore by the landing party is estimated at 500. From the ships, however, a body of cavalry, infantry, and artillery were seen coming out of the town of Semonosaki and taking a course along the Tokaido,* apparently to the aid of the troops in the battery. This supporting force was variously estimated from 3000 to 10,000. In the words of the Chef d'Etat Major of Admiral Jaurais, from whom I received this account of the affair:—
"I did not see them myself, being on shore at the time. Those, however, on board ship saw them distinctly; one officer told me there were 3000, another said there were 6000, while a third assured me there were 10,000." Individually, I should be inclined to adopt the lowest estimate, and subject it also to a very considerable reduction, because, from all I can learn, it is a myth to suppose that the Daimios have anything like the numbers of armed retainers they are represented to have, in proof of which, on the authority of Consul Winchester I have it, that when the "Elgin" and "Rajah" were hired a few days ago to convey troops to Osaca, the government of the Tycoon had great difficulty in scraping together 600 men to send in them. It appears that amongst a Daimio's armed retainers, as they are represented on paper, are included all of the male sex, from old and

---

* This Tokaido is a continuation of the same Tokaido, or "great seaboard road," upon which Mr. Richardson was murdered, nearly 600 miles in another direction.

Y

decrepid men who were once fit to bear arms, to children at the breast, who in course of years will be fit to do so. Altogether I am inclined to think that the military prowess of the Japanese, and their importance as an arm-bearing people, are much over-rated, and that should we be compelled to enter on a trial of arms with them they will be found, like the Chinese, formidable only so long as they are allowed to fight with big guns from behind well planned and strongly defended forts, but the reduction of these involves no great difficulty in these days, considering the powerful artillery that we can bring to bear upon them, as well as the fact that they are all more or less assailable from the rear.

There is no doubt that the Japanese are naturally more prone to the use of arms than the Chinese. Every one of a certain class, holding the position equivalent to that of a Highland clansman of the olden time, learns from an early age the use of the sword, but this knowledge does not appear, so far as we know, to be employed in any more military manner than secret assassinations and open attacks on unarmed foreigners. The Tycoon's Government is certainly now beginning to train troops according to a modification of the European system, but this is only a recent innovation, and these it is probable are more for show than real work, and I have very little doubt that they would bolt with a speed equal to that of their two-sworded brethren if brought in contact with the disciplined troops of the West, as the Chinese have almost invariably done whenever they have attempted operations in the open field.

Even the Chinamen in Yokohama affect pity for the foolhardy course which the Daimios are pursuing in supposing for a moment that they are equal to coping with the powers of the West, and especially with England. One of these gentlemen, the other day conversing with a member of Her Majesty's legation about the present state of matters, made the following judicious observations :— "Those Japan men number one foolo's ; they no savee those ships—they no savee what pieeee fight they makee, supposee that pigeon bigin," which rendered into more intelligible English, means that the Japanese are great fools, and do not know the formidable nature of a collision ("fight pigeon") with our ships of war.

This evening Colonel Neale entertained at dinner the English and French admirals and the various commanders of men-of-war in the harbour. I sat near Captain Macdougall of the "Wyoming," and heard from him an account of his action in the Straits, which coincides with that I have already given. He however does not look upon the destruction of the forts as a matter of any serious difficulty, and is of opinion that three ships of the size of Her Majesty's ship "Encounter" (14-gun corvette) would be an ample force to destroy them—more vessels, he thinks, would be in each other's way. Had he had any ship to have fallen back upon, in the event of his machinery having been struck, he says that he would not have withdrawn as he did; but would have continued engaging the forts, and is of opinion that one by one he could have silenced them. The risk was too great to be attempted unsupported.

July 25th.—This morning Admiral Jaurais received a communication from the Governor of Kanagawa in reply to one that he had sent him yesterday, detailing his proceedings against the forts. The Governor's communication was to the effect that he was very glad to hear of what he had done, but regretted that he had not advanced further up the strait, because had he done so, he would have inflicted still greater chastisement on the Prince of Negato. These expressions of regret tend in some measure to support the correctness of a rumour that is current this morning amongst the Japanese, that it was not the Prince of Negato's fort that the French took, but that of his brother, who is one of the Tycoon's Daimios. Should such be the case, it is unfortunate; but at the same time it is difficult to see how, under the circumstances, the French admiral was to distinguish between hostile and friendly forts, where they are in a line on the same side of the straits.

A conference was held this morning by the representatives of foreign nations having men-of-war in the harbour —namely, England, France, the Netherlands, and America. The conference took place at the French Legation, and it was decided that the four naval commanders should be directed to act in unison, and adopt such measures as seem to them most expedient for re-opening the inland sea to foreign vessels—now closed by the batteries of the Prince of Negato. This conference has no relation to the Prince of Satsuma, as Colonel Neale made it clearly understood that the projected demonstration against Kagosima is an entirely British affair, and that it will be undertaken by Her Majesty's vessels of war only, at the earliest convenient period after the settlement of the question of the opening of the navigation of the inland sea.

In the afternoon I walked by myself to the end of the native town of Yokohama. At the place where a bridge crosses an inlet of the bay into which the northern extreme of the investing canal opens, I found some of the Japanese disciplined troops living in barracks. They were very civil and allowed me to go into the barrack-rooms, which were neat and clean internally, but externally surrounded by swamp and garbage. Nothing could be less offensive than the general bearing of the officers as well as the men: they indulged in a little natural and harmless curiosity, such as examining my clothes and taking out my watch, handling the latter carefully, and politely returning it when they had completed their inspection of it. Their arms appeared to be kept in very good order, and were disposed with regularity in wooden arm-racks. Their cartridge boxes were filled with ball ammunition of their own preparation, the cartridges being made up with Japanese paper. Inside some of the barrack-rooms squads of men were learning the manual and platoon exercise under native instructors.

This system of barrack-room drill struck me as being worthy of introduction into our own service, particularly in India, where want of occupation for the soldier during the greater number of the hours of daylight, constitutes one of the great evils that have to be contended with in his sanitary management. In that country, under a tropical sun, with the thermometer nearly 100° in the shade, eating, drinking, smoking, and sleeping—particularly the latter—constitute almost his only modes of spending his time; in fact, his ideas on the subject of mental and physical exertion closely resemble those of the emancipated negro, who, on being asked how he managed to spend his time now that he was a free man, replied that he laid on his back all day and let time spend himself.

In a communication relating to the means most likely to modify the ill effects amongst soldiers of the use of spirits in warm climates, which by directions of the then President of the Indian Sanitary Commission (the late Lord Herbert), I furnished to the Royal Commissioners early in the year 1860, amongst the recommendations I made was the following—"Enforcing such regulations relating to soldiers in barracks, as will insure their making an amount of physical exertion daily, calculated to promote activity in the excretory functions, and, at the same time, so increase the systemic tear and wear as to afford sufficient employment for the nutritive or nitrogenous portions of their food, and thus obviate such a state of matters as Dr. Mouat* describes to be characteristic of the ordinary routine of a soldier's life in barracks in India, and which is represented according to the following detail—'After sleeping through the night in the very hot, close air of the barracks, he rises at gunfire and goes to parade, after which he employs himself in cleaning his accoutrements till breakfast time—eight o'clock. This meal over, he lies down and sleeps till dinner

* "The British Soldier in India," by Dr. Mouat, Inspector-General of Jails in Bengal.

time, and after dinner he generally retires to his bed again, and sleeps more or less till five o'clock, the temperature of the barrack being frequently as high as 104° Fahrenheit at that period of the day. About five o'clock he has to prepare himself for parade; this over, he saunters out till half-past nine, and then turns in for the night.' This is given by Dr. Mouat as a picture from nature, by Mr. Macnamara, of the ordinary routine lives of the soldiers of the First Bengal Fusiliers at Dinapore." Therefore, with the view of counteracting such an unnatural state of daily existence as that here represented, I cannot see any reason why we should not borrow a leaf from the Japanese, and give our soldiers in India an hour's drill or instruction in their barrack-rooms, or in covered buildings outside if preferred, forenoon and afternoon, in addition to their ordinary parades. This barrack-room drill could be carried out in the warm weather without fatiguing the men, without needless encumbrances of dress, belts, ammunition pouches, &c. Manual and platoon drill might be alternated with "judging distance"* exercise, which, so far as I am aware, there is nothing whatever to prevent being carried out without exposing the men to the sun, against which, whether right or wrong, there is a strong prejudice in India. Monthly or quarterly prizes should be given to the men who have attained the greatest proficiency during the period, on the same principle as is adopted at the annual course of instruction, and thus some direct stimulus would be held out to the men to exert themselves. The expenses connected with such prizes might be defrayed from the "Canteen Fund" (experimentally at any rate), which is generally in a flourishing condition in most of our infantry corps. That there is no point on which the soldier, as a general rule, is more deficient connected with his duties than the capacity for

---

* For the information of the non-military reader, "judging distance" forms the first portion of the course of practical rifle instruction, which every infantry soldier is now-a-days supposed to go through once a year.

correctly estimating distances, I think few who have served with troops in the field since the introduction of the Enfield rifle, will be inclined to deny. The efficiency of this weapon of precision at any range beyond point blank depends on the judgment of the soldier in adjusting the graduated sight with which the rifle is fitted, which, again, is altogether dependent upon his appreciation of distance, which is a practical art, in which experience and constant training can alone render men proficient, and more especially those with not the brightest of natural intellects. At present the soldier goes only once a year through a course of distance-judging, and I do not think that any valid reason can be adduced why it should not be made an almost daily source of instruction, amusement, and emulation to him during a portion of his weary leisure hours in India, where he is precluded from taking exercise in the open air, for a considerable portion of the year, from almost sunrise to sunset—the more so as it constitutes the very groundwork of the efficiency of the soldier of the present day. Some sort of occupation of this kind would lessen the necessity for continuing the system of extreme early rising to which our soldiers are at present subjected in India; too frequently being compelled to get up and dress at the earliest dawn of day—at the very time, in fact, when, after having spent a restless, probably sleepless, night from the extreme heat, exhausted nature is seeking repose. That this is no imaginary picture, my experience as a regimental surgeon in China warrants me in asserting—there the Indian system of early parades was strictly carried out during the hot season, and I know that what I now state was the case.

After leaving the Japanese barracks, I crossed the bridge and walked some way up the road leading to the Governor's residence at Tobay. On the way, I repeatedly met two-sworded men, sometimes singly, sometimes two or three together. I was altogether unarmed, and met with neither insult nor annoyance direct or indirect. I may have been running a risk in going so far beyond the precincts of the settlement, especially without firearms ; I confess, however, to entertaining the idea—it may be an erroneous one—but I have not yet had any personal reason to doubt it, that in moving about amongst Orientals for amusement, it is better rather to trust to the protective influence derived from respecting their prejudices, and avoiding everything likely to give them offence or annoyance, than to carry a revolver. When it becomes really dangerous to move about beyond certain limits without weapons of defence, under circumstances similar to those now relating to Japan, pleasure excursions and visits of curiosity are better altogether avoided. The adoption of the opposite course in both of these respects, I believe to have been the cause of many of our troubles in the East.

CHAPTER VI.

The Gorogio's reply to the French Minister—An American sailor wounded by a Yaconin—The Tycoon and the Daimios—Agriculture—Rapid acquisition of the language by a foreigner—The peasantry—Inconsiderate conduct of equestrians—Naval conference respecting the inland sea question—Japanese shampooing—Its application to the treatment of disease—The blind in Japan—Origin of the Tycoons.

July 26th.—This forenoon M. de Bellecourt received a communication from the Gorogio, being a reply to a despatch he had addressed to the members, relative to the attack on the "Keinchang." The purport of the document is an expression of their regret that such an occurrence should have taken place; adding, by way of consolatory information, that similar attacks have been made upon the American and Dutch flags. The Gorogio then goes on to say, that having learnt that an impression prevails on the part of the foreign ministers, that the Tycoon's Government is unequal to punishing the Prince of Negato for his recent hostile proceedings, they wish it to be understood that such is not the case, and that it is their intention to have all the matters that have recently occurred in the Straits of Semonosaki inquired into. In the meantime, however, they beg that no action may be taken by the French authorities, pending these investigations. This communication is viewed as having been written merely for the purpose of sending a copy of it to the Tycoon, because at the time of its dispatch from Yeddo, the Gorogio must have been in full possession of all the details connected with the destruction of the fort by the French.

Reports are current amongst the Japanese, that Daizen-no-daiboo, and particularly Awadsi-no-kami, are much enraged, and have declared their intention to take vengeance on Yokohama and Nagasaki. The steamer, the brig, and the barque belonging to the Prince of Negato, are said to be severely injured, but are represented as still able to carry their guns. A part of Semonosaki is stated to have been burnt down by three shells from the "Medusa."

In the afternoon, an American sailor, very drunk, was passing down the main street of the foreign settlement, and making tacks from one side of the street to the other, in one of which, he unfortunately came in collision with a Yaconin, who drew the short and least formidable of his two swords, and gave the sailor a cut across the face with it. The Yaconin continued his course, and the sailor his, but bleeding rather freely, and "guessing" that his nose was cut off. This occurred at the door of the Yokohama Hotel, in the presence, I believe, of several foreigners, who appear to have considered discretion the better part of valour, and to have avoided any retaliatory measures towards the two-sworded gentleman. The foreigner, especially when without a revolver, is said to be beginning in Japan to display a capacity for self-control, in reference to acts of violence against the natives, which he is unequal to in China, and which it is reasonable to suppose arises from the fact that Chinamen never by any chance are armed, unless they are soldiers or robbers—whereas, in Japan, a very large proportion of the civil population carry arms, and are, as a general rule, very ready to use them on the least provocation.

July 27th.—The Japanese news to-day is to the effect, that the Princes of Satsuma, Negato, and Tosa, whose territories are respectively in Kiu-sin, Niphon, and Si-kok, have been informed by the Tycoon that they are at liberty to carry out their measures for the expulsion of foreigners, but that he (the Tycoon) declines to hold himself responsible for their acts. The report also is, that at the same time this communication has been sent to them, they have received notice of banishment from both Yeddo and Kioto. They are represented to be now in open rebellion against the Tycoon, and therefore it has been determined to fire upon all foreign vessels passing through the straits. To this rebellion is attributed the recent dispatch of troops to Osaco, for the protection of the Tycoon. As a proof of the hostile feeling of the Tycoon's Government to the Prince of Negato, the Japanese say, that were such not the case, the local authorities would not have furnished pilots to the American and French men-of-war, when they lately went to the straits. It is also stated that three Daimios, named Ho-so-kawa-wakasa-no-kami, Arina-nagats-kassa-no-oske, and Matz-daira-fisen-no-kami, who remain faithful to the Tycoon, have been charged with the destruction of Satsuma, Negato, and Tosa. Such are the conflicting accounts respecting matters *inter se*, and very remarkable is the difficulty which appears to exist at the very scene of action, in ascertaining the truth about them, but taken altogether, everything tends to show that Japan is on the eve of some great political convulsion, apart altogether from the foreign question, which, as I have already stated, the Japanese themselves think is made a cause of discontent, for the purpose of more effectually embroiling the Tycoon, and weakening his power.

In the afternoon I rode some distance into the country, in the rear of the settlement, but within the amphitheatre of hills, and found it to consist chiefly of paddy fields—in other words, swamp under rice cultivation, intersected by a number of narrow, raised pathways, not wide enough for two horses to go abreast. In a few places small patches of ground have been raised, sufficiently high to admit of other crops than rice being raised to a small extent. These little pieces of reclaimed swamp are generally arranged so that the crops alternate with each other—the arrangement being generally a rice field, then a patch of potatoe cultivation, then another rice field, then a patch of beans, and occasionally cotton. The following extract from Kœmpfer is interesting, as showing the state of agriculture in his time (1680 to 1700), and as far as one can judge from superficial observation, it seems equally applicable to its state at the present day:—

"The Japanese are as good husbandmen as perhaps any people in the world. Nor, indeed, is it very surprising that they have made great improvements in agriculture, considering not only the extreme populousness of the country, but chiefly that the natives are denied all commerce and communication with foreigners, and must necessarily support themselves by their own labour and industry. Hence the laws on this head are very particular and severe. Not only the fields and flat country, which are seldom or never turned into meadows or pasture ground, but likewise the hills and mountains afford corn, rice, peas, pulse, and numberless edible plants. Every inch of ground is improved to the best advantage, and it was not without great admiration we beheld in our journey to and from Court, hills and mountains, many inaccessible to cattle, which would lie wholly neglected in other countries, cultivated up to their tops. They are very dexterous and skilful in manuring their ground, which they do in various ways, and with many different substances. Flat, low grounds are ploughed with oxen, steep and high ones by men. As to rice in particular, which is the main food of the natives, what ground they can conveniently spare, and will admit of its culture, is turned into rice fields, particularly low flats which they can cut through by canals, and where they have a command of water, which surprisingly quickens the growth of this plant, it loving a wet muddy soil. The Japanese rice, accordingly, is esteemed the best of all Asia, particularly what grows in the northern provinces, which will keep many years, and which for this reason, they choose to fill their store-houses withal, having first washed it in muddy water and then dried it."

I was accompanied on my ride into the country by Mr. Alexander Von Siebold, a son of the well known Dr. Von Siebold, for many years an employé of the Dutch Government in Japan, and, probably, of all foreigners now alive, the one who possesses the most intimate acquaintance with Japan and its inhabitants. His son, who is only sixteen years of age, in addition to his native tongue, the Dutch, has mastered the English, French, German, and Japanese languages, talking the latter with such fluency as to make it difficult to the Japanese to understand that he is not an Europeanised native. His very perfect colloquial knowledge of Japanese is the more remarkable, from the fact, that two years only have elapsed since he commenced to study the language. In him the phrenological dogma, that the natural capacity for acquiring languages is indicated by large and full eye-balls, finds a well marked illustration. He has been for the last two years attached to the British Legation, and at present acts as private secretary and interpreter to Colonel Neale. He frequently accompanies Admiral Kuper in his rambles into the country, his knowledge of the language being of considerable aid to the Admiral in the pursuit of his entomological researches.

During our ride, we met with unvarying civility from the peasantry, who conversed in a good-humoured manner with Mr. Von Siebold. The more I see of the agricultural population, the more do they remind me of the same class of the Chinese. Owing to the narrowness of the paths, and, in many instances, the swamps on each side of them, the country in the vicinity of Yokohama is not well adapted for riding. The peasants also appear to have a great dread of foreign horses, arising from the unrestrained manner in which they go, as compared with the Japanese horses, which are always led, and consequently not likely to go out of a walk. On our way home, we observed some young foreigners, who looked like Englishmen, riding at a smart pace along one of these narrow causeways, having no regard for several country-people coming along carrying loads, amongst them two old women, who fearing being ridden over, had to get off the pathway on to its bank at the risk of going into the swamp, as also the people with their loads had to do. Greater want of consideration could not have been shown than by these young gentlemen, who never slackened their pace, as the fears of the people became manifest, but went a-head, as if they were performing some chivalrous feat, the delusion being probably aided by the fact of their carrying revolvers.

In the earlier part of the day, Admiral Kuper convened a meeting on board the "Euryalus," of the French, Dutch, and American naval commanders, with the view of deciding on the course of action to be adopted relative to opening the navigation of the inland sea. It was unanimously decided that it is not desirable to adopt any further aggressive steps against the Prince of Negato until the Tycoon's Government unequivocally notifies either its unwillingness or its inability to punish him. Another cause, which renders the adoption of active measures premature, is the fact of the "Coquette" not having yet returned from the Straits of Semonosaki, for which she left about a week ago, in hopes of communicating with Admiral Jaurais. She is expected back in the course of to-morrow or next day, and it is possible she may bring some intelligence influencing the question at issue.

Two days ago, feeling rather fatigued after a long walk I had taken over the hills, it occurred to me to try the efficacy of the Japanese system of shampooing, as a means of dissipating sensations of lassitude from over-exertion,—of the beneficial results of which I had heard a good deal previously. In Japan, the practice of the art of shampooing is a monopoly of the blind. The professors shave the head, and adopt the dress of the medical profession, to which they are considered to be allied, in much the same manner as dentists, cuppers, and aurists are in England. They generally walk about the streets in the evening seeking employment, notifying their presence by ringing a bell. Having secured the services of one of these gentlemen, I was requested to lie down on a sofa; and prior to beginning his manipulations, he asked Mr. Von Siebold what degree of force he should commence with,—whether the minimum, the medium, or the full; his muscular power apparently being graduated much after the fashion of an electro-magnetical machine. Having no acquaintance with the force he was likely to employ, I chose the medium, upon which he commenced a series of powerful and rapid kneadings of one of my limbs, which was so far from being pleasant, as to cause me at once to beg that the minimum force should be substituted. This I managed to bear, the operation consisting of successive graspings of the muscles of the chest and limbs, the digitations being performed with a rapidity resembling a person running over the notes of a piano-forte. The process was by no means an agreeable one, but its effects were very remarkable; all sensations of fatigue having disappeared, and a feeling of perfect elasticity of limb being re-established.

The practice of shampooing is in general use in Japan, and is employed as a remedial agent in the treatment of special maladies,—in fact, it closely resembles the mode of treating disease by muscular movements, introduced to notice about fifty years ago at Stockholm by a Swedish fencing-master, of the name of Ling. Attempts have been made of recent years to introduce this treatment into practice in other parts of Europe under the name of kinesipathy, but it has been by no means favourably received by the medical profession, owing, amongst other causes, to the wide range of disease over which it professes to exercise a curative influence. Ling was more fortunate than his successors have since been. In 1813, he succeeded in procuring the establishment by royal ordinance of the "Gymnastic Central Institute of Stockholm," which was devoted to the carrying out of his views respecting the mechanical treatment of disease by such means as percussion, kneading, vibration, pinching, &c., and it is very probable that a certain amount of success may have attended his practice; as there are hardly any of the many innovations that have been made in modern times on the regular system of medicine that have not some good in them, however little they may be adapted for the cure of disease generally. That the employment in Japan of a method somewhat analagous to kinesipathy, tends to mitigate human suffering there is no doubt, and whatever does so, even to a limited extent, is entitled to consideration, apart altogether from the special "pathy" that it hails from.*

The conferring of a monopoly of the shampooing art on the blind is a wise provision on the part of the Government; the occupation being, of all others, the one best suited for their afflicted state; admitting, as it does, of easy acquirement, and experience being all that is required to beget skill in the art, constant use tending to develope the muscular

---

* Those who have ascended the Pyramids of Egypt may recollect the sensation of relief which is experienced, when, on reaching the top, the Arabs seize their wearied knees, and, by a sort of kinesipathic process, remove from them the feelings of extreme fatigue, which the rude and peculiar nature of the ascent generally produces. In India, shampooing is employed by the native doctors in the treatment of some internal as well as external diseases, but the proceeding is conducted in a more gentle manner than in Japan and China. In the latter country, percussion of the spine constitutes the most important part of the process, and is effected by the operator (who is always a barber) beating a regular tattoo with both his hands over the whole length of the vertebral column. The Chinaman has this operation performed as regularly as he has his head shaved.

power of the fingers, and to confer a manipulating capacity and rapidity truly surprising. I find no allusion made to this art in Kœmpfer's time; from what he says, however, the blind would seem to have been long a favoured class in Japan, and to have constituted one of the most important of the many partly secular, partly ecclesiastical societies that exist in the empire. With respect to the origin of these associations of the blind, Kœmpfer, after giving an account of the religious order of the mountain priests of Japan, goes on to state:—

"There are still many more religious orders and societies established in this country. From the superstitious veneration of the vulgar for their ecclesiastics, and the ease and pleasures of a religious life, it is no wonder that the number of costly temples, rich monasteries and convents, where, under the cloak of retirement and divine worship, the monks give themselves up to an uninterrupted pursuit of wantonness and luxury, is grown to an excess scarce credible. But there are also some particular societies not purely ecclesiastical, nor confined to the clergy alone, but rather of a mixed nature, with an alloy of secularity. Out of many, that of the blind is not unworthy of consideration; a singular, but very ancient and numerous body, composed of all ranks and professions."

In relating the history of this society, he speaks of a certain General, Joritomo by name. This man was the first of the Secular Emperors of Japan, of whom the Tycoon is the modern representative. Joritomo was a Daimio, who, in his turn, appears to have rebelled against the then reigning Dairi or Mikado, who was an usurper. Joritomo succeeded in restoring the rightful heir, by whom he was invested with a temporal control over the empire, under the designation of the Siogoun. The authority of the Mikado, however, would seem not to have been materially affected by this executive appointment, as there is no doubt that at the present day he exercises, when he chooses, supreme governing power, though, apparently, it has been allowed to remain in abeyance for a great number of years, during which the government of the country has resided in the person of the Tycoon alone. But recently it has suited the views of certain influential Daimios to resuscitate the dormant ecclesiastical authority as a means of furthering the displacement of the present secular incumbent.

CHAPTER VII.

Report respecting the return of the Tycoon—Mode of committing suicide a branch of Japanese education—Fight between the betos and the Gaukiro people—Attempt on the part of Japanese traders to procure rifled cannon—Japanese doctor and medical science—Diet of the natives—A profitable land speculation—Errors respecting the disposition of the peasantry—A Japanese official wounded—Return of the Tycoon—Hostile feeling towards foreigners at Miako—Aptitude of the Japanese for mastering the details of machinery—Purchase of the "Lyemoon" steamer—Fire-proof stores—Primitive state of society—Preparations for leaving Yokohama for Nagasaki—Peaceful news—Modes of travelling in Japan—Tattooing—Violent death of the murderer of Mr. Euskin.

July 28*th*.—A report is current to-day that, the Tycoon having succeeded in adjusting his difficulties with the Mikado at Kioto, is shortly about to return to Yeddo. This rumour is believed to be authentic, its origin having been an official source.

This forenoon I met a couple of little children of tender years walking about, each with two miniature swords stuck in his waist sash, indicating that when they grow up they will have the privilege of wearing two swords. It appears that amongst the arm-bearing section of the population, the children, from the earliest years that they are capable of being instructed, are taught not only the use of the sword, but also the most genteel and approved method of committing suicide by Harra Kiru, as it is considered vulgar to perform it as a mere rude process of disemboweling by ripping themselves up. A certain limit is assigned to the abdominal incision, which is usually made with the short sword, in a transverse direction. The actual deprivation of life is effected either by the person himself wounding the great blood-vessels of the throat, or having his head struck off by an attendant after he has recognised the obligation of committing suicide by personally making the abdominal incision.

A great fight commenced yesterday evening and has been going on all day, between the betos (grooms) and the male proprietors of establishments in the Gaukiro. It appears that a feud has existed for some time between them, and that in eleven consecutive engagements the betos have been worsted. This, the twelfth, quarrel, has arisen in consequence of two betos in the employment of the Governor of Kanagawa having got into a squabble in the Gaukiro, which ended in their getting a beating. On the news reaching the betos generally in Yokohama and Kanagawa, they determined to resent this fresh insult to their cloth, and arming themselves with sticks, staves, &c., they went in a body to the Gaukiro, but failed in effecting an entrance, the place having been put in a state of siege. The affair has been going on the whole day, without any decided success on either side. All the betos in the employment of the foreign residents have joined their brethren, and complaints are loud with respect to the neglect the horses are suffering in consequence. On this account a Consular representation was made to-day to the Governor of Kanagawa, who, in reply, said that the affair was one of those disturbances of a purely local and national character occurring within the limits of the Japanese town, that he was at a loss to see that foreigners have anything to do with. The inconvenience is merely a temporary one, and as such must be borne.

July 29*th*.—The betos have received reinforcements from Yeddo, their cause having been espoused by their brethren in the capital. The siege of the Gaukiro has been prosecuted all day, and it is stated that a grand assault is going to be made on it this evening from the side where it can be reached by water.

This afternoon, just as Colonel Neale and myself were going out into the town two Japanese merchants came to the Legation with a quantity of grotesque carvings in ivory. After having expended a few minutes showing their wares, one of them informed Mr. Von Siebold that the real object of their visit was to see if it was practicable for the British Minister to assist them in respect to purchasing some rifled cannon, for which they were commissioned to pay a very high price. They offered Mr. Von Siebold a present of the whole of the ivories, the value of which was considerable, if he would lend his aid towards their procuring even one rifled cannon. On being told that it was impossible to comply with their request, they went away evidently much disappointed. About an hour and a half afterwards, as we were returning from the native town, we met M. de Bellecourt and Admiral Jaurais. While Colonel Neale was talking to them, the same two men passed, and mentioning the circumstances connected with their visit to the Legation, a few questions were put to them, when they immediately renewed their request, and Admiral Jaurais jokingly said, "Tell them to bring off 25,000 francs to my ship, and I will let them have a rifled cannon."

July 30*th.*—It was not supposed for a moment that the remark of the French Admiral about the rifled gun was likely to be viewed otherwise than as a joke. It was, however, taken seriously by the Japanese merchants, who, early this forenoon, were waiting outside the French Legation endeavouring to procure from M. de Bellecourt a letter so that they could go off to the Admiral's ship and get the gun, in accordance with the offer he had made them yesterday afternoon. They were much disconcerted when they were told that it was only in jest that the Admiral had made the remark. They said they would be sure to get into trouble, as they had committed themselves to the Yaconins, by stating that they had succeeded in arranging for the purchase of a rifled cannon, and they did not see how they were to get out of the mess they had got into unless the Admiral would sell them the gun at the price he had mentioned. What they wanted the gun for we could not make out further than that it was for the Government service, and it is not probable that it is wanted for any purpose hostile to foreigners, otherwise the agents of the Government would hardly have the effrontery to endeavour to procure them through the foreign Ministers.

I met a Japanese doctor to-day in the native town, from whom it was ascertained that a few isolated cases of cholera are occurring at present amongst the native population, the cause of the disease being referred to worms in the stomach. The medical faculty in Japan seems to be held in considerable esteem by the natives, who are by no means inclined to trust themselves to the care of foreign physicians, who, they say, do not understand their constitutions. Attention to constitution enters largely into the practice of medicine in Japan, and so much importance is attached to an accurate knowledge of it as a guide to treatment, that Japanese doctors will not risk their reputation by attending their countrymen who have been some time in European employment, on the grounds that the change of diet to which they have been exposed has so materially changed their constitutions as to render it impossible for them to bring the resources of the native medical art successfully to bear on the treatment of ailments contracted under an altered and unnational mode of life.

The diet of the Japanese in this part of the country is very simple, and I believe it represents fairly what it is over the empire generally. It consists almost entirely of rice, fish, and pickled vegetables. They never eat meat, and on no account will drink milk or use it in any way as an article of food, as they look upon it as white blood. It is considered cruel either to kill the ox or the cow, and therefore these animals are kept entirely for the purposes of tillage. I have not heard, however, that the demand which a numerous resident foreign community necessarily gives rise to from day to day for the lives of oxen, has been made a subject of complaint or grievance, the pecuniary considerations involved probably tending to blunt their humanitarian principles. At the present time the slaughter of oxen daily must be considerable, owing to the requirements of the fleet, and two European butchers appear to be driving a very thriving trade.

In the course of conversation, allusion was made to a remarkable powder the Japanese doctors are said to possess; the application of which externally, removes at once muscular rigidity, whether occurring before or after death. The limbs of the dead are stated to be rendered as flexible as during life, immediately after the powder has been rubbed over them.

Notwithstanding the unsettled state of our political relations with Japan, commercial enterprise and land speculation seem by no means paralysed; a small lot of land within the foreign settlement, purchased in 1860 for 1500 dollars, was this day sold for 10,000.

The attack intended to be made yesterday evening on the Gankiro, was frustrated by the authorities taking away all the boats that were to have conveyed the assaulting betos across. To-day matters look more peaceful, and the report is that a compromise has been entered into by the contending parties, the nature of which, however, has not transpired. The betos are now beginning to return to their respective employers, which tends to confirm the report.

July 31*st.*—At a dinner party yesterday, at which I was present, a gallant foreign naval officer expressed the regret he felt at observing that the demeanour of the peasantry in the neighbourhood of Yokohama had altered so much for the worse since he last visited the place. This impression arose from the following circumstance. The other day he took a ride into the country with the Danish Consul and his wife, and after getting a little way out of town, the children shouted at them, and expressions were made use of, which the Danish Consul, who understands a little Japanese, said were not words of a polite nature, and recommended on prudential grounds that they should return. On mentioning the circumstance this morning to M. Von Siebold, he laughed, and told me that the children are now in the habit of shouting out to all foreigners who pass, "An-a-to moo-su," which, freely translated, means beetles and bugs. The poor children mean no offence, but the researches of Admiral Kuper having directed their attention to the study of entomology, they naturally suppose that foreigners generally take an equal interest in the science with the gallant Admiral, and therefore they never lose an opportunity of apprising passers-by that they have a stock of specimens on hand, and a reference to these no doubt constituted the expressions which the Danish Consul, not unnaturally, thought were unpolitely applied to himself and friends. The urchins, I may remark, have a material interest at stake in pressing the sale of their beetles, as they have been accustomed to receive pecuniary remuneration from the Admiral for the specimens they procure for him. This little incident seems to illustrate the erroneous impressions which foreigners are apt to form during a period of political excitement. The rural population is, to all appearance, as amiable and well-disposed as could be wished; wherever one goes, a friendly "Ohio" greets you, and when you leave the equally friendly "Sio-nar-ee;" the former the Japanese salutation on meeting, the latter, that on departing.

I now come to relate an occurrence of a very different nature. Yesterday, three young Englishmen rode on a trip of pleasure to Kanasawa, a very pretty spot on the coast, about twelve miles from Yokohama, having previously sent a boat round by sea, with liquor and provisions. They spent the day there without in any way being interfered with. Towards evening they determined to ride back to Yokohama without their coats, by moonlight, so they rode down a jetty, alongside of which their boat was lying, and in it deposited their coats. On the end of this jetty there was a shrine, and as they were riding off it, a Japanese official came up and spoke to them, in a tone which showed he was remonstrating with them for having ridden on to the jetty, which it seems is private property. One of the party, who, I may remark, is noted for getting into disturbances with the Japanese, knowing a little of the language, made a reply to the man that appears to have incensed him, as he drew his sword and came after them, when, in place of riding away and leaving the man they had irritated to calm himself, as most men of common sense or experience would have done, they drew their revolvers and fired at the man, arresting his progress by wounding him in the arm. Having achieved this bold feat, they rode back to Yokohama, and reported what they had done to Consul Winchester, justifying the act as necessary for self-defence. The matter has been brought to Colonel Neale's notice this morning, and will be made the subject of Consular inquiry. Altogether, it bears the aspect of a very discreditable proceeding. It is rather curious, that it was but yesterday forenoon I made some remarks to Colonel Neale relative to one of the party, expressive of my apprehension that sooner or later he would get himself into some mess, owing to the extraordinary manner in which he had been talking to me about the use of revolvers in Japan. These are the sort of young gentlemen whose indiscreet acts, leading to "violations of the rights of British subjects," have frequently been made the basis for aggressive measures; whereas, in no small proportion of instances, their acts are rather the violation of the rights of aboriginal nations by British subjects.*

This forenoon, the "Jinkee" and "Lyemoon" steamers

* The sequel of this case will be found in a subsequent Chapter.

passed Yokohama, the Tycoon's flag flying at the fore of the former vessel, indicating that the Tycoon was on board, and on his way back to Yeddo.

A few hours after the Tycoon had passed, another steamer arrived from Osaca, and anchored off the foreign settlement. On board of her was the high officer, He-ka-no-kami, who called at Yokohama on the 23rd instant, on his way to Osaca in the "Lyemoon." He landed immediately afterwards, and had an interview with Colonel Neale this afternoon, at which I was present. The object of his visit to Yokohama was to apprize the foreign Ministers that the Tycoon was about to return to Yeddo by sea, and to caution them against firing at his steamers, under the impression that they might belong to hostile Daimios. It appears that he was dispatched from Osaca in advance, five days ago, but his steamer has proved of such indifferent speed, that the Tycoon has arrived before him, which he was not aware of until he landed. In the midst of the interview, some custom-house officials who had been stationed on the heights, hearing of the arrival of He-ka-no-kami, came to the Legation in a state of great excitement, to let him know that the Tycoon had already passed.

In the course of conversation, Colonel Neale, who had known He-ka-no-kami in quieter times, asked him when they were to make their projected tour into the interior: he replied, "After long rains there will be sun, and as rains are now being made by Negato, we must wait until the sun again shines," which he hoped would not be long.

One fact of interest has been ascertained from He-ka-no-kami, which tends to show that the anti-foreign feeling continues to prevail at the capital (Miako). Oga-so-wari, who negotiated the payment of the indemnity money, has been thrown into prison for his connection with the matter. The impression seems to be that the Tycoon has managed to get away from the capital, not from any real improvement in the aspect of his relations with the Mikado, and those in whose hands the latter at present is, but simply because his enemies did not like to risk an engagement with the troops the Tycoon had managed to have about him. The general belief was that he would not be able to return to Yeddo.

The Japanese have certainly a much greater natural aptitude for mastering the details of steamboat mechanism than the Chinese have. It is quite a common occurrence for them to purchase a steamer, put their own crews and engineers on board, number in their own way the important parts of the machinery, get steam up, and without any assistance take the vessel away as readily as if they had been accustomed to the management of steamboats all their lives.

They have a great objection to wood-work being painted. The steam yacht, the "Emperor," presented to the Tycoon by Her Majesty, was beautifully decorated inside, and the first thing that was done with her at Yeddo after she was taken over, was to set a party of carpenters to work and scrape off all the interior embellishments in the form of gilding and paint.

The facts connected with the purchase of the "Lyemoon" steamer are somewhat remarkable—seeing that though she was actually purchased for the Tycoon's Government, from Messrs. Dent and Co. at Shanghai, for 175,000 dollars, the Government of the Tycoon paid 200,000 dollars for her. The agent of Dent and Co. at Yokohama (Mr. Clarke) having been instructed by the firm at Shanghai to sell the "Lyemoon," offered the vessel to the Japanese Government, and with due regard for the interest of his principals, named 240,000 dollars as her price. The Government, however, would not entertain the idea of buying her, the sum demanded appearing much too high. After allowing a little time to elapse, Mr. Clarke availed himself of the American Minister's intimacy at that time with the Tycoon's

Government, to renew the matter and make fresh overtures. General Pruyn is stated to have informed him that there was no prospect of making a deal. It would seem, however, that private negotiations were at the same time entered into with the Tycoon's Government, and their consent obtained to give 200,000 dollars for the vessel; for a Mr. Almand, a son-in-law of the United States Consul at Yokohama (Colonel Fisher), started for Shanghai, taking with him credentials sufficient to succeed in purchasing the "Lyemoon" from Messrs. Dent and Co. for 175,000 dollars. He got possession of her forthwith, and after putting several thousand stand of arms on board of her, as an extra speculation, he started in her for Japan, and the first intimation Mr. Clarke or the public in Yokohama had of the transaction was the arrival of the "Lyemoon," as the property of the Japanese Government, in charge of Mr. Almand. As naturally might be expected, Mr. Clarke was furious at having been so completely outwitted, and in the plainest terms accused his friend, General Pruyn, of being the party who had thus skilfully out-manœuvred him. The General disclaimed all connection with the transaction; but admitted that it was a very sharp proceeding on the part of Mr. Almand, who had no doubt made a very handsome thing out of it. Mr. Clarke would not see it in this light, but threw up the Portuguese Consulship which he was then holding, broke up his establishment, and declared his intention of proceeding direct to the United States to lay the whole matter before the President. This intention, however, he ultimately abandoned.

Amongst the objects of interest in Yokohama, I have omitted to notice the fire-proof stores, which the Japanese are very clever in constructing. The walls, which are of considerable thickness, are formed of a light wooden framework divided into partitions, which are filled with mud, carefully compressed into them. The walls are then plastered over inside and out with a non-combustible preparation of lime, resembling very hard stucco, and fitted with folding windows of sheet-iron. Strong glazed tiles form the roof. In no part of the East have I seen such substantial and well-constructed stores for commercial purposes, and I am told that their fire-proof qualities are undoubted.

This afternoon, passing what looked like a tea shop in one of the streets of the Japanese town, a number of nude figures caught my eye, and on looking in I found it to be a tea-house and bathing establishment combined. While I was standing at the door a portly gentleman, having finished his ablutions, made his appearance in the refreshment-room perfectly naked, and sat down to dry himself with a small cloth he brought with him. As soon as he was seated a young and modest-looking girl walked up to him with a cup of tea on a tray, which he took with the most perfect gravity, and with equal decorum she retired and proceeded to supply another customer who had just appeared—the whole proceeding, to the eye of a stranger, bearing a singularly unsophisticated and primitive character.

News having arrived from Shanghai the day before yesterday, that cholera has so much increased in prevalence there as to be showing signs of re-assuming an epidemic form,—though I am now off the strength of the China command, nevertheless, as I must return to Shanghai on my way to India, I feel it my duty to do so at once, as casualties from sickness or other causes amongst the medical staff, may render my professional services temporarily necessary. I have, therefore, obtained, through Colonel Neale's interest with the French Minister, a passage in his Imperial Majesty's steam corvette the "Monge," which starts to-morrow for Shanghai. This, therefore, is my last evening in Yokohama.

August 1st.—Early this morning Her Majesty's ship "Coquette" returned from her trip to the inland sea. On arriving at the entrance to the Straits of Semonosaki, and seeing no signs of the French admiral, she anchored for a few hours. In the course of the day, while she was thus at anchor, two Japanese officials came off from the shore, and said that if the vessel went through the Straits she would not be interfered with, as they did not wish to have any more fighting, having had enough of it. On her way back to Yokohama the "Coquette" went to Osaca, and sent a boat on shore, but the Japanese would not allow any one to land from it, and pushed the boat off. No other indications of hostility were shown, and as Osaca, though a treaty port, has not yet been opened to trade, the Japanese were quite warranted in opposing foreigners landing there.

This pacific news has materially altered the aspect of affairs respecting the inland sea question, and has enabled the one referring to Satsuma to be again brought forward with a view to immediate settlement. Colonel Neale had an interview with Admiral Kuper, and it has been determined that the squadron will leave Yokohama about the 6th or 7th instant, and proceed to Kagosima, and there deliver to the Prince of Satsuma or his representatives, the letter containing the demands of Her Majesty's Government, which the general impression is will be at once yielded to, as far as relates to the payment of the money. But the execution of the murderer of Mr. Richardson is a matter respecting which several causes may interfere with satisfaction being given.

While out this forenoon in the neighbourhood of the native town, I met a female being carried in what is called a caugo, an ordinary mode of conveyance adopted by the lower orders. It consists of a sort of bamboo litter, in shape not unlike a basket, in which the person sits in a very cramped and uncomfortable looking posture, but one apparently that suits the habits of the people. The caugo is suspended from a pole, which is borne on the shoulders of two men. The only other method of travelling in use in Japan, with the exception of horses, is the norimon, which is an oblong box, built of wicker-work or light wood, and covered outside with lacquer. It is supported by a pole on the shoulders of bearers, and is not unlike the palanquin, or palkee as it is usually called, of India. When horses are used by persons of quality, they merely hold the bridle as a matter of form, the horse being guided by the groom leading it. As a general rule, I believe, the only people who, when riding, are supposed to manage their horses themselves, are soldiers.

The subject of horses reminds me that in describing the betos, I omitted to mention the elaborate tattooing with which, as a general rule, their bodies are covered both back and front. A dragon is one of the favourite designs, and it is not uncommon to see the front of the chest covered with a representation of the head and fore part of the animal, which is represented as encircling the body; the remainder of the dragon being depicted on the back, loins, and even lower down, giving the possessor a singularly grotesque and rather savage aspect. The colours employed in tattooing are chiefly blue, red, and yellow.

There is a professional tattooer in the native town, who enjoys a high reputation as an artist. Some young English officers lately here on leave from China, submitted their arms to him, and left Japan indelibly marked with his skill. One of them showed me on his forearm a dove about half the size of life, and upon the upper part of the same arm a full length portrait of a yaconin, and a butterfly the size of life—the whole beautifully executed and coloured with artistic taste. The operation is described as rather painful, as the artist became occasionally a little excited over his work, especially when executing some of the more delicate touches, to ensure the correctness of which he applied the needle with a little extra force.

This habit of tattooing the person amongst the lower orders, constitutes another point of difference between the Chinese and Japanese. John Chinaman's talents in reference to the art of self-decoration are concentrated in promoting the luxuriance of his tail, and in calling in the aid of art where nature fails in her supply—false tails being as common in China as false teeth are amongst ourselves.

Information has lately been received from Yeddo, that Kio-kawa, the head of the Loonins, who is believed to have been the leader of the attack on the British Legation in June, 1861, and also at a subsequent period the murderer of Mr. Euskin, the interpreter to the American Legation, has himself been assassinated almost on the very spot where the latter deed was perpetrated. He is stated to have been attacked by two men in front, and while he was defending himself a third assaulted him from behind, and cut his head off.

CHAPTER VIII.

Departure for Nagasaki—Division of exchange profits amongst the crew—The currency question in Japan—Encounter a portion of a typhoon—Nagasaki harbour—Peaceful aspect of affairs—The old Dutch settlement of Desima—Singular reception of the Dutch superintendent of trade by the Tycoon at Yeddo—Analogous position of the agents of the late East India Company at Canton—The Japanese town of Nagasaki—Effects of solar influence—Heat apoplexy—Occurrence of cholera at Nagasaki co-existent with salubrity of climate—Observations on cholera.

On the afternoon of the 1st of August, 1863, I sailed from Yokohama in the French steam-corvette the "Monge." Her commander, Captain the Count de Marolles, had recently been promoted for services against the Taepings, in the course of which he had been wounded, and was about to return to France, after handing the vessel over to his successor at Shanghai. He was anxious to make the passage to Nagasaki through the Straits of Semonosaki, but Admiral Jaurais would only give him permission on the understanding that if he was fired at, he was not to continue his progress through, but return at once to Yokohama to apprise him of what had occurred. Being, however, specially desirous of reaching Shanghai in time to catch the French mail steamer that was to leave on the 15th of the month, he did not like to risk having to return to Yokohama, though he had no objection to risk an action with the batteries, if he was allowed to go on; much to his regret, therefore, he had to take the outside passage, and thus forego seeing the beauties of the Inland or Sowonada sea, and the formidable batteries of the Prince of Negato.

The afternoon was beautifully fine, the sky being clear and but little wind blowing. As we were steaming down the Bay of Yeddo a table was placed on deck, at which the first lieutenant and the purser sat down, with a bag of dollars before them. The names of the crew were then called over, and one by one each sailor came forward and received four dollars. My first impression was that it was their month's pay, but the signs of satisfaction apparent on their faces as they pocketed the money, seeming to me hardly consistent with so small a monthly stipend, I inquired as to what the payment was, and learned that it was gained by exchange out of dollar and itzeboo transactions with the Japanese custom-house. To make this intelligible, it is necessary to explain what the currency of Japan is, and the relation in which the coins stand to the Mexican dollar, which is the one now in general use amongst foreigners in China and Japan.

The Japanese coins in circulation at Yokohama and elsewhere are the tempo and the itzeboo, the former an oval shaped copper coin, about the value of $1\frac{1}{4}d.$; sixteen of these go to the itzeboo, a silver coin of an oblong shape, about one inch long and half-an-inch broad. The intrinsic value of the itzeboo is as nearly as possible 1s. 5d. sterling, though at present its nominal value is 1s. 8d. In the tenth article of the British treaty it is provided that "All foreign coin shall be current in Japan, and shall pass for its corresponding weight in Japanese coin of the same description. British and Japanese subjects may freely use foreign or Japanese coin in making payments to each other. As some time will elapse before the Japanese will become acquainted with the value of foreign coin, the Japanese Government will, for the period of one year after the opening of each port, furnish British subjects with Japanese coin in exchange for theirs, equal weights being given, and no discount taken for recoinage." At this period (1858) 311 itzeboos were the equivalent of 100 dollars, and the fixed standard rate of exchange. In minor transactions one dollar represented three itzeboos. Silver also, in relation to gold, was much more valuable in Japan at that time than it now is. The kobang, which is a gold coin of an oval shape, worth about 22s., could be readily purchased four years ago for six itzeboos, and was consequently eagerly bought up by foreign merchants. The Japanese now, however, fully appreciate the relative values of silver and gold, and the kobang at the present time costs 16 itzeboos, more in fact than its intrinsic value, so scarce have they become. Formerly so comparatively little value was attached to them that lacquerware manufacturers were in the habit of chopping them up and introducing small pieces of them into their finer kinds of lacquerware, which now, however, is very scarce, and goes under the name of the "old gold lacquer." This ware, in former days, before the eyes of the Japanese were opened to the value of gold by recent treaty intercourse, was common enough and procurable at moderate price, but things now are completely changed.

The compulsory rate of exchange fixed by treaty in 1858 ceased at Yokohama in June, 1860, and when the dollar thus came into general circulation amongst the Japanese trading community, it was found to be so little appreciated that it was not always practicable to get two itzeboos in exchange for it. By arrangement, however, made on the spot, after the compulsory exchange ceased, the Japanese Government was made to supply the foreign Legations and Consulates with itzeboos in exchange for a certain number of dollars monthly; 5000 dollars to be exchanged, I believe, for each Legation establishment and 1000 for each Consulate, the rate of exchange being fixed at three itzeboos to the dollar, which secured foreign Government residents from loss caused by fluctuations in the money market.

For the mercantile class of the community since June, 1860, the value of the dollar has been altogether governed by the rates of exchange of the day, and as the dollar has

A A 2

been much depreciated ever since, a certain feeling of soreness exists on the part of the foreign merchants that the residents in Government employment are so much more advantageously placed in reference to bullion transactions with the Japanese than they now are. They, however, have had their day, and made good use of it in the buying up of all the gold that was procurable; in fact, were the same relative advantages to be extended to the mercantile community as are now enjoyed by the diplomatic and other foreign Government Residents, that is to say, the right of exchanging their incomes in a similar manner at the Japanese custom-house, it would not be necessary, as I shall proceed to show, to trade in anything else but the conversion of dollars into itzeboos and *vice versâ*, as each transaction of the kind gives a very handsome profit, without incurring any of the risks and troubles usually attendant on goods speculations.

In addition to that referring to furnishing the Legations and Consulates with itzeboos for a fixed number of dollars, a further arrangement has been made with the Japanese Government, that every naval or military officer that the Treaty Powers happen to have for the time in port, or if need be employed on shore, shall be allowed to exchange three dollars per diem at the Japanese custom-houses at the open ports (Yokohama, Nagasaki, and Hakodadi), and every sailor or soldier one dollar per diem; the dollars being taken at the same rate as from the resident foreign officials, namely, three itzeboos to the dollar. This arrangement, seeing that the dollar as a current coin is not worth much over two itzeboos and a half, consequently involves a considerable gain to the fleet; the more so, as it is systematically managed, not by the officers or men themselves, but by the paymasters, who exchange at the custom-house the full amount they are entitled to, namely, one dollar a-day for every seaman and marine borne on the ship's books, and three dollars per diem for every officer. The same system is in force with the foreign troops serving on shore.

The extent of the profit will be readily understood by citing the rate of exchange at the time I left Yokohama, namely, 260 itzeboos to 100 dollars. Thus, for every 100 dollars exchanged by naval or military paymasters, 300 itzeboos are paid by the Japanese custom-house, and for 260 of these they can repossess themselves of their 100 dollars by purchasing them in the ordinary money market; making a clear profit, at the present rate of the itzeboo, equal to about fifteen per cent. sterling on this, the most simple of monetary transactions. Not long ago, the gain was much greater, as itzeboos had risen till less than 200 were equivalent to the 100 dollars.

In the French service every penny thus gained by exchange is divided amongst the officers and men in their relative proportions; thus, the gain to each sailor being four itzeboos on the exchange of ten dollars, gives him twelve itzeboos, or over four dollars per month, in addition to his pay, while three times as much falls to each officer. How the profit by exchange is applied in the British service I am not aware, with the exception that in some of our men-of-war I know a portion of it is applied to improving the diet of the men. This privilege does not extend beyond the periods that vessels of war are actually lying in the treaty ports; but by soldiers or sailors who have been landed for duty on shore, it is enjoyed so long as they continue to be so employed.

The Tycoon's Government lately conceded to Admiral Jaurais the privilege individually of exchanging thirty dollars per diem at the custom-house, at the fixed rate already mentioned, and having done so, they voluntarily did the same to Admiral Kuper, assigning as their reason, that having granted this to the French Admiral, they could not think of doing otherwise to the British Admiral. The Japanese Government having done this of their own accord for Admiral Kuper, General Pruyn did not see why he should not get the same for the senior naval officer of the United States, so he applied to have the like privilege extended to Captain Macdougall, of the "Wyoming," representing him as holding the same relative position at Yokohama as an admiral. The Japanese Government, however, though apparently anxious to make friends with admirals commanding fleets, did not seem to care so much about admirals commanding single ships, so they made inquiries at the other foreign Powers as to whether Captain Macdougall was the same as an admiral or not, and receiving an opinion unfavourable to his recognition in that rank, declined to give the permission the United States Minister had requested for him.

The itzeboos furnished from the custom-house are made up in neat paper parcels, each containing one hundred. The paper used is of country manufacture, and remarkable for its strength and tenacity. It bears ink pretty well, and is applied to a variety of purposes by the Japanese, such as pocket-handkerchiefs, waterproof coats, window glass, &c. In addition to the ordinary itzeboo, there are half and quarter ones in general circulation, which are very convenient sized coins, especially the latter, the value of which is about five pence.

We had hardly got clear of the Bay of Yeddo when the wind freshened to a strong breeze. Towards night of August 3rd, we found ourselves on the outer circle of a typhoon, and all sail had to be taken in except a storm jib, and such was the force of the wind that, with this small patch of canvas only, she ran nine knots an hour.

August 5th.—The weather has been very dirty and squally the whole day, and it was with considerable difficulty this afternoon that the approach to the harbour of Nagasaki was made out. We entered between two points of land, and were soon completely landlocked and sailing in a lake. The scenery was very beautiful, consisting of a series of conical-shaped hills richly wooded, without a trace of level ground being anywhere visible.

An hour nearly had elapsed since we entered the land, and I was standing near the bow of the vessel looking over the bulwarks, wondering where Nagasaki was, when suddenly the harbour opened into view, like the curtain rising in a theatre, and disclosing a gay tableau on the stage—the harbour filled with vessels, and standing out prominent amongst them H.M. ships "Leopard" and "Rattler." On shore, in the foreground, the old Dutch settlement of Desima, with the native town in the rear, and the foreign settlement at right angles on its left; the whole invested by lofty hills, thickly covered with brushwood and light timber of the brightest green, with here and there terraces of cultivation, and a few European bungalows dotted about on their slopes.

The harbour of Nagasaki might be rendered unapproachable, so great are its natural advantages for defence. Near the entrance, we passed under some formidable looking batteries, where about fifty guns are in position; in addition to which there are a number of masked batteries at various other points, respecting which we have no accurate information, as the local authorities will not allow foreigners to examine the heights in the direction in question. The guns that we saw are all carefully protected from wet, by each one having a small wooden shed over it.

We came to anchor a little after five o'clock, and I deferred visiting the shore until the morning, as a drizzling rain was falling, and I heard that during rain it becomes so muddy, as to render walking far from agreeable, especially on the slopes near the base of the hills.

During an experience of foreign travel by no means limited, I can call to recollection no scene that for exquisite beauty is equal to the one witnessed this afternoon. The nearest approach to it that I have seen is the harbour of Rio Janeiro, and next to that, Port Louis, in the Isle of France.

August 6th.—On landing this morning I went to the Acting British Consul, Dr. Myburgh, and delivered to him some despatches that had been entrusted to me by Colonel Neale. As far as I could learn things seem to be going on quietly enough here, and but little apprehension appears to exist in the minds of the foreign community with reference to any attack being made on them, though every now and then there are rumours to that effect as at Yokohama. The desire also to take the life of the British Consular representative would seem to have ceased with the departure of Mr. Morrison, as Dr. Myburgh does not express any fears respecting his own personal safety.

After leaving the Consulate, which is built on the slope of one of the hills, I went and looked at the old settlement of Desima, situated at the extreme end of the harbour, and separated from the native town by a canal running round its rear, which converts it into an artificial island. It is the place where, for nearly two centuries, the Dutch Trading Company carried on their operations without being allowed to move beyond its precincts, except to a very limited extent, and under the following circumstances narrated by Kaempfer :—" Ever since the time of Joritomo, the first secular monarch of Japan, who laid the foundation of the present form of government, it hath been a custom observed, not only by the Governors of the Imperial Cities, and Lord-Lieutenants of the provinces, lands, and demesnes belonging to the Crown, but likewise by all the other Daimios and Scomjos, as they are here called (that is, the lords of all ranks and qualities throughout this vast empire), to go to court once a year and to pay their duties ; the lords of a higher rank, who for the extent of their power and dominions could well be styled kings or princes, to the Emperor himself, the rest only to his prime ministers assembled in council. Both accompany their reverences with presents proportionate to their quality and riches, in token of their acknowledging the supremacy of the Emperor.*

---

* As the question of who is really the Emperor of Japan, responsible for its government, is one not unlikely shortly to arise in connection with the repudiation, by the Mikado, of the treaties entered into by the Tycoon with foreigners, it is as well that I should here mention that the Emperor

The resident of our East India Company, the chief director of our trade for the time being, makes this journey with a physician or surgeon and one or two secretaries, and attended with numerous flocks of Japanese of different ranks and qualities, whom the Governors of Nagasaki, as our magistrates in this country whose instructions and orders we are to follow, appoint, as it were to honour and convoy us as persons that are going to see the Supreme Majesty of the empire; but in fact, and chiefly, to guard and watch us, to keep a good eye over our conduct, to prevent us having any suspicious and unlawful conversation and communication with the natives; from conveying secretly to them crosses, images, relics, or any other things which bear relation to the Christian religion; from presenting them with other European rarities, or from selling the same to them in private; and more particularly to take care that none of us should escape into the country, there either to attempt the reviving and propagating of the Christian faith, or otherwise to occasion tumults and disturbances in prejudice of the tranquillity now established in the empire. So important a trust being laid upon the Japanese companions of our journeys, the reader may easily imagine that none are chosen but persons of known candour and fidelity, and who are otherwise employed in affairs relating to the inspection and regulation of our trade, besides some of the Governor's own domestics. Nay, far from relying merely on their own faithfulness and sincerity, though perhaps never so often approved of, all those that are to go with us, from the leader down to the meanest servant (those only excepted who must look after the horses and are frequently changed), must, before they set out on this journey, oblige themselves by a solemn and dreadful oath, signed as usual

referred to by Kœmpfer is the Tycoon, or Siogoun, as he was called in those days, and that the visit of homage was paid to him at Yeddo, and that no allusion is made to any analogous visit being paid to the court of the Mikado at Kioto (Miako).

with their blood, to give notice to the Government at Nagasaki of whatever they observe to be done, either by the Dutch or by their own countrymen, contrary to the standing laws of the country and the many particular instructions which are given them."

Kœmpfer made the journey to the Emperor's court twice, first in 1691, and again in 1692. In the account he gives of the interview of the Chairman of the Dutch East India Company with the Tycoon, after describing their being ushered into the room adjoining the audience chamber, he goes on to say—" Having waited here upwards of an hour, and the Emperor having in the meantime seated himself in the hall of audience, Sino-Kami and two other commissioners came in and conducted our resident into the Emperor's presence, leaving us behind. As soon as he came thither, they cried out aloud 'Hollanda Captain,' which was the signal for him to draw near and make his obeisances. Accordingly he crawled on his hands and knees to a place shown him between the presents ranged in due order on one side, and the place where the Emperor sat on the other, and when kneeling he bowed his forehead quite down to the ground, and so crawled backwards like a crab without uttering a single word. So mean and short a thing is the audience we have of this mighty monarch. Nor are more ceremonies observed in the audience he gives even to the greatest and most powerful princes of the empire. For, having been called into the hall, their names are cried out aloud, then they move on their hands and feet humbly and silently towards the Emperor's seat, and having shown their submission by bowing their foreheads down to the ground, they creep back again in the same submissive posture." After being thus officially received, the Company's representative and suite, including Kœmpfer, were ordered to proceed to a room where the Emperor and ladies of the Court could see them through a screen, without themselves being seen, and for their amusement perform a variety of antics, Kœmpfer thus describing the scene :—

AN IMPERIAL RECEPTION.

"The Emperor and two ladies sat behind the grated screens on our right, and Bingosama, president of the Council of State, opposite to us in a room by himself. Soon after we came in, and had after the usual obeisances seated ourselves on the place assigned to us, Bingosama welcomed us in the Emperor's name, and then desired us to sit upright, to take off our cloaks, to tell him our names and ages, to stand up, to walk, to turn about, to dance, to sing songs, to compliment one another, to be angry, to invite one another to dinner, to converse one with another, to discourse in a familiar way like father and son, to show how two friends or man and wife compliment or take leave of one another, to play with children, to carry them about in our arms, and do many more things of the like nature. Moreover we were asked many more questions, serious and comical; as for instance, what profession I was of, whether I cured any considerable distempers, to which I answered 'Yes, I had, but not at Nagasaki, where we were kept no better than prisoners.' What houses we had, whether our customs were different from theirs, how we buried our people, and when? to which was answered that we buried our dead in the day-time. How our prince did, what sort of man he was, whether the Governor-General at Batavia was superior to him, or whether he was under his command, whether we had prayers and images like the Portuguese? which was answered in the negative. Whether Holland and other countries abroad were subject to earthquakes and storms of thunder and lightning as well as Japan? Whether there be houses set on fire, and people killed by lightning in European countries? Then, again, we were commanded to read, and to dance separately and jointly, and to tell the names of some European plaisters, upon which I mentioned some of the hardest I could remember. The ambassador was asked concerning his children, how many he had, what their names were, also how far distant Holland was from Nagasaki? In the meanwhile some shutters were opened on the left hand by order of the Emperor, probably to cool the room. We were then further commanded to put on our hats, to walk about the room discoursing with one another, to take off our perukes. I had several opportunities of seeing the Empress, and heard the Emperor say in Japanese how sharp we looked at the room where he was, and that we surely could not but know, or at least suspect him to be there; upon which he removed and went to the ladies which sat just before us. Then I was desired once more to come nearer the screen, and take off my peruke. Then they made us jump, dance, play gambols, and walk together, and upon that they asked the ambassador and me how old we guessed Bingo to be? He answered fifty and I forty-five, which made them laugh. Then they made us kiss one another like man and wife, which the ladies particularly showed by their laughter to be well pleased with. They desired us further to show them what sort of compliments it was customary in Europe to make to inferiors, to ladies, to superiors, to princes, and to kings. After this they begged another song of me, and were satisfied with two which the company seemed to like very well. After this farce was over we were ordered to take off our cloaks, to come near the screen one by one, and to take our leave in the very same manner we would take it of a prince or king in Europe, which being done seemingly to their satisfaction, we went away, after having been exercised in this manner for two hours and a half."

Much as we may be inclined now-a-days to laugh at accounts such as this, showing the manner in which the Dutch succeeded in maintaining a commercial footing in Japan, it is probable that so late as thirty-five years ago our own trade at Canton was carried on under circumstances of not much greater dignity by the representatives there of the late East India Company, certain records of which, remaining amongst the archives of the superintendency of British trade in China, tend to show that the instructions from home sent to the Company's agents at Canton, were such as to warrant their submitting to almost any indignity rather than incur the risk of a stoppage of trade. The extent to which the principle of right and wrong was sunk in a sordid spirit of gain, may be inferred from the following occurrence which took place, if I recollect rightly, in the year 1825. While a salute was being fired from a British vessel lying off the factory at Canton, the wad from one of the guns struck a Chinaman on shore and killed him. The Chinese authorities demanded the surrender of the man who had fired the gun, and to the everlasting shame of all concerned, the unfortunate and unoffending man was given up, and his life sacrificed to the sanguinary laws of China, rather than that any question should arise likely to result in the trade being temporarily stopped. Matters now, however, are completely changed, and not unfrequently pushed to an equally reprehensible extreme in the opposite direction.

The Chinese traders as well as the Dutch were confined within the precincts of Desima, and near its entrance at the present time there is a custom house for the special purpose of supervising the commercial doings of the Chinamen.

After having looked at Desima, which presents no special object of interest, I walked through the native town, which is built in a somewhat detached manner on the hilly slopes, and consists of a number of divisions connected together by flights of steps and bridges. The houses, generally speaking, are of common and flimsy construction, such as a fire would make short work of, especially if there was any wind at the time. The porcelain and lacquer ware for sale in the shops appeared to me very inferior to what I had seen at Yokohama, the only exception being the egg shell China, which is very delicate and beautiful. I saw none of the handsome black porcelain which is procurable at Yokohama. Several Japanese boys, who spoke English pretty well and seemed to be professional guides, followed me through the town, and were most anxious to give me the benefit of their local knowledge and acquaintance with the tastes of foreigners. They recommended a variety of places as worthy of being visited, some of their suggestions tending to show that experience had not led them to entertain the most elevated notions of the morality of foreign visitors.

On returning from the Japanese town, I accompanied Mr. Antonio Loureiro through the modern foreign settlement, which is neatly built on a small piece of level ground that has been recovered from the sea, and formed into a bund. It is here that the places of business are, but the private residences of the foreigners are, for the most part, on the hills overlooking the harbour. In the lower portion of the settlement an embryo club and American bowling alley have lately been started by the foreign residents. Several naval officers were amusing themselves at the latter, which seemed to afford them a healthy form of exercise.* One or two of these American bowling alleys might with great advantage be attached to every one of our military barracks in the East; their construction being simple, the expense trifling, the muscular exercise not too fatiguing, and the protection from the sun complete—the latter being a point to which almost all authorities on Indian hygiene attach great importance. Individually, however, I am inclined to think that the injurious effects of ordinary exposure to the sun, particularly if the head be protected by a light and suitable hat, such as the ventilated pith helmet, are a good deal overrated, and not sufficient importance attached to habits of life and other collateral circumstances, which, in certain constitutions, it is not improbable, may confer the predisposition to be injuriously affected, not only by direct

---

* I recollect being struck with the robust and healthy appearance of one of the number—the late Mr. Edwards, Naval Instructor of the "Leopard." Two or three days afterwards, he was struck by cholera, and in a few hours succumbed to that fatal malady.

solar heat, but by sultry states of the weather, where there has been no exposure to the sun whatever.

Having been, with that characteristic kindness for which his family are well known both in China and Japan, invited by Mr. Antonio Loureiro to stay with him during the detention of the "Monge" in harbour, I accompanied him in the afternoon to his bungalow situated some way up one of the hills, where two ladies with their husbands, who had arrived from Shanghai a week previously, were staying with him for the benefit of their health, and were rapidly convalescing from severe sickness contracted there. One of the ladies left Shanghai in a very critical state, and described to me the change which took place for the better in her symptoms and sensations immediately after landing at Nagasaki, as having been very remarkable. To all appearance the climate is a charming one, and yet at the very time that these invalids from Shanghai are recovering health and strength in it, cases of cholera are of daily occurrence; showing that an atmosphere may contain elements causing death in its most malignant form to some, and at the same time be equal to restoring the prostrated vital powers of others, as well as keep the general mass of the inhabitants in apparently the best of health.

The more I see of this mysterious disease (cholera) the more I feel convinced of its dependence on some unusual condition of the atmospheric electricity, which however alone, I think, is not sufficient to develop the disease, but requires to come in collision with some special condition of the electricity of the human body, and that an electro-chemical change, the product of the two, causes the train of symptoms to which, incorrectly, the term cholera continues to be applied (its etymology implying symptoms that are not usually present in the graver forms of the disease); in other words, the decomposition of the blood by electrical agency transmitted from the atmosphere through the nervous system.

To no physical state of the human system (certain forms of heat apoplexy excepted) does cholera, in its worst shape, seem to me so much allied as that produced by a stroke of lightning—in both of them the blood presenting similar appearances after death. In the latter we have a practical illustration of the blasting effects of the electric fluid in its most violent form, and my belief is that a somewhat analogous condition, in a less acute and severe form, is produced by the contact of the atmospheric and systemic electricities to which I have referred. Fortunately, for the sake of mankind, the possession of this constitutional susceptibility would seem to be the exception and not the rule, otherwise the ravages of cholera would have been very much greater than the records of even the most severe epidemics of the disease show.

It is difficult to decide, in places where cholera is prevailing, whether the morbid electricity of the atmosphere exists in a diffuse form, or only shoots about here and there, picking off victims that come within its sphere of action. Facts connected with the history of epidemics can be cited tending to support both views, but taken altogether the balance of evidence is in favour of its existing in certain portions of the atmosphere more than in others.

This view of the existence of an atmospheric electrical cause operating on a systemic one — the sum of the two constituting cholera—has not, so far as I am aware, been previously advanced in explanation of the cause of the disease, and it has been arrived at by me, after careful observation and endeavours to connect its occurrence with those agencies, to which, in medical and sanitary literature, it is usually referred; namely, injudicious diet, bad water, contagion, and local filth—the result having been that far from having ascertained a single fact tending to identify the disease with any of these causes, facts in the aggregate have satisfied me that they have no direct connection whatever with its causation. That they may have an indirect connection, as far as relates to developing an individual predisposition to the disease, is possible, though I cannot say that I have been able to find proof of it during my own experience; inasmuch as I have seen places where the most important of the conditions in question were in full operation totally escape cholera, and localities free from them severely visited.

There is no disease in the investigation of which the *post hoc propter hoc* argument has been so indiscriminately and unphilosophically brought into play, as in that of cholera. For instance, when a person, especially in the better class of society, is attacked, the first question generally asked relates to what has been eaten previously, and should perchance a fruit tart or a cucumber have constituted a portion of the food, the attack is usually attributed to that, without pushing the investigation any farther, and inquiring how many other people also on the same day ate fruit tarts or cucumbers without experiencing any injurious consequences.

If these views are correct, it is manifest that the labours of sanitarians to remove what they believe to be the causes of cholera are not likely to be attended with success, and that the true field for investigation and research will lie in endeavouring to ascertain the special physical conditions which render certain individuals susceptible of the choleraic influence, and confer immunity on the majority of the human race. Cholera has been known to run up one side of a barrack-room and pick off a certain number of victims, leaving the greater number untouched, while the men on the opposite side of the room have escaped altogether. The same has been observed in the case of streets and villages at home. I have seen it in China shoot into a ward of the hospital and pick off two men out of five-and-thirty. I have known it also pass through a barrack-room and in its course take only three men out of sixty. There is no doubt that it frequently, though by no means invariably, displays a marked predisposition to hover over water, and also to follow the courses of rivers; but I have also seen it occur under conditions of a totally opposite nature, and where the individuals attacked were, as far as the eye could judge, enjoying every sanitary advantage.

As well might we by scientific means attempt to control the action of the winds and the waves, and bid them blow and roll as we would wish, as hope to banish from the atmosphere the cause originating cholera when, guided by the hand of nature, its cycle comes round. That the researches of advancing science, particularly if conducted by a Faraday, may ultimately discover the co-relations existing between the electrical conditions of the human body and the choleraic electricity of the atmosphere is possible; and if so, then perhaps, as we protect our ships, our houses, and our powder magazines from one form of the electric fluid, some analogous protecting agent may be discovered capable of averting from combination with our systems electrical agency of another and uncognisable nature.

In reflecting on a disease which has so completely baffled human skill as cholera, one feels warranted in indulging in guesses after truth, and as the principle of making it compulsory on the part of soldiers in India and China to wear protecting agents, under the name of "cholera belts," [*] is at the present time recognised—which, however, do not seem to be attended with any practical benefit—the idea occurs to me, that in the present complete state of our ignorance respecting the disease, it would not be an irrational subject of investigation, to endeavour to ascertain whether, in places subject to visitations of cholera, the wearing of the medicinal galvanic chains that are now in common use, or some light metallic apparatus similar to them, might not exercise a protecting influence. Electricity and

---

[*] These consist merely of a broad piece of coarse flannel bound round the abdomen, and secured by strings of tape.

galvanism have been extensively tried for the cure of cholera; it is not unreasonable, therefore, to entertain the possibility, at least, that some such agency might prevent it.

CHAPTER IX.

Visit to the Japanese steam factory at Nagasaki—English tea establishment—Commercial relations of the Prince of Satsuma with foreigners at Nagasaki—Interview with two of Satsuma's high officers—Anxiety expressed by them to avert the visit of the British squadron to Kagosima—Leave Nagasaki—Arrive at Shanghai.

August 7th.—Visited the Japanese steam factory. It is under Dutch superintendence, and the machinery for it was made at Amsterdam. We were admitted without any trouble, and allowed to go all over the establishment, which is on a scale of considerable extent. It was certainly a remarkable sight in this remote part of the world to see Japanese artizans at work at the various operations connected with the manufacture of marine steam-engines; such as turning iron shafts, cylinders, and the like. Attached to the engineering works there is a foundry, where we saw Japanese engaged in casting. Near it there is a glass work, in which we found glass tubing and chimneys for moderator lamps in course of being made. Large quantities of old glass, chiefly broken bottles, seemed to be kept in store for conversion into new material, being first reduced into fine powder, and further refined by a careful process of sifting through a fine gauze sieve.

In another portion of the establishment, two large boilers, beautifully constructed, and composed entirely of copper plates, were being completed for the Prince of Satsuma, to replace the iron boilers of the "*England*" steamer, which he had recently purchased, and had the satisfaction of finding out afterwards that the boilers were so defective as to require immediate removal. These copper boilers, though very expensive in the first instance, are most economical in the end, as they will last thirty years,—in fact, see the vessel out, whereas iron ones are expended in about seven years.

We visited also a part of the establishment where a Japanese gunsmith was at work with some musket barrels, endeavouring to convert them into spiral grooved rifles, according to a breech-loading sample which he had. He seemed, however, to have made but little progress, his labours not having extended beyond designing some implements with which he purposed making the attempt.

The "Amerika," a Russian steam-corvette, was lying off the factory, about to be fitted with a pair of new iron boilers, which her commander informed us he had succeeded in getting manufactured by the Japanese Government for 600 dollars, he giving them the aid of his own engineers. He endeavoured to get the boilers made at Shanghai in the first instance, but the sum demanded was 25,000 dollars, which he considered such an imposition that he determined to try the Japanese factory, and had succeeded beyond his expectations. He further informed us that he had paid at Shanghai 21,000 dollars for a new mast and the docking and coppering of his vessel, he finding the copper.

The Japanese have already made at this factory a complete set of machinery for a steam-corvette, but as yet they have not built the vessel that the engines are intended to propel.

On recrossing the harbour, and proceeding to the foreign settlement, we visited the tea-firing establishment attached to the firm of Messrs. Glover and Company. We found upwards of 1000 Japanese men and women at work. This establishment is the only one of the kind yet started in Japan, and it is merely the translation to that country of the system which has been long in operation on a great scale in China.

The Japanese tea, I am informed by Mr. Glover, is as yet weak in strength, but is gradually improving from year to year, its cultivation being more carefully attended to as the foreign demand for it increases. Heretofore, it has been allowed, in a great measure, to grow wild along the side of hedges.

The workers in the factory receive five tempos daily, equal to about eightpence sterling. At present, at Nagasaki, sixteen tempos go to the itzeboo, and two itzeboos and five tempos to the dollar.

The Messrs. Glover have frequent commercial transactions with the Prince of Satsuma, and lately sent him a present of a gold watch and chain. Amongst some of the supplies that he has recently requested them to procure for him is an European arm-chair, for which he has formed a fancy, having seen one on board one of his steamers. The Messrs. Glover being very anxious respecting the issue of our demands on Satsuma at Kagosima, and knowing, from the circumstances under which I had been residing at Yokohama, that I was better informed on the matter than any one at the time in Nagasaki, asked me if I would accompany one of the firm to the Japanese town, and personally explain to two of Satsuma's officers, who were then residing there, the existing state of matters, as they felt much afraid, from what they had stated, that though Satsuma individually was most anxious to avoid hostilities, and ready privately to pay the money, still, if the fleet went to Kagosima, and made a public demand for it, hostilities would result, as he would lose face (as the Chinese say) with his own people, and get into trouble with the Mikado, if the money was paid under compulsion. One of the officers in question, named Mi-no-di, was then Satsuma's chief agent at Nagasaki, and comptroller of his finance ; the other, named Gho-dhi, was an executive officer and personal friend and associate of Satsuma's, by whom he had recently been invested with the command of his steam yacht, the "Sir George Grey," in which he was in the habit of making frequent trips.

As I did not see that I could do any harm, and might possibly do some good, I consented to go as requested with Mr. Thomas Glover, who has acquired some colloquial knowledge of the language. We proceeded to a private house in the Japanese town, where Gho-dhi was at the time residing with a Japanese who talks English pretty well, and who has been employed in the native interpretorial service. On entering, Mr. Glover, in conformity with the custom of the country, took his boots off, so as not to soil the padded matting with which all Japanese floors are covered.

On going up-stairs, Gho-dhi, who seemed to be on most friendly terms with Mr. Glover, came forward, and after shaking hands with me, conveyed through the interpreter expressions of welcome. We were immediately requested to be seated, and we sat down on the window-sill in preference to the matted floor. Tea and fruit were then brought in on small lacquer trays, after which Mr. Glover proceeded to explain that the object we had in coming, was to inform them of the approaching visit of the British squadron to Kagosima, with the letter demanding the indemnity money, and to caution them above everything against making any hostile demonstration on the arrival of the ships; because, if a single shot was fired from the batteries on the vessels, the town of Kagosima would be destroyed. He said that they were aware of the intention of the English to send ships to Kagosima to deliver the letter referred to, and that he knew that the Prince of Satsuma was very uneasy on the subject, as he was afraid that he would not be able to control the men in his batteries, who, in spite of his orders to the contrary, might fire upon the vessels. I pointed out to him that the easiest way of avoiding this risk, would be to remove the men altogether from the batteries, and place them in barracks in the town, where they would be removed from the temptation of acting on their own responsibility, when they saw the vessels approaching. He at once admitted this plan to be the correct one to adopt, and said that without delay he would adopt measures to prevent a collision taking place, and that he could almost guarantee that the ships would not be fired at on their arrival in the anchorage. He then put a variety of questions to me, all bearing on the practicability of averting the ships coming at all, and asked if it would not be possible to pay the money privately, because, if the demand for it was made in public, the matter must be referred to the Mikado and Tycoon, and that the Prince of Satsuma would be compelled to act in accordance with their decision. Gho-dhi then went on to express the obligations he felt to me for the considerate spirit which had influenced me in coming to him, as well as for the information and advice I had given; also, that he would at once despatch a special courier overland to Kagosima, and convey to the Prince of Satsuma what had passed at our interview. Before I left, however, he expressed himself as being very anxious that I should see Mi-no-di, as he was the chief envoy of the Prince at Nagasaki. He then sat down on the floor, and took writing materials out of a box, and with remarkable rapidity wrote a somewhat lengthy letter to Mi-no-di, after the manner of a scroll, which is the Japanese mode of writing. The length of this note was nearly six feet; the characters being large, and the writing wide. This communication was given to the interpreter, and I was asked to go with him alone; Mr. Glover and Gho-dhi remaining behind, having some private business to settle.

When we reached Mi-no-di's house, several servants came to the door, and the visit of a foreigner seemed to excite a good deal of surprise. The interpreter sent in Gho-dhi's letter, and in a few minutes we were ushered into a room beautifully matted, and presenting a perfect model of cleanliness. In this room there were a table and four European arm-chairs, the first that I had seen in a Japanese dwelling, and which seemed to show the leaning of the native mind towards certain customs of the West.* After we had been in the room about five minutes, Mi-no-di, a fine burly-looking old man, with a sword stuck in his sash, came in. The interpreter immediately prostrated himself before him, bringing his head in contact with the ground, in much the same way as the Chinese perform the kow-tow; indicating that a wide difference existed between their respective social positions. Mi-no-di shook hands cordially with me, being apparently familiar with this European custom. After making me sit down, he commenced at once to go over the same ground that had been already gone over with Gho-dhi, especially with reference to the possibility of preventing the coming of the ships. In a short time we were joined by Mr. Glover, Gho-dhi, and a third party, also a high officer of Satsuma's. They all seemed to take the greatest interest in the question, and I was asked whether, supposing the money could not be paid in dollars, that would occasion any difficulty. I said that I did not think it would, as I had every reason to believe that the equivalent in itzeboos would be received. In the course of our conversation tea was brought in first, afterwards champagne, and sponge cake. The wine seemed to have come from Holland, and was given to us in European claret glasses. Champagne appears to be a wine suited to the Japanese taste, as they all drank it with evident relish.

The two interviews extended over two hours and a half, and as I was afraid of losing my passage to Shanghai, I had to take my departure before they were nearly tired of talking on the matter, continuing to go again and again over the same ground that we had originally started on. They

* In China tables and arm-chairs are in universal use all over the empire, and it is singular that in this respect the Chinese should differ from all other Orientals.

were very anxious to know if, by sending the money to Yokohama, they could not succeed in stopping the ships coming. I said I thought not, for two reasons—in the first place, that it was almost certain that the ships had already sailed for Kagosima, and in the second place, that the orders of the British Government were, that the demands were to be made at Kagosima, and these demands embraced other questions than the mere payment of the money, but were of a nature that would admit of easy adjustment, if the desire was manifest on their part for a friendly settlement of the matter. Before leaving, my name was requested and written down by each of them, and through the interpreter they conveyed to me certain expressions of friendship, which, rendered into English by him, were to the effect, that "they were my great friends, and that they hoped I would revisit Japan, and that they might again see me." On taking my departure, they displayed an amount of warmth and cordiality that I feel unwilling to take so crooked a view of human nature, even in Orientals, as to believe was mere empty acting. One of the last remarks they made was an assurance to the effect that no steps would be left untried on their part to prevent the ships being fired at as they approached the anchorage, and that they would, with the information they now possessed, guarantee that such an occurrence would not take place, but that the letter of demands would be peacefully received. Nothing could seem more sincere than their desire to avoid hostilities, and bring about an amicable adjustment of existing difficulties. They would not, however, commit themselves to any expression favourable to the demands being complied with, otherwise than privately, repeating again and again that a public demand for the indemnity made by vessels of war would compel Satsuma to refer the question to the Mikado, the result of which, they were afraid, would be unfavourable to peace.

On our way back, Mr. Glover informed me, that he had

had several conversations with them on the indemnity question, since it became known that British ships of war were going to Kagosima, and that the question had been asked by them whether, by paying the money to Messrs. Glover's firm, to the credit of the British Government, the difficulty could not be got over, and the visit from the ships averted. This, of course, it was explained to them the firm had no power to do, but Mr. Glover expressed himself as being confident, that if they had consented to receive the money, it would have been paid.

Towards sunset the "Monge" steamed slowly out of Nagasaki harbour. On the left we passed a regularly constructed fort, and a long battery of guns mounted *en barbette*,* on the top of a hill amongst some trees, neither of which fortifications had been observed as we entered. In a short time we passed close to a small rocky islet of a conical shape, with a few trees upon it, called Papenberg (Mount of the Priests) by the Dutch, from its having been the spot on which some two thousand Christians were landed at the period of the expulsion of the Jesuits from Japan, and put to death by being driven *en masse* into the sea.

August 10*th*.—We entered the Wang-po river and anchored a little above Woo-sung. On landing, I procured a sedan-chair and some Chinamen to carry my baggage, and started overland for Shanghai, a distance of about ten miles. The road the men took lay along narrow pathways, amongst one continuous mass of rice and cotton cultivation. The sun was very strong, but its influence was much modified by a cool and refreshing breeze that was blowing at the time over the paddy fields.

On reaching Shanghai, I found that in determining to return there, I had anticipated the wishes of the commandant of the garrison, Colonel Hough, of the Second Belooch battalion, by whom I was requested to resume the duties of senior medical officer from which I had been relieved

* Exposed on the top of a parapet unprotected by embrasures.

four weeks previously; one medical officer in the interval had been invalided, another was lying ill of fever from sunstroke. Cholera was still prevalent, and the horizon in and around Shanghai had suddenly become less tranquil in consequence of the desertion of the former commander of the disciplined Chinese (Burgevine) to the Taepings, which had necessitated the summoning of the General from Hong-Kong, the detention of the 67th Regiment at Shanghai, and the sending out of a patrolling force in the Soo-chow direction of the thirty-mile radius round Shanghai that it has been settled by the English and French Governments shall be kept clear of Taepings.

I shall not here enter into details of the circumstances occurring in connection with these events, as they are foreign to the subject of this narrative, and I only allude to them as explanatory of the circumstances under which I remained in China, and thus, from the best sources of information, became cognizant of the serious results of the British demonstration before Kagosima within a few days of their occurrence. In common with many others I had entertained the hope that the issue would have been different, notwithstanding the misgivings expressed to me at Nagasaki respecting the consequences, if the demand for the indemnity was made in a public and warlike manner, in place of being negotiated under the rose, which there is no doubt Satsuma's people were most anxious to effect. This, however, could not have been done without giving a complexion to the affair, at variance with the object which Her Majesty's Government had in view in preferring its demands.

CHAPTER X.

Kagosima—Attempt of the Tycoon's Government to detain the squadron—The letter of demands sent in to Satsuma—His minister's reply—Admiral Kuper's despatch—Two of Satsuma's officers voluntary prisoners—The Armstrong gun in naval warfare—Admiral Kuper unjustly censured—A traveller's experience of the British abroad.

August 23rd.—I received a letter from Colonel Neale, dated the 18th of August, giving me an account of the eventful occurrences and dangers through which the squadron had just passed.

Prior to proceeding to Kagosima, Colonel Neale considered it right to acquaint the government of the Tycoon with his intentions. In reply, he received the following request that the expedition might be postponed :—" On receipt of your despatch of the 3rd of August, we fully understood that you intend to go within three days to the territory of the Prince of Satsuma with the men of war now lying in the Bay of Yokohama, in order to demand satisfaction for the murder of a British merchant on the Tokaido last year. But owing to the present unsettled state of affairs in our empire which you witness and hear of, we are in great trouble, and intend to carry out several plans. Supposing, now, something untoward were to happen, then all the trouble and care both you and we have taken would have been in vain and fruitless; therefore, we request that the said departure may be delayed for the present." This document was dated Yeddo, the 4th of August, and signed by four ministers for foreign affairs. Immediately after this communication was received by Colonel Neale, a vice-minister arrived from Yeddo, and had an interview with him on the 5th of August, but singular to say, far from urging further arguments against the expedition, he stated that the Tycoon's Government purposed sending one of its own steamers with the squadron, having a high officer on board. No such steamer, however, made its appearance.

On the 6th of August Colonel Neale and the members of the Legation embarked on board the "Euryalus," and the squadron detailed for Kagosima sailed the same day.

On the 11th the squadron, under easy steam, entered the Bay of Kagosima, described as one of great beauty and considerable width at its entrance, and anchored about seven miles below the town, after having had much difficulty in finding a suitable place, owing to the depth of the water.

At seven o'clock the following morning the vessels weighed anchor and steamed for the town of Kagosima, anchoring off it about two hours afterwards. It presented a strongly fortified appearance, having a line of forts in front of it, from one of which the flag of the Prince of Satsuma was flying.

Shortly after anchoring, some two-sworded officials came off to the flag-ship, who, after asking why the vessels had come, concluded by saying that they believed it was for the purpose of delivering a letter to the Prince, who they stated was at the time residing inland about fifty miles distant. Colonel Neale gave them a letter containing the demands of the British Government, and fixed twenty-four hours as the period within which it was to be replied to.

The following day officials came off several times to say that it was impossible to get the Prince of Satsuma's answer in so short a time, and Colonel Neale therefore added on six hours to the time originally fixed. Having effected this, their next step was a strong endeavour to get Colonel Neale and Admiral Kuper to go on shore, and there receive the answer and personally discuss the matter in a building that had been prepared for their reception. This invitation was, of course, prudently declined.*

In the evening the answer arrived, written on a scroll of paper fifteen feet long. As the document required translation, the bearer of it was informed that if he sent off the next morning, a reply would be given, whether it was considered satisfactory or not. The document, on translation, proved to be to the following effect:—

"*Translation of a Despatch in Japanese from* KAWA KAMI TAJIMA, *Minister of* MATSUDAIRA SHIURIMO DAIBOO, PRINCE OF SATSUMA, &c., &c., *to* COLONEL E. ST. JOHN NEALE, *H.B.M.'s Chargé-d'Affaires*, &c., &c., &c.

"It is just that a man who has killed another should be arrested and punished by death, as there is nothing more sacred than human life; and although we should like to secure them (the murderers), as we have endeavoured to do since last year, it is impossible for us to do so owing to the political differences at present existing between the Daimios of Japan, some of whom even hide and protect such people. Besides, the murderers are not one but several persons, and therefore find easier means of escape.

"The journey to Yeddo (undertaken by Shimidzu Saburo) was not with the object of committing murders but to conciliate the two courts of Yeddo and Kioto; and you will

* It has since been stated, but whether from reliable sources of information or not, I cannot say, that the invitation on shore was an attempt to lead Colonel Neale and Admiral Kuper into a snare, and that, had they landed, every arrangement was made for their capture by the lifting of drawbridges within the castle, where it is alleged the interview was to have been held. The squadron would then have been communicated with to the effect that the prisoners would be beheaded if a shot was fired from any of the ships at the town; and it is further stated, that if the treachery had succeeded the captives were to have been imprisoned at Kirisimi, a stronghold of Satsuma's some fifty miles inland. This statement appeared in the "Japan Commercial News," published at Yokohama immediately after the return of the squadron from Kagosima.

therefore easily believe that our Master (Shimadus) could not have ordered it (the murder). Great offenders against the laws of their country (Japan) who escape, are liable to capital punishment. If, therefore, we can detect those in question, and after examination find them to be guilty, they shall be punished, and we will then inform the commanders of your men-of-war at Nagasaki or at Yokohama, in order that they may come to witness their execution. You must, therefore, consent to the unavoidable delay which is necessary to carry out these measures. If we were to execute criminals condemned for other offences, and told you that they were the offenders (above referred to), you would not be able to recognise them; and this would be deceiving you and not acting in accordance with the spirit of our ancestors.

"The (Provincial) Governments of Japan are subordinate to the Yeddo Government, and, as you are well aware, are subservient to the orders received from it.

"We have heard something about a Treaty having been negotiated, in which a certain limit was assigned to foreigners to move about in; but we have not heard of any stipulation by which they are authorised to impede the passage of a road.

"Supposing this happened in your country, travelling with a large number of retainers as we do here, would you not chastise (push out of the way and beat) any one thus disregarding and breaking the existing laws of the country? If this were neglected, Princes could no longer travel. We repeat that we agree with you that the taking of human life is a very grave matter. On the other hand the insufficiency of the Yeddo Government, who govern and direct everything, is shown by their neglecting to insert in the treaty (with foreigners) the laws of the country (in respect to these matters) which have existed from ancient times. You will, therefore, be able to judge yourself whether the Yeddo Government (for not inserting these laws) or my master (for carrying them out) is to be blamed.

"To decide this important matter, a high official of the Yeddo government, and one of our government, ought to discuss it before you, and find out who is in the right.

"After the above question has been judged and settled, the money indemnity shall be arranged.

"We have not received from the Tycoon any orders or communications by steamer that your men-of-war were coming here. Such statements are probably made with the object of representing us in a bad light. If it were not with this object you would certainly have them in writing from the Gorogio, and if so we request you to let us see them. In consequence of such mis-statements great misunderstandings are caused.

"All this surprises us much! Does it not surprise you?

"Our government will act in everything according to the orders of the Yeddo government.

"This is our open-hearted reply to the different subjects mentioned in your despatch.

"29th day of the 6th month of the 3rd year of Bunkew (13th August, 1863).

"Signed, KAWA KAMI TAJIMA, 'Scisse' (Minister).

"Translated by ABEL A. J. GOWER and A. VON SIEBOLD."

About half-past eight o'clock on the morning of the 14th, a boat came off from the town to ascertain how the answer had been received. The reply, I believe, was to the effect that the answer was so far from satisfactory that no further communication would be held with them except under a flag of truce. In the meantime, Colonel Neale had placed the adjustment of matters in the hands of Admiral Kuper, and no better description can be given of the subsequent course of events than the following extracts from the gallant Admiral's despatch to the secretary of the Admiralty:—

"'EURYALUS,' GULF OF YEDDO, *Aug.* 22.

"SIR,—I request you will acquaint the Lords Commissioners of the Admiralty that, having embarked Lieutenant-Colonel Neale, Her Majesty's Chargé-d'Affaires, and such of the members of the Legation as he wished to accompany him, I sailed from Yokohama on the 6th inst. with the 'Euryalus,' 'Pearl,' 'Coquette,' 'Argus,' 'Perseus,' 'Racehorse,' and 'Havoc' for Kagosima, the capital of the Daimio, Prince of Satsuma.

"Several Japanese officials having come on board to inquire into the object of our visit, Lieutenant-Colonel Neale delivered to them the despatch addressed to the Prince of Satsuma embodying the demands made upon him by Her Majesty's Government. Twenty-four hours were allowed for a reply, and the intervening time was made use of by us in obtaining as much local information as circumstances rendered possible; and towards the evening Captains Borlase and Josling, Commander Wilmot and Captain Brine, Royal Engineers, went farther up the Gulf in boats, and discovered three steamers of the Prince of Satsuma anchored close to the shore, in a bay about seven or eight miles from our anchorage, but quite out of sight.

"During the 13th the Japanese officials came on board several times with various excuses for delay in sending a reply to the demands, as well as to endeavour to induce Colonel Neale and myself to go on shore to hold a conference; which, however, knowing the treacherous nature of these people, we from prudential motives thought fit to decline, offering, nevertheless, to hold the conference on board my flag-ship, or to move the 'Havoc' close in shore for the purpose, which they declined. It was also observed that preparations were being made for hostilities. They had commenced at daylight to assemble large bodies of men in the batteries, and to point the whole of the guns (numbering from 70 to 80) upon the squadron; and five large junks belonging to the Prince, and employed in the trade with the Loo Choo Islands, were warped out of the inner harbour and anchored out of the line of fire, between the batteries and the squadron. In consequence of these manifestations, so undoubtedly hostile in character, I considered it expedient to be on my guard against any act of treachery; and as it had been decided by Lieutenant-Colonel Neale and myself that hostilities should not be commenced by us unless we were obliged to take the initiative, and as from the depth of water and the direction of the wind and tide, it would have been difficult, if not impossible, to keep the ships' broadsides on the batteries, I directed steam to be got up and the squadron to be ready to weigh at a moment's notice.

"At about 3 P.M. we observed a number of boats coming out of the inner harbour, and, on approaching the squadron, they were found each to contain a few water-melons and eggs and two or three fowls, intended probably to represent the supplies with which they had promised to furnish us. One of these boats pulled off to each ship of the squadron, but, instead of going alongside to sell the few supplies they contained, they merely pulled round the ships and returned to the shore, it being evident, from the presence in each boat of a large number of yaconins, or soldiers, that their object was simply to obtain by closer observation a knowledge of the strength of the various ships, and of their state of preparation for hostilities. This rendered it still more necessary to be on our guard.

"Shortly following this occurrence an official said to be of high rank, and who stipulated for the admission to the ship of a guard of 40 men, came on board. I offered no objection to the guard accompanying the official, but had a guard of Marines to face them on the opposite side of the quarter-deck. This officer, who was the bearer of the reply to Lieutenant-Colonel Neale's despatch, appeared to be in a state of great nervous anxiety, and no sooner had he taken his seat in the cabin than another boat was observed pulling hastily off from the shore, and waving flags as signals to the preceding one. On coming alongside it was ascertained, as stated by the Japanese, that, as there was some mistake in the despatch, it was to be taken on shore again for alteration, and the official accordingly left the ship without delivering it. Feeling perfectly convinced that this was a mere ruse to detain the ships in their present position, which would enable the batteries during slack water to fire upon us with comparative impunity, I directed the squadron to weigh and to be prepared to return the fire of the batteries. But, finding they did not open fire upon us, which was probably owing to the change in our position having completely thrown them out in the direction and elevation of their guns, I endeavoured to find an anchorage above the town, but the water proved to be so deep that I was obliged to return opposite to the town, and anchored in 21 fathoms, about 1,000 yards nearer to the Sakura side. The letter from the authorities at Kagosima was brought on board in the evening by the same officer as before, who attempted to explain his strange conduct by saying that it was a misunderstanding, and that the letter he then delivered to Colonel Neale was the same he had previously brought on board.

"In the forenoon of the 14th a strong breeze from the eastward had sprung up, and the rapid falling of the barometer indicating the probable approach of a typhoon or heavy gale, the top-gallant masts were sent on deck.

"I have now to report to their lordships the further progress of the events following the receipt, on the evening of this day (14th instant), of a despatch from Her Majesty's Chargé-d'Affaires, and its enclosures, in which I was requested to enter upon such measures of coercion as I might deem expedient and best calculated to awaken the Prince of Satsuma to a sense of the serious nature of the determinations which had brought Her Majesty's squadron to the Bay of Kagosima.

"The 'Pearl,' 'Coquette,' 'Argus,' 'Racehorse,' and 'Havoc,' were sent at daylight on the 15th, under the orders of Captain Borlase, to seize the three steamers already referred to.

"Captain Borlase was further directed to avoid as much as possible all unnecessary bloodshed or active hostility. The steamers were accordingly taken possession of without opposition, and brought down to our anchorage during the forenoon of the 15th, lashed alongside the 'Coquette,' 'Argus,' and 'Racehorse,' which vessels anchored in the same bay as before, the object had in view being the detention of these steamers as reprisals, until the Prince of Satsuma should either comply with the demands, or make overtures to Her Majesty's Chargé-d'Affaires which might lead to their settlement.

"At noon, during a squall, accompanied by much rain, the whole of the batteries on the Kagosima side suddenly opened fire upon the 'Euryalus,' the only ship within range; but although many shot and shell passed over and close around her, no damage was done beyond cutting away a few ropes. Finding that the springs on the cable would not keep the ship broadside on, and as it was impossible, with the comparatively small force at my command, to engage the batteries under weigh and at the same time to retain possession of the steamers, I signalled to the 'Coquette,' 'Argus,' and 'Racehorse' to burn their prizes, and then to the whole squadron to weigh and form the line of battle according to seniority, the 'Havoc' being directed to secure the destruction of the three steamers.

"Previous to this the 'Perseus,' having slipped her cable, was directed to fire on the north battery until the signal was made to form line-of-battle, which service was executed by Commander A. J. Kingston with great promptness.

"Although the weather was now very dirty, with every indication of a typhoon, I considered it advisable not to postpone until another day the return of the fire of the

Japanese, to punish the Prince Satsuma for the outrage, and to vindicate the honour of the flag; and everything being now ready, I proceeded towards the batteries, opening fire upon the northernmost one, with considerable effect, and passed at slow speed along the whole line, within point-blank range. Owing probably to the unfavourable state of the weather, the ships astern did not maintain their position in as close order as I could have wished, and the 'Euryalus' was consequently exposed to a very heavy and well-directed fire from several of the batteries at the same time, and suffered somewhat severely. About this time also, and while in the thickest of the action, I deeply regret to state that I was deprived at the same moment of the assistance of Captain Josling and Commander Wilmot, both of whom were killed by the same shot while standing by me on the bridge of the 'Euryalus,' directing the fire of the quarters, and setting an example of coolness and gallantry which was emulated throughout the entire ship.

"By the time the 'Euryalus' got abreast of the last or southernmost battery I could observe the town to be on fire in several places, and the weather having now assumed a most threatening appearance, I considered it advisable to discontinue the engagement, and to seek a secure anchorage for Her Majesty's ships. The 'Havoc' was then ordered to set fire to five large junks belonging to the Prince of Satsuma, which Lieutenant George Poole accomplished in a most satisfactory manner; and these, as well as a very extensive arsenal and foundry, for the manufacture of guns, shot and shell, together with large storehouses adjoining, were also completely destroyed.

"During the whole of the succeeding night it blew almost a hurricane, but all the vessels of the squadron rode it out without accident, with the exception of the 'Perseus,' which vessel dragged her anchors off the bank into sixty fathoms water, and was compelled to slip her cable during the following forenoon, when the gale had somewhat moderated.

The gale subsided gradually during the 16th, and as I had observed the Japanese at work, apparently erecting batteries on the hill above the anchorage, enveloped in trees and bushes, and which might have inflicted much damage upon the small vessels lying within pistol-shot of the shore I became anxious for their safety, and determined to move the squadron out to the anchorage we had occupied on the night of our arrival in the Gulf, for the purpose of repairing damages, fishing spars, and refitting previous to proceeding to sea.

"The squadron accordingly weighed at 3 P.M. of the 16th, and passing in line between the batteries of Kagosima and Sakurasima, steamed through the channel, and anchored to the southward of the island, taking advantage of the occasion to shell the batteries on the Sakura side which had not been previously engaged, and also the palace of the Prince in Kagosima. A feeble fire only was returned from the batteries which had not been closely engaged in the first attack, and this happily without effect upon Her Majesty's ships."

Our total loss amounted to two officers and seven men killed, and fifty-two men wounded, four of them mortally.

I had written to Colonel Neale an account of my interview with Satsuma's officers at Nagasaki. By a singular coincidence, two of my friends were, at the moment he received my letter, voluntary prisoners on board the "Euryalus." They were on board the "Sir George Grey" at the time of her capture, and requested to remain in the "Euryalus" rather than go on shore. The captives were Gho-dhi and the interpreter, whose name I have since learned is Kasiwah; he is a doctor by profession, and accompanied the embassy to England in 1862. They were taken to Yokohama, and, under cover of night, on the 24th of August, landed at Kanagawa. Colonel Neale mentioned that, during the passage, a good deal was extracted from them, but nothing very consistent or tangible was ascertained; which, however, is the usual characteristic of information derived from Japanese sources.

The reports that reached Shanghai with reference to the Armstrong gun at Kagosima,—the first occasion of its having been tried in naval warfare,—were not of a favourable nature, and more especially in regard to the 110-pounder gun, as compared with the ordinary muzzle-loading 68-pounder, the comparison being represented as having been much to the disadvantage of the former, on board of certain vessels whose armament admitted of the respective merits of the two guns being fairly tested. Altogether, the general tone of the statements then in circulation was calculated to throw considerable doubt not only on the efficiency of the gun at the range at which it was used, but also on the suitableness for naval guns of lead-coated projectiles, owing to the loss of bulk to which the process of cleaning necessary on shipboard exposes them, and the consequent increased windage and loss of velocity and penetrating force which result. In a former chapter, I alluded to the fact that the Armstrong shell does not invariably burst into the thirty-nine segments of which it is constructed; and this I am certain of, that assertions to the effect that wounds produced by segments of Armstrong shells are equal in severity to wounds caused by fragments of ordinary shells are incorrect. I think it may be safely admitted, as an axiom in physics, that the greater the resistance offered to an explosive compound, such as the bursting-charge of a shell, the greater will be the force with which the fragments of the containing body are scattered about; it therefore seems to me not at all probable that the resistance to the explosion of gunpowder in a conical iron case, built of thirty-nine separate pieces, cemented together, and covered over with a thin coating of lead, can be equal to that offered by a hollow globe of cast-iron, such as the ordinary shell is formed of. I recollect an officer of the Royal Artillery mentioning to me at Tien-tsin, that immediately after the capture of the Taku Forts, as he was walking round the outside looking at the damage done by our fire, he observed where one of the 12-pounder Armstrong shells had exploded underneath one of the mantlets that the Chinese used for covering their embrasures, and that, to his surprise, the fragments had to all appearance separated with so little force as not to have penetrated the hide of which the mantlet was formed.

On the news of the affair of Kagosima reaching England, strong expressions of opinion were published condemnatory of the proceeding. The measures adopted by Admiral Kuper were alleged to have been characterised by unnecessary ruthlessness. However much the destruction of property which attended the bombardment of Kagosima is to be deplored, this I am sure of, that no one is likely to have felt regret at it more acutely than the gallant Admiral himself. There are not three men in England actuated by kinder or more philanthropic feelings towards the Japanese than Colonel Neale, Admiral Kuper, and his second in command, Captain Borlase. To assail Admiral Kuper as the agent personally responsible for the burning of Kagosima is, to say the least of it, unjust. Those acquainted with the nature, mode of construction, and materials of Japanese towns, will readily understand that the very act of opening fire on the batteries was inseparable from the burning of the town, especially if there was much wind at the time. It was the full conviction that the destruction by a conflagration of Kagosima, would be an unavoidable consequence of the squadron firing on the batteries, that chiefly influenced me in going to Satsuma's officers at Nagasaki, and in impressing upon them the certain fate that would befall the town should the ships be fired at as they approached. It is much easier to censure the course of action taken at Kagosima, than to show how, with due regard to the honour of the British flag, any other course could, under the circumstances, have been adopted. The Admiral in the first instance, on having the matter placed in his hands, adopted the mildest measure of coercion that he could, namely, the seizure of the steamers. When, however, the whole line of batteries fronting the town opened on his squadron, what would the people of England have said had Admiral Kuper removed his ships from the range of Satsuma's guns, and assigned as his reason for not returning the fire, that he could not do so without incurring the risk of burning down the town? Would the press or the public have been satisfied? I think not; my impression being, that had Admiral Kuper evinced any such practical humanitarianism, the outcry against him would have been tenfold what the other course has developed, and more than probably coupled with disagreeable allusions to the fate of Admiral Byng.

That this Satsuma complication, from beginning to end, is one to be deeply regretted every right-minded person ought to feel.

My experience in the East, especially in China, convinces me that it is only by a *bonâ fide* spirit of conciliation that a real and permanent influence is to be gained over Orientals. The principles inculcated for the carrying out of its Eastern policy by the British Government are conciliatory in the extreme, but its beneficent intentions are in too many instances frustrated by the arrogance, superciliousness, violent temper, want of tact, and general incompetency for the management of men, of those into whose hands the execution of its measures falls. The spirit of conciliation has long appeared to me the element, of all others, the most deficient in the English character in the East.

In dealing with the Chinese (and the same probably applies to the Japanese and Orientals generally) it has always seemed to me that we are too much in the habit of viewing questions at issue through an European medium only, and that we do not make sufficient allowance for the stereotyped form of the Oriental mind, and for the *bonâ fide* obstacle which it offers to their seeing things in the same light in which they appear to us—the natural consequence of mental organisms built up as it were of a fixed and determined number of ideas, the displacement of these to make room for a new one being only attainable by a slow and gentle process of reasoning, by going over the same ground again and again with patient endurance, until at last we succeed in getting a new idea to take root. The shoal upon which our Eastern diplomacy so often becomes stranded, is the ready means which unsuccessful negotiators have of bringing in the pressure of material force to carry measures to which their moral influence has proved unequal.

A knowledge of the native language also appears to me to have been too indiscriminately taken as a guarantee for diplomatic capacity, and I think I could state instances where mischief has resulted from the diplomatic employment of injudicious and unconciliating linguists, in place of their services having been restricted within purely interpretorial limits. An intimate acquaintance with an Oriental language, or a brain stuffed full of book-learning, by no means implies the possession of that combination of tact, discretion, and judgment which, under the name of common sense, is so essential to success in dealing with Orientals; and hence it is, that of all tests of fitness for the public service, competitive examination is perhaps the most fallacious. The quality of brain which shines most at one of these ordeals, may prove that least practically adapted for the very post that a high class examination has gained for it. The absorbent form of brain, which, like a sponge, readily imbibes whatever is submitted to its action, and also like a sponge, on being squeezed equally readily lets it out, constitutes the type of mind which is now preferred for the public service, to the exclusion of brains that may be infinitely superior.

SUPPLEMENTARY CHAPTER.

Consular trial at Yokohama—Affairs in Japan in September, 1863—The Prince of Negato—The Tycoon unfolds his foreign policy—Threatening notice from the Loonins—The Satsuma difficulty amicably settled—Congratulatory despatch from the Tycoon—Shimadzo Sabooro's explanations—Indemnity for the "Pembroke" being fired at—The Tycoon's palace destroyed—Charges brought against him by Daimios—A second embassy to Europe—The first ambassadors' opinions of Europe and the Europeans—Arrival of the Japanese embassy at Shanghai—Concluding observations.

UP to the period of my leaving China (11th September, 1863), no change had taken place in the aspect of affairs in Japan, nor had any incident of interest occurred since the destruction of Kagosima, with the exception of the trial before the consular court at Yokohama of the three Englishmen engaged in the wounding of the Japanese officer before mentioned. The trial took place on the 9th of September, the judges in the case being Consul Winchester and three of the British mercantile community, styled "Assessors." The prosecution was conducted in the name of "The Queen upon the information ex officio of the Governor of Kanagawa." The charge against the three defendants was "Shooting at and wounding, or being accessory to the shooting and wounding of, Morotamon, a Japanese officer, on the evening of the 30th of July, 1863, at Kanasawa, within the consular district of Kanagawa." The defendants pleaded "Not Guilty." Morotamon appeared in court with his arm bound up, and his evidence was chiefly to the effect that the defendants were trespassing on a private road, and that on his remonstrating with them he received an insulting reply from one of the party, and drew his sword in self-defence. The decision of the Court was that "there was an appearance of danger sufficient to justify the use of means of self-defence."

During the remainder of the month of September, nothing of any interest occurred, with the exception that the Prince of Negato, though he had desisted from firing on foreign vessels, was still showing hostility to foreigners, by endeavouring to injure the trade of Nagasaki by preventing native junks from passing through the inland sea, either to or from Nagasaki. This measure, however, gave so much dissatisfaction to his own subjects, and the feeling against it became so demonstrative, that he did not persist in carrying out the measure.

Towards the end of October, the rumours that had been so long in circulation respecting the expulsion of foreigners began to assume a substantial form. On the 24th of the month, General Pruyn and M. Von Polsbroek, the Ministers respectively of America and the Netherlands, were invited by the Gorogio to attend a conference at Yeddo, when, after a little circumlocution, they were informed that the order for the expulsion of foreigners had been withdrawn, but that it was the wish of the Tycoon that Yokohama should be given up as a foreign settlement, and trade in future confined to Nagasaki and Hakodadi. The two Ministers expressed their surprise that the representatives of England and France had not been invited to attend on the occasion of so important a communication being made, and the explanation they received was, that as Holland and America were the oldest friends of Japan, it was thought best that they should be first informed. The Gorogio then went on to express a strong hope that the Ministers of the various treaty powers would meet the Tycoon's wish, and on their own responsibility give orders for the vacating of Yokohama, without waiting for instructions from their respective governments; adding, that if foreigners remained at Yokohama a revolution was inevitable, and one that the Tycoon was powerless to repress; also, that the admission of foreigners to trade at a point so near the capital had been an experiment, which was not found to answer, and therefore would have to be given up. The two Ministers undertook to inform their respective governments regarding the request the Tycoon had made, and the conference ended.

Whether this desire that foreigners should quit Yokohama is a *bonâ fide* one on the part of the Tycoon and his government, it is impossible to say; it is by no means improbable that it is not, but that it has been forced upon them by hostile Daimios. A similar communication was conveyed in writing to the other foreign representatives, but not apparently with the intention of carrying matters farther than merely making the request, and then waiting replies from the several governments. About the same time, the following notice was posted about Yokohama, supposed to have emanated from the anti-foreign party.

"A few years ago, the Tycoon and his ministers made treaties with foreign nations without the consent of his superior (the Mikado), and the above-named have largely profited by commerce with foreigners without considering the sufferings they have brought upon their country; they have trafficked in copper cash, silk, wax, oil, and salt, in fact, all the most important produce of the country have they bought and sent to Yokohama and Nagasaki for sale to foreigners, and have thereby so enhanced the prices that everybody suffers. To many poor families it is as though the country was oppressed with famine; they cannot live together as heretofore, but are obliged to separate to seek a subsistence; and yet, after all their hardships, some have actually died of starvation. We cannot blind ourselves to their sufferings. But it may be asked, why we wish to punish persons who have traded under the licence of the Tycoon? It is because they have forgotten their obligations to their country and to the Mikado, and for their own selfish purposes have become careless of the sufferings of others, that they have condescended to deal with government officials, and also with foreigners, who are lower than the brute beasts, and the mischiefs they have compassed is more than we can tell of. We in our persons represent the sufferings of the Japanese people, and in their name have put to death Yawa-taya Wobei. At Osaca, Nagasaki, Johsiu, Ida, Naghama, Ohjee, Yokohama, and within all places and provinces of the east and west, we (the Loonins*) will examine the merchants, and exterminate all who have dealt with or shown any leaning either towards foreigners or their trade."

November opened with more cheering prospects; overtures of a peaceful nature being made to Colonel Neale by the Prince of Satsuma, which resulted in his sending several of his high officers to wait on Colonel Neale, with whom they had two long interviews, the first taking place on the 9th of November. At first they expressed themselves in terms indicating that they were under the impression that, in seizing and burning the steamers without giving any notice of such an intention, the British had not treated the Prince of Satsuma fairly. They ultimately, however, acknowledged, after hearing Colonel Neale's explanation regarding the circumstances under which the steamers had been seized, and that there was no intention, in the first instance, of destroying them, that the matter stood in a more favourable light than it had hitherto appeared to them. The last interview took place on the 11th of November, and ended in the envoys agreeing to all

---

* In a former note I have mentioned that the Loonins are outlaws who have thrown off their allegiance to their respective Daimios, and constituted themselves patriots. It is, therefore, just possible, that in their case Dr. Johnson's definition of patriotism may be correct, namely—"the last refuge of a scoundrel."

Colonel Neale's demands, and further expressing, on the part of the Prince of Satsuma, a desire to send several of his young nobility to England for their education.

The Tycoon's government, immediately on being informed by Satsuma's envoys that their negotiations had come to a satisfactory conclusion, addressed a congratulatory despatch to Colonel Neale, expressing the hope that nothing more would occur to interrupt the good feeling that was thus re-established between the two nations. Envoys from Shimadzo Sabooro also waited on Colonel Neale, with the object of explaining that he had been erroneously identified as the individual immediately responsible for Mr. Richardson's murder, which, it is presumed, was represented as an act of excitement on the part of his retainers at the obstruction offered to their progress by the foreigners on horseback. That he should have entertained such violent feelings of dislike to foreigners as to order their murder on the high road has always seemed to me difficult of explanation, seeing that, but a week previously, he was not only engaged in mercantile transactions with them in Yokohama, but even took a pleasure trip in the "Fiery Cross" steamer, previous to purchasing the vessel from Messrs. Jardine and Matheson.

In November the Tycoon consented to pay an indemnity of 10,000 dollars for the attack made by the armed vessels of the Prince of Negato on the American steamer, "Pembroke," which seems rather hard on the Tycoon, seeing that he had nothing whatever to do with the matter. The Prince of Negato had been already severely chastised by the "Wyoming" destroying two of his vessels.

Though matters relating to foreigners continued tranquil throughout December, and Satsuma had ratified the obligations entered into by his envoys by paying down the £25,000, yet the political horizon was far from settled in Japan; on the 25th of the month the Tycoon's palace at Yeddo was burned to the ground, and he himself compelled to seek refuge in a remote house in the suburbs, being fearful of traversing the streets to another palace. The following document conveys some idea of the sentiments entertained towards the Tycoon by certain of the Daimios, and it tends also to show some of the grounds upon which their alleged grievances against foreigners rest. It is a series of accusations brought against the Tycoon by several of the hostile Daimios, and embodied by them in a petition to the Mikado.

"Both you and Harrisooh (the late American Minister, Mr. Harris) said that cotton would be sold for a mere nothing, and that silk and manufactured goods would not cost us anything. The daily necessities of life would be brought to our country from all quarters of the globe, and our farmers would not be required to sow and reap. We anxiously wait these miracles, and at present enjoy advantages which you never mentioned, namely, that those articles which you and Harrisooh promised to give at very low prices are now three times as expensive as they formerly were.

"You monopolize the import and export duties completely; and we had a right to suppose that those duties, which, according to your statements and those of your financier, Harrisooh, would enrich the Japanese nation, ought to cover expenses, such as building fortifications and buying men-of-war, which you say must inspire the barbarians with the respect due to our great country. But what have you done for the last three years? What has been the tenor of all your despatches? 'Japan must be fortified, fortifications must be built, the artillery and navy increased. Money is required. The presence of foreigners occasions great expenses: entertainments must be given to the Ministers, the petty consuls cannot be forgotten, and foreigners must be made to respect and fear our great nation by witnessing the boundless resources of the country and the majesty of its ruler.' If we could only see those fortifications, those men-of-war, we would complain less about the expense; but everything is postponed and nothing executed. You think that drawings and plans will scare foreigners and cause them to flee from our country; but we doubt it, for they nearly equal us in this art. You sometimes talk to us about political economy, and we candidly own you give us excellent advice; unfortunately, we have numerous proofs that you do not follow the advice that you give us. Why was such an incredible sum of money spent for all the vain and useless pomp which accompanied the sister of the Mikado on her journey to Yeddo preparatory to her marriage with the Tycoon? Why was so much money expended in rebuilding the palace of the Tycoon? We shall not mention the various ways in which the public money is wasted, as this would cause our nation to blush, and the Mikado to mourn. Public rumour, however, says that numerous thefts have been committed by the highest officers of the Tycoon; if any protest against the course which is now pursued, they are instantly and mysteriously silenced for ever. As you always remind us of the great principles of political economy when you demand pecuniary supplies, pardon us for making the following remarks:—Owing to the troubled state of the country, the presence of the Daimios at Yeddo was formerly highly necessary. This is not the case at present, and still our lords are travelling to and from the capital. The personal fatigue, vexation, and the expense of the immense retinue which always accompanies them, can no longer be supported. The time has come that these ruinous journeys should cease, and that the lords of Japan declare themselves unable to defray the expenses which you impose upon them.

"As foreign trade has nearly ruined us, and as fortifications and numerous other unforeseen expenses are deemed necessary in all the ports that have been opened to the barbarians, we not only demand that the new ports, Osaca, Negata, and Yeddo, shall not be opened, but that Kanagawa be closed. You always assert that we are opposed to friendly intercourse with foreign nations; but this is utterly false. We willingly consent to open the whole of Japan, if this step does not occasion expenses which surpass our means. We have not murdered our adherents who were favourably inclined towards the opening of Japan to foreigners. You teach the young to despise and insult foreigners; and although you always tell us that the foreign nations are powerful and greatly to be feared, a high functionary of the 'Tori' lately said that, with the exception of the Russians, all the foreigners could be insulted with impunity."

The year 1864 opened by two vice-ministers of state and three Daimios, holding the rank of Governors of Provinces, having an interview with Colonel Neale, for the purpose of informing him of the intention of the Tycoon to send an embassy to Europe to endeavour to persuade the treaty powers to resign the right of residence at Yokohama, and confine their trade to Nagasaki and Hakodadi. They said that the Japanese were hostile to foreigners; that the Tycoon's Government was exposed to grave difficulties on account of this feeling; and that the foreign treaties, which were made experimentally, had failed and would have to be abandoned. Colonel Neale is stated to have denied that any understanding had ever existed relative to the treaties being of an experimental nature, adding, that while, of course, the Tycoon was at full liberty to send ambassadors to England, in the meantime he might rest assured that the provisions of the existing treaty with Great Britain would be strictly enforced.

At the very time that arrangements were being made for an embassy to Europe to induce the treaty powers to abandon trade at Yokohama, the Tycoon's Government, by a paradox which could only occur in China or Japan, made a treaty with Switzerland, and entered into commercial conventions with America and France; reducing, and in some instances abolishing, the duty on several kinds of imports.

The following is a translation of the introduction to an account which was published at Yeddo in March, 1863, of the visit of the first ambassadors to Europe in 1862:—

"The races of the west all closely resemble each other. They all clothe themselves in the same manner, eat with the same ceremonies, &c. They differ little in the darkness of their complexion and colour of their hair. Their arms are the same. The French appear to value them more than their neighbours, and we were told that they are most skilled in their use. In truth, the movements of the French soldiers appear more active and lively than those of the soldiers of the other nations. Their sabres are much inferior to ours; but they do not appear to attach much importance to them, and prefer firearms. We never saw sword or spear exercise; to make up for this, they attach a sort of sabre to the end of their guns, and use it where we use the spear.

"Their rites or ceremonies appear very light, although it would be wrong to say that there are none; but the most striking thing about them is, that these ceremonies are almost the same for personages of rank as for common men. They lift their hat, and make a slight movement of the head: such is the salutation for every one. It would appear that there is but little respect for, or distinction of class. Thus, in our audience with the Emperor of France and other sovereigns, their Majesties were not separated from us by any veil. The consort of the sovereign was even there, neither veiled nor concealed, seated on a seat as high as that of her husband. Notwithstanding this, the nobles were extremely polite in France, even too much so sometimes, especially at dinner, where, in order to please them, it was necessary to eat and drink more than was agreeable. As to the other men, they were less polite. The greater number stared at and touched us, and passed remarks on us in our hearing; nor did they conceal that they thought us very ugly.

"Of the women, some are very handsome,—for example, the Empress of France. They are however, in general, less so than in America. Their noses are sometimes higher than those of the men; they walk like men, taking long steps; look men in the face, and laugh a great deal, sometimes very loud. In order to make themselves look taller, they make their bonnets stick up on their heads. Even the modest women dance a great deal. They hook on to the arms of the men; and there are days when every man has a woman hanging on his arm. Are they their own wives? We think so. In general the women enjoy great liberty. What we say of the women of France applies to those of all Europe. The latter, with the exception of the Dutch, are inferior to the French. We will not speak of the costume: it is impossible to understand it. In the evening it is not always decent.

"The men are stiff, and a little proud or rough. However, the respectable as well as the lower classes carry no arms. A respectable man seldom carries about him any marks of his rank. It would seem that all classes, even the upper ones, frequent *cafés*. Even the superior officials go to the theatre, for which they have a great passion. We have regretted more than once not having understood what was said there. Almost every one was armed with opera-glasses, which were often directed at us,—doubtless, through absence of mind.

"The shopkeepers are haughty, and saluted us only in a very middling degree. They did not like us to derange the articles in their shops much, and doubtless reckoned on our buying a great deal from them. We were able to see that the mechanicians and useful tradesmen were more respected than the mere shopkeepers.

"The articles of diet are almost the same as with us; however, they eat but little rice and fish, but, on the other hand, much meat and pastry. We were extremely disgusted at Paris and elsewhere, to see beef and mutton still bloody exposed in the most public shops. To eat beef is often medicinally useful; but why present it to the eyes of all the world? Is it not sinful thus to despise so useful an animal? It was truly shocking to several of our party.

"However, the cookery of the French is good, and their wine excellent. The wine is the best thing they have, and does not yield in anything to our saki.

"The dress of the men appears at first ridiculous and curtailed; however, it must be convenient and economical.

"In Paris, as in London, every one walks very fast, as with us when there is a fire. Their houses are so high that they must fall on the first earthquake; they appear, nevertheless, to be proof against fire. We will speak of the marvellous things we saw in the order in which they were seen by us."

When the Japanese Ambassadors were in Europe, it was remarked, wherever they went, with what avidity they listened to and took notes of whatever the interpreters explained to them. Immediately on their return to Yeddo, their various notes were handed over to one of their number as editor, and after being arranged by him, the work appeared under the title of "History of the Travels of the Japanese Commissioners in Europe,—by Fou-yah." The translation of the introduction from the Japanese was made by a member of the French Legation, and it was originally published in the *Patrie* newspaper.

Early in February, it was stated that a Council of Daimios was about to assemble at Osaca for the purpose of considering the affairs of the nation generally, and that, as a matter of course, the foreign question was to form an important element in their discussions. Though the Loonins at this time had ceased to occasion alarm to the inhabitants of the foreign settlements, acts of incendiarism at Yeddo, Yokohama, and Osaca were very common. At

Yokohama foreign property was not interfered with, the conflagrations being confined to native houses.

On the 13th of February, the new Ambassadors and *suite*, numbering in all twenty-seven persons, arrived at Shanghai in the "Monge." The Ambassadors proper are three in number; in addition, there is an assistant, or sort of member in waiting, holding the rank of a Provincial Vice-Governor. The object of their mission is still stated to be the consent of the treaty powers to evacuate Yokohama; but it is hinted that they have said privately that neither they nor the Tycoon have any expectation of succeeding. The measure, it is believed, is only carried out to enable the Tycoon to say to the Mikado, that he has done his utmost to carry out his wish respecting the expulsion of foreigners.

On the 18th of February, Sir Rutherford Alcock arrived at Shanghai *en route* to Yokohama to resume his official position, after an absence of two years from Japan. Immediately on his arrival, Colonel Neale returns to England to enjoy well-merited repose, after the harassing period he has passed through, and the succession of dangers which have attended his two years' tenure of office as Her Majesty's Chargé-d'Affaires in Japan. The important services rendered by him during that period have received the acknowledgment of Her Majesty's Government, by the Order of the Bath having been conferred upon him in connection with Kagosima.

That there is, apart altogether from the question of hostility to foreigners, some well-founded grievance on the part of the feudal nobility of Japan in regard to the manner in which foreign trade is at present conducted, there would seem to be no doubt. The problem then to be solved is, how to render foreign trade beneficial to the people and acceptable to Japan generally. That the Government of the Tycoon is equal to effecting this, there are the strongest reasons for doubting.

We have sufficient proofs that diplomatic success achieved

at the cannon's mouth is not permanent in its results, and requires from time to time the reintroduction for its maintenance of the same mode of argument by which it was originally attained. Something of the European regard for human life is extending itself to the East, and a feeling is gradually springing up at home unfavourable to the extension of commerce where it can only be supported by periodical demonstrations of physical force.

In conclusion, should it seem to any that the comments I have made on the bearing of our countrymen in the East are couched in terms of undue asperity, or tainted with exaggeration, I would wish to say, that my endeavour has been to place the matter in the least offensive and personal light consistent with a plain statement of facts; and I will only add, that it is little use our mourning over events like those of the Kagosima, if the recharging of the shell, to the explosion of which such occurrences may be likened, is allowed to go on unchecked. We must cease to believe that our countrymen are always right, and that Orientals must of necessity be invariably in the wrong. The longer the hallucination is indulged in, the more difficult will it become to arrest the growth of the seeds of discord which are constantly germinating in the East, and, periodically budding forth, frequently bringing with them catastrophes from which our national sense of justice and humanity recoils.

THE END.

BRADBURY AND EVANS, PRINTERS, WHITEFRIARS.

www.ingramcontent.com/pod-product-compliance
Lightning Source LLC
Chambersburg PA
CBHW030542300426
44111CB00009B/826